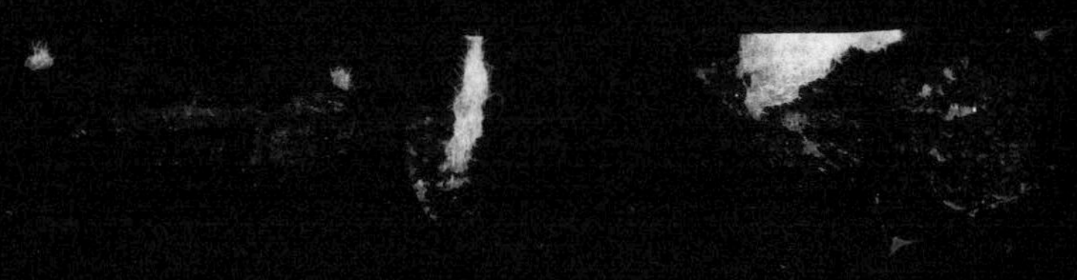

THE INTERNATIONAL DESIGN YEARBOOK

1996

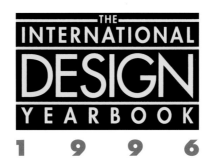

THE INTERNATIONAL DESIGN YEARBOOK

1 9 9 6

Editor: **Alessandro Mendini**

General Editor: **Conway Lloyd Morgan**

Assistant Editor: **Jennifer Hudson**

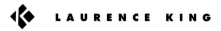

LAURENCE KING

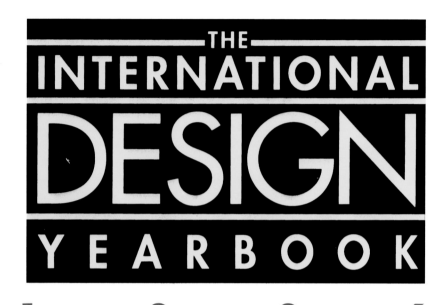

Published 1996 by Laurence King Publishing
an imprint of Calmann & King Ltd
71 Great Russell Street
London WC1B 3BN

A catalogue record for this book is available from the British Library.

ISBN 1 85669 080 6

Based on an original idea by Stuart Durant
Designed by Mikhail Anikst
Printed in Hong Kong

Photographic Credits

The publisher and editors would like to thank the designers and manufacturers who submitted work for inclusion; Junko Popham for her help in collecting the Japanese contributions, and the following photographers and copyright holders for the use of their material:

Takashi Abiko 4.30. Alessi 3.32. Aloisi 5.1, 2. Hiroshi Aoki 2.57. Jan Armgardt 1.23, 85, 86. Satoshi Asakawa 1.75. Aldo Ballo 3.54. Rien Bazen 1.26, 117; 4.24. © Roland Beaufre 1.12. Toussaint Benedetti 5.15. Bette GmbH & Co. KG, Delbrück 5.46. Alessandro Bon 5.5, 64. Bernd Borchardt 2.11. Grazia Branco 5.29. © C.A.A.C. The Pigozzi Collection; photos: Claude Postel 1.10. Santi Caleca page 10; 3.27, 37, 52, 53; 5.71. Stefano Casati page 12 (bottom right). C.E.M. 1.84. Darren Centofanti 2.23. Amos Chan 4.50, 65. Bitetto Chimenti 1.28. Collection Stadtsgalerie Stuttgart page 8 (left). David Cripps 3.17. D. James Dee 4.57. Thomas Deutschmann page 11 (top). Rainer Diehl 3.66; 5.70. Caren Dissinger 2.45, 47. Philippe Durand 1.76. Uwe Düttmann 4.10, 11. Tim Edwards 1.31; 2.28. Rick English 5.17, 18. Anna Eoclidi 2.26. C. Fei 2.14. Siggi Fischer 5.26. Georg Fontana 3.42, 43. Dominique Feintrenie 1.39. Dan Burn Forti 1.25, 79, 110. Fotolinde 4.45. Monica Fritz 4.58. Nobu Fukuda/Yoshio Hayashi 5.51. Yuuzo Fujii 5.19. Michael Gerlach 1.113. Massimo Giacon 3.6, 7; 4.60. Carlo Gianni 1.73. Rob Gray 4.3. Leon Gulikers 1.29, 38. Walter Gumiero 2.48. Ashley Hall 1.97; 2.49. David Hall 5.13. Hans Hansen 1.63; 2.20. John Hatt page 146. Scott Henderson 5.84. © Udo Hesse 3.63, 4. Yuki Higuchi 4.36–39. Hitch Mylius Ltd 1.42. Tim Imrie 1.45, 48. Interspazi, Asolo, Italy 4.4. Italimage 5.58. Setsu Ito 5.36. Markus Jans 1.95. Mark Jenkinson 5.86. Georg Kai 5.7–10. Eleanor Kearney 3.55. Christoph Kicherer 5.65 (page 209). N. Koliusis 2.52. Rene Koster 1.69. Regina Kumn 5.81. John Lazzarini 3.15. Jennifer Lee 3.4. © Erica Lennard 1.107. Michael MacIntyre page 112. David Maclay 1.100. Matteo Manduzzio 1.71. Peter Mathis page 170. Liz McLoud page 78. Sue McNab 4.40–42. Dennis McNicol 1.47. Jann Merlin 2.18; 3.65. C. Metrah 2.61. Yoram Mitelstadt 1.108; 2.36, 37. Hirofumi Miyamoto 5.48, 62. John Moldauer 5.82. Joe Montana 1.37. Nacása & Partners Inc. 1.16, 118; 3.19–23. Hiromi Nakano page 7 (left). Paul Newman 5.42. Bart Nieuwenhuys 3.47. Lars Oer 1.91; 2.51; 5.27. Ohuchi Photo Studio 5.14. Paulina Pasanen 3.14. Guido Pedron 3.11. T.P. Persman 2.38, 39. Philips International B.V. 5.6, 73, 91. PR-Studio, Pasi Haaranen 5.11. Marino Ramazzotti 1.82. Joachim Rensing 1.128; 2.53. Markus Richter 5.38, 66. Christian Richters 3.40. Mark Safron 4.63. Michael St John 3.9. Katsuji Sato 4.25–29. Pietro Savorelli 3.16. Elisabeth Scheder-Bieschin 1.114. E.G. Schempf 1.92. Rudi Schmutz 4.6–8. Schneider/Hanuschke 3.58. Jan-Chr. Schultchen 2.35. Gregor Schuster 3.3. Schnakenburg & Brahl 1.17, 18, 41, 121. © Thierry Secretan page 14; 1.2–4. Yoshio Shiratori 2.60. Michael Sieger 3.38, 39. Michael P. Smith 1.1 (inset), 14. Steven Speller 1.77, 78; 4.59. STAFF 2.32, 33. Dexter Stewart page 17. Beba Stoppani 1.105; 2.46; 4.49. Studio Ombra page 11 (bottom). Iyer Swaminathan 5.61. Patrick Szalai 2.8. C. Themessl 2.16. Toshinori Toshima 5.87. Emilio Tremolada 1.20; 2.3, 4, 22, 43, 58. Matteo Tresoldi 3.62. Nick Turner 5.37, 40. Tom Vack page 12 (top right); 5.85. Hans van der Mars 1.44, 60, 70, 74; 3.46, 56; 5.25. © Pierre Verrier 1.72. VIA 1.123. Hans Vos 2.2. © Roger Vulliez 2.44. William Whitehurst 4.46. Rupert Williamson 1.112. Christian Winsel 5.23. D. Wolfenden 2.5. Peter Wood 1.106; 2.1, 10. Miro Zagnoli 1.63; 2.31. David Zanardi 2.40.

Contents

Design as an Odyssey

Alessandro Mendini

People are always talking about trends: future trends and current tastes, new needs, changing desires. In the consumer world, trends are the point where design, style, product and user converge. Market success is evidence that a project has caught on and set up a trend. But trends are always a bit mysterious. Every success is aleatory and temporary, since every new trend contradicts its predecessors or moves in alongside or into conflict with those contiguous to it. So at any time numerous trends and tendencies can be at work. We have to try to understand how the different disciplines of design express trends, which are first and foremost a social phenomenon.

The most rigid discipline is that of architecture. As its works have longer lives than those of other areas of design, its organization in time is more stable and transformations of style are curbed. Then there is graphic design, which is less slow than architecture in its mutation, but similarly bound by functional principles and expressive restrictions. Next comes fashion, which quickly self-consumes, whilst remaining tied to "seasonal" styles that are conventions of taste. The freest expression of trends is certainly that of art. Neither having nor claiming to have immediate or functional references, art is better able to prefigure cultural and social tendencies.

Where does industrial design fit into this scheme of trends measured against the models of their temporality? I believe it can be placed at an average point that fluctuates between the "useless" freedom of art and the "useful" restraint of objective, almost architectural progress. In its averageness, design must, like art, have the capacity to anticipate, but also, like architecture, to preserve.

Allan McCollum
50 Perfect Vehicles
Installation, 1989
Stedelijk Van
Abbemuseum, Eindhoven

Seriality

The conflict between uniqueness and seriality seems to have become the eternal battle of the modern world. The unique piece, the work of art and the unrepeatable original have become symbols of an artistic or artisan past, whilst the mass-produced object, the series-made product, the duplicate, are symbols of the industrial present.

But what if original and serial were not in conflict? Supposing art and industry did not necessarily have to be enemies? Are the two poles bound to wage a war without any dialogue? Perhaps the time has come to consider whether we have got past the period when art provocatively aped industry in order to denounce the fall of the original work's unique "aura", and during which the multiplication of consumer products smacked of an insult to aesthetic value.

Today we are in a position to let art, crafts and industry live together. In the complex and stratified universe of late modern consumption, many industrial products have regained the right to be used as unique and unrepeatable objects, even in ordinary homes. And conversely, many of the works that spring from the value of artistic or artisan uniqueness are multiplied and serialized in a process of social communication. An artist's multiple, the ceramic of an artisan potter, a piece of industrial furniture, co-existing in the domestic space, point to a dialogue between uniqueness and seriality. Art and industry can be seen and experienced as parallel, not necessarily alternative, roads, just as the features of a portrait are always unique in themselves whilst bearing a likeness to the family from which the portrayed person descends.

Mark Kostabi
Mass Production
1990
137.2 x 167.6cm
54 x 66in

Informatics

Information science, computers, and more generally, communications media, are radically transforming the patterns of contemporary experience. The styles and pace of our lives are being subjected to an extraordinary perceptive and cultural revolution. Archives are losing their physicality, and certain architectural genres, such as the office building, are becoming obsolete. The social subject is being transformed into a communicational one. Man seems to be a figure with the gift of ubiquity accomplished by means of placeless information.

But how does an electronic tool become an object of common experience? As always happens, in the early stages of consumption electronic equipment assumed the air of a technology to be revered. Cold and black, computers or hi-fi systems presented themselves like sacred icons before which users should stand in awe and humiliation. There are times when technology witnesses such public devotion. But then, after a while, the tools themselves are gradually transformed. Coming into widespread social use, they lose their aloofness and acquire a new familiarity. Thus today the face of technology is changing. The design of electronic goods has begun to shed the chilly and abstract appearance of its experimental origins, to take on colours and to adopt domesticated forms, presenting itself in a more light-hearted way.

This development indicates how technology has pervaded daily experience to the point of being camouflaged by it. Electronic goods are being miniaturized and becoming transportable; they have an informal appearance and accompany everyday acts in the manner of toys. The task of design today is to design the technological games of communicational man.

Keith Haring
China set
1989

Rituality

After the typically rampant functionalism of the pioneering days of technology, design now has to tackle the conception and production of goods to encourage private uses, individual motives and even new personal experiences. But the goods are still too often thought of, designed and used within the restraints of functionalist reduction. In that respect, objects exist only as tools; the horizons of their purposes are closed and narrow. It is necessary, therefore, even in advanced contemporary design, to recapture and develop man's former tendency to use objects according to ritual attitudes. Perhaps this is the origin of "decor": the sense that every object requires specific, "decorous" acts, an etiquette of movements, a rituality of postures.

A number of great cultural traditions maintain this link with ceremonialism, and there is no ceremonialism that does not have its specific objects. The Far East, most of all, retains a clear affection for a rituality that combines religious, spiritual meanings and the care of corporal gestures. The West, with its functionalist ideology, has in the course of time removed from objects their ritual value and ceremonial resonance. Today, in consequence, what is required is an effort to reintroduce a certain ceremonial slowness, a more meditated rituality into the domain of accelerated functionalism. Objects must comply with, and yet supersede, technical requirements, to be transformed into the small and discreet priests of the many daily rites which even contemporary experience requires.

Haim Steinbach
Sweetest Taboo, 1987
Plastic laminated wood shelf, marble and brass urns, cast-iron cookware
Collection Stadtsgalerie Stuttgart

Eclecticism

The world is random in itself, and there is also a randomness in nature, which is referred to as "biological diversity". There are natural, already composite materials, and others that combine at will to produce better levels of resistance, performance and quality. Designed goods, too, need to respond to this material eclecticism, by using natural and synthetic materials together, and trying out different combinations and assemblages.

The world is also random from a temporal, chronological point of view. There are ancient materials and new ones, and in production systems archaic and advanced techniques coexist, with very ancient and very new modes of processing and transforming materials. Wood, pieces of trees, stones, earth are natural archaic elements. Steels, plastics, resins are synthetic elements, young materials. All these elements can be combined today, in a textural and technical eclecticism situated between the natural and the artificial, ancient and modern, archaic and brand new. The fascination of these joint presences in a design product stems not only from polymaterial richness, but also from the vanquishing of time thereby achieved: the eclecticism of ancient and new materials, coupled with the eclecticism of archaic and technological production processes, leads to a sort of syncretism between periods that may be very far apart chronologically.

A product which, together with automated technologies, embraces ancient techniques of hand lathes or steam hammers for iron beating, may perhaps today speak the language of a new tradition. Materials and techniques, used in their natural, synthetic and temporal extremes, can provide us with the object-symbols of contemporary spatial and chronological eclecticism.

Above
Wim Delvoye
De Kast van Utrecht
Installation, 1988–1989

Narratives

An object is not identified merely with its practical end-purpose. Every object is the fruit of contingencies, utopias, design hazards and expressive moods. Every object traces its own parabola, from conception to creation through a useful life or lives, to its final decline. The message which the object seeks to get across in this way is a story, embracing its broad destiny and bestowing an almost literary identity upon the silent forms and materials of design.

This narrative must be enhanced. The project must be made into fiction as if it were the I, the narrator of a novel. The potential narratives of the object coalesce in choices of form, in stylistic character and structural identity, but above all they are expressed in surface, colour, decoration. If in a psychological novel the plot is conveyed by the surface of descriptions of characters and their dialogues, similarly, in objects, design communicates through their visible, perceptible, sensible surface.

In particular, it is by working on the surface of products that their stature can be broadened from functionality to literariness. The aim is to submerge the cold and violent consumption of things into a narrative, evocative, psychic and emotive flow. Thus hypermodern man, too, may learn to move about in the universe of objects as in an infinite odyssey. Today, in a world reduced and deconfigured by technology and information, the Homeric task of design is all the more urgent. This is why I talk about "Design as an Odyssey": to transform the boundless contemporary catalogue of goods into a landscape to be crossed on a journey of discovery and poetry.

Oklahoma srl
Bench
Painted metal, PVC
1992

Cutting Harlequin's Coat

Conway Lloyd Morgan

Alessandro Mendini
Corkscrew,
Anna G.
1994

Alessandro Mendini's surname refers to what was probably once an ancestor's profession, that of menders, often of clothes, something akin to the English rag-picker or French *ravaudeuse*, who would patch up new clothes out of old pieces. The kind of tailor, in effect, who would have made Harlequin's coat, a crazy patchwork of colours and materials. Indeed the image of Harlequin fits Mendini well. Not only for his love of colours and variety, but also for his ubiquity, wit and sensibility. For Harlequin, in the original *Commedia dell'Arte*, is a literally Mercurial figure, present everywhere, involved in everything, at turns happy and sad, but ready with a trick or a stratagem. The arrival of his flashing coat on stage signals a dénoument, the answer to the riddle, the solving of a problem.

Alessandro Mendini was born in Milan in 1931. He trained as an architect and in 1965 joined Nizzoli Associati, working with them on housing developments and competitions. He was already working on exhibition design, with projects on Gaudí, Erich Mendelsohn and young American architects shown in Milan in the late 1950s and early 1960s. His writing career took shape with his work at *Casabella*, starting in 1970, then as editor of *Modo* (from 1977) and finally *Domus*, where he was editor from1979 until founding Atelier Mendini with his brother Francesco in 1989. At the same time he was working actively as a designer, with the various design groups of the early 1970s, and then with Studio Alchimia from 1979 until 1991. His first one-person show of paintings was held in Milan in 1986, the latest in Brussels in 1993. His most recent projects as an architect are the Groningen Museum in Holland, which opened in 1994, the "Busstops" project in Hanover, Germany, in 1992, showrooms for Mobel Meyer and offices for Alessi in 1993 and most recently the pavilion Tre Architetti Domotici with Jean Nouvel and Emilio Ambasz in parallel with the 1995 Venice Biennale.

This rapid survey of an immensely varied and productive career omits, in fact, two of Mendini's most important roles in contemporary design, his work as art director for Swatch and for Alessi. These two companies, in the one case producing watches and accessories, and in the other cookware and tableware, brought design out of the showcase and into the high street, in the same way as Habitat did in the 1960s in Britain and France, and IKEA in Sweden a decade later. Although contemporary design ideas are regularly aired in the lifestyle press and discussed in specialist reviews, these four companies, at different times, brought contemporary design objects within the ambit of ordinary people. Mendini's role as arbiter elegantiae at Alessi and Swatch has had much to do with the banquet of design available today.

One way to understand the complexities of Mendini's approach to design, the complexities that have led him to extend his definition of designer into architecture, painting, consultancy, writing, art direction and editorial work, is through his own design. Take for example his "Busstops" project. The city of Hanover decided to celebrate their new urban transit system with a series of shelters and stops commissioned from leading architects and designers, including Jasper Morrison, Frank Gehry and Ettore Sottsass. Mendini's design for a stop in the Steintorplatz was a regular square arch of yellow and black cubes, surmounted by tall golden cones. The shape and colour of the structure make no concessions to the surroundings: the whole thing, like a constructivist unicorn in an urban zoo, is simply a bright visual object. It is not to be seen through the spectacles of post-Modern irony, nor is it making a didactic statement: it just is. For Mendini's view is that architecture is object, but not object in the sense of minor decorative elements disconnected from a larger whole, but objects as the keys to our personal rituals, whether domestic or urban, work or social, personal or collective. For Mendini, objects must be affective: being effective is not enough. Objects are the carriers of the fetishisms, dramas and mysteries that make up our lives. The way objects appear, their necessary decoration, needs to be continuously re-appraised, re-sourced, re-invented, for them to continue, in their totality, to have a valid meaning for us.

This reappraisal of objects can be seen in the famous *Proust* chair, first shown in 1978, and once described as an "explosion of confetti". Its ample and repetitive curves are deliberately kitsch; its decorations, though applied by hand, recall Formica. The wit in this approach is subtle: the chair gently asks us to revise our ideas about comfort, about history and about taste. It is also an object that has evolved: first made with the confetti finish, then in black and yellow, then bronzed. And the decorative finishes have also been applied to other objects, including a teddy bear, a bookshelf and a lamp. What marks this chair, then, as a contemporary work is partly its self-knowledge (the overall application of a finish to a form that would traditionally have been divided, for example) and partly its extensibility (*Proust*, unlike Marcel, has descendants). Above all it is the way in which the object presupposes a discourse with the viewer, assumes that it does not only function but also engages the emotions, that makes the *Proust* armchair a key expression of Mendini's ideas.

Above
Atelier Mendini
(with **G. Gregori**)
Busstop, Steintorplatz,
Hanover, 1994

Left
Bruno Gregori
Entrance to the Groninger Museum,
1988–1994

One of the latest appearances of the *Proust* motif is in a commercial surface laminate, entitled Proust Groningen, produced by Abet in 1994, and used as external cladding on the Groningen Museum. The Museum, constructed on an island in the canals of northern Holland, houses both a permanent collection of contemporary fine and decorative art and temporary exhibitions. Mendini's delight in colour, and his belief in the importance of colour in communicating ideas, flows all over this building, from the silver pinnacles surmounting the golden yellow storage tower at the centre, to the mosaic decoration of the main staircase and the *pointilliste* main entrance. For Mendini, any design emerges as much from a collective imagination as an individual one. The collective imagination, for him, is composed of infinite quantities of three elements – forms, decorations and colours. Ornament and colour are what inject energy and vitality into the ordinary, be it a routine, an object, or a building. And because this experience of colour and ornament is a collective one, it makes sense to work in a collective way.

Alessandro Mendini
Above
Coffee maker from the *Philips by Alessi* series, 1994
Left
Vanicoro from the *Easy Home* collection
Memphis, 1995
Below
Swatch Watch, *Lots of Dots*
1992

A key principle in Mendini's design activity is the shared project. At Groningen, Coop Himmelblau, Philippe Starck and Michele de Lucchi were among the architects invited to contribute parts to the overall project, for example. Mendini's own design practice is deliberately not called a studio, but an atelier, referring to a traditional confederacy of master craftsmen, rather than a hierarchy of masters and apprentices. This co-operative approach is typically Italian, a useful counterweight to the Morrisian fallacy that design and architecture are solitary pursuits. The mutual passions, and counterpassions, generated within the group are what made Memphis designs successful, Michele de Lucchi once told me. Mendini takes this a step further: a group work is not just the *cadavre exquis*, the work by several hands beloved of the Surrealists. Rather the group work is greater than the sum of the individual contributions to it, he maintains, and the more so the less hierarchical the group is. The Modern Movement's vision of ordered teamwork under a leader is not a true group. Despite a return in the 1990s to independent work by many other designers, Mendini insists that the Atelier keeps its balance between giving individuals space to develop, and between working together in a freeform way on projects from architecture to graphic and editorial design to products.

Mendini not only diverges from William Morris on the question of individuality, he also disagrees with the perceived dichotomy between craft and industry. For him they are not in opposition, the black satanic mills crushing the independent artisan, as the Arts and Crafts Movement, quoting Blake, was to claim. Mendini sees the two approaches today as moving in parallel, with no sense of confrontation. One development he finds particularly interesting is the cross-over between them, when a craftsman uses a high-technology material or process, or when an industrial object becomes a craft one through design. An example of the latter is his own *Caffettiera*: a mass-produced aluminium coffee-maker transformed into a design work through the application of coloured panels.

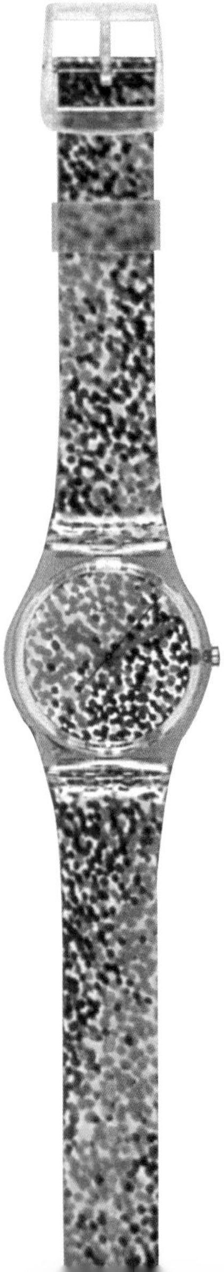

An extension both of the group project and the importance of the object can be found in shared works such as *33 Mirrors* and *100% MakeUp*. In the latter, one hundred identical vases were decorated by one hundred different designers from around the world, and produced in a first series of one hundred each, and then in an unnumbered series (the first series were deliberately cheaper than the second!). This strange marketing ploy is best explained as a way of presenting the whole project as a snapshot of design at the end of a century, a universal statement rather than a particular one. This idea of design as only adding human value is also expressed in Mendini's *Utopian Vase* project: standard vases, hand decorated, simply fired, and sold by the makers themselves – who could be anybody – at cost, without a mark-up for a designer name. This is not just a political statement, it is also an attempt to bring design back into a relationship with society in which design provides the necessary vocabulary of ideas, emotions and shared experiences.

Mendini's belief in the importance of the creative group, and his skills as an organizer and leader, show through in his work for Swatch and Alessi. For Swatch he has not only co-ordinated the involvement of designers in creating each year's collection, but also, through the design of exhibition stands, shop interiors and special events, created an *image de marque* which has helped Swatch reach its astonishing position in the market. More importantly, the Swatch idea of an accessible, individual product found in Mendini a sense of direction, in the hands of a designer for whom the supposedly "banal" taste of the public was a subject of key interest, and whose work has regularly challenged our perceptions of popular culture, investing it with its proper creativity and dignity.

For Alessi, Mendini has provided the gateway for a number of younger designers to enter a collection which already features Graves, Starck and Sottsass. He has also introduced a series of programmes, moving away from individual design statements to families of work, notably in the series of objects jointly produced by Philips and Alessi in 1994. In this collection his own piece, a jaunty human corkscrew in green and yellow, *Anna G.*, is both a personal dedication and a declaration of the literally human face of design. It encapsulates the ambiguities between individual craftsman and mass production, between the fetters of taste and the bounds of wit, between personal statement and social response, that are the very stuff of Mendini's approach to design. "Our real problem", Mendini has written, "is not with the terms of a given design project, but rather with this great project that is life and the living of it. It is a question of ceremony, a ceremony that must be expressed through design.... Design, separated from the styles which articulate it, is the soul within the material. Our string of possessions, an indispensable part of the human attitude to change, to the human sense of difference, can be seen as an enormous painter's palette full of colours." Or seen as Harlequin's gloriously spangled coat, which Mendini carries with ease, humour and grace.

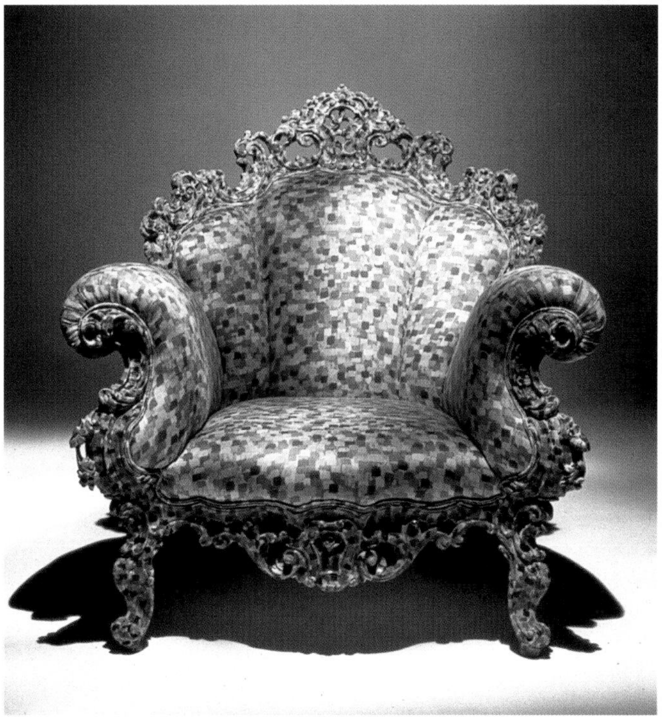

Alessandro Mendini
Armchair, *Proust*
Cappellini International, 1993

f u r n i t u r e

Imagine a circle, Mendini suggests. Within its broad circumference are the smaller circles that represent architecture, technology, society, fashion and art. Design, to have meaning, must be within this larger circle, and so must interact with the other circles. Sometimes it will be closer to one than another – nearer to fashion than to technology, for example, or nearer to architecture than to art. At the same time it cannot merely overlap one subsidiary circle: design cannot be just about technology, or just about society. This is not a negative way of defining design, rather a contextual one, a way of insisting on the importance of design as playing a central and a linking role between these other, important areas.

Looking at the overlap between design and society, Mendini particularly highlights in his selection of furniture the notion of "new ethnologies", the emergence of new cultural forms linked to specific social groups. Kane Kwei's coffins (page 18) are a typical example, since they do not derive from the traditions of African art. The YA/YA group's work with teenage designers in New Orleans, looking for design inspiration from the street, is another. This tendency opens up the frontiers of design, outside the traditional First World framework, towards new areas of creation. The idea of generalized design – everyone their own designer – has already been proclaimed for graphic design by Neville Brody: there is no reason why furniture design cannot be next. Mendini's selection highlights individuality within the wider circle of design, if not always within the old rules.

1 **Carlos Neville**
Chair, *Hot Seat*
Wood, acrylic paint
h 114cm w 48cm d 47cm
h 45in w 19in d 18½in
Young Aspirations/Young Artists (YA/YA) Inc., USA
(One-off)

2

3

4

Kane Kwei's coffins are both a secular and a spiritual celebration. The forms evoke the fame of the occupant – an eagle for a chief, a hen for the mother of a large family, a pirogue or a fish for a fisherman, a cocoa pod for a farmer. Their stylistic vocabulary is wholly independent of the traditions of art in Ghana, but does reflect the religious and social mix of the country. These splendid objects validate, in their bright pomp, the importance of family ties and traditions. Kwei's followers, such as Paa Joe and Laï have carried on the idea of figurative coffins, and it has been recognized by art dealers and collectors, and recently celebrated in Thierry Secretan's book *Going into Darkness* (Thames & Hudson, 1994). The coffins are entirely carved by hand and eye, with no preliminary design drawings. They represent a genuinely new craft motif, one of the "new ethnologies" of the late twentieth century.

The central success of the 1960s cartoon "The Flintstones" (and the failure of the 1990s film version) lay in its precise transformation of contemporary social attitudes and technologies into a single medium – rock. Natanel Gluska's hewn *Sculpt Chairs* achieve the same lateral shift. Made of wood, they look as if they should be in almost any other material. Had this trick been played in another way, it would have seemed cynical, but in the wholly natural medium of wood the wit and the craftsmanship shine through.

2-4 **Samuel Kane Kwei**
Coffins
Wood
(One-offs)

5 **Natanel Gluska**
Sculpt Chair
Beechwood
h 105cm w 81cm d 70cm
h 41⅜in w 31⅞in d 27½in
(One-off)

6 **Natanel Gluska**
Sculpt Chair
Beechwood
h 73cm w 70cm d 62cm
h 28¾in w 27½in d 24⅜in
(One-off)

5

6

7

8

9

7, 9 **Beata Bär, Gerhard Bär, Hartmut Knell**
Armchair
h 68cm w 90cm d 85cm
h 26¾in w 35⅜in d 33½in
Bär & Knell Design, Germany
(Limited batch production)

8 **Beata Bär, Gerhard Bär, Hartmut Knell**
Sofa
Recycled mixed plastics
h 85cm w 165cm d 68cm
h 33½in w 65in d 26¾in
Bär & Knell Design, Germany
(Limited batch production)

10 **Samuel Kane Kwei**
Cabinets
Wood
h 38cm w 60cm d 49cm
h 15in w 23⅝in d 19⅜in
(One-offs)

10

10

11

12 **Claude Bouchard**
Plant container, *Mammouth*
China, enamels
h 23cm w 28cm d 8.5cm
h 9in w 11in d 3⅜in
Emaux d'Art de Longwy, France
(Limited edition of 30)

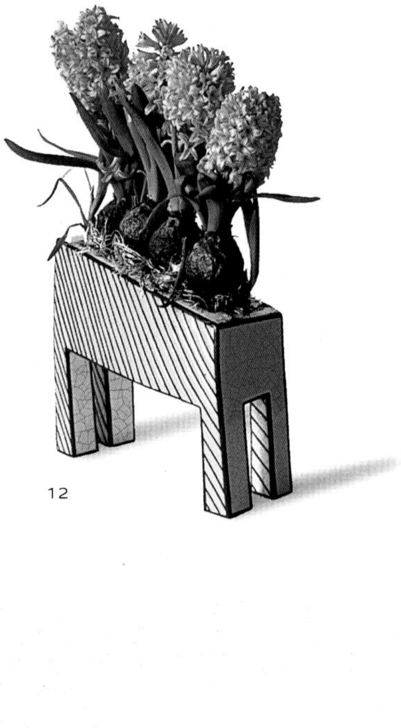

12

11 **Nuala Goodman**
Screen, *Madonna and Child*
Wood, tempera, wax, varnish
h 150cm w 100cm d 30cm
h 59in w 39⅜in d 11¾in
(One-off)

13 **Johanna Gunkel**
Screen
Plastic garbage
h 158cm w 87cm d 57cm
h 62¼in w 34¼in d 22½in
(One-off)

14 **Rondell Crier**
Chair, *Line Creator*
Wood, acrylic paint
h 152cm w 106cm d 76cm
h 60in w 42in d 30in
Young Aspirations/Young Artists
(YA/YA) Inc., USA
(Prototype)

13

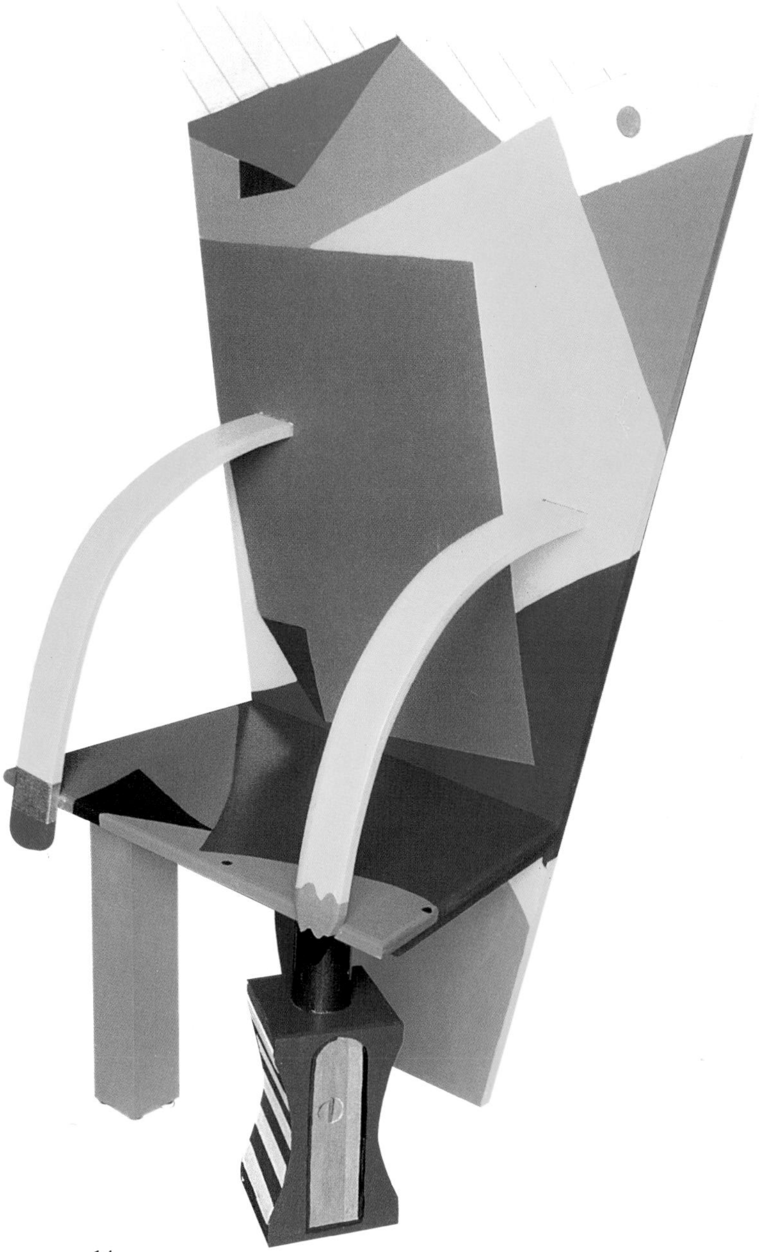
14

Expression can work through minimalism: Antonio Citterio's stacking tables for Kartell arrive at their form through emotion, not through reduction. With Konstantin Grcic's monochrome occasional table (page 26), it is as if the use of plain black enables the shapes to articulate and express themselves more clearly, in the way that Foucault speaks of "representations with the power to open within themselves a space in which they could analyse themselves". Such an intense internal dialogue, seen in Rolf Sachs' chair, for example, moves beyond abstraction into a true system of signs.

16

16

15

15 **Rolf Sachs**
Armchair with side-table, *Easy Chère*
MDF
h 77cm w 100cm d 60cm
h 30¼in w 39⅜in d 23⅝in
(Limited batch production)

16 **Yoko Kinoshita**
Table, *Doppio*, designed for YOS Inc.
Steel, plexiglass
h 70cm w 90cm d 90cm
h 27½in w 35⅜in d 35⅜in
Ishimaru Co. Ltd, Japan
(Prototype)

17

17 **Erik Krogh**
Reclining chair, *Spring-3*
Galvanized steel
h 90cm w 65cm l 145cm
h 35¼in w 25⅝in l 57⅛in
BJ-Metal, Denmark
(Limited batch production)

18 **Erik Krogh**
Reclining/rocking chair, *Leonardo*
Galvanized steel
h 65cm w 52.5cm l 180cm
h 25⅝in w 20⅝in l 70⅞in
BJ-Metal, Denmark
(Prototype)

19 **Antonio Citterio**
Tables, *Tris*
Chrome steel tube, thermoplastic technopolymer
h 33.5, 35.5, 38.5cm w 48.5cm d 48.5cm
h 13¼, 14, 15⅛in w 19⅛in d 19⅛in
Kartell, Italy

18

19

19

20 **Oscar Tusquets**
Table, *Volatil*
Multi-layered beech
h 52.5, 72.2, 84cm w 60cm
d 53cm
h 20⅝, 28⅜, 33in w 23⅝in
d 20⅞in
Driade, Italy

21 **Eric Jourdan**
Cabinet
Wood
h 120cm w 30cm d 45cm
h 47¼in w 11¾in d 17¾in
Néotù, France
(Limited batch production)

20

21

22

24

25

26

27

28

22 **Terence Woodgate**
Console, *Place*
Beech
h 87cm w 40cm l 180cm
h 34¼in w 15¾in l 70⅞in
Cappellini, Italy

23 **Jan Armgardt**
Bench, *Waiting For...JA40P*
Plywood, paper, felt
h 84cm l 160cm d 37cm
h 33⅛in l 63in d 14⅝in
Jan Armgardt Design, Germany
(Limited batch production)

24 **Konstantin Grcic**
Side-tables, *Mono*
Steel
h 65cm w 38cm
h 25⅝in w 15in
SCP Ltd, UK

25 **Tom Dixon**
Multi-function cabinet
MDF
h 185cm w 75cm d 50cm
h 72⅞in w 29½in d 19⅝in
Space, UK
(Limited batch production)

26 **Gijs Bakker**
Stool, *Draaikruk*
Stainless steel, terrazzo
h 75cm di 40cm
h 29½in di 15¾in
Verwo Projecten, The Netherlands

27 **Konstantin Grcic**
Side-table, *School*
Aero-ply, maple
h 67cm w 46cm d 34cm
h 26⅜in w 18½in d 13⅜in
Architektur & Wohnen, Germany
(Limited batch production)

28 **Andreas Brandolini**
Table, *Artu*
Steel, wood
h 72cm l 160, 200, 240cm
d 80, 90, 100cm
h 28⅜in l 63, 78¾, 94½in
d 31½, 35⅜, 39⅜in
Noto-Zeus, Italy

a love of decoration is sometimes mistaken for a passion for the past, for tradition. Mendini's enthusiasm for ornament and decoration is at the core of his approach, but for him anything he designs is part of a collective imagination, "for all cosmic shapes belong to a universal, endless river". Tradition is not part of this in the way that myth and instinct are: "the transience of our values conducts us straight from the old antiquarian to the new 'futurarian'....A brand new piece of furniture can be perceived at one and the same time as new object and as antique." Borek Sípek's *Yves* chair, which plays elegant games with traditional decoration, is just such a piece, as is Ruine Design's *D'Artagnan* table (page 31).

29 **Borek Sípek**
Bookcase/chair, *Yves*. Original Chinese chair with additions by Sípek
Copper, rosewood, mother-of-pearl
h 150cm w 48cm d 60cm, h 59in w 18⅞in d 23⅝in
Steltman Editions, The Netherlands, (Signed one-off)

30 **Bohuslav Horak**
Bookcase, *Nasikmo*. Wood, acrylic
h 130cm w 120cm d 35cm, h 51⅛in w 47⅛in d 13¾in
Anthologie Quartett, Germany

31 **Nick Allen**
Stool, *Ionic*. Distressed, copper-plated aluminium, fabric
h 48cm w 61cm d 49cm, h 18⅞in w 24in d 19⅜in
(Limited batch production)

29

30

31

34

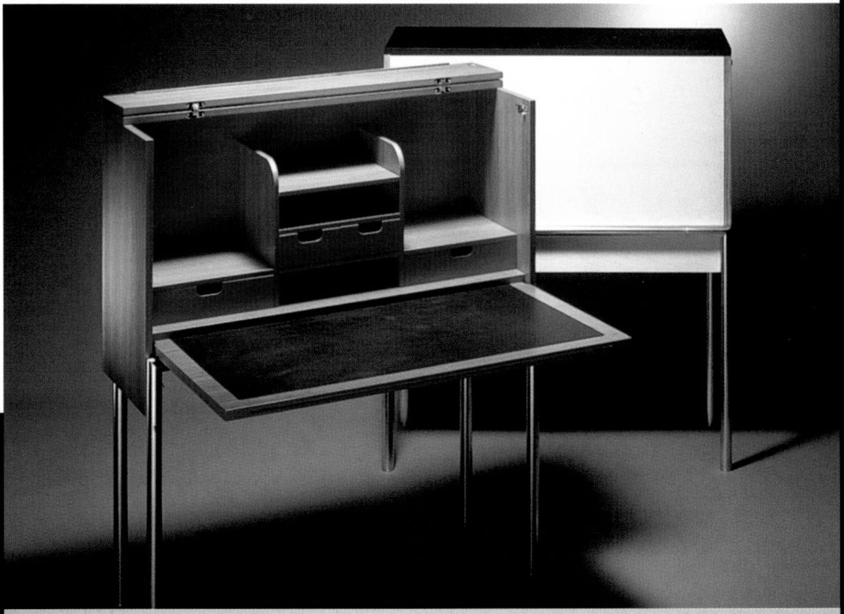

32

35

33

36

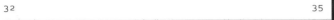

The *D'Artagnan* table by Ruine Design does not hesitate to add a buckle where a swash would do. Its curves are as voluptuous as a Hollywood starlet's, its choice of colours and materials as dazzling as Errol Flynn's sword-play. But what saves it from pastiche is both the sculptural quality of the final shape, and the deliberate contrasts introduced by using a glass table-top and by the mixture of traditional and modern materials in the base.

37

32 **Delo Lindo**
Armchair, *Stanislas*
Beechwood, pressed plywood, anodized aluminium
h 83cm w 56cm d 62cm
h 32⅝in w 22in d 24⅜in
Soca Line, France

33 **Delo Lindo**
Stacking chair, *Ambroise*
Chrome, pressed plywood
h 85cm w 48cm d 43cm
h 33½in w 18⅞in d 16⅞in
Soca Line, France

34 **Konstantin Grcic**
Secretaire, *Orcus*
Steel, plywood veneered in maple or pear
h 121cm w 104cm d 38, 100cm
h 47⅝in w 41cm d 15, 39⅜in
Classicon, Germany

35 **Maria Christina Hamel**
Table, *Armadillo*
Mahogany, mosaic
h 72cm l 192cm
h 28⅜in l 75⅝in
Bisazza, Italy

36 **Terri Pecora**
Collection of containers, *Cose Semplici*
Rattan
Large: h 70cm l 120cm d 50cm
h 27½in l 47¼in d 19¾in
Sech Ratan, Italy

37 **Cheryl and Paul Ruine**
Dining table, *D'Artagnan*
Bronze, glass
h 79cm w 132cm d 81cm
h 30in w 52in d 32in
Ruine Design Associates, USA
(Limited batch production)

40

38

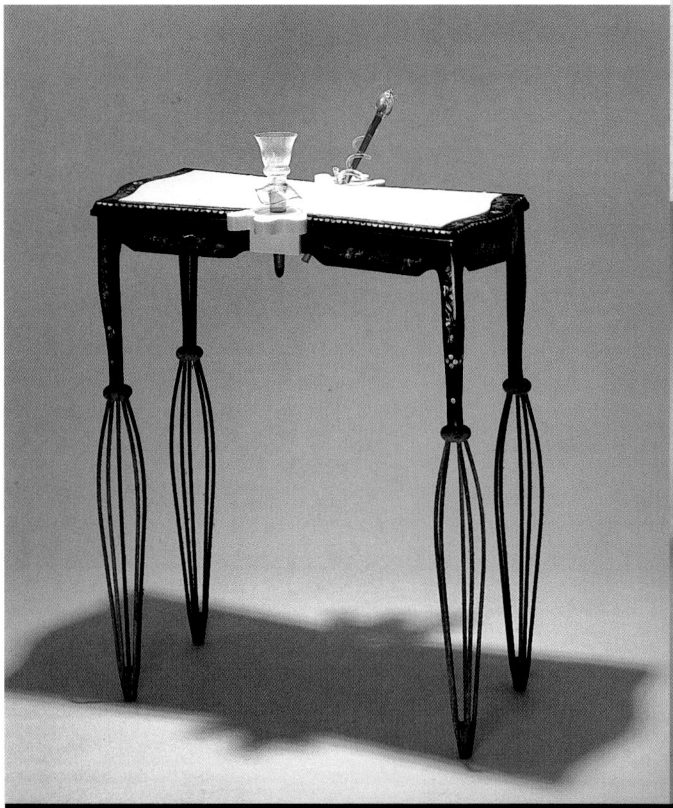

41

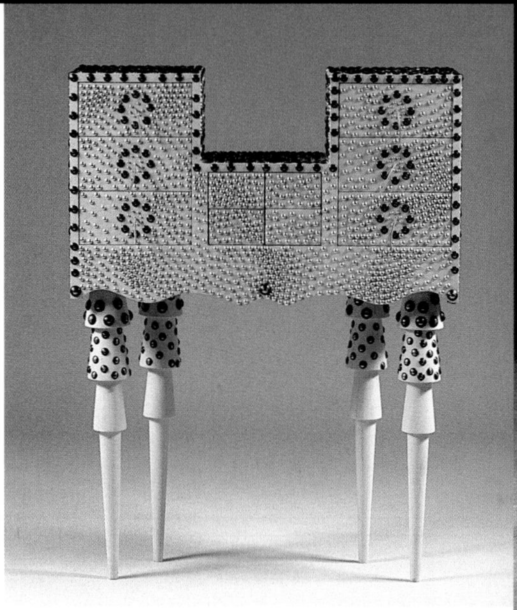

39

42

43

38 **Borek Sípek**
The China Table
Original Chinese table with additions by Sípek
Rosewood, mother-of-pearl, corian, copper
h 97cm w 79cm d 41cm
h 38¼in w 31⅛in d 16⅛in
Steltman Editions, The Netherlands
(Signed one-off)

39 **Abdi Abdelkader**
Chest of drawers, *Roca*
Wood, nails, leather
h 140cm w 110cm d 40cm
h 55⅛in w 43¼in d 15¾in
(Prototype)

40 **Denis Santachiara**
Rocking armchair, *Mama*
Steel, polyurethane, fabric
h 77cm w 77cm d 105cm
h 30¼in w 30¼in d 41⅜in
Baleri Italia, Italy

41 **Marno Gudiksen**
Chaise longue
Acrylic, folded foam polyethylene
h 40cm w 66cm l 200cm
h 15¾in w 26in l 78¾in
(One-off)

42 **Nigel Coates**
Chair and sofa from *The Slipper Collection*
Beech, plywood, polyester
h 85cm w 128, 65cm d 75cm
h 33½in w 50⅜, 25⅝in d 29½in
Hitch/Mylius Ltd, UK

43 **Dwight Huffman**
Cabinet, *NYPD*
Recycled chipboard, aluminium, diamond plate
h 61cm w 71cm d 41cm
h 24in w 28in d 16in
Haute House, USA
(One-off)

44

45

48

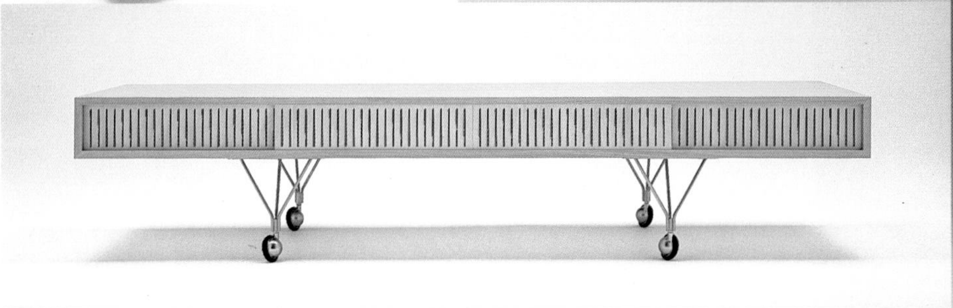

46

47

49

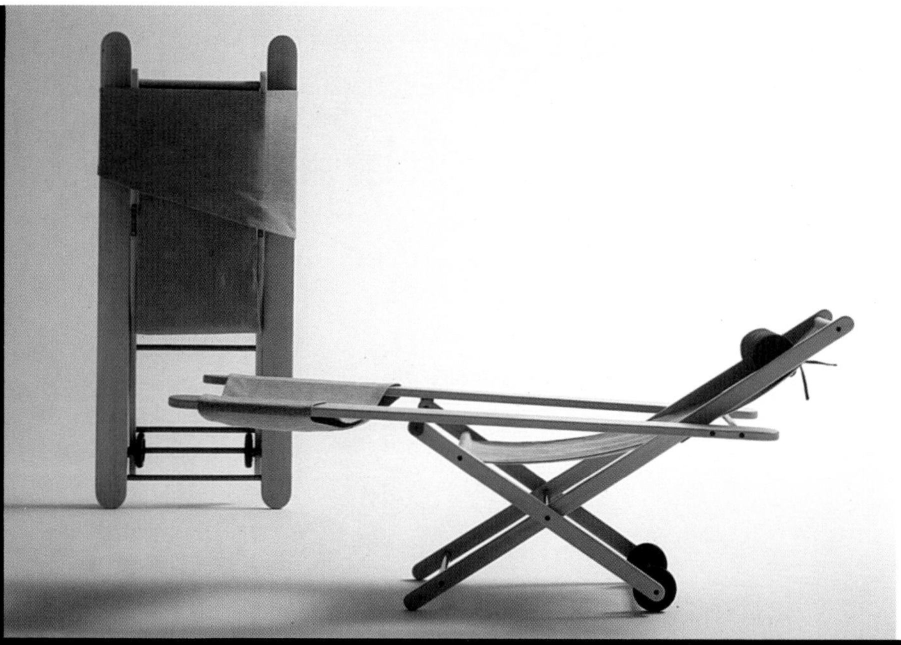

50

44 **Richard Hutten**
Stool, *DD83*
Maple, foam
h 40cm w 50cm d 50cm
h 15¾in w 19⅝in d 19⅝in
Droog Design, The Netherlands
(Batch production)

45 **John Coleman**
Desk/dressing table
Macassar ebony
h 73cm w 137cm d 53cm
h 28¾in w 53in d 20⅞in
(Prototype)

46 **Katsushi Nagumo**
TV stage
Senwood with polyurethane finish, stainless steel
h 40cm w 200cm d 55cm
h 15¾in w 78¾in d 21⅝in
Daitsu Co. Ltd, Japan

47 **David Trubridge**
Bench and table, *Hornpipe*
Radiata and Oregon pine, acrylic paint
h 80cm w 196cm d 55cm
h 31½in w 77⅛in d 21⅝in
David Trubridge Ltd, New Zealand
(Prototype)

48 **John Coleman**
Collector's cabinet
Bog oak, red oxide on steel
h 117cm w 46.5cm d 33.5cm
h 46in w 18¼in d 13¼in
(One-off)

49 **Suzanne Wessely**
Chair
Beech
h 80cm w 42cm d 45cm
h 31½in w 16½in d 17¾in
Royal College of Art, UK

50 **Vico Magistretti**
Folding chaise longue, *Baobab*
Veneered beechwood
h 81cm w 73cm l 186cm
h 31⅞in w 28¾in l 73¼in
Campeggi srl, Italy

Books, they say, do furnish a room, but for books one needs shelves. Furniture, then, often needs to be about order as much as about ideas. But simple, necessary objects do not have to be dull. Aldo Rossi's bookcase is rescued from any risk of the ordinary by carefully minimal details, clear proportions and bold colour, for example. It shows that the idea of modular furniture is no longer confined to the rigid hierarchies of Modernism, but can be expressed in new visual ways, even within the necessities of order, as in the bookcases by Thomas Sandell (page 40), or through new eyes as in Chi Wing Lo's work (page 43).

51

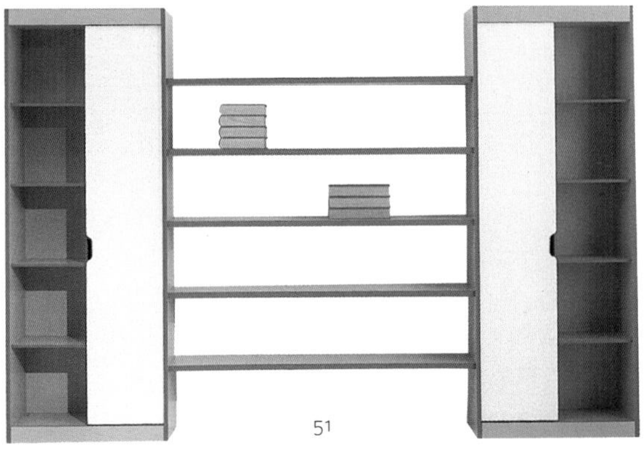

51

51 **Jasper Morrison and James Irvine**
Alfabeto System
Wood-covered melamine
h 211, 85cm
l 319, 240cm w 38cm
h 83, 33½in
l 125⅝in, 94½in w 15in
Cappellini, Italy

52 **Aldo Rossi**
Bookcase, *Cartesio*
Metal, wood
h 186cm w 141cm
d 45cm
h 73¼in w 55½in
d 17¾in
Unifor, Italy

52

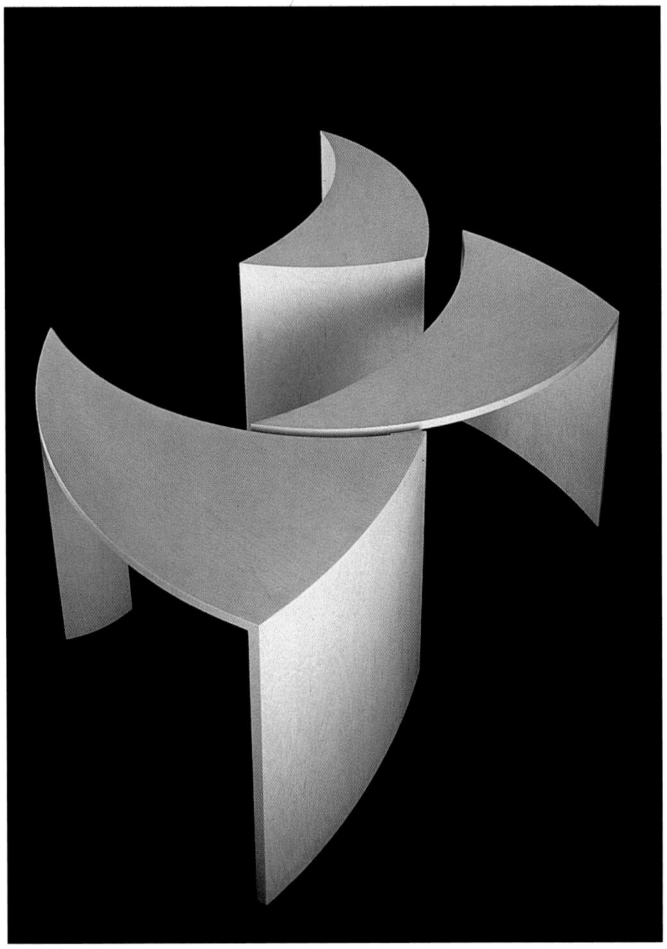

53

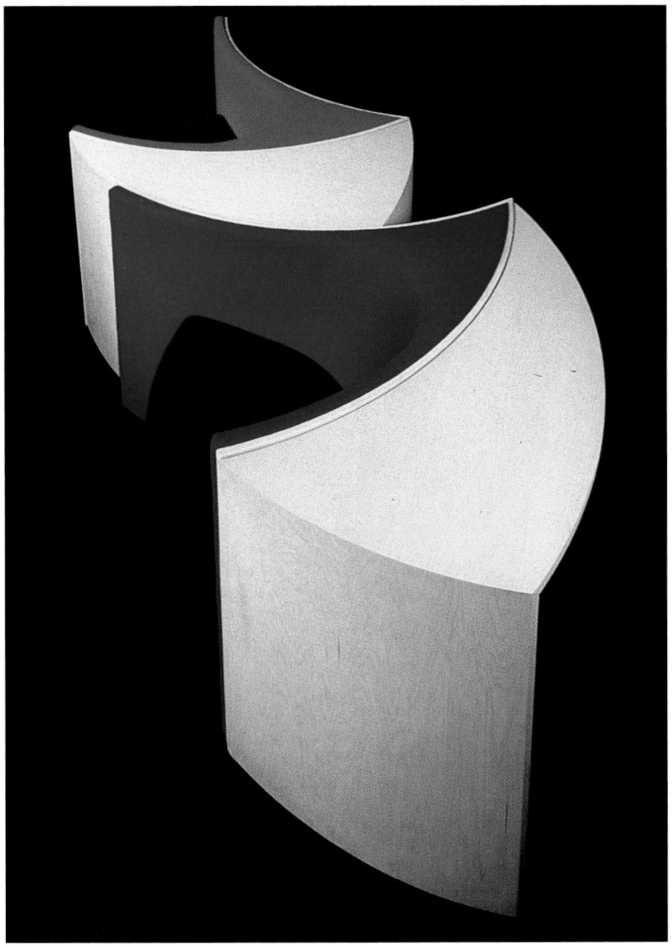

53

53 **Eero Aarnio**
Armchair and table, *Delfin*
Birch, fabric
h 68cm w 99cm d 114cm
h 26¾in w 39in d 44⅞in
Adelta/Finlandcontact, Germany

54 **Bang Design**
Shelving system, *Radius*
Veneered board, plywood
Various sizes
Anibou Pty Ltd, Australia

54

54

55

55

55 **Thomas Sandell**
Bookcases
Birch veneer, fibreboard
h 177, 103cm w 90cm d 32.5cm
h 69¾, 40½in w 35⅜in d 12¾in
IKEA, Sweden

56 **Defne Koz**
Cupboard from the *Tomo* collection
Wood, chrome
h 128cm w 120cm d 60cm
h 50⅜in w 47¼in d 23⅝in
Alparda, Turkey

57 **Olivier Leblois**
Chair, *216*
Cardboard
h 91cm w 32cm d 45cm
h 35⅞in w 12⅝in d 17¾in
Quart de Poil, France
(One-off)

56

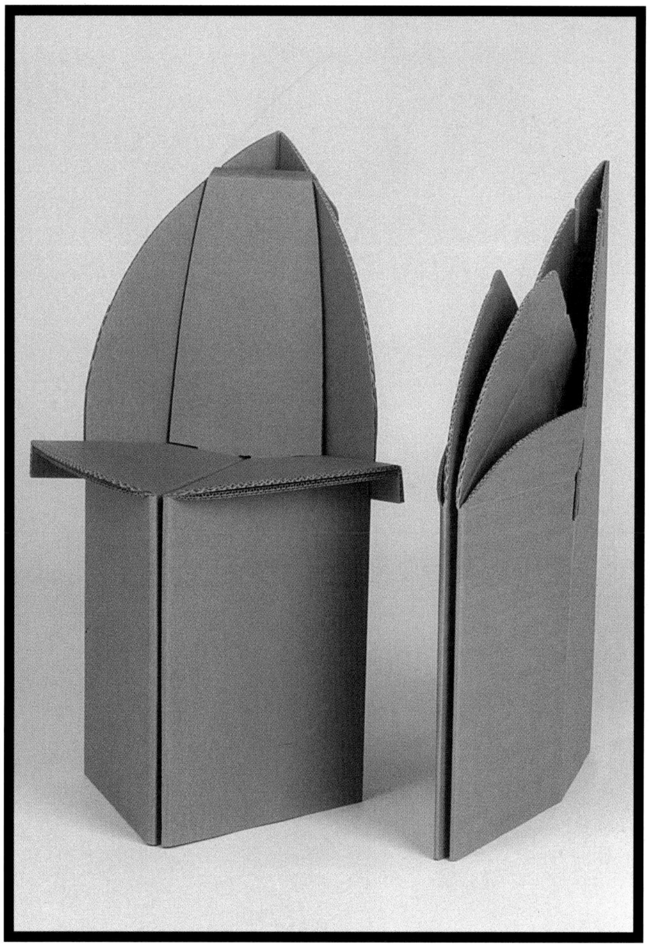

57

58 **Thibault Desombre**
Furniture range, *Izara*
Stainless steel, natural teak
Chair: h 82cm w 43cm d 50cm
h 32¼in w 16⅞in d 19⅝in
Armchair: h 82cm w 52cm d 52cm
h 32¼in w 20½in d 20½in
Bar stool: h 99cm w 46cm d 51cm
h 38in w 18½in d 20⅛in
Round table: h 74cm di 70cm
h 29⅛in di 27½in
Soca Line, France

59 **Christina and Anders Leideman**
Cabinet, *Binary*
Sand-blasted glass, plywood, birch/cherry
h 45cm w 45cm d 17.5cm
h 17¾in w 17¾in d 6⅞in
Collage & Co., Sweden
(Prototype)

60 **Jaap van Arkel**
Tilted cupboards, *DD07*
Steel plate
h 44, 57, 70cm w 31, 29, 27cm d 17, 18, 20cm
h 17⅜, 22½, 27½in w 12¼, 11⅜, 10⅝in d 6¾, 7⅛, 7⅞in
Droog Design, The Netherlands
(Prototype)

61 **Chi Wing Lo**
Chest of drawers, *Eon*
Maple, metal
h 100cm w 150cm d 45cm
h 39⅜in w 59in d 17¾in
Giorgetti SpA, Italy

62 **Chi Wing Lo**
Corner chest, *Nyn*
Maple, metal
h 140cm w 48cm d 48cm
h 55⅛in w 18⅞in d 18⅞in
Giorgetti SpA, Italy

63 **Philippe Starck**
Footrest, *Dr Oola*
ABS
h 5cm w 38cm l 50cm
h 2in w 15in l 19⅝in
Vitra (International) AG, Switzerland

58 61
59 62
60 63

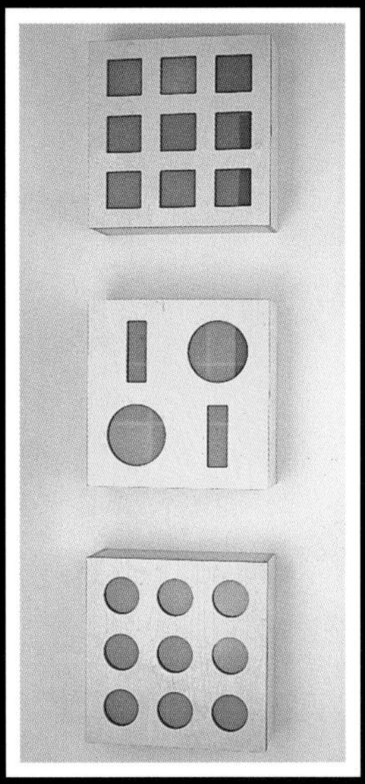

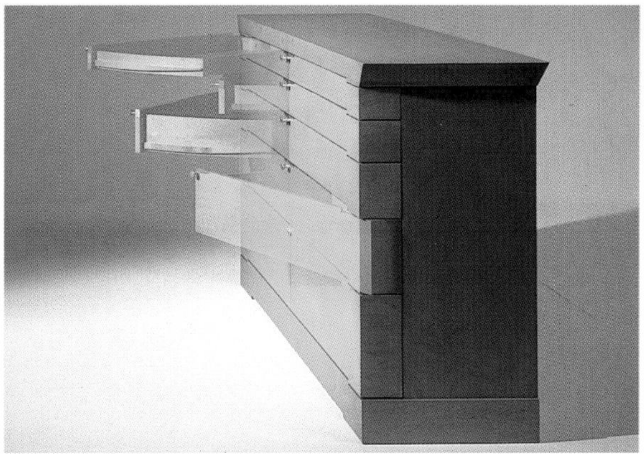

Chi Wing Lo's new storage pieces for Giorgetti show a non-European sensibility applied to Western furniture. This is not just a matter of detailing, such as the arched doors that echo the shape of Chinese grain storage jars. It lies more in a different handling of spaces and volumes, a perception of spatial organization that does not take traditional European forms as a fixed starting point. The pieces express a semantic of storage that, through swinging drawers and curved spaces, challenges our normal perceptions.

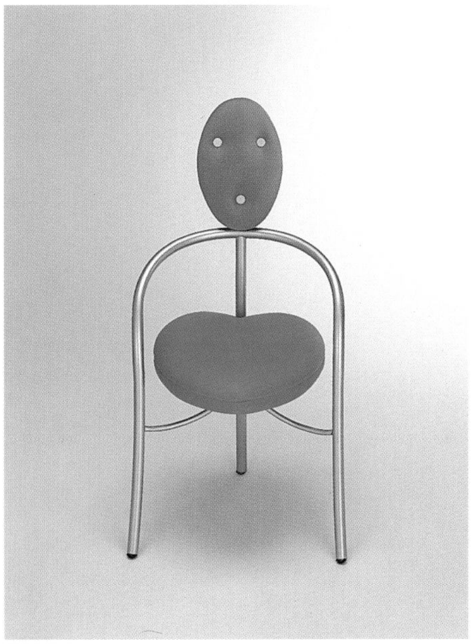

65

Individual expression in a piece of furniture design does not have to be a hot statement: it can be cool, for example the literally reflective understatement in Ron Arad's mirror tables (page 46), or the classical reserve of Kazuko Fujie's bench (page 51). Sometimes, as in Martijn Fransen's neat reworking of hard and soft in an armchair for Droog Design (page 50), intellect and wit are brought into play as much as emotion. In such cases restraint allows the creative personality of the designer to show through. As Mendini puts it: "for some time now my motto has been: simplify, simplify, simplify!" Using the metaphor of a farm, he suggests that "everyone sows his own experience. Seen against this natural background, our project sheds its skin of complexity, becomes something cyclical and simple."

64 **Philippe Starck**
Chair, *Peninsula*
Mahogany-stained beechwood, cotton
h 89cm w 40cm d 46cm
h 35in w 15¾in d 18⅛in
XO, France

65 **Sinya Okayama**
Chair, *Mr Lady*
Tubular steel, fabric
h 91.5cm w 54cm d 59cm
h 36in w 21¼in d 23¼in
Interior Object Inc., Japan

66 **Gaetano Pesce**
Tables, *Triple Play*
Cast resin, resin, steel
h 36, 29, 22cm di 40cm
h 14⅛, 11⅜, 8⅝in di 15¾in
Fish Design, The Netherlands
(Limited batch production)

64

66

67

67 **Ron Arad**
Tables, from the *38 Tables* series
Mirror, polished stainless steel, steel
h 72cm w,l varied
h 28⅜in w,l varied
Ron Arad Studio/Marzorati Ronchetti, UK
(Limited batch production)
Lamps by Ingo Maurer (see page 82)

67

67

68

68 **Sinya Okayama**
Sideboard, *Como*
Veneered ash, stainless steel
h 100cm w 125cm d 27cm
h 39⅜in w 49¼in d 10⅝in
Interior Object Inc., Japan

69

70

These two pieces, by Richard Hutten for Droog Design, make an uncompromising pairing, pillorying well-known symbols. In the year that marks the fiftieth anniversary of the end of the Second World War they offer a sombre reminder of suffering under Nazism, and perhaps also a reminder of the wars of religion that swept across The Netherlands in earlier centuries. They suggest a darker side to the dry humour familiar from Droog's spare and simple designs, though they are executed with the customary flourish of competence.

69 **Richard Hutten**
Couch, *S(h)it On It*
Steel, lacquered MDF
h 75cm w 110cm d 110cm
h 29½in w 43¼in d 43¼in
Droog Design, The Netherlands
(Limited batch production)

70 **Richard Hutten**
Couch, *The Cross*
Maple, polyurethane
h 75cm w 120cm l 200cm
h 29½in w 47¼in l 78¾in
Droog Design, The Netherlands
(Limited batch production)

71 **Norbert Wangen**
Armchair, *Attila*
Wood, stainless steel
h 73cm w 63cm d 56cm
h 28¾in w 24¾in d 22in
(Limited batch production)

71

72

74

73

72 **Chérif**
Sofa, *Grenade*
Fabric, wood
h 67cm w 180cm d 52cm
h 26⅜in w 70⅞in d 20½in
Les Editions Marchal, France

73 **Biagio Cisotti and Sandra Laube**
Cupboards, *Blob*
Wood, metal, plastic
h 180, 100cm w 85, 40cm d 40cm
h 70⅞, 39⅜in w 33⅜, 15¾in d 15¾in
B.R.F., Italy

74 **Martijn Fransen**
Easy chair, *DD61*
Polyurethane, beech
h 75cm w 75cm d 55cm
h 29½in w 29½in d 21⅝in
Droog Design, The Netherlands

75

75 **Kazuko Fujie**

Bench from the *Morphe* series, *Moment-V*

Aluminium, rubber, laminated timber

h 150cm l 854cm d 274cm

h 59in l 336¼in d 107⅞in

Minerva Co. Ltd/Yamamoto Metal Manufacturing Co. Ltd, Japan

(One-off)

76 **Frédérick Du Chayla**

Sofa, *Meridienne Fasi*

Wood, foam, fabric

h 80cm l 140cm d 80cm

h 31½in l 55⅛in d 31½in

Studio Totem, France

76

77

78

77 **Mary Little**
Armchair, *Kim*
Steel, polyurethane foam, fabric
h 87cm w 70cm d 70cm
h 34¼in w 27½in d 27½in
(One-off)

78 **Mary Little**
Armchair, *Tom*
Steel, polyurethane foam, fabric
h 90cm w 60cm d 60cm
h 35⅜in w 23⅝in d 23⅝in
(One-off)

79 **Tom Dixon**
Boat bench and chaise
Galvanized steel
Bench: h 45cm l 180cm d 50cm
h 17¾in l 70⅞in d 19⅝in
Chaise: h 120cm l 180cm d 56cm
h 47¼in l 70⅞in d 22in
Space, UK
(Limited batch production)

79

For Mendini, architecture is design at a different pace. Pieces like Enzo Mari's *Lubecca* bookcase, or Jan Armgardt's recycled chair (page 56) do not hesitate to use an architectonic vocabulary, while Ashley Hall's *RSJ Table* (page 61) takes a positive delight in solving constructional problems, without, however, the function appearing as an afterthought. The same conceit animates Ginbande's *Pic-Nic* table for Sawaya & Moroni (page 59), which folds into an elegant Japanese umbrella for transport.

80

81

80 **Ugo Marano**
Square mosaic, *A Prima Vista*
Enamelled glass
h 50cm w 50cm
h 19⅝in w 19⅝in
Bisazza, Italy

81 **Anna Gili**
Sagittario
Glass mosaic
h 80cm w 80cm
h 31½in w 31½in
Bisazza, Italy

82 **Enzo Mari**
Wall-mounted bookcase, *Lubecca*
Steel, aluminium alloy
h 85cm w 75cm d 20cm
h 33½in w 29½in d 7⅞in
Zanotta SpA, Italy

83 **Johanna Grawunder**
Desk
Plastic laminate custom designed by Rudolf Stingel
for Abet Laminati,
anti-mosquito lamps, clear plastic
h 70cm w 145cm d 32cm
h 27½in w 57⅛in d 12⅝in
Design Gallery Milano, Italy
(Limited batch production)

82

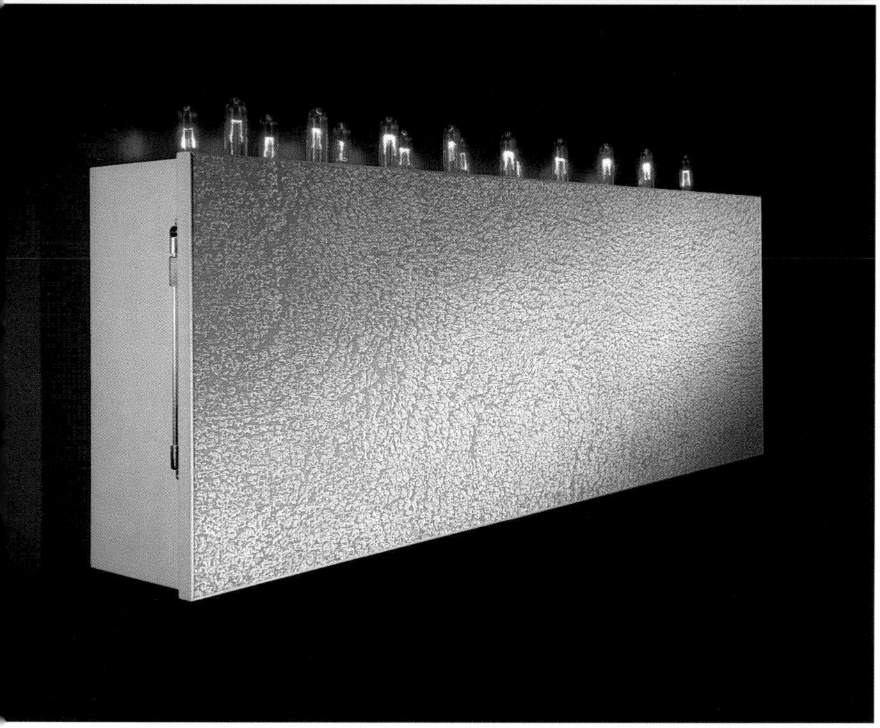

83

When designing her new collection, presented at the Design Gallery Milan during the 1995 *Salone*, Johanna Grawunder set out with two objectives. Firstly she wished to produce a series of pieces of furniture that also incorporated light. Secondly, she wished to show that standard industrial materials could be used in new and different ways, a cross-over of technologies that Mendini and others see as a key to current design activity. She herself describes the work as "Explosion-proof, precision-built, universal type industrial lighting, shop equipment, and power tools designed and built for general purpose applications." (See also page 99.)

85

84

86

87

88

84 **Piero Gaeta**
Armchair, *Poldina*
Wood, polyurethane, fabric
h 82cm w 72cm d 72cm
h 32¼in w 28⅜in d 28⅜in
C.E.M. Cantù, Italy

85 **Jan Armgardt**
Resting Bench JA41P
Plywood, paper, felt
h 76cm w 113cm d 37cm
h 29⅞in w 44½in d 14⅝in
Jan Armgardt Design, Germany
(Limited batch production)

86 **Jan Armgardt**
Chair, *Reader's Place JA39P*
Plywood, paper
h 75cm w 60cm d 70cm
h 29½in w 23⅝in d 27½in
Jan Armgardt Design, Germany
(Limited batch production)

87 **Verner Panton**
Chair
Leather
h 83cm w 58cm d 58cm
h 32⅝in w 22⅞in d 22⅞in
Polythema, Germany

88 **Paul Tuttle**
Easy chair, *Nenufar*
Steel, polyurethane
h 74cm w 68cm d 73cm
h 29⅛in w 26¾in d 28¾in
Strässle Söhne AG, Switzerland

89 **Massimo Morozzi**
Cupboards, *Kasimir*
Teak wood
h 185cm w 138cm d 60cm
h 72⅞in w 54⅜in d 23⅝in
Mazzei, Italy

90 **Geoff Hollington**
Stacking chair, *MSc*
Steel
h 72cm w 36.5cm d 47cm
h 28¾in w 14⅜in d 18½in
SCP, UK

91 **Robert Wettstein**
Child's chair, *Vorwitz*
Birch
h 75cm w 25cm d 60cm
h 29½in w 9¾in d 23⅝in
Structure Design, Switzerland
(Limited batch production)

92 **Stefan Lindfors**
Stacking chair from the Kemper Museum
Fibreglass, reinforced plastic, sand-cast aluminium
h 85cm w 65cm d 59cm
h 33½in w 25⅝in d 23¼in
First Products, USA

93 **Ginbande**
Table, *Pic-Nic*
Wood, nickel-plated metal
h 61cm w 65.5cm d 65.5cm
h 24in w 25¾in d 25¾in
Sawaya & Moroni, Italy

90

91

89

92

93

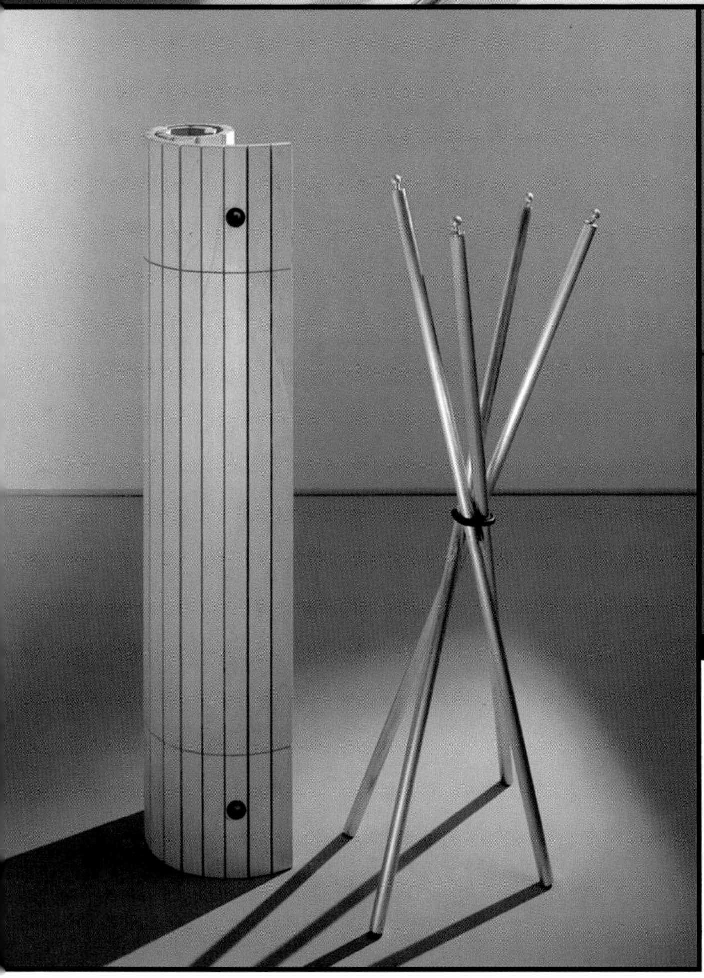

93

94 **Jasper Morrison**
No. 5 series of tables
Douglas fir
h 90, 53cm w 48, 38cm d 53cm
h 35⅜, 20⅞in w 18⅞, 15in d 20⅞in
SCP, UK

95 **Konstantin Grcic**
Extending table
Stainless steel, maple
h 75cm l 130–820cm d 90cm
h 29½in l 51⅛–322⅞in d 35⅜in
Requisitenbau Franke, Winkler, Germany
(One-off)

96 **Piet Hein Eek**
Cupboard series
Various sizes
(One-off)
From left to right:

Wallpaper cupboard, wallpaper, hardboard
Heatingroom cupboard, sheet iron
Asylum cupboard, deal
Church window cupboard, oak, polyester
Vondel cupboard, oak
Bathroom window cupboard, steel
Philips Mono cupboard, oak
Toilet windows cupboard, oak
Ship cupboard, oak
Ironwork cupboard, scrabwood (deal)
Window cupboard, oak
Rubber doors cupboard, oak, rubber
Heating room cupboard, iron sheet
Refrigerator cell door cupboard,
aluminium, beech
Stucco cupboard
multiplex wood, stucco, pine

97 **Ashley Hall**
RSJ Table
Glass, RSJ, galvanized T-section
h 45.5cm w 106cm d 74cm
h 17⅞in w 41¾in d 29⅛in
Ashley Hall Design, UK
(Limited batch production)

94

95

96

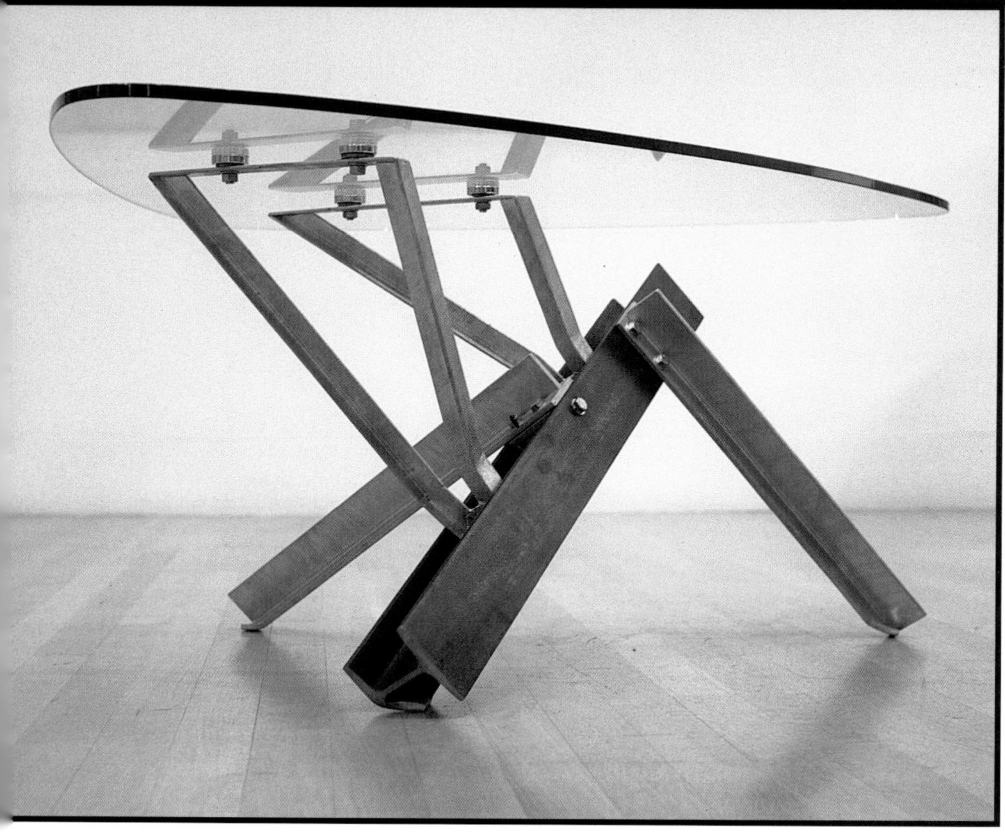

97

New materials and traditional technologies make a combination that fascinates Mendini, an analogy with "the labyrinth of conflicting characteristics" that he sees as defining contemporary humankind. Jane Atfield's chairs, which execute traditional shapes in recycled plastic, and Aldo Cibic's chair in steel and mosaic all celebrate in their individual way this "mystic, robot and neo-natural figure" (pages 64–5). But combining two disparate elements is not a process of conflict, rather one of acceptance of actuality. It becomes a means of using contemporary experience, with all its *anomie* and violence, as a vehicle for optimism and hope, an activity central to design.

98

99

100

98 **Johanna Grawunder**
Coffee table
Fibreglass, black-lacquered base, fluorescent lamps
h 45cm w 120cm d 50cm
h 17¾in w 47¼in d 19⅝in
Design Gallery Milano, Italy
(Limited batch production)

99 **Johanna Grawunder**
Cabinet
Aluminium, fluorescent ceiling light
h 225cm w 60cm d 85cm
h 88⅝in w 23⅝in d 33½in
Design Gallery Milano, Italy
(Limited batch production)

100 **Danny Lane**
Figurative bedside tables
Rusted steel, glass
h 50cm w 110, 120cm d 80cm
h 19⅝in w 43¼, 47¼in d 31½in
(One-off)

101

101

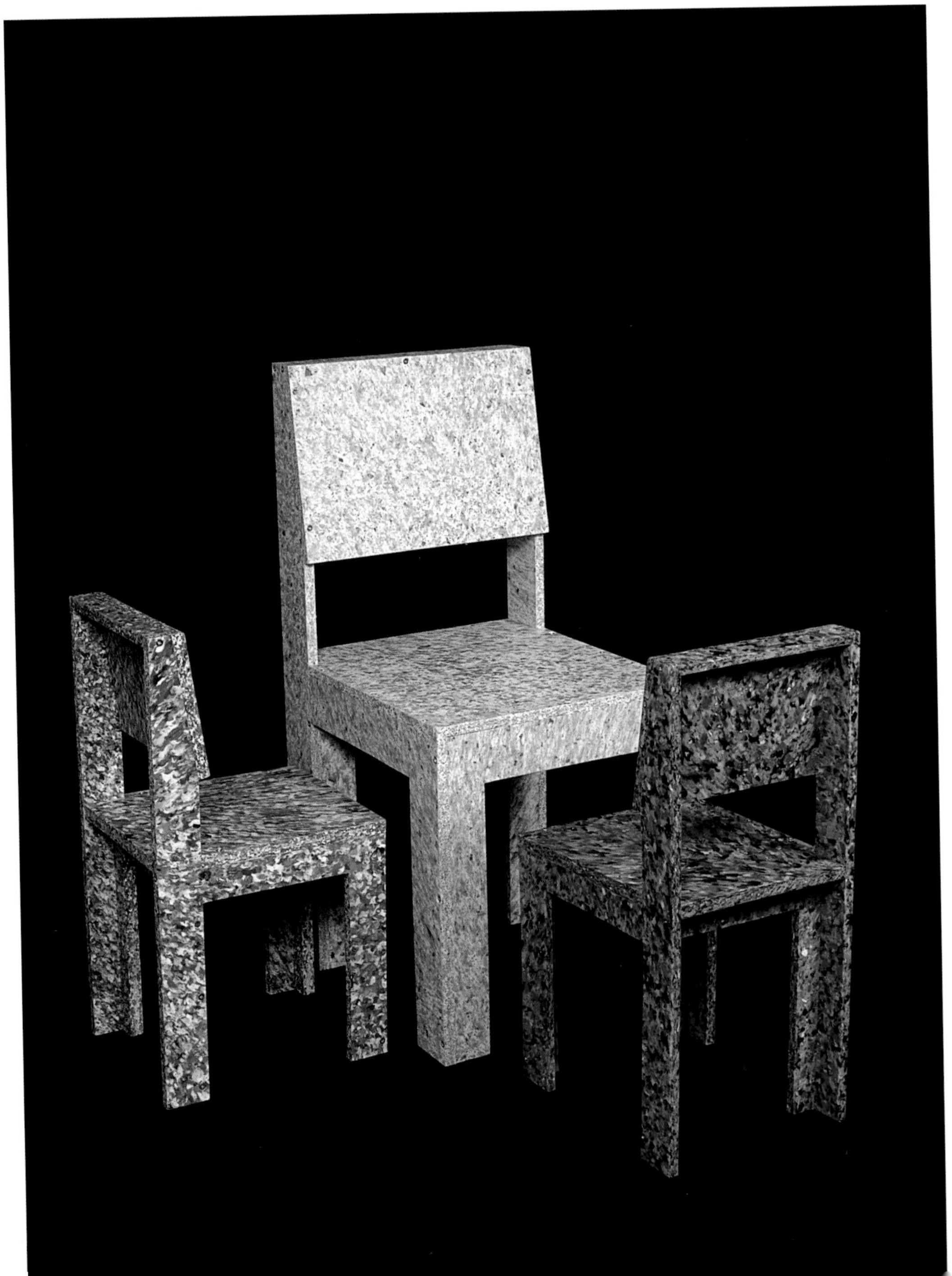

101 **Jane Atfield**
Chair and table, *RCP2*
Recycled plastic
Chair: h 81cm w 38cm d 45cm
h 31⅞in w 15in d 17¾in
Children's chair: h 55cm w 26cm d 30cm
h 26⅝in w 10½in d 11¾in
Children's table: h 50cm w 60cm d 60cm
h 19⅝in w 23⅝in d 23⅝in
Made of Waste, UK
(Limited batch production)

102 **Aldo Cibic**
Chair, *Antalya*
Aluminium, glass mosaic, steel
h 102cm w 45cm d 45cm
h 40⅛in w 17¾in d 17¾in
Bisazza, Italy

102

A chair in mosaic and steel would seem to sacrifice style to comfort, but Aldo Cibic's vigorous and opulent object for Bisazza is more comfortable than it appears, with the steel back having sufficient spring to support the spine easily. Bisazza is a traditional mosaic fabricator, but in recent years they have commissioned new and original work from designers in Italy, mainly for their own collection. Designers chosen have included Anna Gili and Ugo Marano (see page 54), and the works have shown how fruitful a combination of contemporary designers and traditional techniques can be.

103

104

103 **Anna Gili**
Table, *Terra Acqua Fuoco*
Stainless steel, mosaic "Opus Veneziano"
h 42, 49, 56cm
h 16½, 19¼, 22in
Bisazza, Italy

104 **Riccardo Dalisi**
Table, *Tabula*
Steel, glass mosaic, mahogany
h 73cm di 124cm
h 28¾in di 48¾in
Bisazza, Italy

105 **Masayo Ave**
Table, *Filly*
Wood, 3D Shibori textiles "Kumo" and "Karamatsu"
h 90cm di 60cm
h 35⅜in di 23⅝in
(Limited batch production)

106 **Danny Lane**
Table, *Little Sun*
Rusted steel, antique glass
h 60cm w 45cm d 50cm
h 23⅝in w 17¾in d 19⅝in
(One-off)

107 **Denis Colomb**
Night table
Stainless steel
h 50cm l 40cm d 40cm
h 19⅝in l 15¾in d 15¾in
Denis Colomb Créations, France
(Prototype)

105

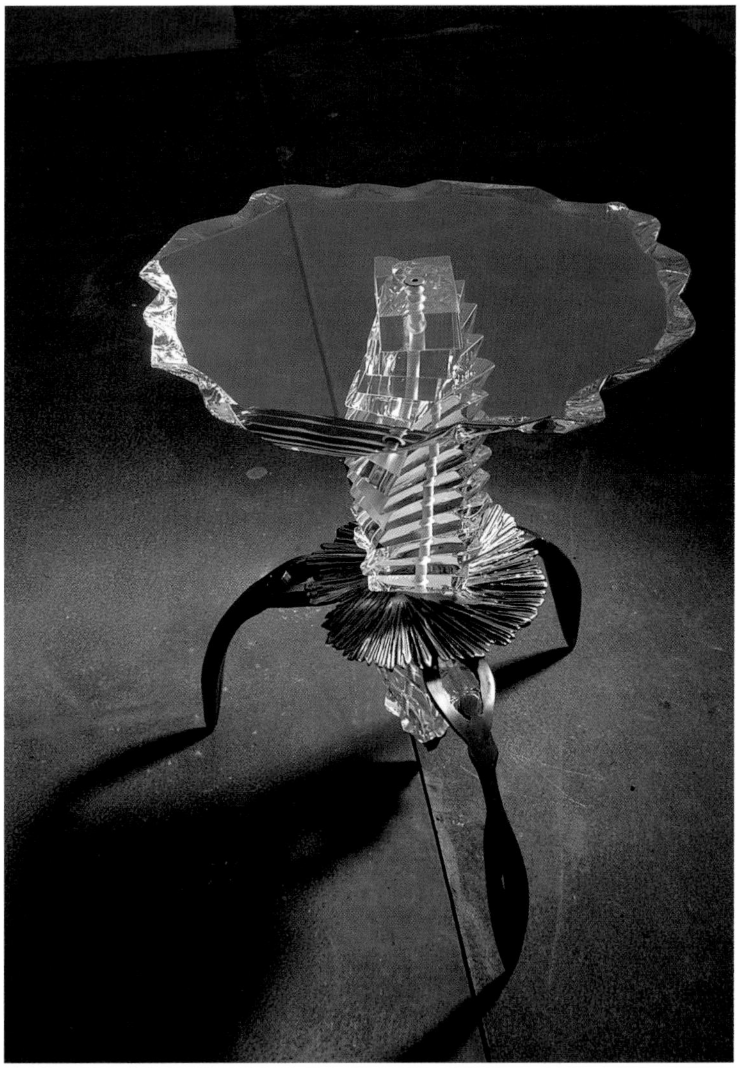
106

107

Successful design often uses simile rather than metaphor; that is to say it buries its connections with other disciplines or media within itself. Take Rolf Sachs' bed (page 76): it has something of the nomad's tent, something of the futon, something of the child discovering a book with a torch under the bedclothes. Such sources – if sources they are – are not paraded, rather they resonate through the design, giving it a human mode and dimension. For Mendini, such links between the human and natural world and the designed object are essential, decisive even, in creating the rituals of domestic life, whether in Antonio Da Motta Leal's metamorphosis of Brazilian flora and fauna into tables (page 70), or through Ayala Sperling-Serfaty's transmuted flora. This necessary interaction assimilates the human and natural worlds into design, "the great project", in Mendini's words, "that is life and the living of it.... Optimism about the future of design seems to me necessarily linked to acceptance of this desire for objects that express our humanity."

108

109

108 **Ayala Sperling-Serfaty**
Table, *Green Moss*
Sawdust on wood
h 45cm w 90cm l 110cm
h 17¾in w 35½in l 43¼in
Aqua, Israel
(One-off)

109 **Vlastislav Hofman**
Chair
Stained oak, leather
h 80cm w 45cm d 47cm
h 31½in w 17¾in d 18½in
Interier Maly, Czech Republic
(Limited batch production)

110 **Tom Dixon**
Chair, *Slatty*
Nickel-plated steel
h 100cm w 40cm d 40cm
h 39⅜in w 15¾in d 15¾in
Space, UK
(Limited batch production)

110

Antonio Da Motta Leal's tables on aluminium frames with tops in Brazilian semi-precious stone are evidence of an independent design experience in South America, derived in part from European and North American examples, but also from local influences. There has been active promotion of graphic and product design in Brazil in the last fifty years, with the establishment of a museum of art and design in the 1950s and the first design schools in Rio de Janeiro and São Paulo in the 1960s. Conferences, visiting teachers and exchange programmes followed and in 1995 the first exhibition of Brazilian design was held in Italy.

111

111

111

111 **Antonio Da Motta Leal**
Table
Cast aluminium, onyx, dolomite
h 48cm w 55cm d 55cm
h 18⅞in w 21⅝in d 21⅝in
Da Motta Studio, USA
(Limited batch production)

112

113

112 **Rupert Williamson**
Chair, *Arran*
Rosewood
h 90cm w 85cm d 70cm
h 35⅜in w 33½in d 27½in
R.W.F., UK
(One-off)

113 **Wulf Schneider & Partner**
Chair, *290F*
MDF, beech
h 80cm w 56cm d 51cm
h 31½in w 22in d 20in
Gebrüder Thonet GmbH, Germany

114 **Philipp Mainzer and Florian Asche**
Table, *T4 Bigfoot*
Oak
h 73.5cm l 230cm d 93cm
h 29in l 90½in d 36⅝in
E15, UK

115 **Kotaro Shimogori**
Chair, *Taiko*
Wood
h 91cm w 43cm d 43cm
h 36in w 17in d 17in
IDT, USA
(Limited batch production)

116 **Jirí Pelcl**
Chaise longue, *Salamander*
Wood, leather
h 100cm w 60cm l 160cm
h 39⅜in w 23⅝in l 63in
(One-off)

117 **Gijs Bakker**
Table, *Bolpoottafe*
Maple wood
h 77cm w 77cm d 75cm
h 30¼in w 30¼in d 29½in
(Limited edition of six)

114

114

115

117

116

118

119

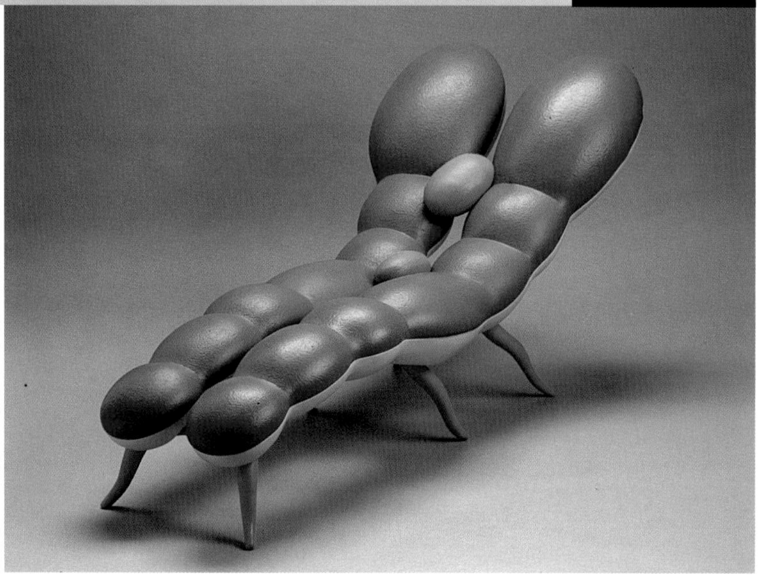

120

118 **Masanori Umeda**
Sofa, *Sakura*
Cherrywood
h 80cm w 113cm d 71.5cm
h 31½in w 44½in d 28⅛in
YOS Collection, Japan

119 **Paolo Giordano**
19 Cushions
Wrought iron, cushions
h 91cm w 142cm d 70cm
h 35⅞in w 55⅞in d 27½in
(One-off)

120 **Marc Harrison**
Sun lounger, *Big Ears*
Acrylic membrane, resin, foam
h 90cm l 200cm d 70cm
h 35⅜in l 78¾in d 27½in
ANTworks, Australia
(One-off)

121 **Nanna Ditzel**
Stacking chair, *Trinidad*
Wood, steel
h 83cm w 50cm d 62cm
h 32⅝in w 19⅝in d 24⅜in
Fredericia Stolefabrik A/S, Denmark

122 **Vladimir Ambroz**
Chair, *Ultralight*
Ceramic fibre, polyester
A.M.O.S., Czech Republic

123 **Vincent Beaurin**
Chair, *Noli Me Tangere*
Polyurethane
h 55cm w 50cm d 40cm
h 21⅝in w 19⅝in d 15¾in
Via, France
(Prototype)

124 **Makoto Komatsu**
High stool
Steel, wood
h 70cm w 30cm d 30cm
h 27½in w 11¾in d 11¾in
B.C. Kôbô Co. Ltd, Japan
(Limited batch production)

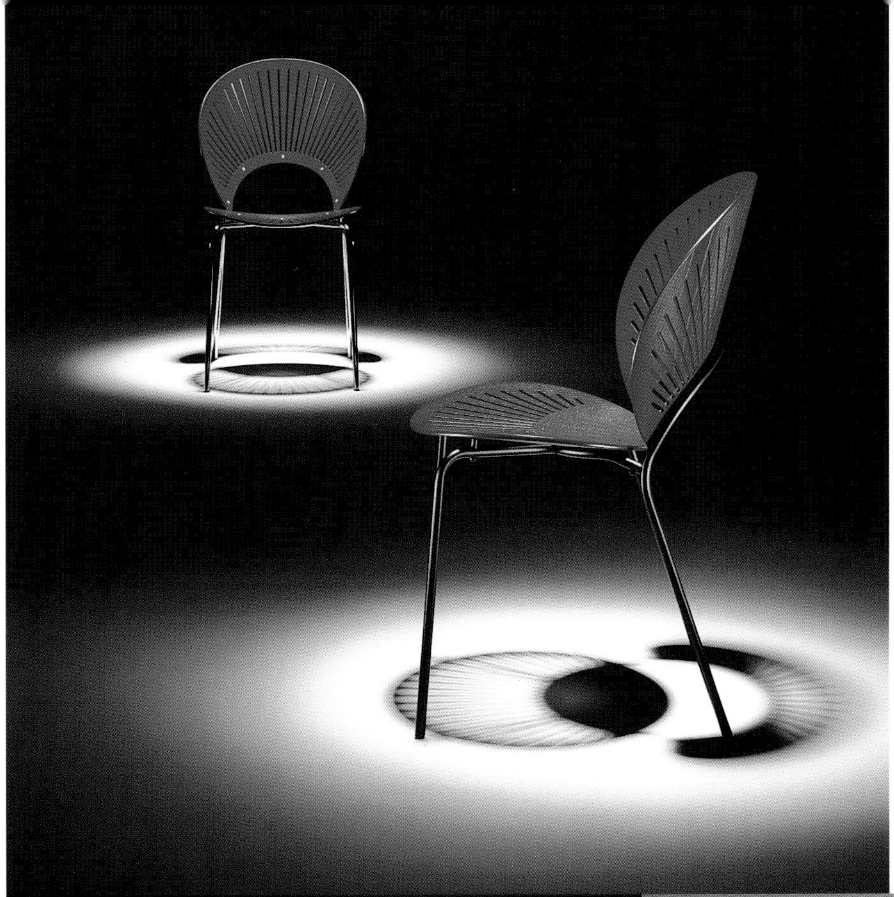

121

123

122

124

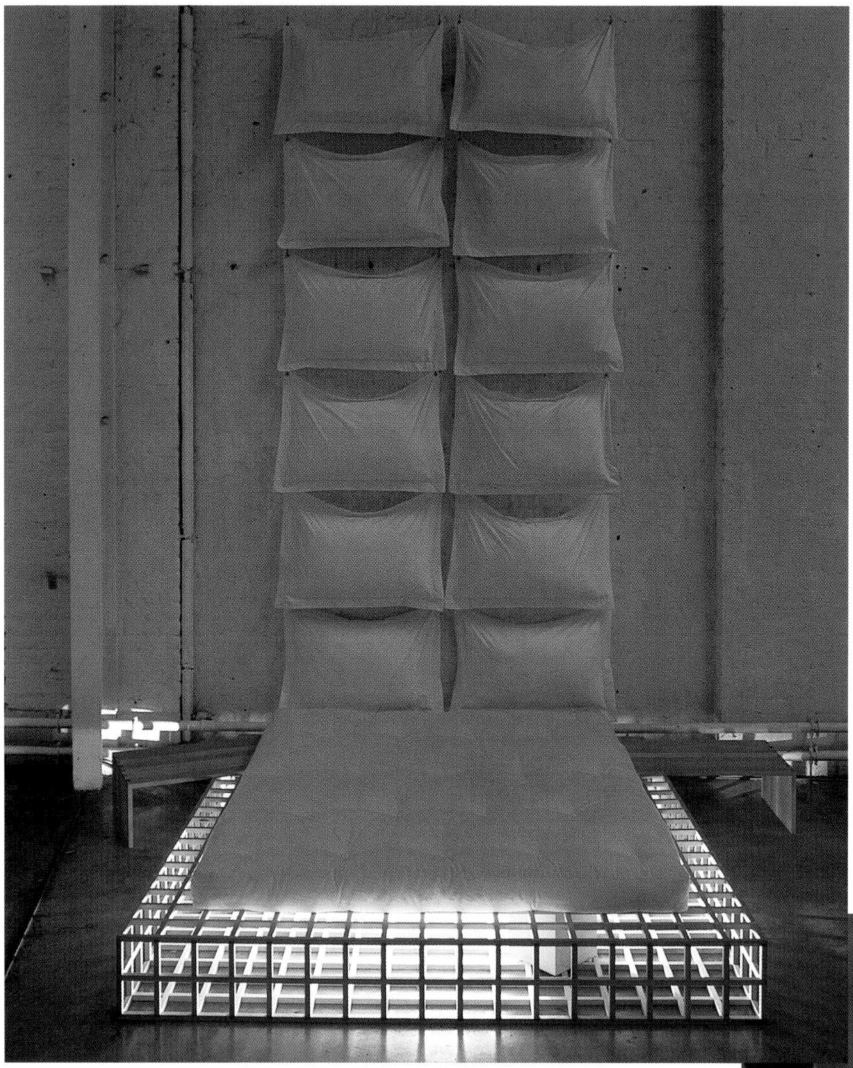

125

126

125 **Rolf Sachs**
Bed with night tables, *Vice*
Maple, futon
h 25.4cm w 200cm l 220cm
h 10in w 78¾in l 86⅝in
(Limited batch production)

126 **Ron Arad and Javier Mariscal**
Armchair, *Sof Sof*
Steel, flame retardant polyurethane, metal
One seat with one arm:
h 96cm w 88cm d 93cm
h 37¾in w 34⅝in d 36⅝in
Moroso, Italy
(Prototype)

127 **Michal Fronek and Jan Nemecek**
Cabinet, *Tin Can*
Stainless steel
h 200cm w 30cm d 40cm
h 78¾in w 11¾in d 15¾in

128 **Bohuslav Horak**
Coat stand, *Spring*
Iron, lacquered beech
h 180cm di 65cm
h 70⅞in di 25⅝in
Anthologie Quartett, Germany

129 **Paolo Giordano**
5 Feet Table
Wrought iron, wood
h 78cm w 120cm d 70cm
h 30¾in w 47¼in d 27½in
Asia Edition, Italy
(Limited batch production)

127

128

129

l i g h t i n g

Faking chaos is perhaps a necessary design tactic these days: chaos because both our scientific and our emotional understandings of the contemporary world emphasize its complex and aleatory nature, its real multiplicity and virtual duplicity, its endless parallel mirrors between medium and message; and faking because however hard the designer tries to convey the chance and complexity of the world, the design has to be fixed, has to be cut from metal, built in concrete, printed on paper, in a single, final form. For all the alchemies of design, every experiment has to show an end result. As Mendini puts it, the ceremony of design is "the strainer through which we can reduce a flood of contemporary enigmas to a tenable synthesis, a vision." Lighting design, with its central role in our experience of space, its vast available technology and its ability to express ornament and decoration, can both illuminate chaos and enrich its complexities, as in the work of Ingo Maurer, Weyers and Borms and Danny Lane.

1 **Danny Lane**
Chandelier, *Sword of Damacles*
Float glass
Xenon bulb
h 750cm di max 110cm
h 295¼in di max 43¼in
Structural Engineer: Whitby and Bird
Lighting consultant: Tim Warner
(One-off)

2 **Weyers and Borms**
Chandelier, *Fish Fuck In It*
Iron, polyester, mixed media
(bubble blower, audio tape)
32w 220v circular tube light
1 x 60w, 1 x 100w, 2 x 10w 220v bulbs
h 80cm w 60cm l 350cm
h 31½in w 23⅝in l 137¾in
(One-off)

2

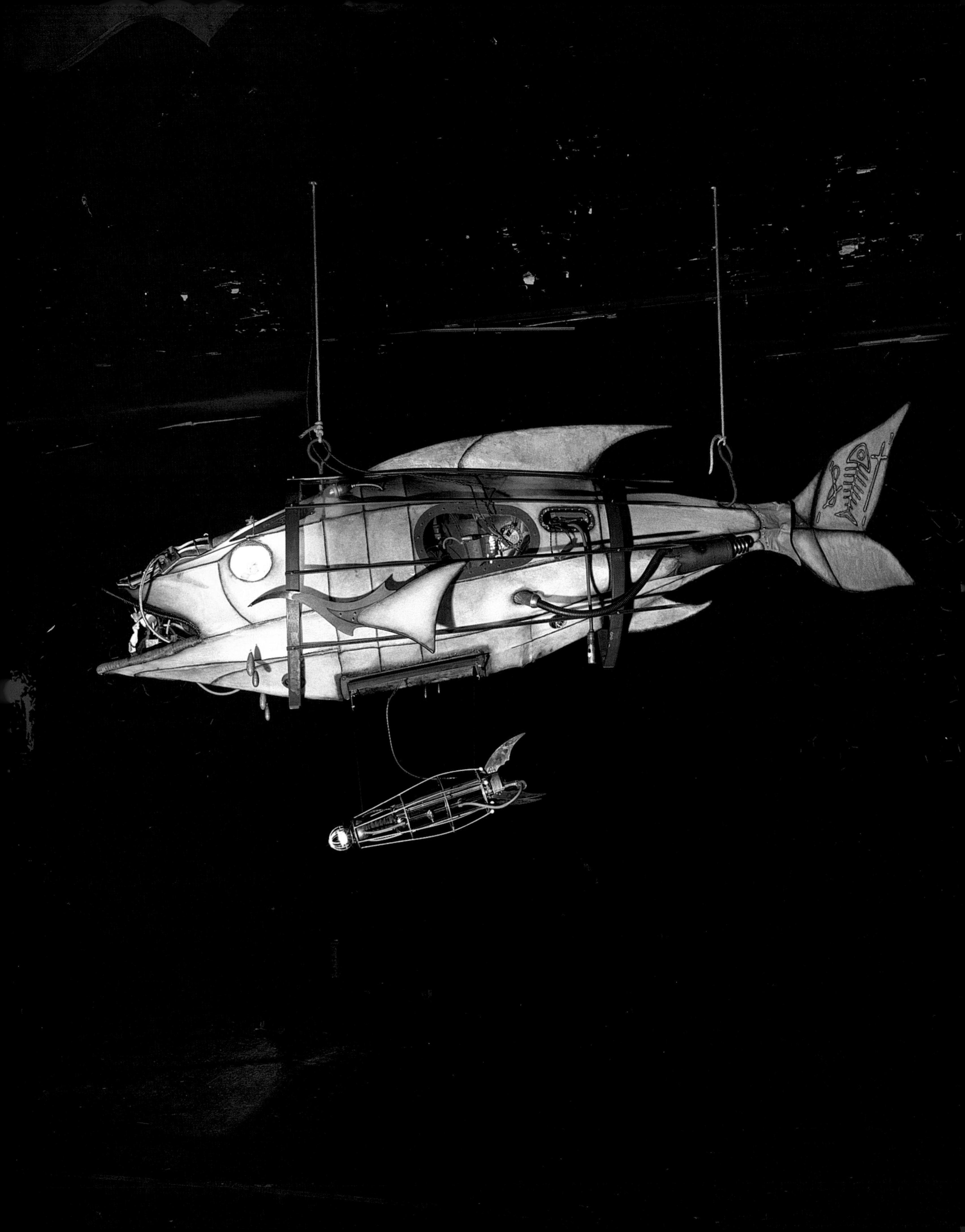

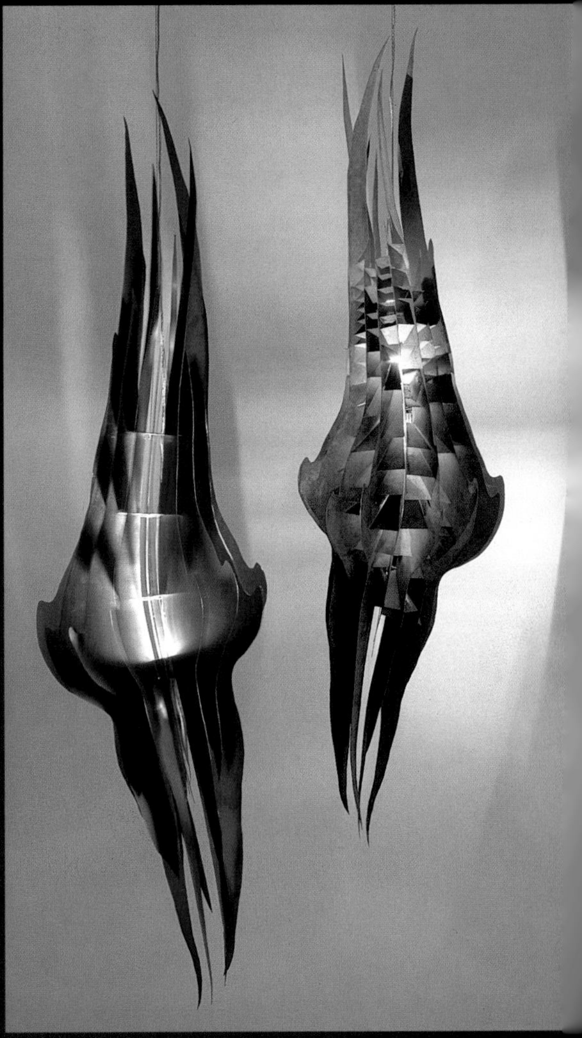

5

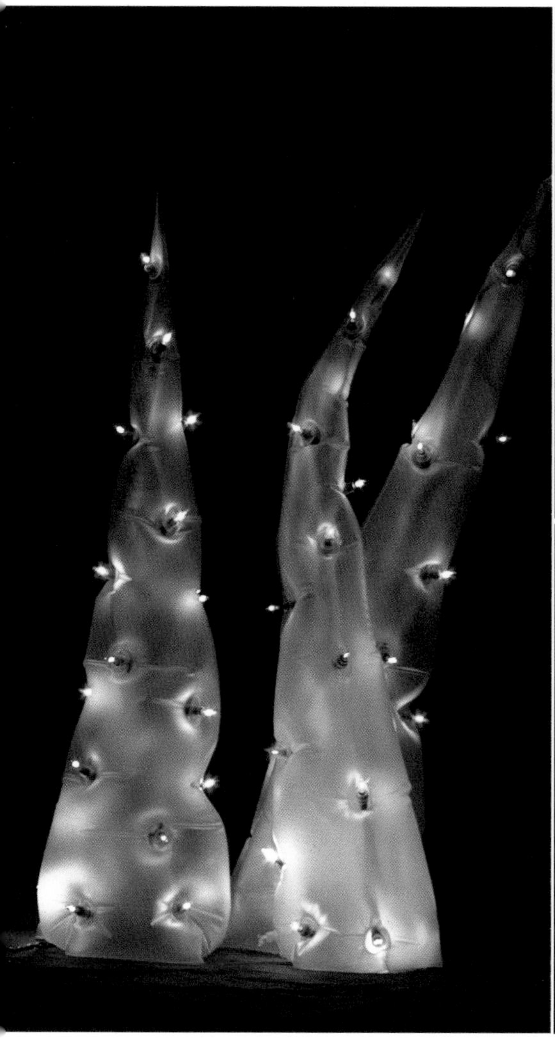

6

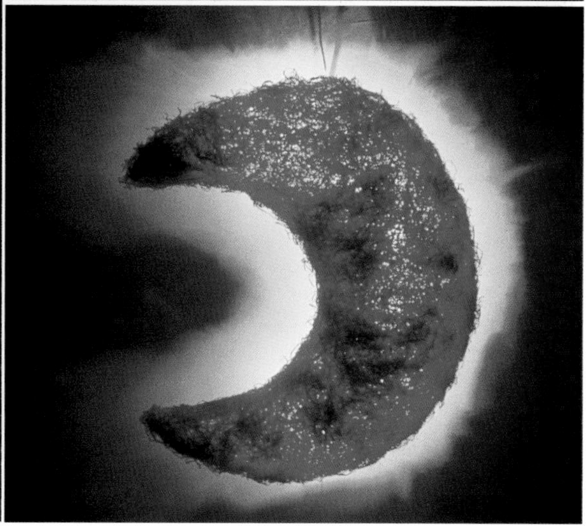

7

3 **Ingo Maurer**
Suspension lamp, *Orgia d'Oro*
Gold-plate
Total 600w 230v frosted and
clear halogen bulbs
h 100cm di 60cm
h 39⅜in di 23⅝in
Ingo Maurer GmbH, Germany
(Limited batch production)

4 **Ingo Maurer**
Suspension lamp, *Magnoon*
Metal
300–900w 230v halogen and blue
fluorescent bulbs
h 300cm di 70cm
h 118⅛in di 27½in
Ingo Maurer GmbH, Germany
(Limited batch production)

5 **Katrien Van Liefferinge**
Table lamp, *Luminosa*
PVC
Coloured fairy lights
h 30–60cm w 20–40cm l 30–60cm
h 11¾–23⅝in w 7⅞–15¾in l 11¾–23⅝in
(Limited batch production)

6 **Masafumi Katsukawa**
Table lamp, *Manda I/Manda II*
Pyrex glass
20w 12v bulb
h 28, 35cm w 18cm d 8cm
h 11, 13¾in w 7⅛in d 3⅛in
(Prototype)

7 **Gaetano Pesce**
Wall lamp, *Moonshine*
Shredded paper, resin, steel, iron
Coloured bulb
h 69cm w 50cm d 20cm
h 27⅛in w 19⅝in d 7¾in
Fish Design, The Netherlands
(Limited batch production)

3, 4- *inset*

8

9

8 **Weyers and Borms**
Chandelier, *Dobrou Chut*
Copper, glass,
polyester, motors
12v bulbs
h 35cm w 110cm l 150cm
h 13¾in w 43¼in l 59in
(One-off)

9 **Weyers and Borms**
Chandelier, *Syndrome*
Iron, glass, polyester, water,
pump, loudspeakers
2 x 10w 110v bulbs
3 x 40w candle model bulb,
1 x 40w clear bulb,
1 x 60w 220v spotlight
h 150cm di 160cm
h 59in di 63in
(One-off)

Jules Verne's predictions on the late twentieth century have just been rediscovered and published. Weyers and Borms' work might have been produced to coincide with just that event. The whirling propellors and turning arms on their lights epitomize a nineteenth-century view of mechanical technology, filtered by Hollywood: the *Syndrome* chandelier would fit the stateroom of the *Nautilus* in any remake of *20,000 Leagues under the Sea*. The young Belgian designers' choices of colour and form suggest a submarine influence, but their lamps are reminiscent of the bioluminescent creatures of the deep sea, rather than anything terrestrial. Since several of these one-off pieces were commissioned for a hotel in the seaside resort of Zeebrugge, this is perhaps quite appropriate.

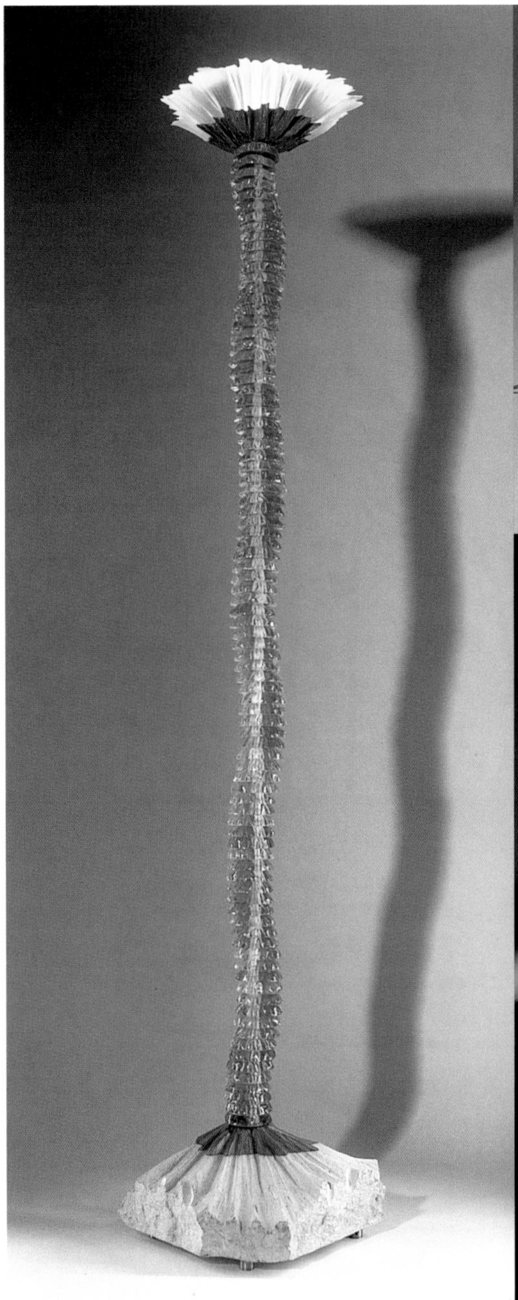

10

11

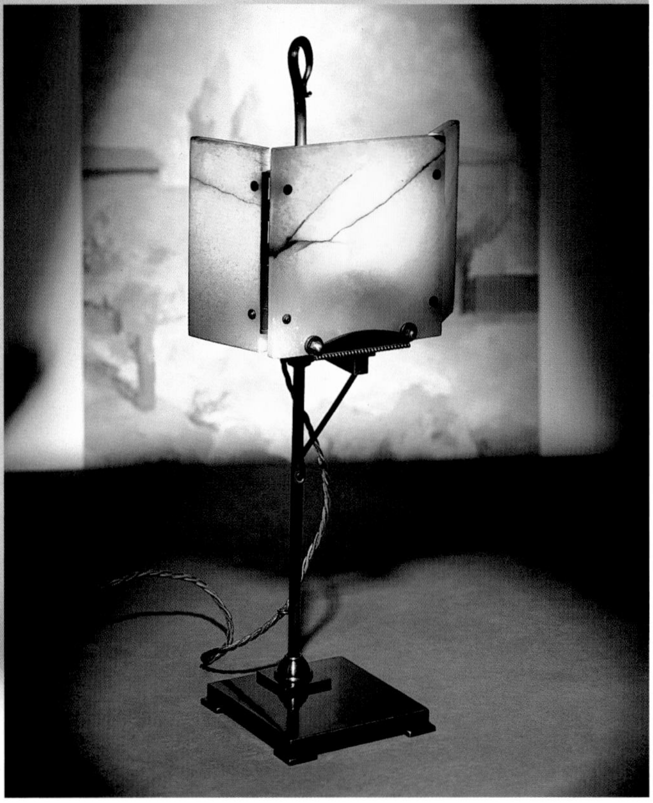

12

10 **Danny Lane**
Floor lamp, *Palm Light*
Glass, stone, steel
Halogen capsule
h 210cm w 35cm d 35cm
h 82⅝in w 13¾in d 13¾in
(One-off)

11 **Frank Schreiner**
Table lamp, *Light Companion*
Wood, brass
Max 40w bulb
h 45cm w 30cm d 15.4cm
h 17¾in w 11¾in d 6in
Stiletto Studios, Germany

12 **Michael Graves**
Table lamp, *Villa Giulia*
Patinated brass, onyx
100w bulb
h 50.8cm w 15.2cm d 13.3cm
h 20in w 6in d 5¼in
Baldinger, USA
(Limited batch production)

13 **Weyers and Borms**
Chandelier, *Lunatics*
Iron, polyester, paper, motor
75w 220v halogen bulb
12 x 25w top-mirrored gold bulbs
h 90cm di 100cm
h 35⅜in di 39⅜in
(One-off)

13

Even magic needs to be structured, just as the apparent simplicity of light to our senses dissolves into the real complexities of its physics. What could be simpler to imagine than a lamp on the end of a wire or at the top of a stand, and yet more difficult to design with balance and grace? Providing a minimal platform, which can also be integrated into the visual richness of the modern home, is the challenge answered by designers such as Terri Pecora, Nick Allen and Tobias Grau. The traditional vocabulary of luminaires – uplighting, pendant, supported – is articulated through simple forms, so making us more aware of the design challenges involved. Uplighters, for example, need to be both stable and invisible: there is no point putting a light on a pedestal and then living in its shadow.

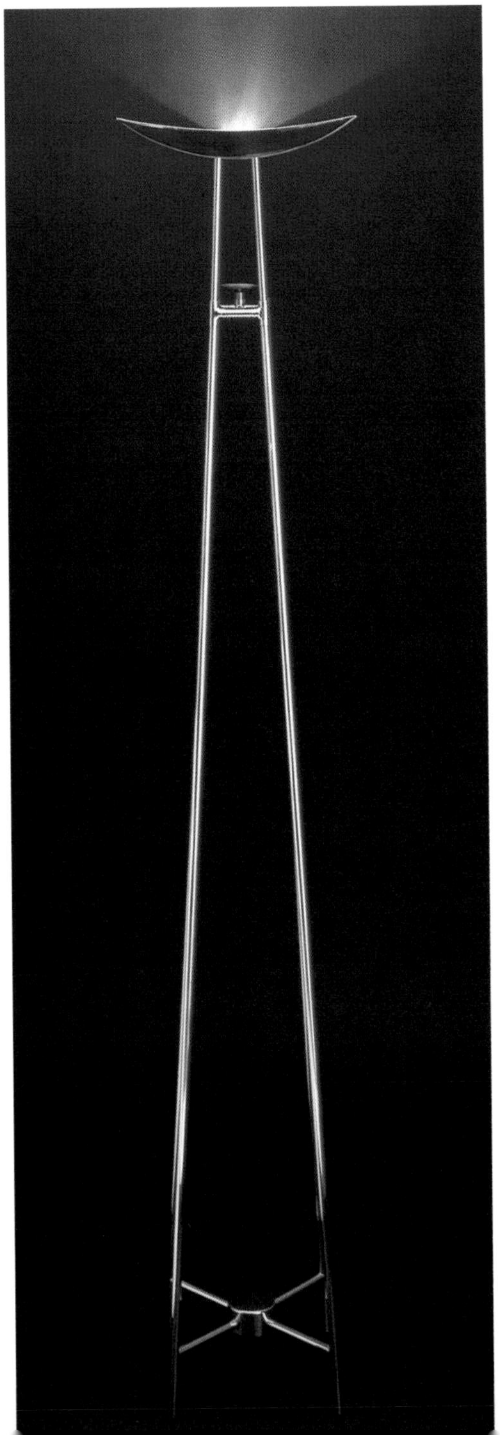

14

15

16

14 **Andrea Ponsi**
Floor lamp, *Vul*
Copper
250w halogen bulb
h 190cm w 35cm l 25cm
h 74¾in w 13¾in l 9⅞in
Andrea Ponsi Design, Italy

15 **Terri Pecora**
Ceiling/suspension lamp, *Yes*
Aluminium
Halogen bulb
h 20cm w 8cm
h 7⅞in w 3⅛in
Mito, Italy

16 **Hermann Czech**
Wall light, designed for the Palais Schwarzenberg
Brass, opaline glass
60w 220v bulb
h 32cm w 20cm
h 12⅝in w 7⅞in
Woka Lamps Vienna, Austria
(One-off)

17

18

17 **Alberto Meda**
Floor lamps, *Uni-X Family*
Aluminium, glass, polycarbonate
300w halogen bulb
h 186cm di 31cm
h 73¼in di 12¼in
Luceplan SpA, Italy

18 **Olivier Gagnere**
Table lamp, *Girbaud*
Bronze, chromed metal, parchment
60w bulb
h 57cm di 35cm
h 22½in di 13¾in
Néotù, France

19 **Vico Magistretti**
Table lamp, *Silica*
Metal, glass
9w compact fluorescent bulb
h 30cm di 16cm
h 11¾in di 6½in
FontanaArte, Italy

20 **Franco Clivio**
Desk light, *Lucy*
Solid cast aluminium, plastic
18/50w 12v low-voltage halogen bulb
(small head)
Compact fluorescent bulb (large head)
h max 76cm w max 69cm
h max 29⅞in w max 27⅛in
Erco Leuchten GmbH, Germany

20

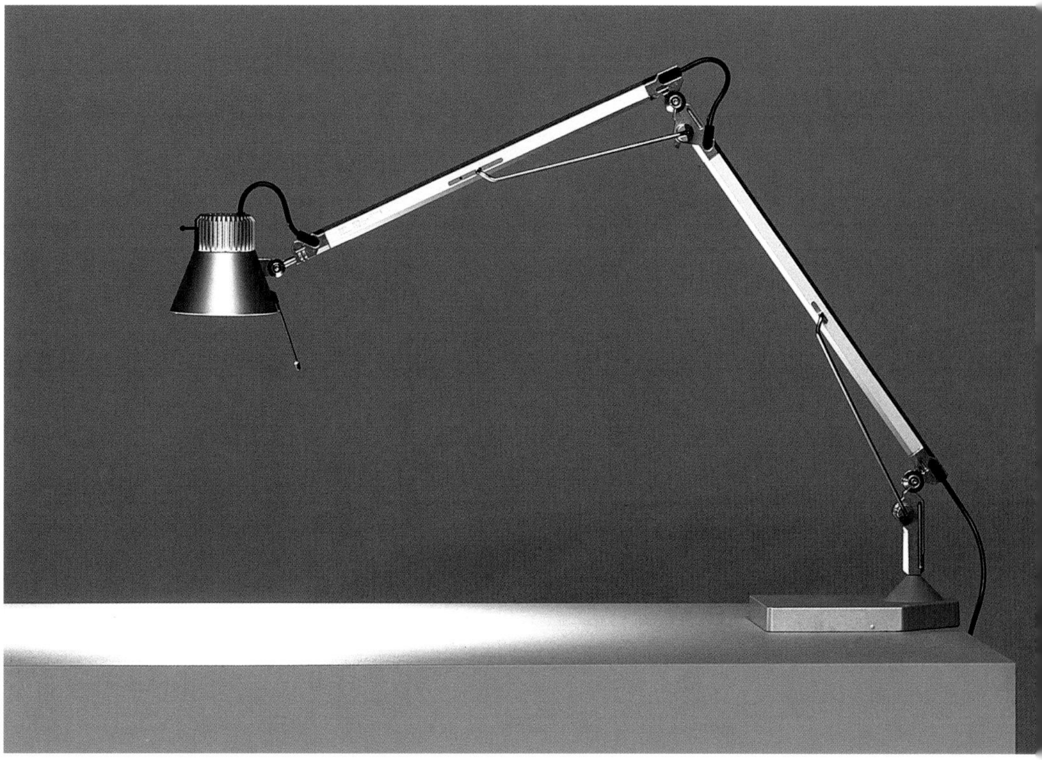

The desk lamp presents a traditional design conundrum: you want light over the workspace without the lamp stand cluttering it up. The luminaire has to move back and forwards, again without moving the stand. Franco Clivio's new solution to this old problem pays proper homage to the classic Anglepoise design, while finding a formal vocabulary in tune with the new compact fluorescent bulb in the lampholder.

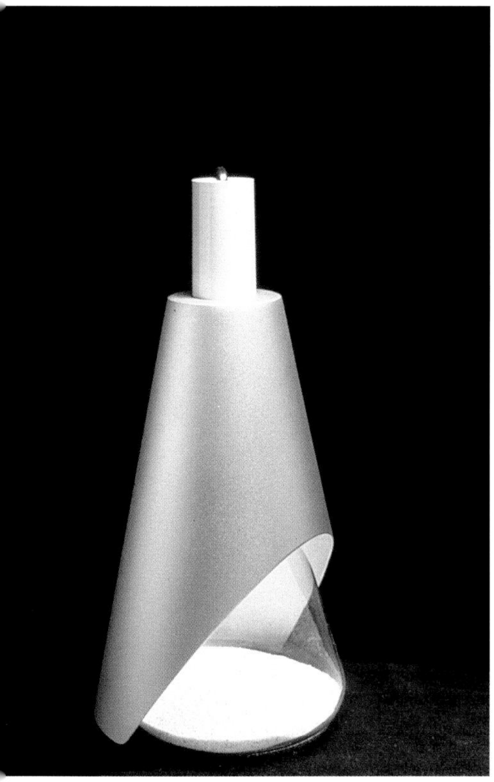

19

21

Agnoletto and Clerici's table lamp adds a touch of the surreal to the moonlight theme: the colour combination suggests a Christmas pudding, while the prominent cable recalls the fuse of an old-fashioned anarchist's bomb. This witty light is a reminder of how many layers of meaning even a simple shape can contain, just as Jane Atfield's *Flight Box* transforms the designer's light box with memories of green fields.

22

21 **Jane Atfield**
Wall lamp, *Flight Box*
Birch plywood, recycled plastic
23w bulb
h 37cm w 37cm d 15cm
h 14⅝in w 14⅝in d 5⅞in
(Limited batch production)

22 **Agnoletto and Clerici**
Table lamp, *Moon*
Glass, metal
60w or 100w bulb
di 25cm
di 9⅞in
Amedei Tre SNC, Italy
(Prototype)

23 **Greg Healey**
Desk lamp, *Jumpy Light*
Aluminium, stainless steel
50w 12v bulb
h 90cm w 25cm
h 35⅜in w 9⅞in
(Prototype)

24 **Design Network**
Extensible standard lamp, *Stadium 1*
Bardiglio crushed marble, steel
2 x 75w 220v halogen bulbs
h 170–250cm w 29cm di 26cm
h 66⅞–98⅜in w 11⅜in di 10¼in
Pallucco Italia SAS, Italy

24

23

25 **Karim Rashid**
Floor lamp, *Lucinda*
Hand-blown glass, walnut, stainless steel
100w incandescent bulb
h 190cm di 25cm
h 74¾in di 9⅞in
(Limited batch production)

26 **Anna Eoclidi**
Table/floor lamp, *Contessa*
Aluminium, hand-blown glass,
stainless steel
50w 12v halogen bulb
h 120cm w 15, 20cm di 20cm
h 47¼in w 5⅞, 7⅞in di 7⅞in
(One-off)

27 **Tobias Grau**
Floor lamp, *Pur Mickey*
Plastic, glass, steel
50w 220–240v bulb
h 175cm di 33cm
h 68⅞in di 13in
T. Grau KG GmbH & Co., Germany

28 **Nick Allen**
Floor lamp, *Maasai Light*
Steel, bronze
20w halogen bulbs
h 200cm w 61cm d 49cm
h 78¾in w 24in d 19¼in
(Limited batch production)

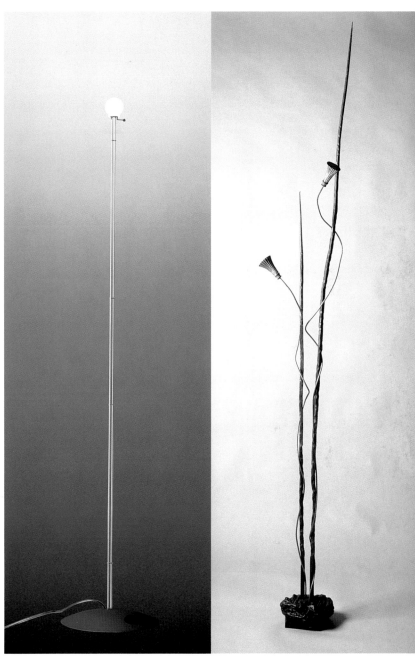

27

28

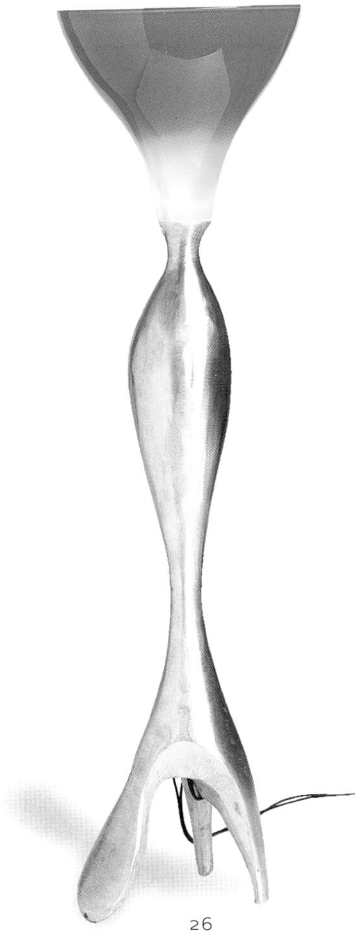

25

26

Light is such a common metaphor in speech and thought that it is not surprising that lighting design often turns to metaphor. This is sometimes direct, as with Jean-Charles de Castelbajac's *Moon* and *Storm* (page 100), and sometimes indirect, as in Isao Hosoe's *Heron* table lamp, or Ayala Sperling-Serfaty's *Night Lights* (page 100). At other times the metaphor becomes sculptural, for example Johanna Grawunder's classic cubes (page 99). Here celebrating technology moves on into a celebration of formal values, in which the light source itself plays a defining role.

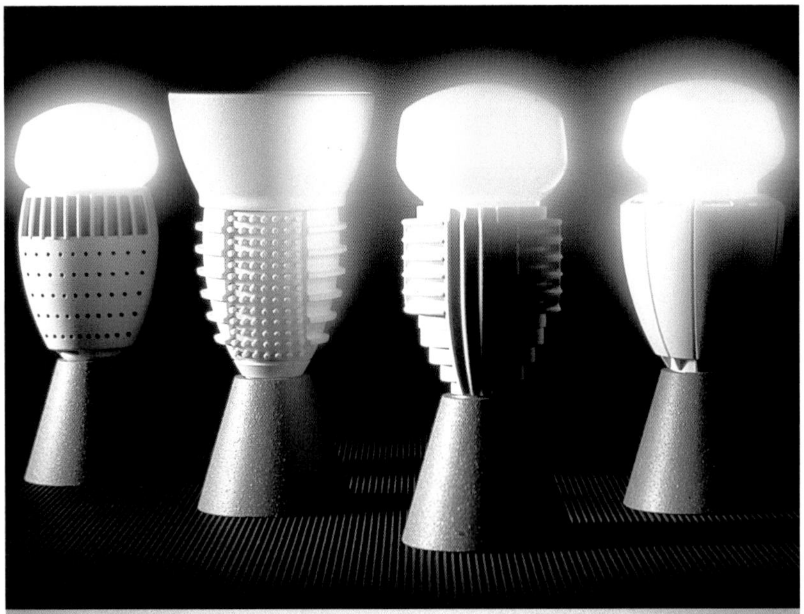

29

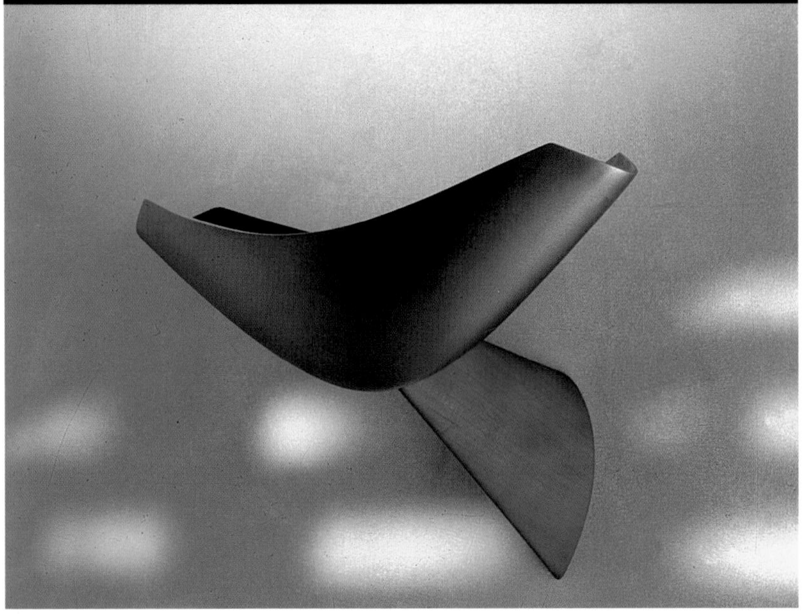

30

29 **Jochen Backs (IDEO Product Development)**
Electrical light source, *E-Lamp*
Die-cast chassis,
injection-moulded ABS coating
h 15.2cm d 7.3cm
h 6in d 2⅞in
Diablo Research Corporation, USA
(Prototype)

30 **Josep Lluscà**
Wall lamp, *Servul*
Metal, wood
300w halogen bulb
h 18cm w 29cm d 17cm
h 7in w 11⅜in d 6¾in
Flos SpA, Italy

31 **Isao Hosoe**
Table lamp, *Heron*
Nylon reinforced with fibreglass
50w 12v halogen bulb
h 64cm w 54cm
h 25¼in w 21¼in
Luxo Italiana SpA, Italy

31

32

Hartmut Engel's two suspension fittings from the *Dancer* spotlight series show how judicious handling of the luminaire casing can add eloquence to an otherwise purely technical object. The stepped fins of the floodlight give it a dynamic appearance, while the rounded modelling of the spotlight echoes the pencil beam of light it produces.

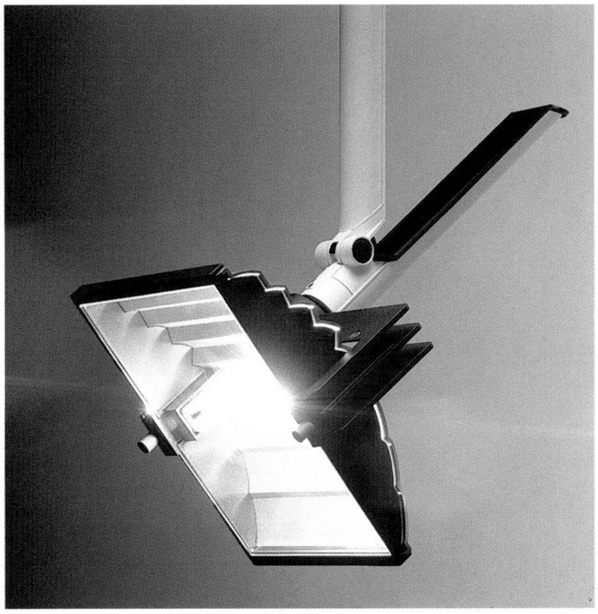

33

32, 33 **Hartmut Engel**
Spot systems,
Dancer 33 and *Dancer 25*
Die-cast aluminium,
polycarbonate, plastic
Dancer 33 (right):
26w 240v or 150w 240v
compact fluorescent halogen bulb
Dancer 25: max 100w 240v
tungsten halogen bulbs
Various sizes
Staff, Germany

34 **Johanna Grawunder**
Table lamp
Fibreglass, lacquer
Fluorescent bulb
h 30cm w 30cm d 30cm
h 11¾in w 11¾in d 11¾in
Design Gallery Milano, Italy
(Limited batch production)

35 **Feldmann & Schultchen**
Wall lamp, *Flexlight*
Polycarbonate, foil
40w 220v bulb
h 15cm w 40cm l 40cm
h 5⅞in w 15¾in l 15¾in
Brainbox, Germany

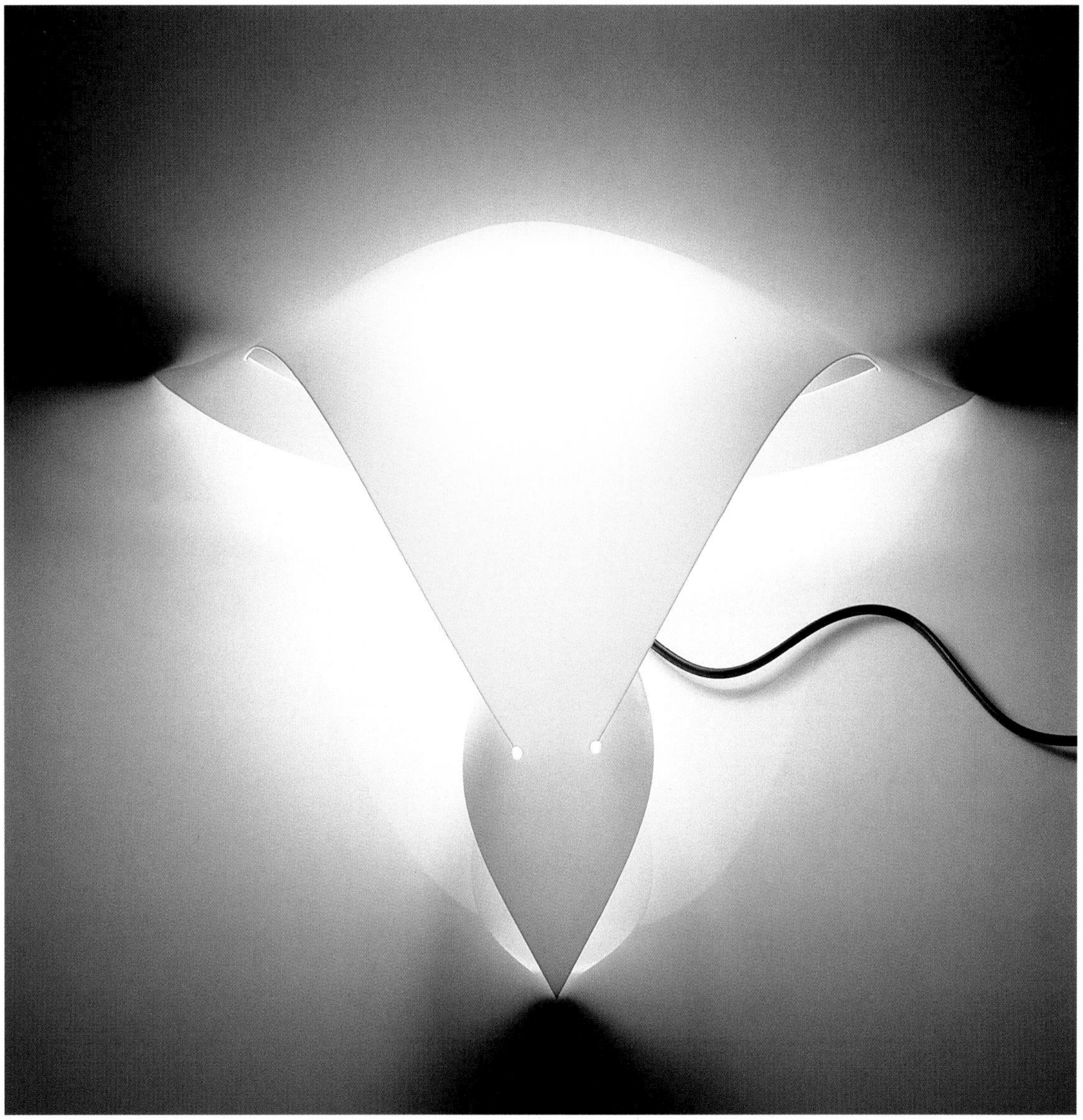

35

34

36

38

37

39

36 **Ayala Sperling-Serfaty**
Table lamp, *Night Light 6*
Metal, silk
40–60w 230v bulb
h 20cm di 30cm
h 7⅞in di 11¾in
Aqua, Israel
(Limited batch production)

37 **Ayala Sperling-Serfaty**
Floor lamp, *Night Light 2*
Metal, copper
Max 300w 230v bulb
h 38cm di 48cm
h 15in di 18⅞in
Aqua, Israel
(Limited batch production)

38, 39
Jean-Charles de Castelbajac
Moon and *Storm*
Resin
60w bulb
Moon: h 35cm l 35cm
h 13¾in l 13¾in
Storm: h 38cm l 34cm
h 15in l 13⅜in
Brossier-Saderne, France

40 **Kazuyo Komoda**
Table lamp, *Libro da Comodino*
Aluminium, Teflon
20w 12v halogen bulb
Open: h 15cm w 27.5cm d 17cm
h 5⅞in w 10⅞in d 6¾in
Closed: h 3.5cm w 13cm d 17cm
h 1⅜in w 5⅛in d 6¾in
(Prototype)

41 **Marc Harrison**
Wall/floor/table lamp,
Aphid Illuminant
Flexible plywood, polycarbonate
Compact fluorescent or
incandescent bulb
h 30cm w 12.5cm l 30cm
h 11¾in w 4⅞in l 11¾in
ANTworks, Australia

40

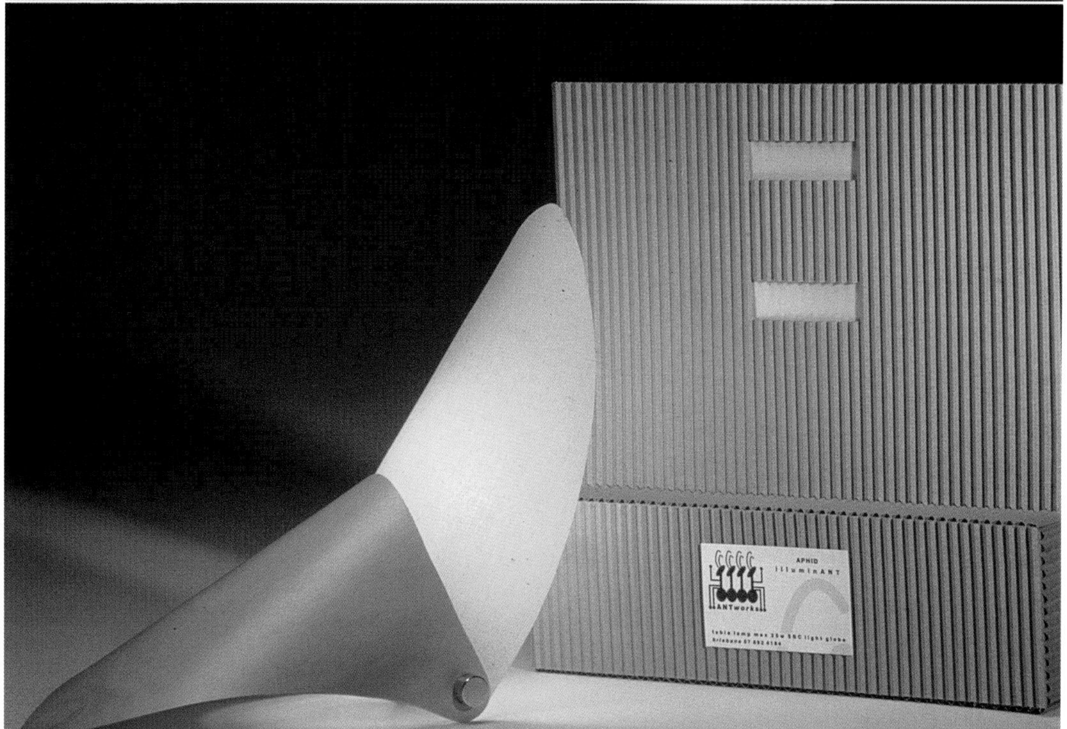

41

Light is colour, Newton's prism tells us. Colour in lighting can provide animation and contrast in an overall decorative setting. Whether in a major fitting, such as Gregory Prade's astonishing insect shape (page 105), or in a discreet reading lamp by Giovanni Levanti, colour in fitting and light plays the same role as ornament or decoration in furniture, offering a further layer of imagery, references and reflections that makes up our personal, subtle perception of our own space.

42

42 **Piero Gaeta**
Table lamp, *Gost*
Glass, metal
60w incandescent bulb
h 25/37cm di 9/14cm
h 9⅞/14⅝in di 3½/5½in
Le Cose Nostre srl, Italy

43 **Giovanni Levanti**
Table lamp, *Cromatica*
Aluminium, coloured paper
75w cool beam bulb
h 56cm w 42cm l 26cm
h 22in w 16½in l 10¼in
Domodinamica srl, Italy

43

44

45

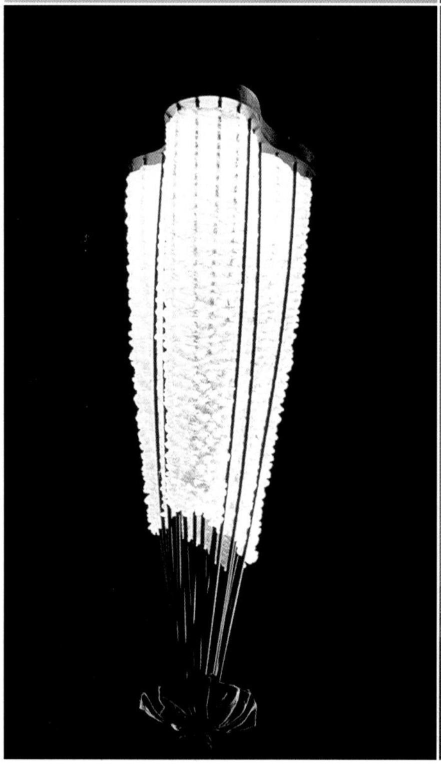

46

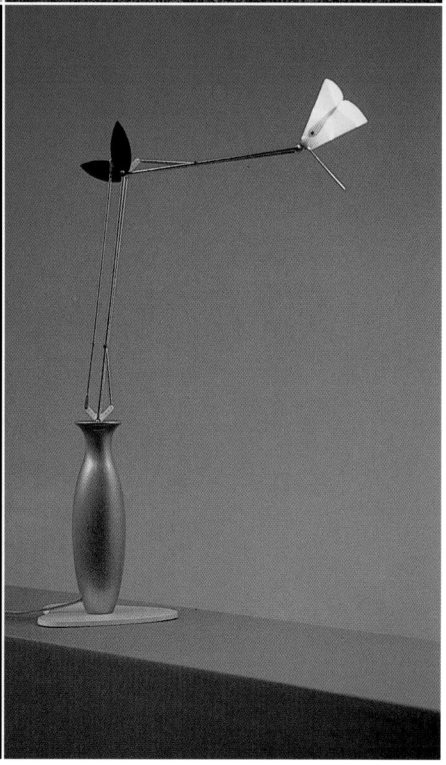

47

44 **Nestor Perkal**
Floor lamp, *Fort Apache*
Chestnut wood, porcelain
150w bulb
h 165cm w 50cm
h 65in w 19⅝in
Lou Fagotin Editions, France
(Limited batch production)

45 **David D'Imperio**
Table lamp, *Aquifer*
Wood, brass, aluminium
2 x 20w 12v halogen bulbs
h 61cm w 15.2cm d 15.2cm
h 24in w 6in d 6in
David D'Imperio, USA
(Limited batch production)

46 **Masayo Ave**
Floor lamp, *Mymble*
Wood, Shibori textile "Miura"
60w bulb
h 110cm w 32cm d 32cm
h 43¼in w 12⅝in d 12⅝in
(Limited batch production)

47 **David D'Imperio**
Desk lamp, *Virosa*
Wood, brass, steel, aluminium
20w 12v halogen bulb
h max 86.3cm w (base) 15.2cm
l max 61cm di (base) 7.6cm
h max 34in w (base) 6in
l max 24in di (base) 3in
David D'Imperio, USA
(Limited batch production)

48 **Pietro Laviani**
Suspension lamp, *Slim 1*
Glass, metal
Max 150w bulb
h 120cm w 26cm d 12cm
h 47¼in w 10¼in d 4¾in
Mito, Italy

49 **Ashley Hall**
Table lamp, *Nacelle*
Polycarbonate, acetate
9w 240v bulb
h 28.5cm w 16cm d 12.5cm
h 11¼in w 6¼in d 4⅞in
Ashley Hall Design, UK
(Prototype)

50 **Gregory Prade**
Wall lamp, *77 Moons*
Stainless steel, glass
w 16cm l 25cm
w 6½in l 9⅞in
Primavera Light, Germany

48

49

50

In Mendini's terms, we need "the new neo-natural outlook, by which I mean a return to the vision of our natural world as the key to our basic survival, as well as to spiritual enrichment". This vision is both the physiological action of perception, and our self-awareness of our place in nature and the world. What better way to illuminate such a vision than through the natural light of a candle, whether in Bohuslav Horak's baronial splendour or Jane Atfield's simplicity of shape. Or to insist on the intimate quality of soft light, as in Howard Montgomery's *Sopus* (page 110). For if it is light that links us to the world, it can also be light that links us to ourselves.

51

51 **Robert Wettstein**
Candleholder, *Lupa*
Leather, glass
h 30cm di 14cm
h 11¾in di 5½in
(Limited batch production)

52 **Svitalia Design**
Candlestick, *Lucidino*
Cast aluminium
h 15cm di 6cm
h 5⅞in di 2⅜in
Svitalia, Switzerland

53 **Bohuslav Horak**
Chandelier, *Lilia*
Lacquered aluminium
h 90cm di 105cm
h 35⅜in di 41⅜in
Anthologie Quartett, Germany

52-*inset*, 53

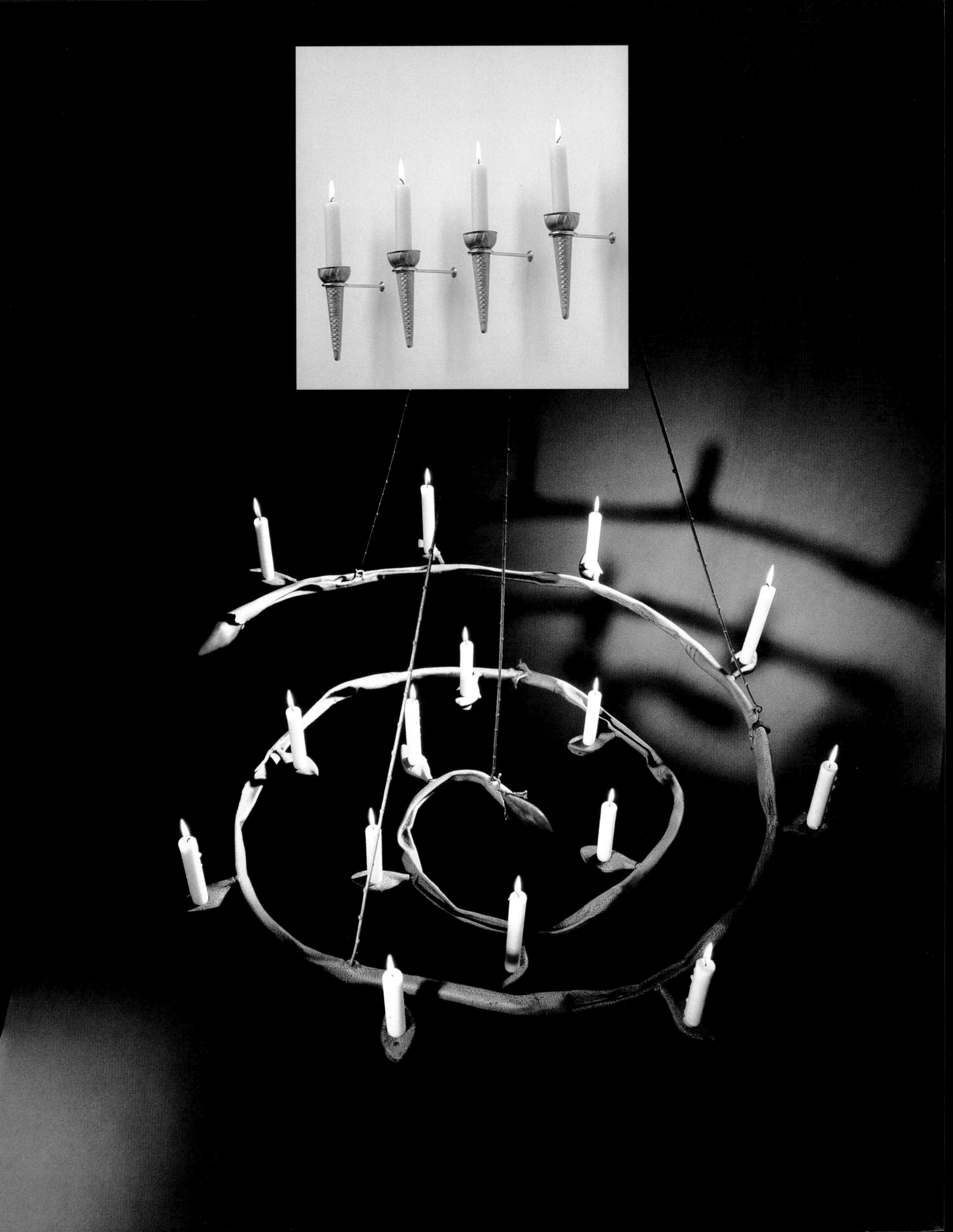

54 **Jane Atfield**
Candleholders
Wax, aluminium, cork disc
h 19cm di 7cm
h 7½in di 2¾in
Space, UK
(Limited batch production)

55 **Guinter Parschalk**
Floor lamp
Steel, Japanese paper, synthetic paper, resin finish
40w incandescent bulb
h 60cm l 25cm
h 23⅝in l 9⅞in
Radix Comercial Ltda, Brazil
(Limited batch production)

56 **Michele de Lucchi**
Folding table lamp, *Trefili*
Aluminium, rubber, cardboard
60w bulb
h 37cm w 10cm d 13cm
h 14⅝in w 3⅞in d 5⅛in
(Limited batch production)

57 **Zeukyau Shichida**
Floor lamp, *Okina*
Bamboo, Japanese paper (*Washi*)
h 54cm di 16cm
h 21¼in di 6¼in
Kwau Shau An, Japan

58 **Sergio Calatroni**
Wall lamp, *Nature*
Bronze
100w 220v bulb
h 100, 84cm w 25cm
h 39⅜, 33⅛in w 9⅞in
Afro City, Italy
(Limited batch production)

Michael Innes writes of "waxworks uneerily aware of their own waxiness". Jane Atfield's candleholders, made themselves of wax, enact a similar "obscure psychological manoeuvre". It is as if the reminder that candle and holder are all one is somehow unsettling, for all the subtle elegance with which they have been executed.

54

55

57

56

58

59

In contrast to the *toko na mai*, the corner of darkness that is at the heart of the traditional Japanese interior, the West looks to the hearth as the centre of the home. Howard Montgomery's *Sopus* and Masanori Umeda's *Be-Byobu* provide new interpretations of this tradition. In the former, a 50–400 HZ electro-luminescent panel is mounted inside a soft, translucent plastic housing, which acts as both diffuser and pillow. With *Be-Byobu*, the floor mounting of the lamp provides an immediate metaphor for the light of a fire.

59 **Howard Montgomery**
Alarm/reading light pillow, *Sopus*
Polyfibre, Jersey, Dacron
50–400 Hz electro-luminescent panel (EL)
h 17.7cm w 83.8cm l 55.8cm
h 7in w 33in l 22in
(Prototype)

60 **Masanori Umeda**
Screen light, *Be-Byobu*
Lacquered MDF, steel,
Japanese paper laminated on resin
60w bulb
(each panel) h 142cm w 57.5cm d 17cm
h 55⅞in w 22⅝in d 6¾in
Be-Echizen, Japan

61 **Yamo**
Suspension oil lamp, *Isara*
Silver-plated metal, steel
di 12cm
di 4¾in
Yamo, France
(Limited batch production)

60

61

市光
市朋

t a b l e w a r e

"One of my favourite historical periods," Mendini told me during the selection meeting for the Yearbook, "is the English Victorian era." Not, he went on, because of the styles of the period, but because of the way in which the taste of the time celebrated the interior: not only a table, but a table with a cover and then a tablecloth over it; not a curtain at the window but a series of layers of textile between interior and exterior. This respect for the rituals of the home, emphasized by the mantlepiece layered with knick-knacks and mementoes, is an expression of what Mendini calls the ideal home: "it is a state of perpetual becoming, always itself and yet not itself. Our furniture is a state of mind, intimately bound up with the reality of our existence as home dwellers. Furnishing our home is a way we have of 'pollinating' the immediate space around us, an extra security that arches over and around our outer skin." Bohuslav Horak's elemental bowl, or Laura de Santillana's elegant dishes (page 116), convey this sense of place, of moving beyond function and beyond decoration.

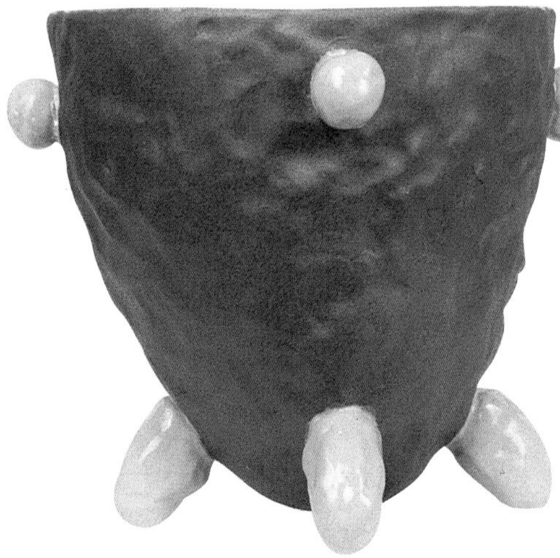

1

2

1 **Bohuslav Horak**
Bowl, *Primitive*
Ceramic
h 30cm di 28cm
h 11¾in di 11in
Anthologie Quartett,
Germany

2 **Nuala Goodman**
Hand-painted boxes
Left to right: *Boxing Women, Pyramid, Heart, Tree of Life, Faces in Blue, Fat Man*
Sesame wood,
tempera, varnish
h 33, 19cm w 14cm d 14cm
h 13, 7½in w 5½in d 5½in
Twergi, Italy

THE TREE OF
JEDERMANN

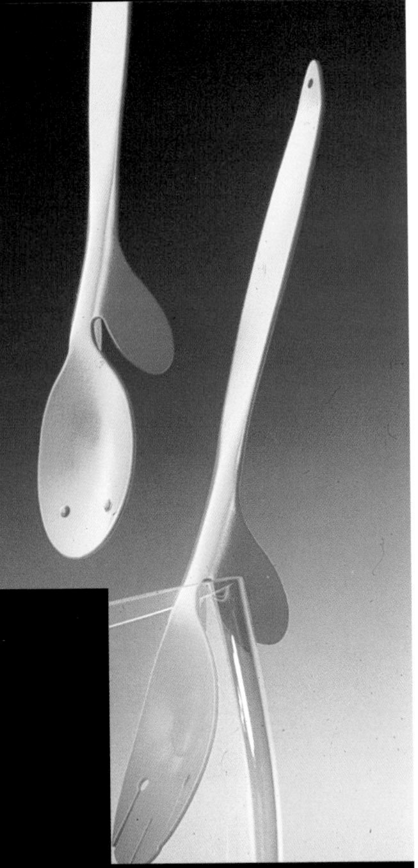

3

4

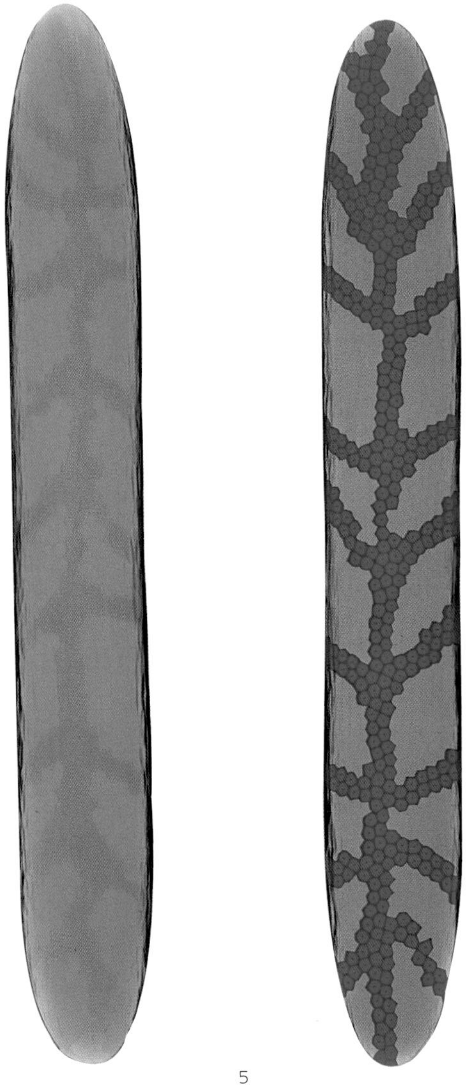

5

3 **Metz/Schlett/Kindler**
Salad servers, *Egon and Kalle*
Plastic
h 6cm w 5cm l 25cm
h 2⅜in w 2in l 9⅞in
WMF, Germany
(Prototype)

4 **Jennifer Lee**
Sand-grained pot
Stoneware clay, oxides
h 13.2cm di 11.1cm
h 5¼in di 4⅜in
(One-off)

5 **Laura de Santillana**
Dishes, *Murrina Vessels*
Murrina pearls
w 8, 6, 5cm l 55, 33cm
w 3⅛, 2⅜, 2in l 21⅝, 13in

6 **Massimo Giacon**
Teapot, *Hole 1*
Porcelain
h 18cm w 15cm d 3cm
h 7⅛in w 5⅞in d 1⅛in
Alessi, Italy
(Prototype)

7 **Massimo Giacon**
Teapot, *Hole 2*
Porcelain
h 18cm w 15cm d 3cm
h 7⅛in w 5⅞in d 1⅛in
Alessi, Italy
(Prototype)

8 **Gaetano Pesce**
Try Tray
Cast resin
h 3cm di 38cm
h 1⅛in di 15in
Fish Design, The Netherlands
(Limited batch production)

9 **Kevin Goehring**
Teapot from the
Barcelona Blanca series
Glazed earthenware
h 16.5cm w 16.5cm l 29.2cm
h 6½in w 6½in l 11½in
Square One, USA
(Limited batch production)

6

7

8

9

10

11

12

13

10 **Gunnel Sahlin**
Carafe
Porcelain
h 22cm di 13cm
h 8⅝in di 5⅛in
IKEA, Sweden

11 **Anna Gili**
Vases, *Tom and Gerry*
Silver
h 28.5, 18.5cm di 10, 9cm
h 11¼, 7¼in di 3⅞, 3½in
De Giovanni Argenteria, Italy

12 **Bohuslav Horak**
Glass, *Viktorka*
h 12cm di 8cm
h 4⅝in di 3⅛in
Anthologie Quartett, Germany

13 **Gunnel Sahlin**
Cup and saucer
Porcelain
Cup: h 8cm di 9cm
h 3⅛in di 3½in
Saucer: h 2cm di 16cm
h ¾in di 6⅓in
IKEA, Sweden

14 **Annaleena Hakatie**
Bowl, *Tight-rope Walker*
Glass
h 18cm w 42cm d 20cm
h 7⅛in w 16½in d 7⅞in
Department of Industrial Design,
University of Art and Design, Helsinki

15 **Geoffrey Mason**
Boys will be Boys
Glass, copper
h 28.5cm di 64.5cm
h 11¼in di 25⅜in
(One-off)

14

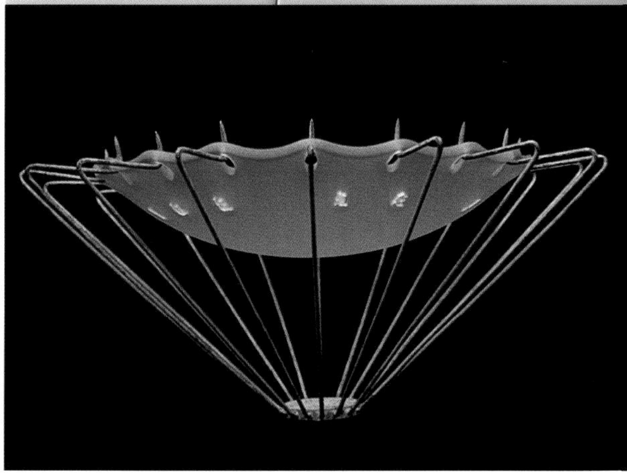

15

Geoffrey Mason's *Boys will be Boys* does not need its rather heady title. The object itself juxtaposes its visible assembly of copper rod and glass plate with an apparent instability, while the points on the rods dare the user to make use of the supporting surface. Described as a reinterpretation of a Chinese ritual bronze vessel, and poised somewhere between a trampoline and a circus tent, the object invites speculation as to its true form while endlessly offering alternative metaphors for its shape.

16

For an object to have a place in the rituals of the home, decoration or ornament are not absolutely necessary. Often decoration can, like Proust's soggy madeleine, enrich the link between a particular item and an aspect of living that we want to celebrate. But abstract form can be charged with as much significance. Zaha Hadid's plates or Anna Gili's goblet (pages 124–5) have this quality of memory, an echo, Mendini would say, of a collective unconscious of forms. Other forms make more direct evocations: Shigeru Uchida's remodelling of tea-ceremony ware, for example (pages 122–3).

16 **Paola Palma and Carlo Vannicola**
E-Vases
Ceramic
h 24cm w 24cm d 6cm
h 9½in w 9½in d 2⅜in
Flavia srl, Italy

17 **Michael Rowe**
Vase
Brass, tin
h 26cm w 44cm d 36cm
h 10¼in w 17⅓in d 14⅛in
(One-off)

18 **Sergio Asti**
Plate from the *Nuvola* series
Porcelain
di 31cm
di 11¾in
Richard-Ginori srl, Italy

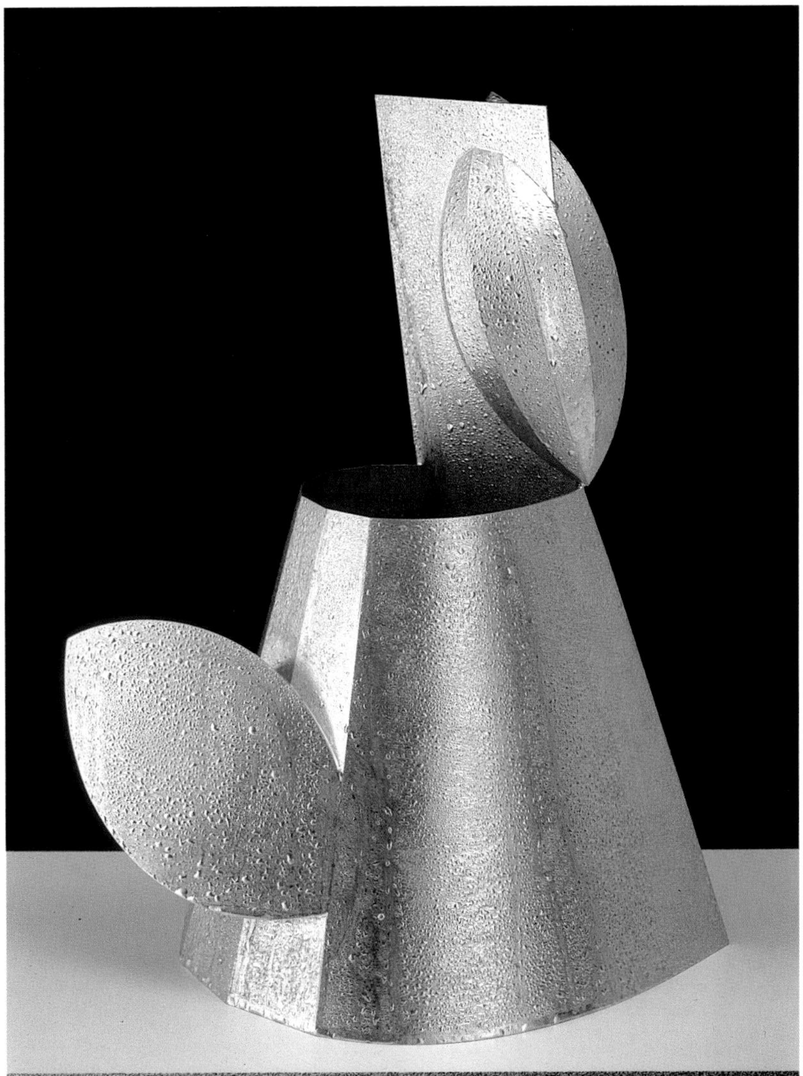

17

18

19

21

22

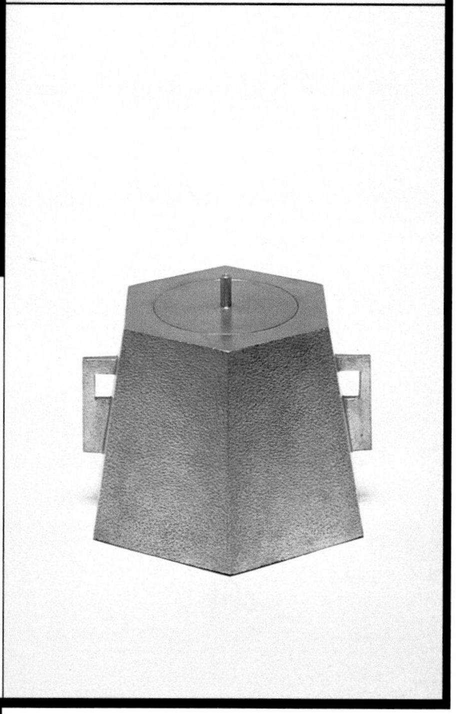

20

19–23
Shigeru Uchida
Tea Ceremony
Studio 80, Japan

19 Pitcher, *Yoho Mizutsugi*
Aluminium
h 16cm w 12cm d 12cm
h 6½in w 4¾in d 4¾in

20 Bowl for sweets,
Kashiki
Japanese lacquer
h 7.5cm di 35cm
h 3in di 13¾in

21 Kettle, *Rokkaku Suehiro Gama*
Aluminium
h 16.5cm w 23cm d 23cm
h 6½in w 9in d 9in

22 Vase, *Rokkaku Suehiro Hanaire*
Copper, aluminium, Japanese lacquer
h 24cm w 80cm d 80cm
h 9½in w 31½in d 31½in

23 *Paper Cube Lamp*
Japanese paper
h 20cm w 20cm d 20cm
h 7⅞in w 7⅞in d 7⅞in

24 **Katsuhiko Ogino**
Vases
Porcelain
h 21, 29cm w 30, 20cm
d 8, 6cm
h 8¼, 11⅜in w 11¾, 7⅞in
d 3⅛, 2⅜in
Ceramic Japan Inc., Japan

23

24

25

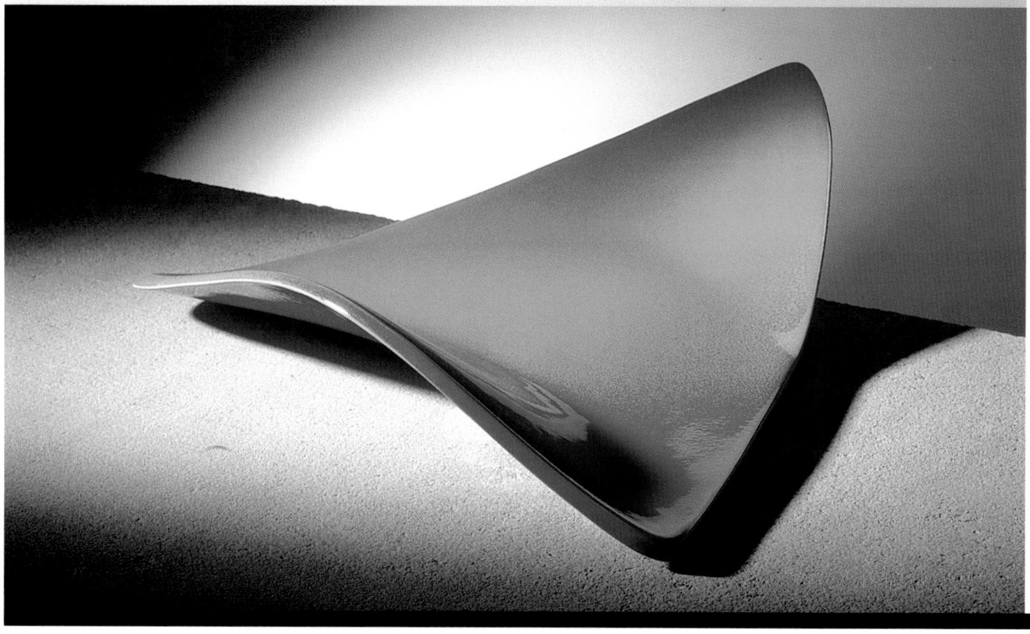

25

Though her corpus of built work is increasing, notably with the recent Fire Station for Vitra, the Iranian-born architect Zaha Hadid first came to prominence with her astonishing deconstructivist drawings. No-one should now doubt her ability to move from two dimensions into three. These dishes for Waechtersbacher Keramik show a finely calculated sense of space – a reflection perhaps of her first training as a mathematician – with some of the dishes only resting on the surface at three points. The technical skill required to create the freely floating forms in clay is also very considerable.

25 **Zaha Hadid**
Tableware
Ceramic
Plate: h 5.5cm w 28cm d 44cm
h 2⅛in w 11in d 17¼in
Cup: h 3cm w 7cm d 13cm
h 1⅛in w 2¾in d 5⅛in
Saucer: h 1.5cm w 9cm d 21.5cm
h ⅝in w 3½in d 8½in
Waechtersbach, Germany

25

26

27
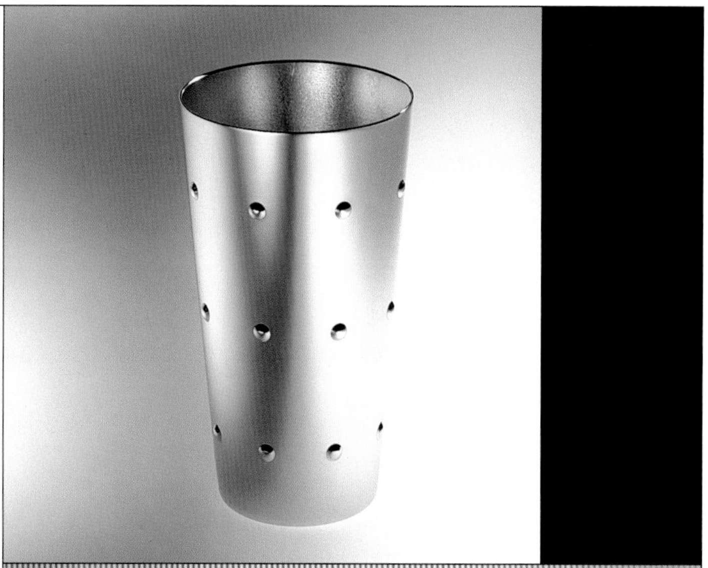

28
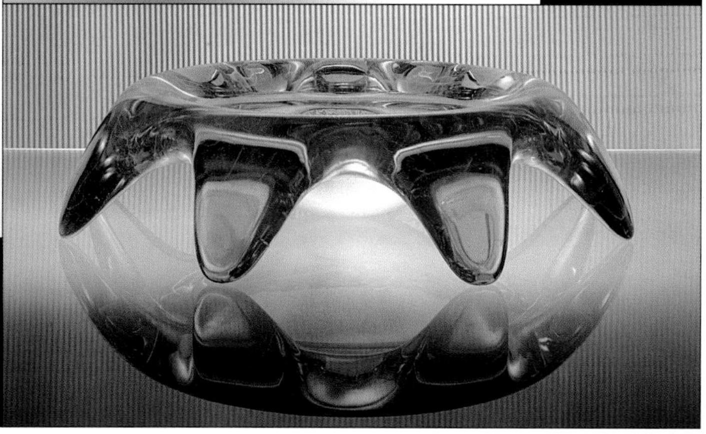

26 **Toshiyuki Kita**
Tea caddy, *Cha à la Carte - Aska*
Pewter
h 14.4cm di 10.3cm
h 5⅝in di 4in
Suzuhan Co. Ltd, Japan
(Limited batch production)

27 **Anna Gili**
Goblet, *Win*
Stainless steel
h 12cm di 7cm
h 4¾in di 2¾in
Alessi, Italy

28 **Michal Fronek and Jan Nemecek**
Bowl, *Grand Fathers*
Glass
h 8cm di 35cm
h 3⅛in di 13¾in
R & L, Czech Republic
(Limited batch production)

The concepts of ceremony and narrative are linked, in the sense that ceremony becomes wholly empty and meaningless in the absence of the continuing context that narrative or history provides. And narrative, in the form of tradition, supports ceremony even when historical reason has fallen away. Ceramic decoration has a similar hold on memory, and even new decorations, such as those by Michael Graves (page 128), seem to fit into a known canon, to be welcome as familiar even when they are quite new.

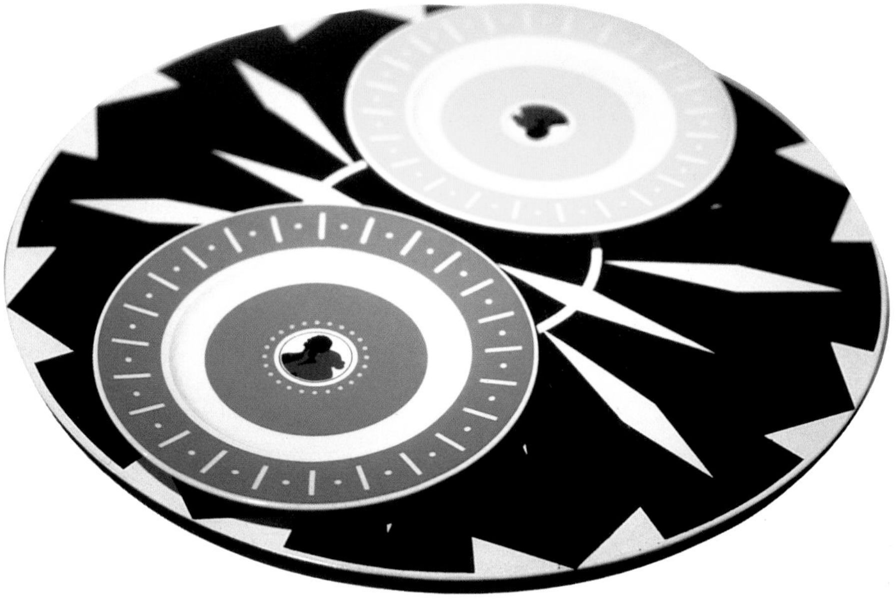

29

29 **Alessandro Guerriero**
Dinner for Two
Porcelain
Plate: di 21cm di 8¼in
Marsberger Glaswerke Ritzenhoff GmbH, Germany

30 **Ravage**
Dinner services,
Algonquin (top) and *Pascal*
Porcelain
Plates: di 27.5, 21.5cm
di 10⅞, 8½in
Bowl: di 27cm
di 10⅝in
Cup: h 6cm di 8.5cm
h 2⅜in di 3⅜in
Saucer: di 16cm
di 6½in
Made under licence with Sasaki, USA

30

30

31

32

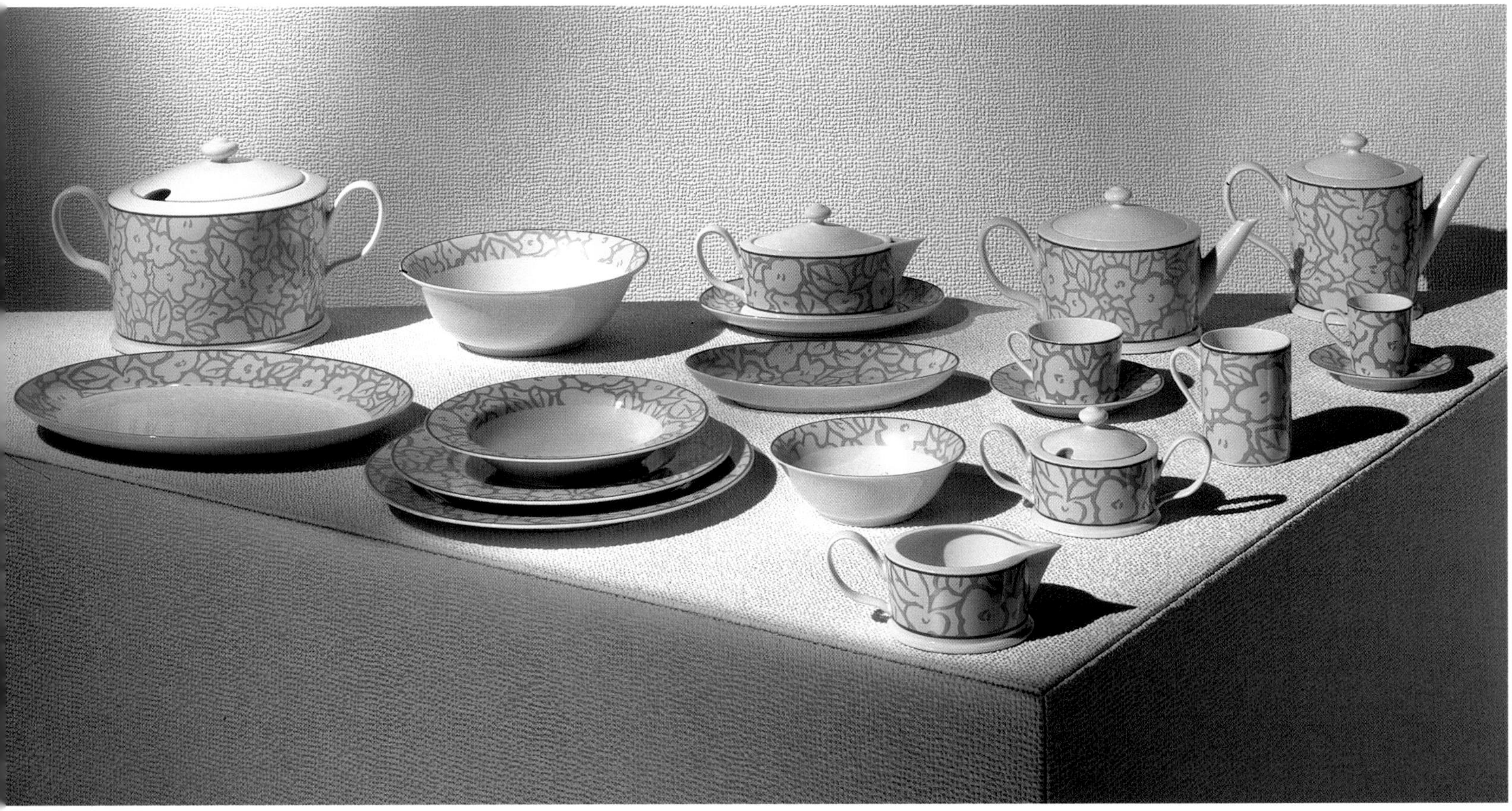

31 **Randi Kristensen**
Plate, *Sea*
Porcelain
di 21cm
di 8¼in
(One-off)

32 **Michael Graves**
Dinner service, *Deanrey*
Porcelain
Soup tureen: di 20cm
di 8in
Espresso cup: di 5.5cm
di 2¼in
Alessi, Italy

33 **Riccardo Dalisi**
Figurines, *Circo Totocchio*
Murano glass
h 17cm
h 6¾in
Bisazza, Italy

34 **Maria Christina Hamel**
Candleholder, *Ellis*
Ceramic
h 35cm w 25cm d 12cm
h 13¾in w 9⅞in d 4¾in
(Limited batch production)

35 **Volker Albus**
Plate, *Piatto Fax*
Porcelain
d 2cm di 24cm
d ¾in di 9½in
Fine Factory, Italy

36 **Urs Schweizer**
Plate, *Piatto Fax*
Porcelain
d 2cm di 24cm
d ¾in di 9½in
Fine Factory, Italy

33

34

35

36

37 **Stefano Giovannoni**
Table mats, *Coins*
Aluminium
h 2cm di 18cm
h ¾in di 7⅛in
Alessi, Italy

38, 40
39

38 & 39 **Nathalie du Pasquier**

(Above left and below)

Dinner for Two

Porcelain

Plate: di 21cm

di 8¼in

Coffee cup: h 5.5cm di 8cm

h 2⅛in di 3⅛in

Marsberger Glaswerke Ritzenhoff GmbH, Germany

40 **Dieter Sieger**

(Above right)

Faccetta, from the *Cult Terrazzo* series

Porcelain

Plate: di 21cm

di 8¼in

Saucer: di 15.2cm

di 6in

Coffee cup: h 6.3cm di 7.7cm

h 2½in di 3in

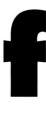

For Mendini the "new plastics...can assume an infinite variety of identities". A material that can take on many shapes – artificial leather, simulated wood, man-made silk, imitation marble – satisfies perfectly our need for ambiguity: for ambiguities of form and purpose can strengthen the ritual aspect of objects, by making us look beyond the functional. Ambiguity lies at the heart of Fish Design's resin vases (page 134), for each one emerges from the manufacturing process different from the others, a mixture of randomness and choice within a fixed shape. Hella Jongerius's *Soft Vases* also challenge us with their contradiction of purpose and material (page 135).

41 **Carsten Jorgensen**
Salad server, *Dent de Lion*
NAS
w 5cm l 31cm
w 2in l 12¼in
Bodum (Schweiz) AG, Switzerland

42 **Stefano Giovannoni**
Box, *Marybiscuit*
PMMA, thermoplastic rubber
h 11.5cm w 28cm d 22cm
h 4½in w 11in d 8⅝in
Alessi, Italy

43 **Stefano Giovannoni**
Vase
Murano glass
h 40cm w 23.5cm d 11.5cm
h 15¾in w 9¼in d 4½in
Progetto Oggetto Cappellini, Italy

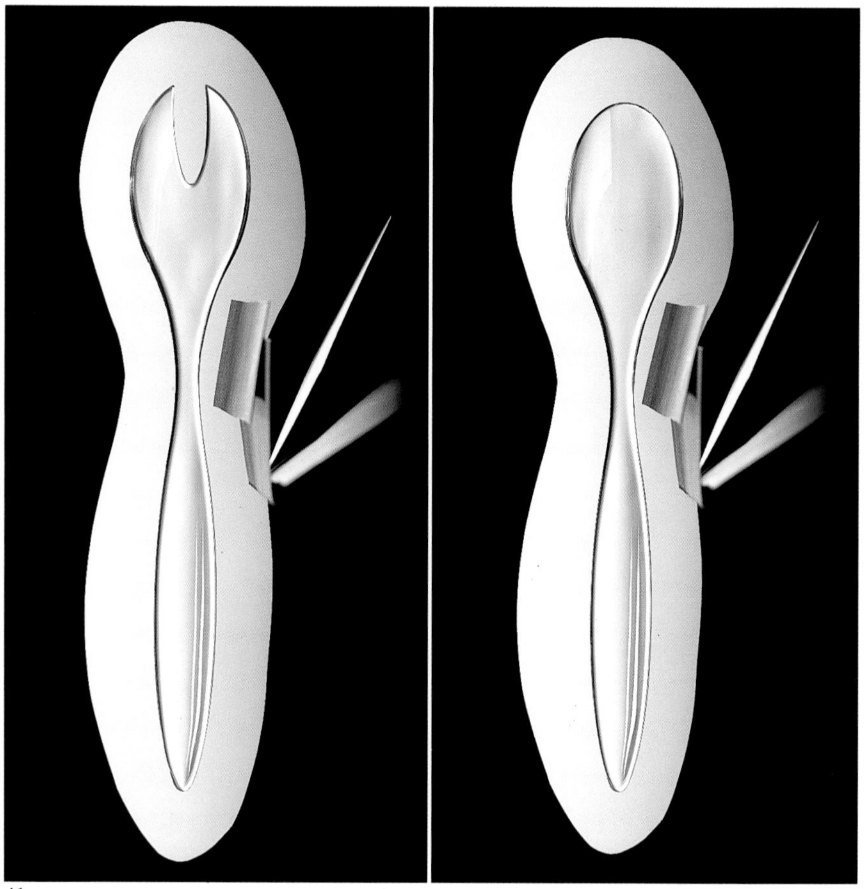
41

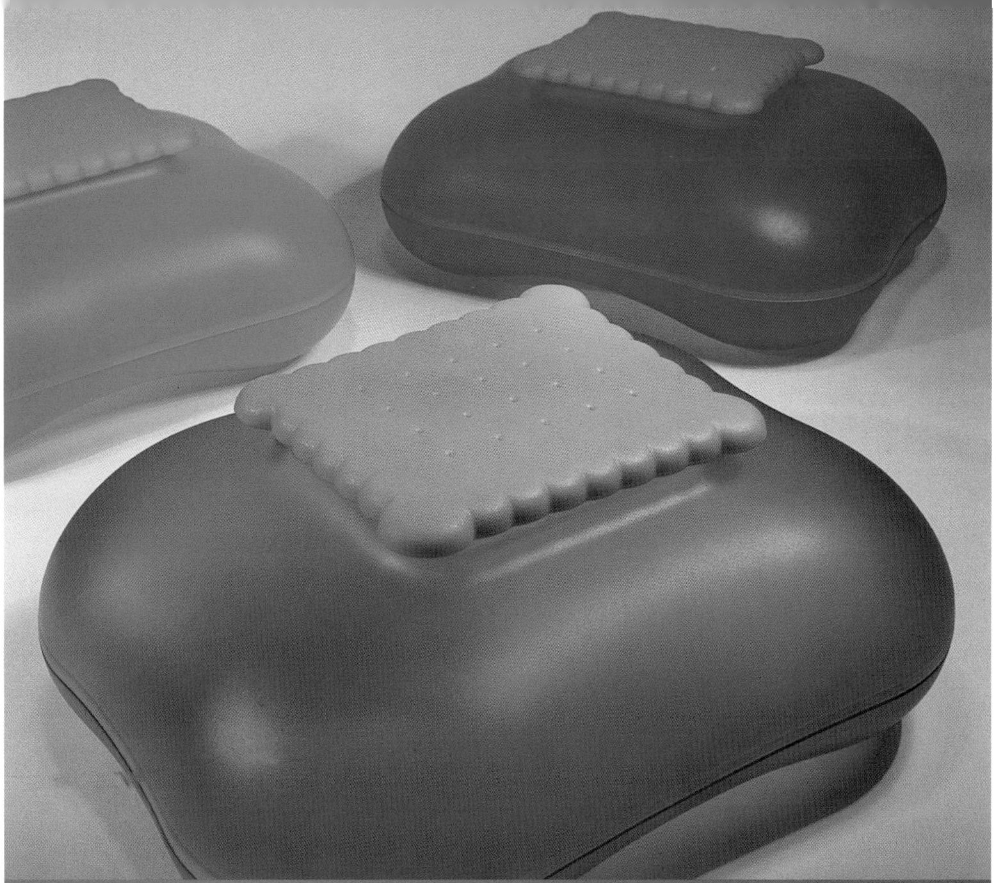

42

43

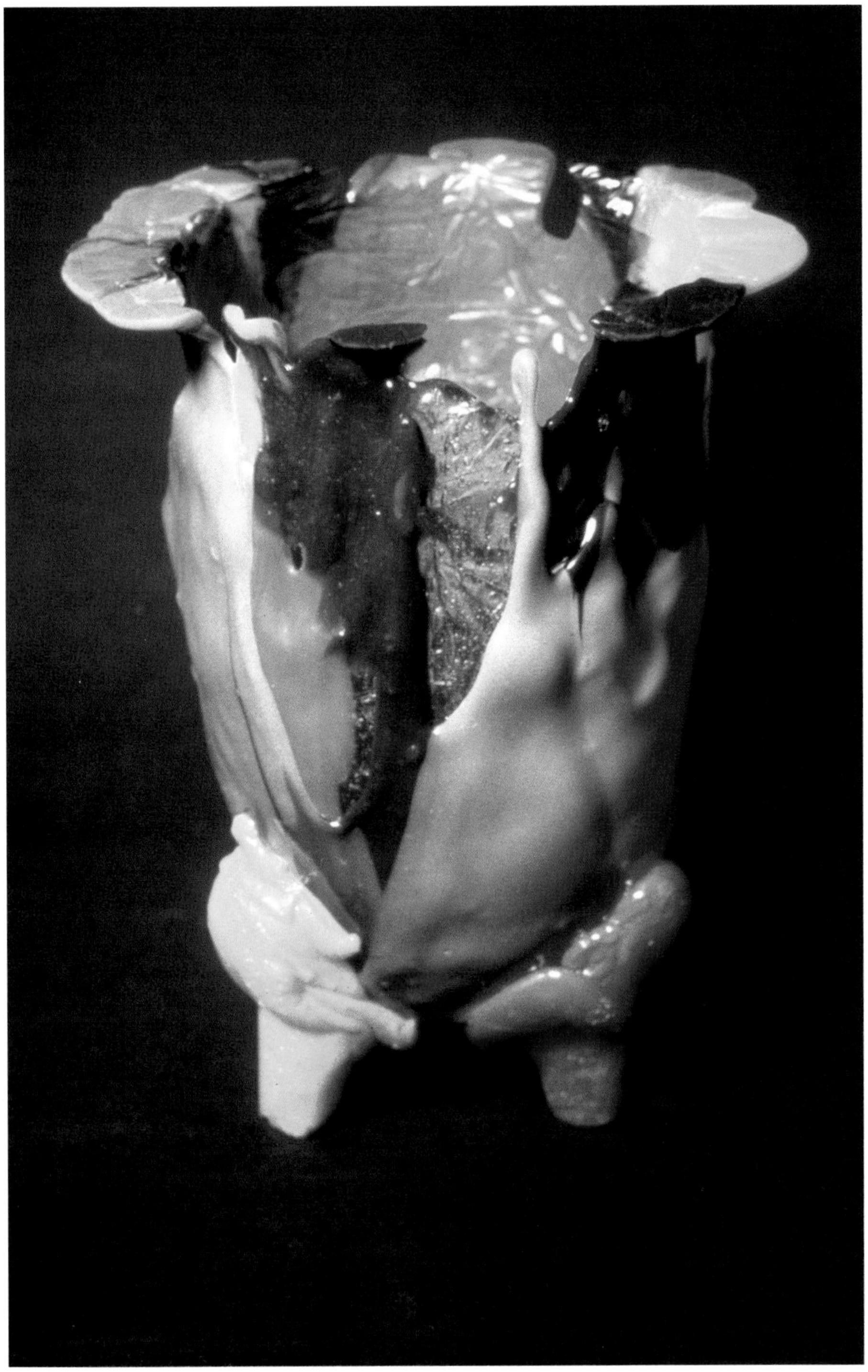

44

Fish Design is a new Amsterdam-based initiative spanning two continents. The colourful furniture, tableware and lamps are, of course, from designs by Gaetano Pesce, and are executed in flexible resin in a factory in Mexico. But this is not only a simple case of outsourcing. A deliberate element of chance was left in the manufacturing process, mainly in the choice and proportion of colours, and also in the completeness of the final shape. This left part of the final design responsibility to the Mexican workforce, thereby empowering them in the process. And at the same time each item became a unique piece, since the manufacturing system could not guarantee that each item would turn out exactly the same as its predecessor. A cynic might argue that this is simply making the best of an unsteady process, but the bright colours and vigorous shapes tend to banish such thoughts.

44 **Gaetano Pesce**
Vase, *Amazonia*
Flexible resin
h 29cm di 26cm
h 11⅜in di 10¼in
Fish Design, The Netherlands
(Limited batch production)

45 **Defne Koz**
Tray, *Aski*
Aluminium, brass
h 40cm di 30cm
h 15¾in di 11⅞in
Ala Rossa, Italy

46 **Hella Jongerius**
Soft Vase, DD09
Soft polyurethane
h 18, 10cm di 22, 12cm
h 7⅛, 3⅞in di 8⅝, 4¾in
Droog Design, The Netherlands
(Prototype)

47 **Hella Jongerius**
Soft Vase, DMD89
Soft polyurethane
h 27cm di 15cm
h 10⅝in di 5⅞in
DMD, The Netherlands

46

45

47

"We know the wine in the bottle is red, as the bottle is dark; we know the wine is white because the bottle is clear," the Futurist Filìa once wrote. Transparency and reflectance add drama to the art of the table, exposing and concealing what is in front of us. Arnout Visser's *Salt Glass* gently mocks our notions of time (page 139). Eleanor Kearney's plump pewter jar invites us to lift its rounded lid, while Enzo Mari's bottles for oil and vinegar are a classically neat restatement of a traditional but relevant form (page 138).

48

49

48 **Helmut Wolf**
Rock crystal object
Rock crystal, natural pyrite
h 20cm w 29cm d 26cm
h 7⅞in w 11⅜in d 10¼in
Eva-Maria Melchers, Germany
(One-off)

49 & 50
Sofia Uddén
Glass and carafe
Glass: h 12.5, 11.5, 9.5cm
di 5.5, 5, 4.5cm
h 4⅞, 4½, 3¾in di 2⅛, 2, 1¾in
IKEA, Sweden

51 **Maria Christina Hamel**
Glass, *Rigatino*
Glass
h 7, 8.5, 9.5, 10cm
di 4, 6, 7, 8cm
h 2¾, 3⅓, 3¾, 3⅞in
di 1⅝, 2⅜, 2¾, 3⅛in
Bisazza, Italy

52 **Pierangelo Caramia**
Tea infuser, *Happy Egg*
Stainless steel, polyamide
l 23.5cm di 3.6cm
l 9¼in di 1⅜in
Alessi, Italy

IKEA's *PS* collection, launched at the 1995 Milan *Salone*, is a much-trumpeted essay in validating the company's business and design ethic of producing quality furniture, houseware and cookware at affordable prices. By commissioning a new collection from young Scandinavian designers they also wanted to affirm their Scandinavian origins, as the company, founded fifty years ago in Älmhult, increasingly moves on to a wider world stage. To many, IKEA's interest in design was well-known – the company regularly credits designers in its catalogues, for example, and has won a string of design awards for its products. And it tirelessly promotes its Swedish origins, not least through product names – *Lack* for a minimal shelving system is one of my favourites. While most of the work in the new collection maintains IKEA's fine design tradition, the whole exercise in Milan seems to have rather too self-conscious and serious an air, like someone arriving at a party rather late and in the wrong clothes. IKEA does not need the endorsement of the Corso Montenapoleone to clear its design credentials.

50

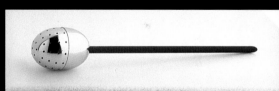

52

54

Finding new forms for traditional materials is something Mendini sees as part of the meeting point between the artisan and industrial approaches to design. Eleanor Kearney's pewter container, with its simple form and complex use, fits this well: it can be both a jar and a jug, and the lip is adapted to pour at any angle. A simple pewter ball acts as a stopper. The lightly polished surface has a good tactile quality, and the object is the right size to fit well into the hand. Kearney has specialized in pewter tableware since studying design at college: "I enjoy", she says, "the challenge of working with a material with a long tradition, but also finding new ways of working with the metal."

55

56

53 **Constantin Boym**
Canisters, *Tin Man*
Stainless steel, wood
h 19.7cm di 10.5cm
h 7¾in di 4⅛in
Alessi, Italy

54 **Enzo Mari**
Oil dispenser, *Domestica*
Stainless steel, Pyrex
h 18cm di 7cm
h 7⅛in di 2¾in
Zani & Zani, Italy

55 **Eleanor Kearney**
Jar
Pewter sheet
h 13cm w 8.5cm
h 5in w 3⅜in
A. R. Wentworth (Sheffield) Ltd, UK
(Limited batch production)

58

56 **Arnout Visser**
Salt Glass, DD13
Glass
h 19cm di 5cm
h 7½in di 2in
Droog Design, The Netherlands
(Prototype)

57 **Borek Sípek**
Vase, *Jór*
Bohemian glass
h 35cm di 10cm
h 13¾in di 4in
Ajeto-Bohemia SRO, Czech Republic

58 **Peter Schmitz**
Bowls
Silver
h 23, 14, 10cm di 33, 16, 12cm
h 9, 5½, 3⅞in di 13, 6¼, 4¾in
Metall & Gestaltung, Germany
(Limited batch production)

michael Graves' new collection for Alessi has a rather ponderous grace, and is saved from being overbearing by its dry use of colour. Annette Berliner's dish is saturated with hand-painted colour (page 145). If, for Mendini, the world is a "container of fragments", then colour is one of the key aesthetic senses that orders and organizes this accumulation, introducing a motif of association and ceremony into the rich, multi-layered patterns of everyday life.

59

59

Michael Graves

Tableware series, *Euclid*

ABS plastic

Vacuum glass jug:

h 23cm w 25cm d 17.5cm

h 9in w 9⅞in d 6⅞in

Salad bowl:

h 15cm di 40cm

h 5⅞in di 15¾in

PMMA salad set:

w 7.5cm l 31cm

w 2⅞in l 12¼in

Kitchen box:

h 13cm w 11.5cm d 11.5cm

h 5in w 4½in d 4½in

Kitchen box:

h 23cm w 11.5cm d 11.5cm

h 9in w 4½in d 4½in

Stainless steel napkin holder:

h 7cm w 23cm d 21cm

h 2¾in w 9in d 8¼in

Square tray:

h 3cm w 36cm d 36cm

h 1¼in w 13¾in d 13¾in

Bottle stand:

h 23cm w 14cm d 14cm

h 9in w 5½in d 5½in

Alessi, Italy

60 **Gae Aulenti**
Vase, *Ritorto*
Bubbled glass, iron
h 20cm l 66cm
h 7⅞in l 26in
Venini, Italy
(Limited batch production)

61 **Gae Aulenti**
Vase, *Torto*
Bubbled glass, iron
h 32cm l 50cm
h 12⅝in l 19⅝in
Venini, Italy
(Limited batch production)

62 **Giorgio Gregori**
Awa
Ceramic
h 45cm di 32cm
h 17¾in di 12⅝in
Kaleidositalia srl, Italy

60

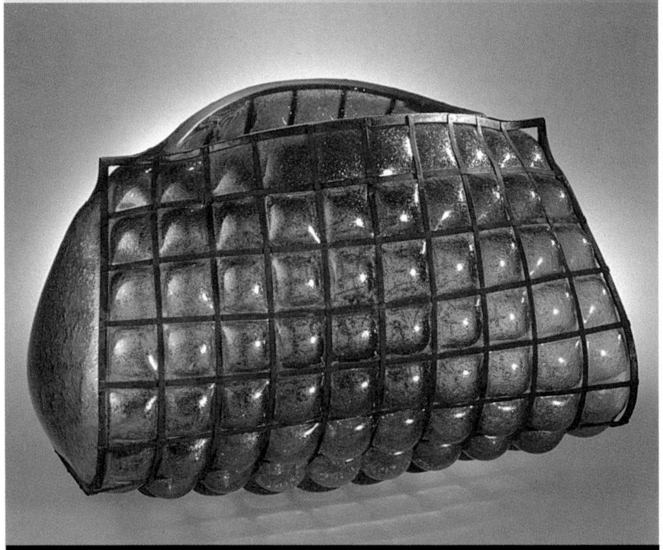

61

Gae Aulenti's two vases, in blue glass with iron-wired frames, play on the theme of the variation of materials. One is shaped like a purse, but in a solid rather than a flexible material, the other is an inedible ice-cream cone (or perhaps an unfoldable paper wrapping for flowers). Whatever the metaphor, the meaning is the same: the application of refined materials to mundane objects transforms our perception of the objects, while the ordinariness of the visual source makes us reconsider our hierarchy of materials.

63 **Heike Mühlhaus**
Vase, *Flower Birthday*
Ceramic
h 40cm
h 15¾in
Cocktail, Germany
(Limited batch edition)

64 **Heike Mühlhaus**
Vase, *It's Your Birthday*
Ceramic
di 45cm
di 17¾in
Cocktail, Germany
(Limited batch edition)

65 **Alain and Thierry Manoha**
Vase, *Balustré*
Ceramic
h 37cm di 15cm
h 14⅝in di 5⅞in
Néotù, France

62

63

64

65

66

67

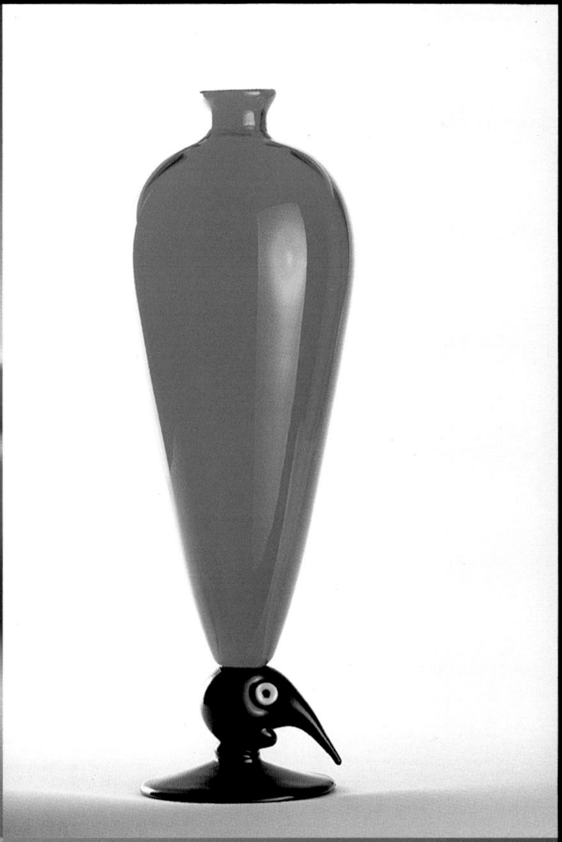

68

69

66 **Stephan Koziol**
Napkin holder, *King Arthur*
Acrylic
h 7.5cm w 7.7cm d 1.6cm
h 2⅞in w 3in d ⅝in
Koziol GmbH, Germany

67 **Ugo Marano**
Vase, *Solo per Te*
Murano glass
h 39cm l 57cm di 11cm
h 15⅜in l 22½in di 4⅜in
Bisazza, Italy

68 **Ugo Marano**
Vase, *Per Amore*
Glass
h 49cm di 14cm
h 19½in di 5½in
Bisazza, Italy

69 **Toshiyuki Kita**
A la carte tray, *Pepemellina*
Melamine
h 1.7cm w 27.1cm d 22cm
h ⅝in w 10⅝in d 8⅝in
Kokusaikako Co. Ltd, Japan

70 **Louise Gibb**
Penny
Glass mosaic
w 50cm l 50cm
w 19¾in l 19¾in
Bisazza, Italy

71 **Annette Berliner**
Dish
Ceramic
h 8cm di max 58cm
h 3⅛in di max 22⅞in
(Limited batch production)

70

71

t e x t i l e s

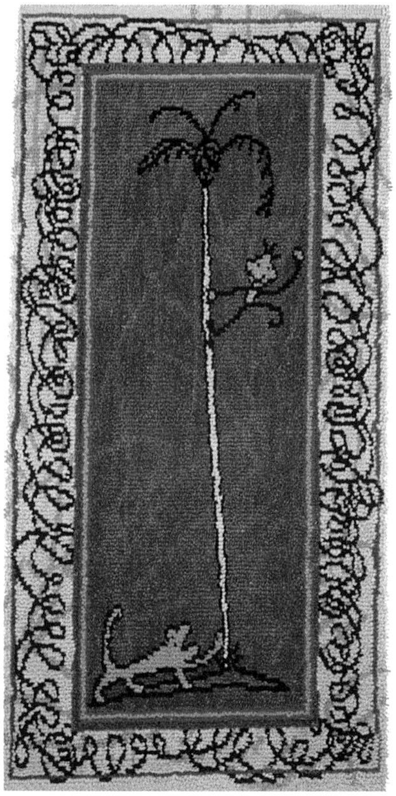

1

"I would like to sing the praises of the carpet. That is, I would like to convince you that the carpet is one of the most characteristic objects of the age in which we live. The carpet today is our existence reduced to its bare essentials.... But also, by definition, a carpet is a thing of decoration." Since one of the earliest applications of programming was in weaving on Jacquard looms, and as handweaving and dyeing is still honoured practice today, textiles do have this eerie ambiguity between ancient and modern technologies, between figuration and abstraction, and between roles as objects of appreciation and of use. Do you look at a carpet or sit on it? The very different carpets designed by Konstantin Grcic, Javier Mariscal and Christine Van der Hurd in this year's selection show that the potential of the "brush of many colours" so admired by Mendini is in good and varied hands.

2

1 **Javier Mariscal**
Rug
Wool
w 60cm l 120cm
w 23⅝in l 47¼in
Nani Marquina, Spain

2 **Randi Kristensen**
Carpet, *Bees*
Wool
w 170cm l 240cm
w 66⅞in l 94½in
Zanettin Tappeti, Italy

3 **Christine Van der Hurd**
Carpet, *Kashmir*
Wool
w 83.8cm l 251.4cm
w 33in l 99in
(Limited batch production)

4 **Renata Bonfanti**
Wall textile, *Eccentrica*
Wool, linen
w 50cm l 185cm
w 19¾in l 72⅞in
Renata Bonfanti SNC, Italy
(Limited production)

5 **Andrée Putman**
Carpet, *Staccato Lin*
New Zealand wool
w 170cm l 240cm
w 66⅞in l 94½in
Toulemonde Bochart,
France

3

4

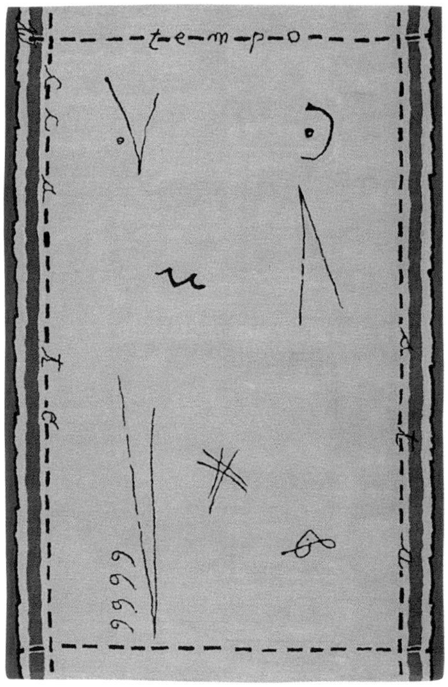

5

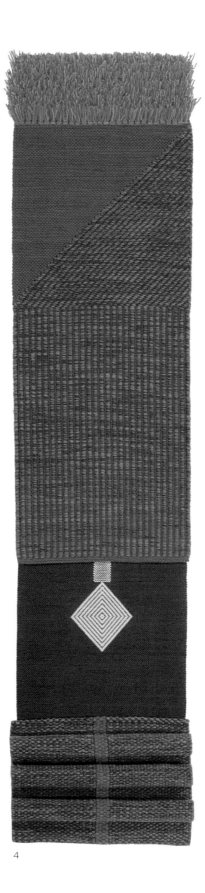

6

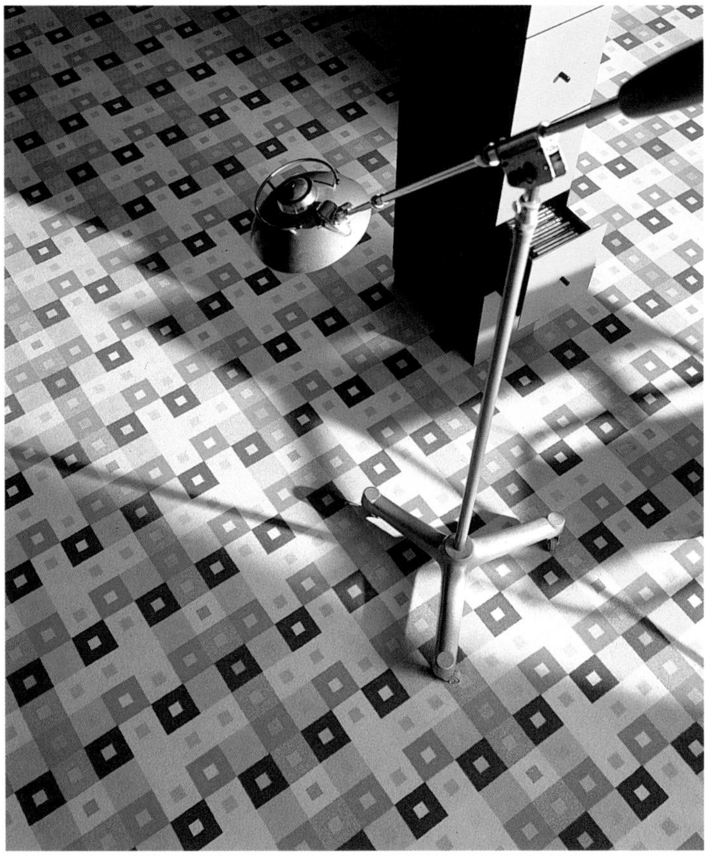

7

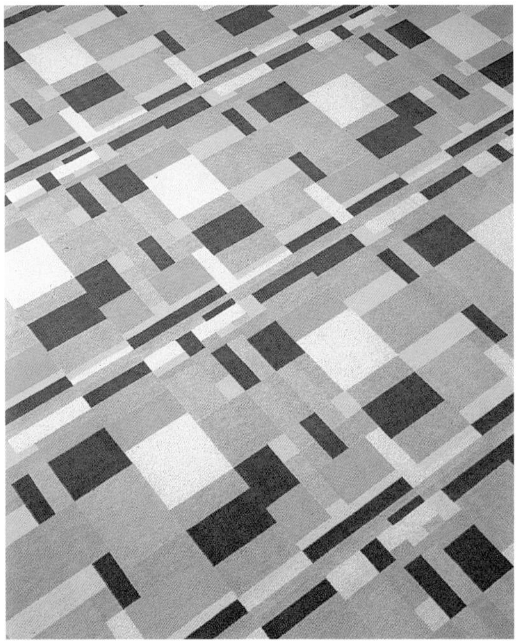

8

6 **Kitty Fischer**
Bauhaus Women – from the *Classic* range
Machine-tufted and printed
heavy contract carpet
Dupont's Antron Classic polyamide fibre
w repeat 80cm l repeat 47.5cm
w repeat 31½in l repeat 18¾in
Vorwerk & Co., Germany

7 **Monica Bella-Broner**
Bauhaus Women – from the *Classic* range
Machine-tufted and printed
heavy contract carpet
Dupont's Antron Classic polyamide fibre
w repeat 100cm l repeat 95cm
w repeat 39¼in l repeat 27¼in
Vorwerk & Co., Germany

8 **Gertrud Arndt**
Bauhaus Women – from the *Classic* range
Machine-tufted and printed
heavy contract carpet
Dupont's Antron Classic polyamide fibre
w repeat 133.5cm l repeat 95cm
w repeat 52½in l repeat 37¼in
Vorwerk & Co., Germany

9 **Konstantin Grcic**
Side-table with matching rug
Wool
l 130cm di 70cm
l 51⅛in di 27½in
Authentics artipresent GmbH, Germany

10, 11
Vorwerk
Modena fantasia (left) and
Impala fantasia (right)
from *The Home Collection*
Aquafil Aqualon, polyamide, wool
w 200, 400, 500cm
w 78¾, 157½, 196⅞in
Vorwerk & Co., Germany

9

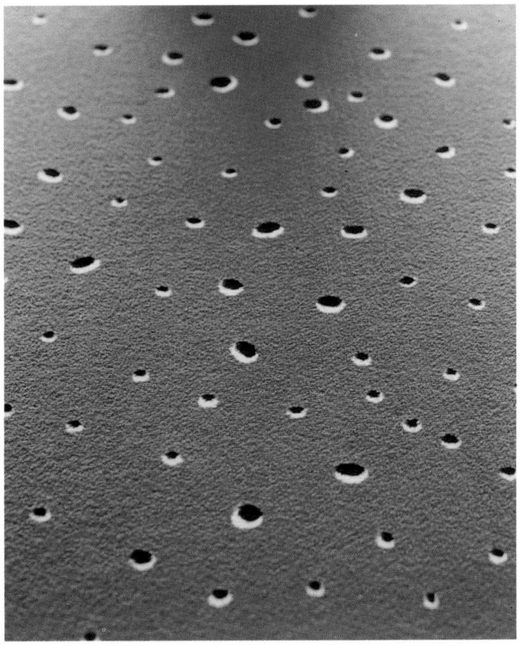

10

11

12

12 **Yoshiki Hishinuma**
Knit, *Bird Eats Flower*
61% mohair, 31% nylon,
8% melted wool

13 **Yoshiki Hishinuma**
Knit, *Triangle*
72% melted wool,
28% nylon

14 **Yoshiki Hishinuma**
Transfer print with shrink process,
Flower
Polyester

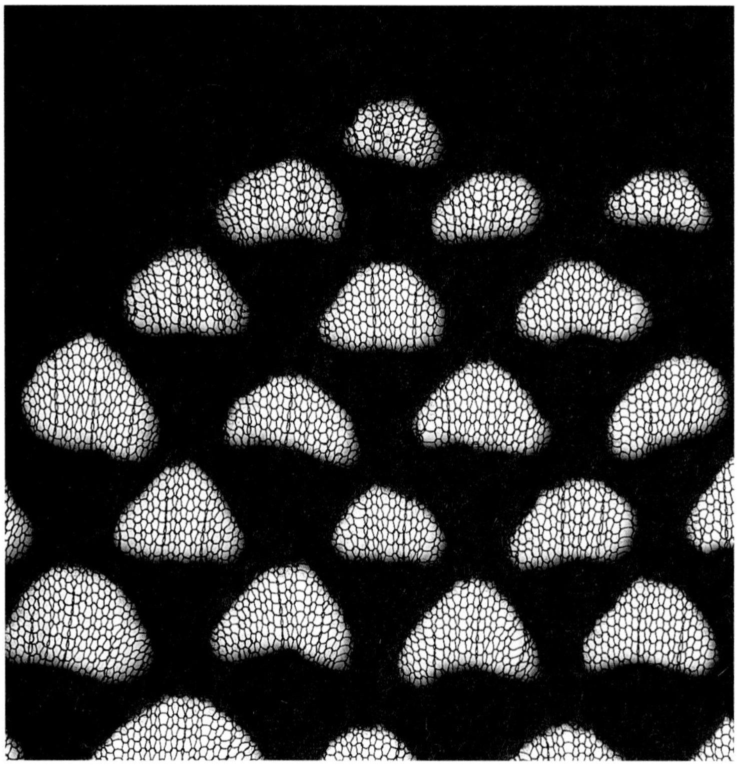

13

14

16

15 **Yoshiki Hishinuma**
Transfer print with shrink process, *Orchid*
Polyester

16 **Yoshiki Hishinuma**
Melted and transfer-printed velvet, *Melted Velvet-1*
80% rayon, 20% polyester

17 **Yoshiki Hishinuma**
Transfer print with shrink process, *Desert-1*
Polyester

18 **Yoshiki Hishinuma**
Transfer print with shrink process, *Bao Babu*
Polyester

17

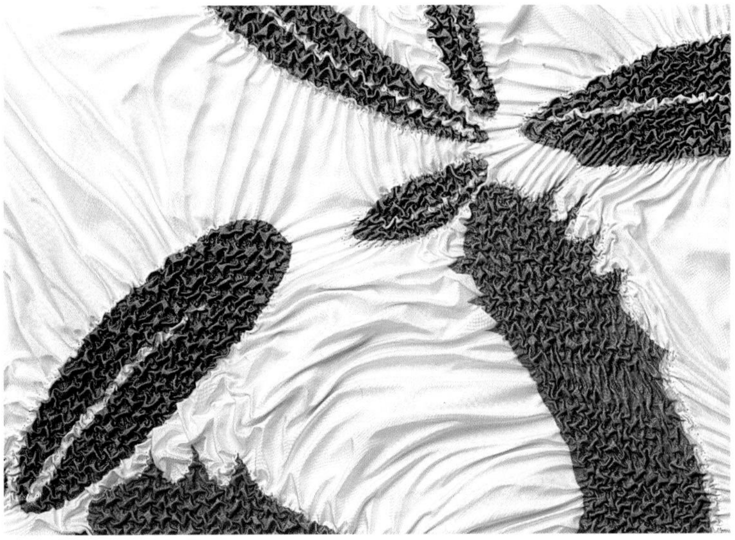

18

15

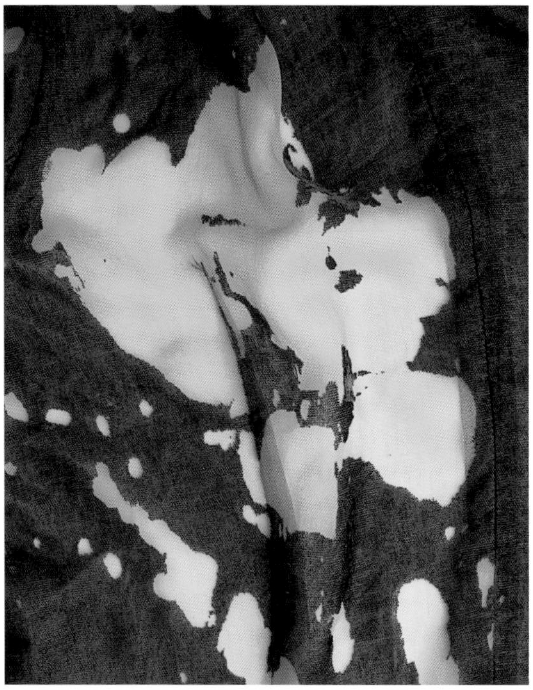
19

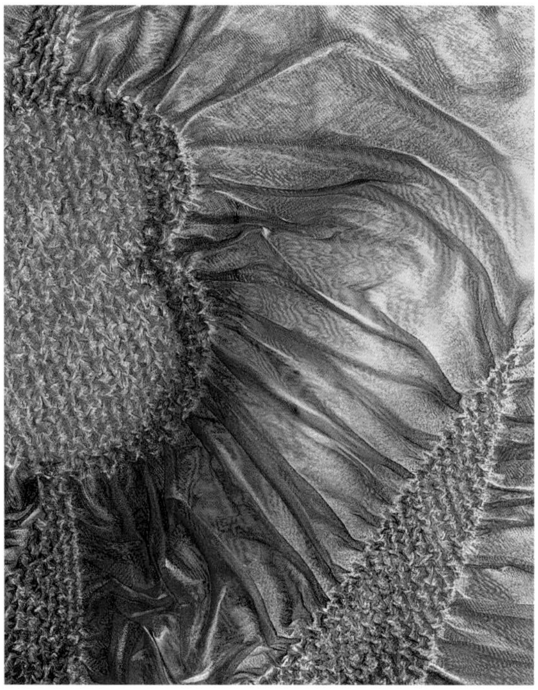
21

20

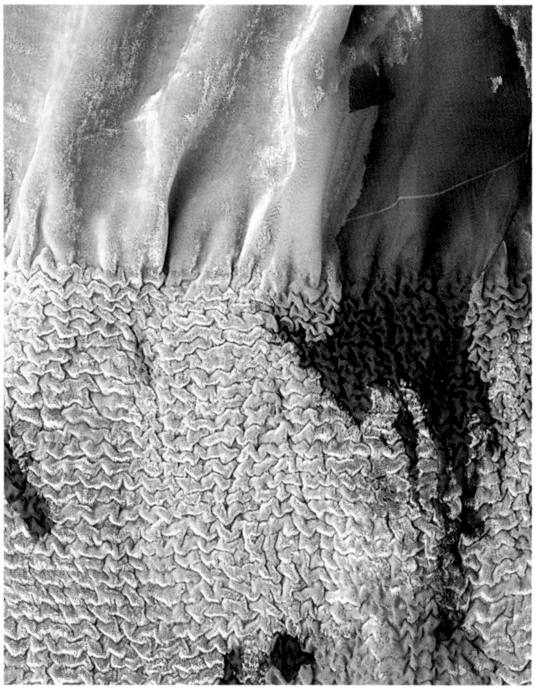
22

19 **Yoshiki Hishinuma**
Melted velvet, *Flower*
70% rayon, 30% polyester

20 **Yoshiki Hishinuma**
Transfer print with
shrink process, *Impressionism*
Polyester

21 **Yoshiki Hishinuma**
Transfer print with
shrink process, *Flower*
Polyester

22 **Yoshiki Hishinuma**
Melted and transfer-printed
velvet with shrink
process, *Stone*
70% rayon, 30% polyester

23 **Yoshiki Hishinuma**
Transfer print with
shrink process, *Clover*
Polyester

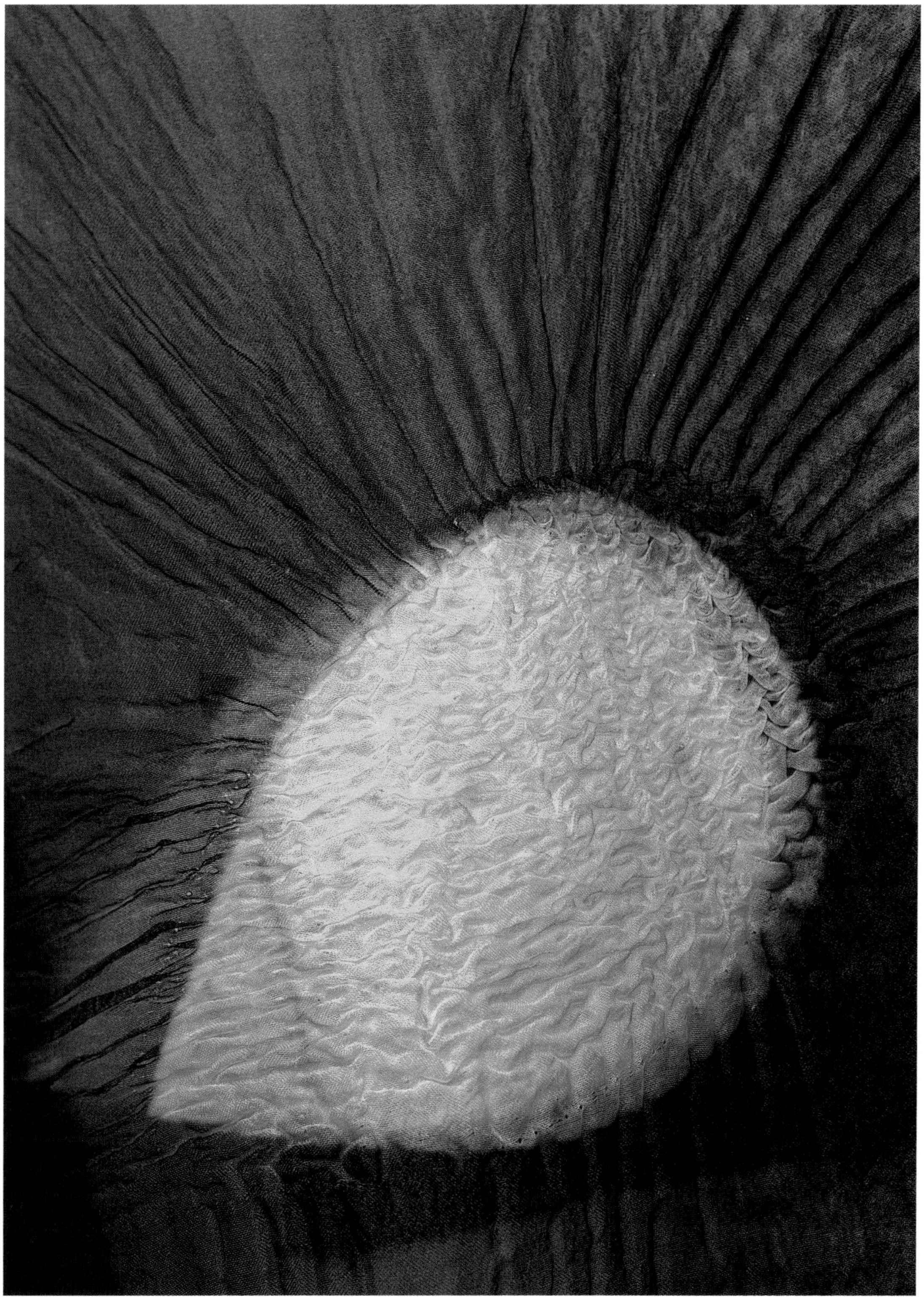

23

Koji Hamai's textile designs hover between fashion and furnishing, and he has always been interested in new materials. His *Titanium* jackets with their use of metal mesh move almost beyond textiles, just as Gijs Bakker's *Non Cloth* takes a minimal definition to the opposite extreme. We have become so accustomed to the extraordinary surface and colour effects of Hamai and other Japanese designers that their high degree of taste and craftsmanship seems to be a norm. In fact it should be recognized as a discipline continually in renewal, through contacts with new design sources as in the Maki sisters' work, and through new interpretations of old techniques.

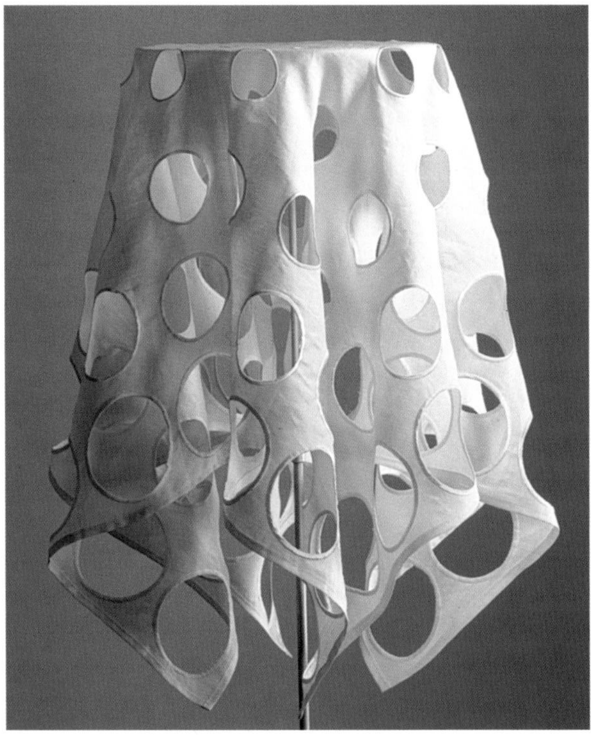

24 **Gijs Bakker**
Tablecloth, *Non Cloth*
Linen
w 150cm | 150cm
w 59in | 59in
DMD, The Netherlands

25 **Koji Hamai**
Shelters 3
Stainless steel, polyester
w 100cm | 300cm
w 39⅜in | 118⅛in
Hamai Factory Inc., Japan

26 **Koji Hamai**
Titanium Shelters Jacket
Titanium, polyester
w 60cm | 100cm
w 23⅝in | 39⅜in
Hamai Factory Inc., Japan

27 **Koji Hamai**
Titanium Shelters Pants
Titanium, polyester
w 60cm | 150cm
w 23⅝in | 59in
Hamai Factory Inc., Japan

28 **Koji Hamai**
Dry Fish
Polyester, stainless steel
w 100cm | 300cm
w 39⅜in | 118⅛in
Hamai Factory Inc., Japan

29 **Koji Hamai**
Recycled felt
w 150cm | 500cm
w 59in | 196⅞in
Hamai Factory Inc., Japan

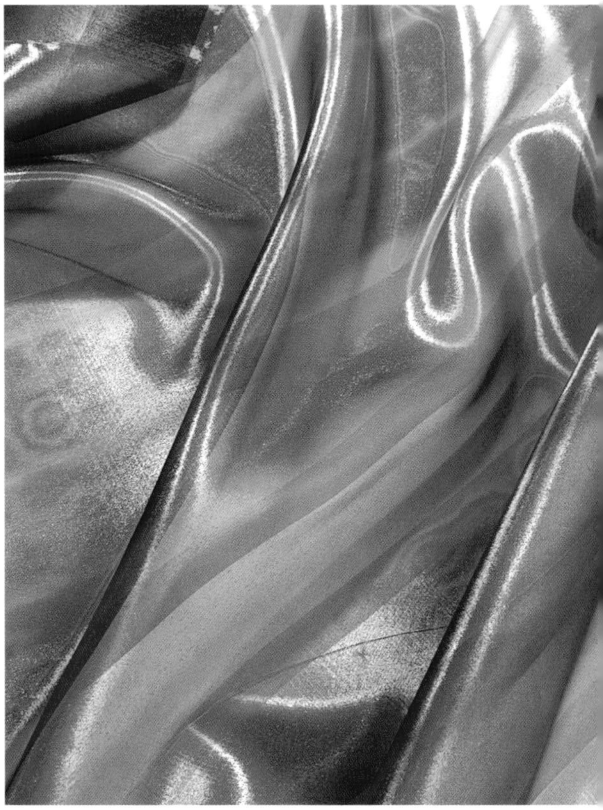

25

26

29

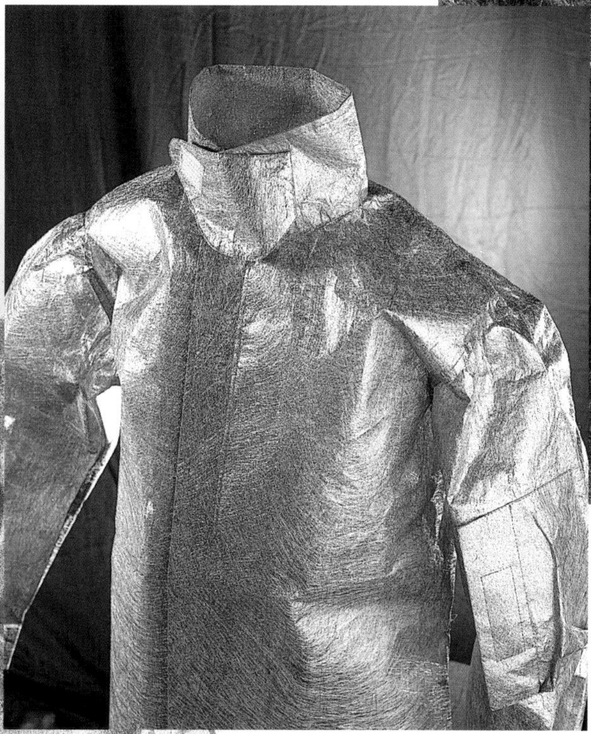

28

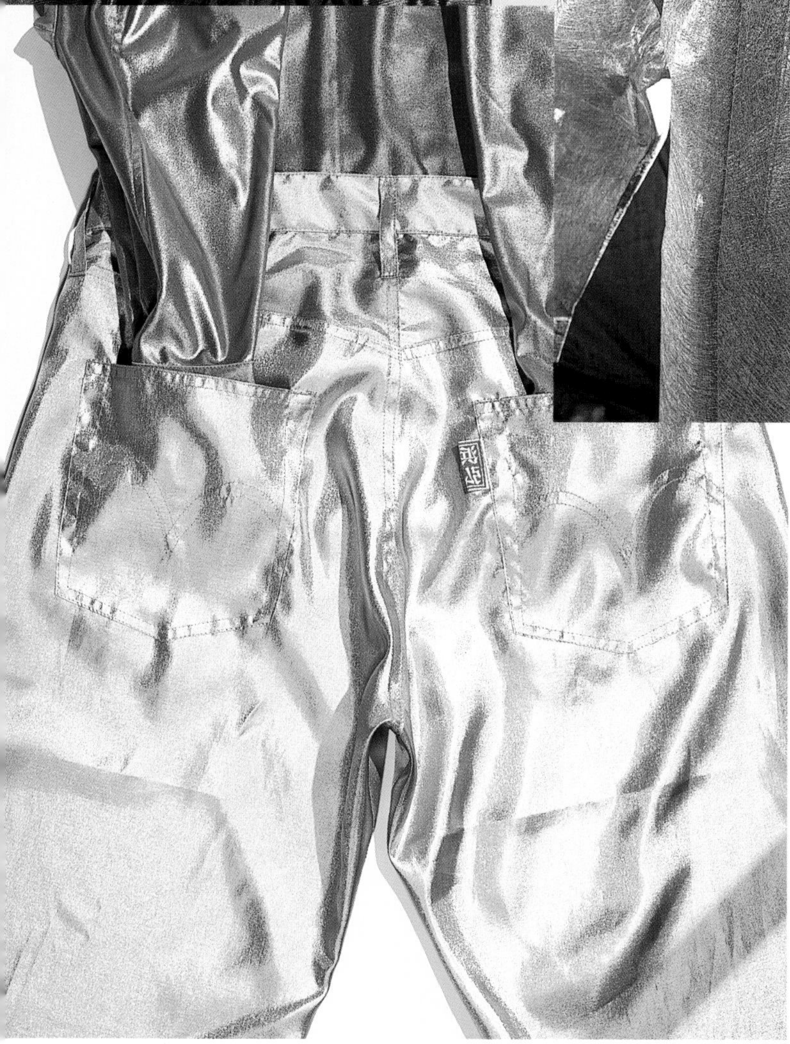

27

30

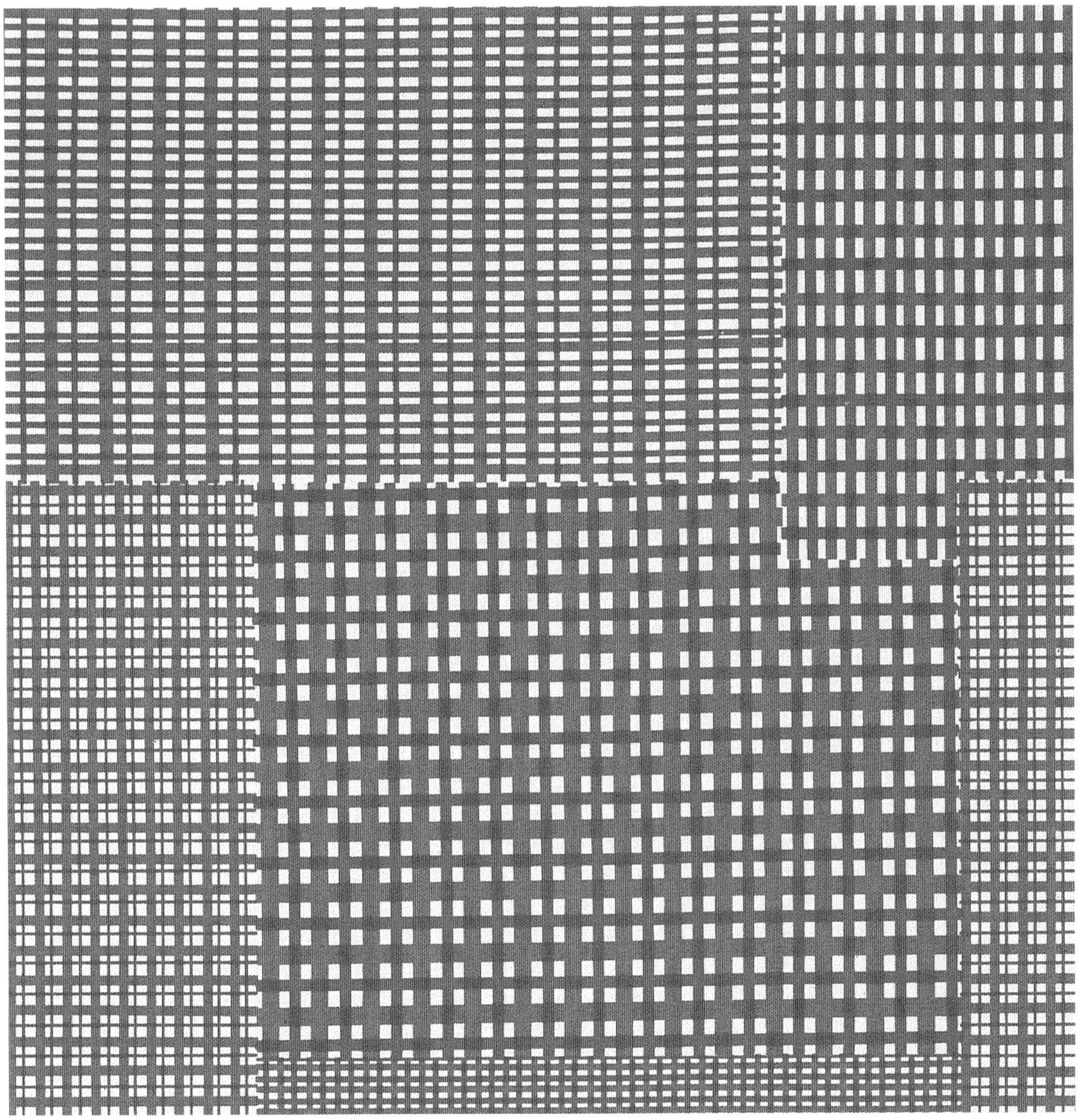

Sadly the news of Hiroshi Awatsuji's death came through as the selection for the *Yearbook* was being made. He was 66, and for over thirty years had been a major figure in Japanese textile design, though he himself preferred the term "surface designer". Unlike some of his colleagues – Junichi Arai, for example – for whom texture is all-important, Awatsuji concentrated on the use of pattern and colour. As he said in an interview with Junko Popham for the *Yearbook* a few years ago, "I believe in the strength of surface design. Design for texture sounds to me like whispering quietly, whereas a print can express something more instantly and strongly. I am fascinated by textile design because it is not just art but a wrapping which is for use by people." Many of Awatsuji's designs were produced by Fujie-Textile, and have had a lasting effect on interior design standards in Japan. He always drew his designs full size, by hand. "When I have an idea my hand never stops moving to chase and capture it. That is how I create my designs."

30 **Hiroshi Awatsuji**
Interior design fabric, *Farm*
Cotton
w 139cm
w 54¾in
Fujie Textile Co. Ltd, Japan

31 **Junichi Arai**
Fabric A
Polyester

32 **Junichi Arai**
Fabric B
60% nylon, 40% polyester

33 **Junichi Arai**
Fabric C
Polyester, aluminium

34 **Junichi Arai**
Fabric D
Polyester, aluminium

35 **Junichi Arai**
Fabric E
Red: Nylon, aluminium
Other colours: Polyester, aluminium

31

33

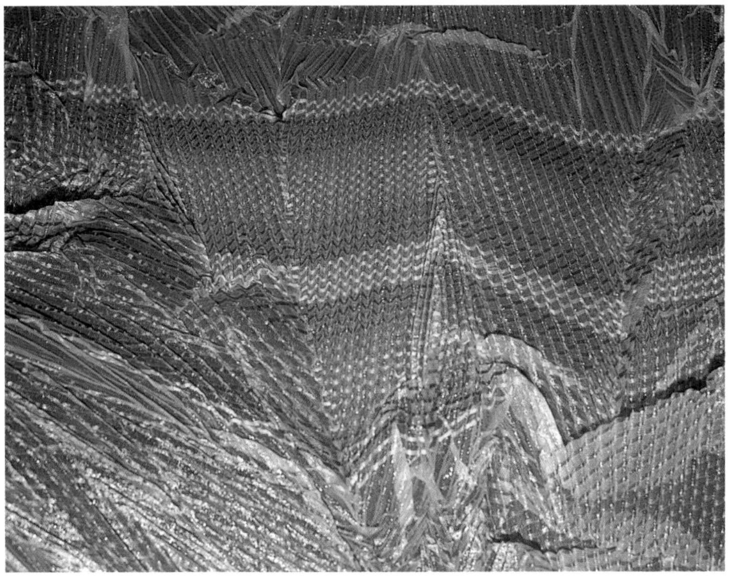

32

34

35

36

38

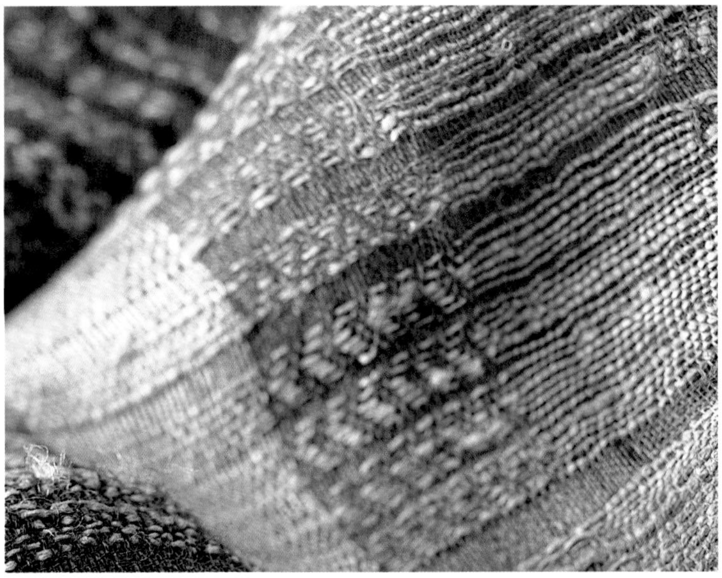

36

39

37

39

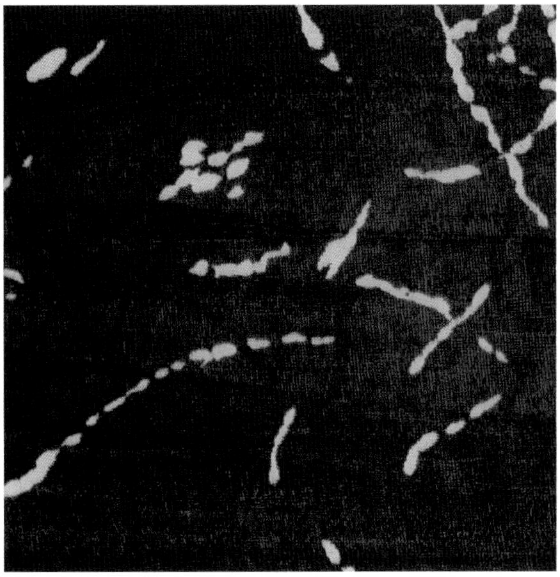

40

41

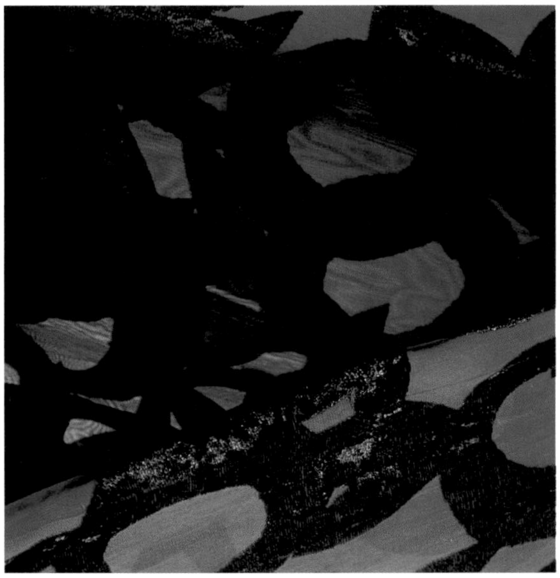

42

36 **Chiaki Maki**
Jacquard hand-woven shawl, *Shady*
Silk, wool, linen
w 70cm l 200cm
w 27½in l 78¾in
Maki Textile Studio, Japan

37 **Chiaki Maki**
Hand-woven shawl, *Akiha*
Silk, wool
w 80cm l 200cm
w 31½in l 78¾in
Maki Textile Studio, Japan

38 **Kaori Maki**
Multi-harness weave, *Pranshu II*
Wool, malda silk, spun silk
w 45cm l 150cm
w 17¾in l 59in
Maki Textile Studio, Japan
(Limited batch production)

39 **Kaori Maki**
Jacquard woven shawl, *Diksha I*
Wool, spun silk, malda silk
w 60cm l 200cm
w 23⅝in l 78¾in
Maki Textile Studio, Japan
(Limited batch production)

40 **Reiko Sudo**
Fashion fabric, *Erves*
Polyester, rayon
w 90cm repeat 45, 48cm
w 35¾in repeat 17¾, 18⅞in
Nuno Corporation, Japan

41 **Reiko Sudo**
Fashion fabric, *Moth-Eaten*
Cotton, polyester
w 85cm repeat 61cm
w 33½in repeat 24in
Nuno Corporation, Japan

42 **Reiko Sudo**
Fashion fabric, *Bamboo*
Polyester, rayon
w 90cm repeat 200cm
w 35¾in repeat 78¾in
Nuno Corporation, Japan

Textile design is, like painting, largely two-dimensional, and, for Mendini, is therefore free to borrow the wider licences of art. This includes the right to be directly figurative, as in the work here by Hilton McConnico and Heinz Röntgen, in which the textile surface is treated like a canvas. It also makes room for the sculptural, whether in Jan Truman's copper-wire jewel, or Masayo Ave's sea-anenome in Shibori textile (page 166), a project devised in parallel with Mary Little's furniture (page 52), and shown in Milan in 1995.

43

44

45

46

47

43 **Hilton McConnico**
Carpet, *Petites Feuilles Pourpre*
Wool
w 180cm l 270cm
w 70⅞in l 106½in
Toulemonde Bochart, France

44 **Heinz Röntgen**
Furnishing fabric embroidery, *Arva*
35% cotton, 65% polyester
w 150cm
w 59in
Nya Nordiska, Germany

45 **Marc van Hoe**
Jacquard woven upholstery fabric,
3 Head Man
Cotton, linen
w 14cm l 17.5cm
w 5½in l 6⅞in
Waesland NV, Belgium

46 **Knoll Textiles Design Studio**
Upholstery fabric, *Legacy*
51% cotton, 28% polyester, 21% viscose
w 137.2cm repeat 92cm (vertical)
70.2cm (horizontal)
w 54in repeat 36¼in (vertical)
27⅝in (horizontal)
Knoll Textiles, USA

47 **Pia Wallén**
Blankets, *Crux*
Wool
l 213cm d 132cm
l 83⅞in d 52in
Edition Asplund, Sweden

48

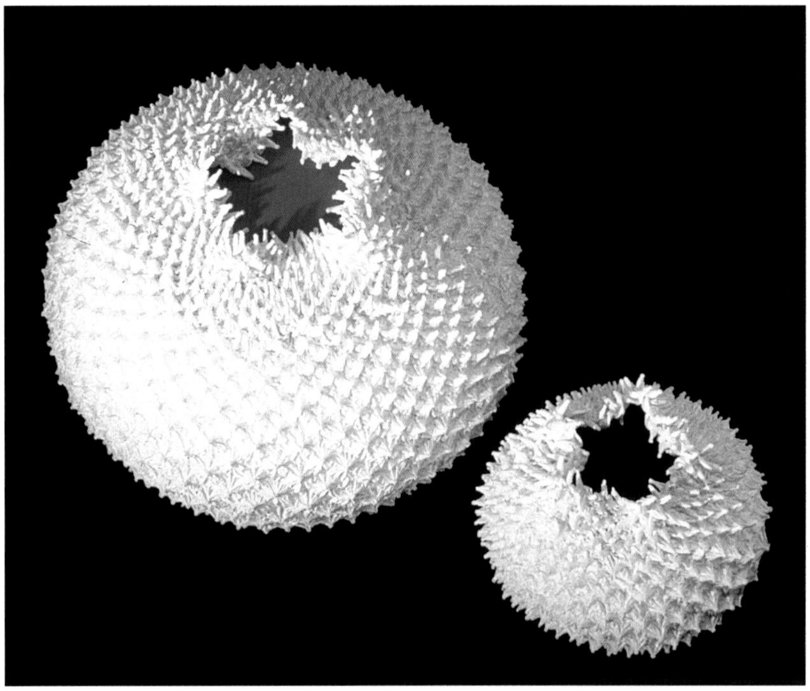

49

50

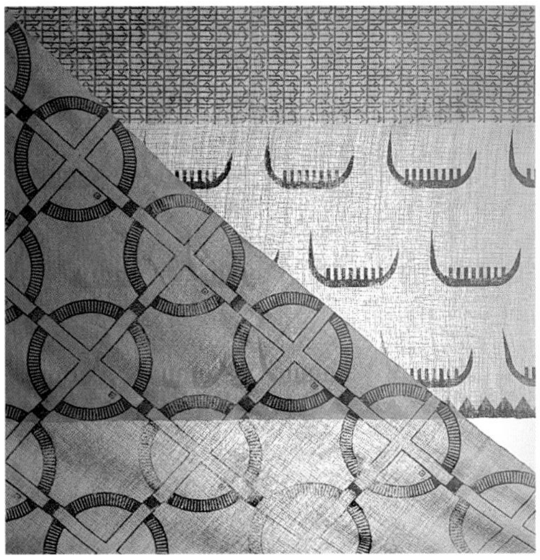

53

51

54

52

55

48 **Jan Truman**
Sculptural knitted-wire brooch
Gold-plated and enamelled copper wire, amethyst gemstones, glass beads
w 9cm l 10cm
w 3½in l 4in
(One-off)

49 **Masayo Ave**
Cushions, *Tofts*
Polyurethane, nylon, Shibori textile "Kumo"
Large: h 38cm d 20cm
h 15in d 7⅞in
Small: h 20cm d 10cm
h 7⅞in d 4in
(Limited batch production)

50 **Jack Lenor Larsen**
Upholstery fabrics, *Matrix*, *True Grits*, *Fairways*, *Herald Square*, *Intermission*
Cotton, linen
Matrix: w 149.8cm; w 59in
True Grits: w 149.8cm; w 59in
Fairways: w 149.8cm repeat 5cm
w 59in repeat 2in
Herald Square: w 149.8cm repeat 1.9cm
w 59in repeat ¾in
Intermission: w 137.2cm; w 54in
Jack Lenor Larsen, USA

51 **Iris di Ciommo and Circe Bernardes**
Arte Nativa
Printed cotton
l repeat 130cm
l repeat 51⅛in
ANA – Arte Nativa Aplicada, Brazil

52 **Ravage**
Scarf, *Leatitia's Children*
Silk
w 90cm l 90cm
w 35⅜in l 35⅜in
Printed by Italseta, Italy

53 **Mette Mikkelsen**
Curtains. Linen, copper print
h 400cm w 120cm repeat 110 x 350cm
h 157½in w 47¼in repeat 43¼ x 137¾in
(Prototype)

54 **Gary Bukovnik**
Curtain fabric, *Yvette's Poppies*
Cotton
w 140cm repeat 69cm
w 55⅛in repeat 27⅛in
Kvadrat Boligtextiler A/S, Denmark

55 **Gary Bukovnik**
Curtain fabric, *Tulips*
Cotton
w 140cm repeat 69cm
w 55⅛in repeat 27⅛in
Kvadrat Boligtextiler A/S, Denmark

56

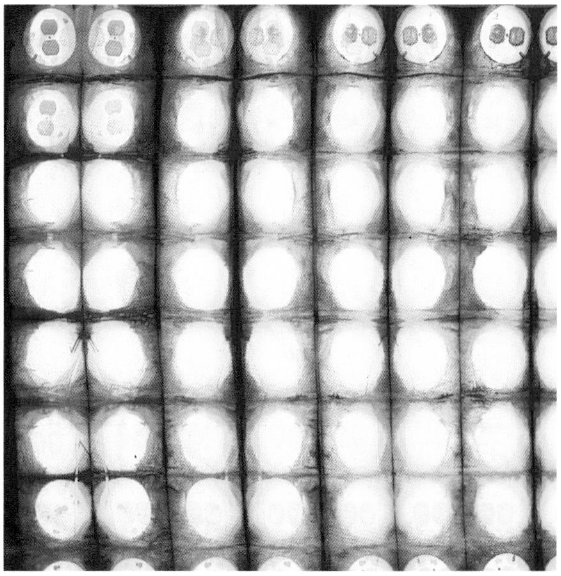

57

56 **Heinz Röntgen**
Furnishing fabric embroidery, *Lia-Daisy*
90% polyamide, 10% viscose
w 140cm
w 55⅛in
Nya Nordiska, Germany

57 **Carol Westfall**
Silk print, *Strobes*
Silk crêpe, Sabraset silk dyes
w 152.4cm repeat 17.7cm
w 60in repeat 7in
(One-off)

58 **Gabriella Giandelli**
Printed silk, *India*
w 30cm
w 11¾in
Memphis Milano srl, Italy

59 **Louise Gibb**
Silk print, *I'm The Best*
w 120cm
w 47¼in
Repeat 16cm across, 19cm down
Repeat 6½in across, 7½in down
Bolgheri Franchise for
Memphis Milano srl, Italy

60 **Massimo Giacon**
Wallpaper, *Wilma*
Printed paper
Measurements unavailable
Sannelli e Volpi, Italy
(Prototype)

61 **Helle Abild**
Computer-generated
heat-transferred print, *Oil*
Cotton
w 90cm repeat 4cm
w 35⅜in repeat 1½in
(One-off)

62 **Helle Abild**
Computer-generated
heat-transferred print, *Nature*
Cotton
w 90cm repeat 4cm
w 35⅜in repeat 1½in
(One-off)

63 **Adriane Nicolaisen**
Computer dobby loom weave,
Linen Lace
Rayon, silk, linen
w 121.9cm repeat 45.7cm
w 48in repeat 18in
Handwoven Webworks, USA
(Limited batch production)

64 **Helle Abild**
Computer-generated
heat-transferred print,
Electric Eye
Cotton
w 90cm repeat 4cm
w 35⅜in repeat 1½in
(One-off)

65 **Jack Lenor Larsen**
Upholstery fabric, *Pillows*
Polyester
w 165cm
w 65in
Jack Lenor Larsen, USA

58

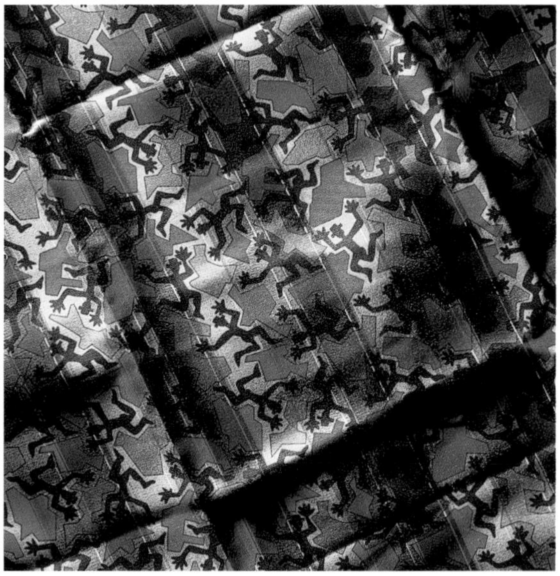

59

60

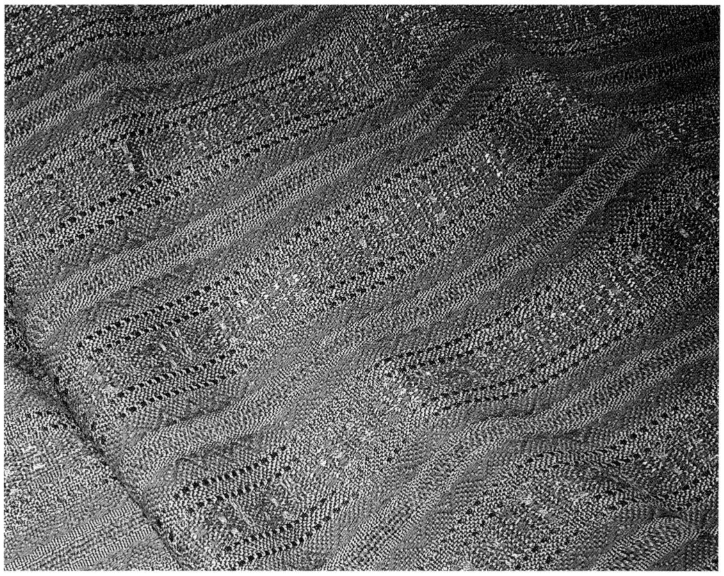
63

61

64

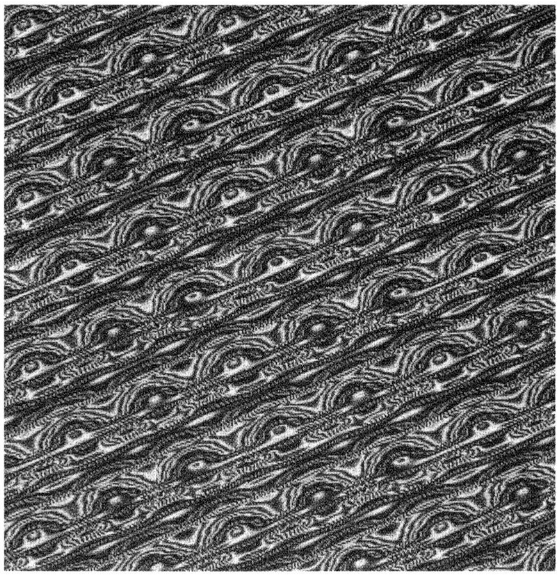
62

65

products

The impact of new technologies on design is a subject that fascinates Mendini: not only do they offer designers fresh ways of working, but also the challenge of interpreting new devices. Compare, for example, the re-edition of Le Corbusier's globe, an evaluation of the world by the Modern Movement (page 185), and the new electronic information screens from Toshiba (pages 183 and 184): here design is responding to changing levels of our perception of knowledge, from a sphere to a web. This process started with electronic command systems and miniaturization, thanks to which function no longer dictates form. The shapes of many objects are no longer determined by their mechanics. The new collection of electronic products designed by Philippe Starck for the French electronic group Thomson represents this radical change, with Starck devising a whole range of new forms, a new product semantics for audio and television equipment.

1 **Philippe Starck**
Radio, *LaLaLa*
Bakelite
l 27.8cm
l 10⅞in
Thomson, France
(Limited batch production)

2 **Philippe Starck**
Radio, *Moa Moa*
Bakelite
h 11.6cm w 13.4cm
h 4½in w 5¼in
Thomson, France
(Limited batch production)

3 **Philippe Starck**
Television and video recorder, *La Tour*
Screen: 40cm
Screen: 15¾in
Thomson, France

4 **Philippe Starck**
Portable colour television, *Zéo*
h 38.9cm l 38.3cm d 36.7cm
h 15¼in l 15⅛in d 14½in
Screen: 36cm
Screen: 14⅛in
Thomson, France

1

2

3

4

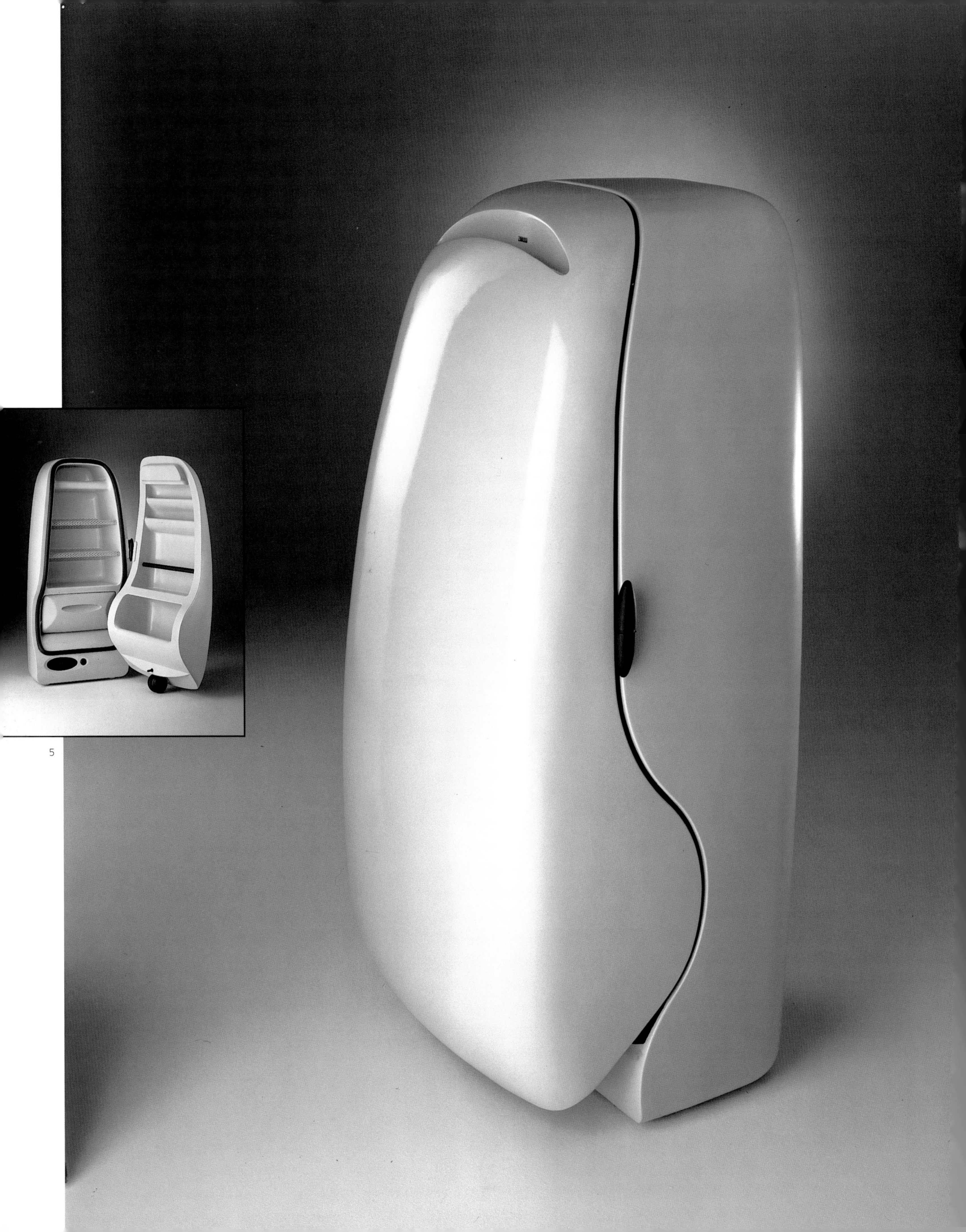

5

6

5 **Roberto Pezzetta**
Refrigerator, *Oz*
h 123cm w 62cm d 60cm
h 54⅜in w 24⅜in d 23⅝in
Zanussi Elettrodomestici SpA, Italy
(Prototype)

6 **Philips Corporate Design**
Moustache trimmer, *Definition HS 040*
P.O.M., corrosion resistant chromium steel, ABS
h 14cm w 3.6cm l 3.9cm
h 5½in w 1⅜in l 1½in
Philips International BV, The Netherlands

7

7 **Andreas Brandolini**
Christmas-tree decoration, *Lorraine Ball*
Glass
h 6cm l 6cm
h 2⅜in l 2⅜in
Anthologie Quartett, Germany

8 **Claudio Giunnelli and Marcello Panza**
Christmas-tree decoration
Glass
h 6cm l 6cm
h 2⅜in l 2⅜in
Anthologie Quartett, Germany

8

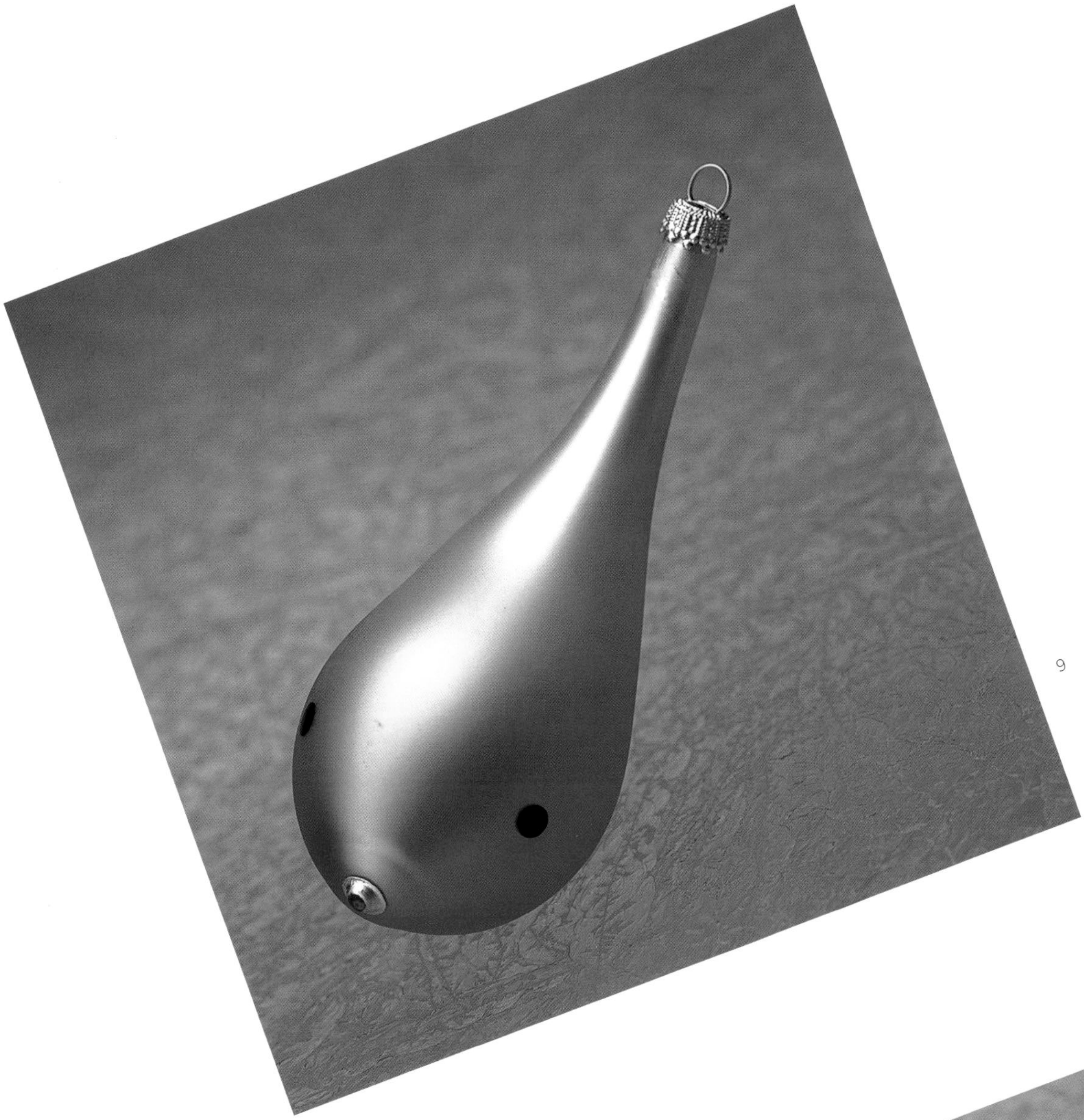

9

9 **Maria Christina Hamel**
Christmas-tree decoration, *Fish*
Glass
h 6cm | 6cm
h 2⅜in | 2⅜in
Anthologie Quartett, Germany

10 **Robert Wettstein**
Christmas-tree decoration, *Snow Ball*
Glass
h 6cm | 6cm
h 2⅜in | 2⅜in
Anthologie Quartett, Germany

10

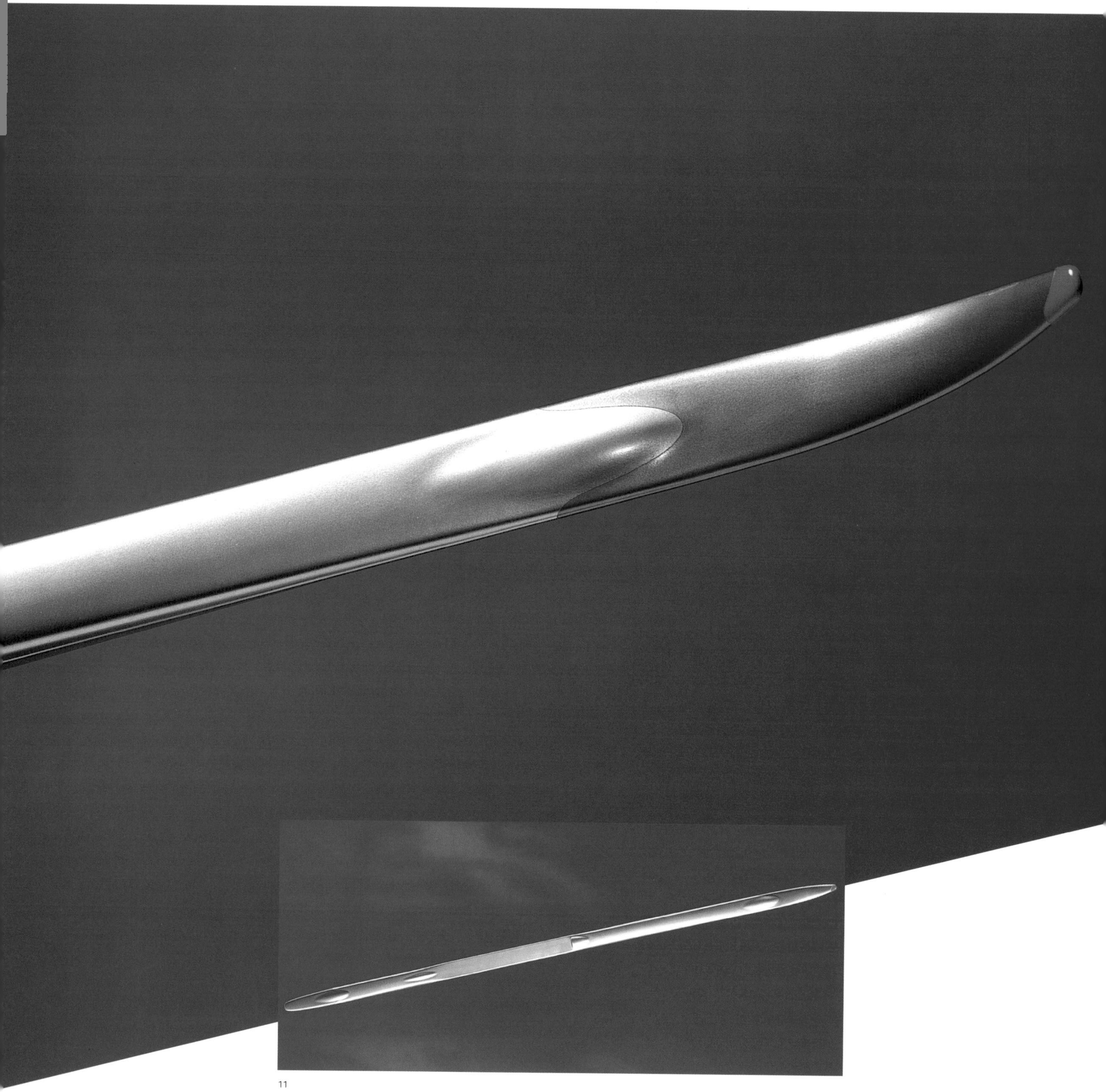

11

The market for skis exceeds a million pairs annually, and skiing, particularly slalom and downhill, has become an important television sport worldwide. This justifies considerable long-term research and development into new materials, construction and design. Creadesign's new ski for Karhu will not be available commercially for one or two years. It uses a mix of carbon fibre and plastics as material, and new moulding technologies to integrate tip and tail pieces into the main body. The new racing ski is 20 to 30 centimetres shorter than the current standard sizes, and Karhu believe it will create a "totally new cross-country skiing culture".

11 **Creadesign Oy**
Ski, *Karhu Cubix*
Carbon fibre, plastic
w 5cm l 180cm d 6cm
w 12in l 70⅞in d 2⅜in
Karhu-Titan Oy, Finland
(Prototype)

12 **Yamaha Product Design Laboratory**
Ski, *Yamaha Proto T.T.*
PBT, fibreglass, epoxy carbon resin, steel
l 183–201cm
l 72–79⅛in
Yamaha Corporation, Japan

13 **Jasper Morrison and Matthias Dietz**
Skirting board
Aluminium
h 8cm l 400cm d 2cm
h 3⅛in l 157½in d ¾in
Art-Line Wohndecor GmbH, Germany

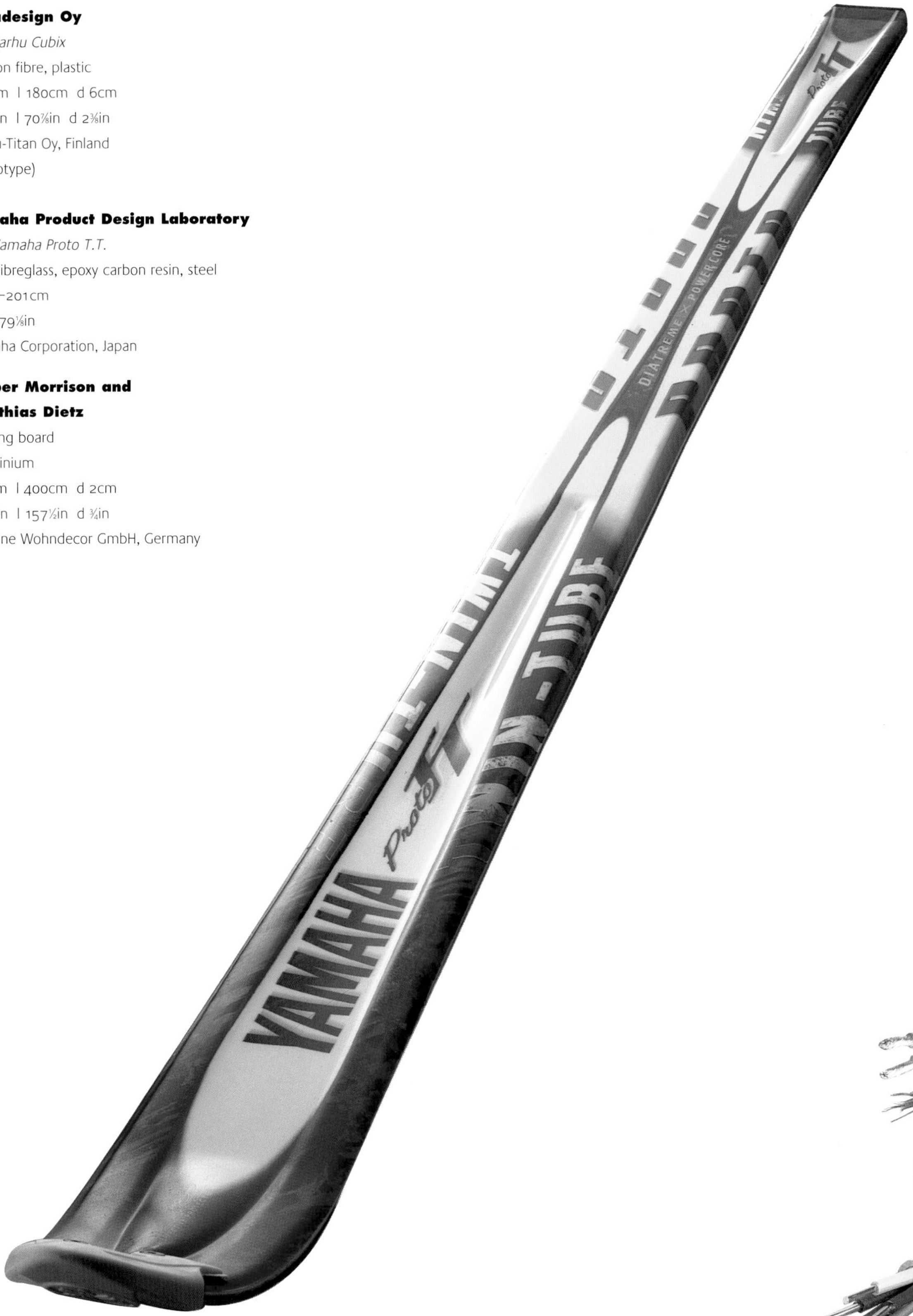

12

13

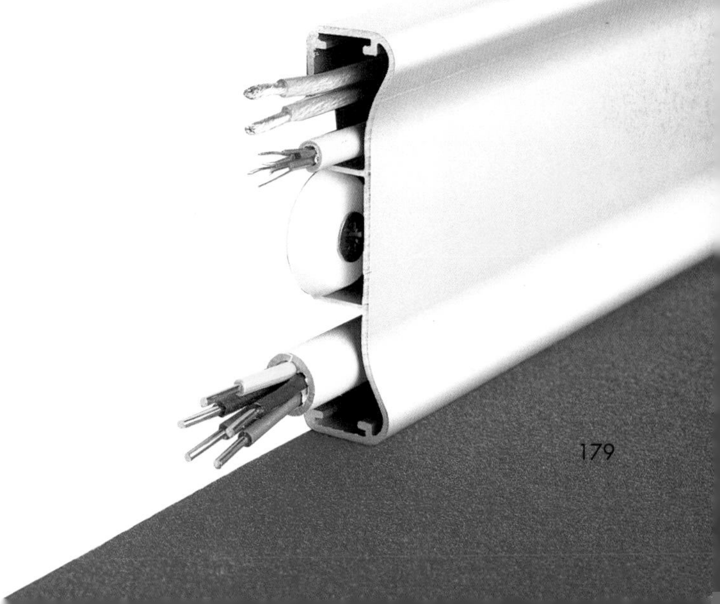

14

Panasonic
VisionPro 6500

15

SAMSUNG ZOOM LENS
38-140mm AUTO MACRO
SAMSUNG

16

17

17 **Yves Béhar, Gil Wong, Jeff Salazar, Glenn Wong, Max Yoshimoto (Lunar Design)**
Personal computer,
Hewlett Packard Home PC
ABS, sheet metal
Monitor: h 40.5cm w 36.9cm l 39.3cm
h 16in w 14½in l 15½in
CPU: h 11.6cm w 42.5cm l 38cm
h 4⅝in w 16¾in l 15in
Tower: h 41.6cm w 20.2cm l 45.6cm
h 16⅜in w 8in l 18in
Hewlett Packard Company, USA

18 **Yves Béhar, Brett Loveday (Lunar Design)**
Digital telephone
Polycarbonate, ABS
Base: h 4.7cm w 19.8cm l 21.5cm
h 1⅞in w 7¾in l 8½in
Handset: h 3.2cm w 6cm l 15.5cm
h 1¼in w 2¼in l 6⅛in
Taihan Electric Wire Co., Korea

14 **Kyushu Matsushita Electric Design Centre**
Video teleconferencing system,
KXC-M6500N
Moulded ABS
h 42.4cm w 14.1cm d 18.1cm
h 16¾in w 5½in d 7⅛in
Kyushu Matsushita
Electric Industrial Co. Ltd, Japan

15 **LCD Design Consultants**
Torch, *ATX*
Polycarbonate
l 20.6cm di 7cm
l 8⅛in di 2¾in
Martin Cunel SA, France

16 **Christian Schwamkrug**
Compact zoom camera, *ECX-1*
Plastic
h 8.2cm w 15cm d 7.5cm
h 3¼in w 5⅞in d 3in
Samsung Aerospace Industries Ltd, Korea

18

19

19 **Television Division Design Department**
Liquid crystal colour television
Plastic, zinc
h 28.6cm w 29.6cm d 19cm
h 11¼in w 11⅝in d 7½in
Matsushita Electric Industrial Co. Ltd, Japan

20 **Ninaber, Peters, Krouwel Industrial Design**
Energy mirror
Steel plate, glass
Basis module: h 70cm w 35cm d 7cm
h 27½in w 13¾in d 2¾in
Consumer module:
h 70cm w 48cm d 7cm
h 27½in w 18⅞in d 2¾in
Ecofys, The Netherlands
(Limited batch production)

21 **Toshiba Corporation Design Centre**
Image Instrument
h 17.5cm w 25.2cm d 4.4cm
h 6⅞in w 9⅞in d 1¾in
Toshiba Corporation, Japan

Architects and building managers are increasingly concerned about efficient energy consumption in buildings, not only as a matter of cost but also because of wider environmental concerns. Gathering and analysing this information is difficult, while part of a good energy policy is to communicate to the users of the building the need for minimum energy consumption. Ninaber Peters Krouwel's "energy mirror" is intended to meet this need. Its LED and LCD displays show the consumption of gas, electricty and water, and monitor temperature and humidity. Thus both users of and visitors to a building will have a clearer understanding of energy consumption and so be encouraged to economize.

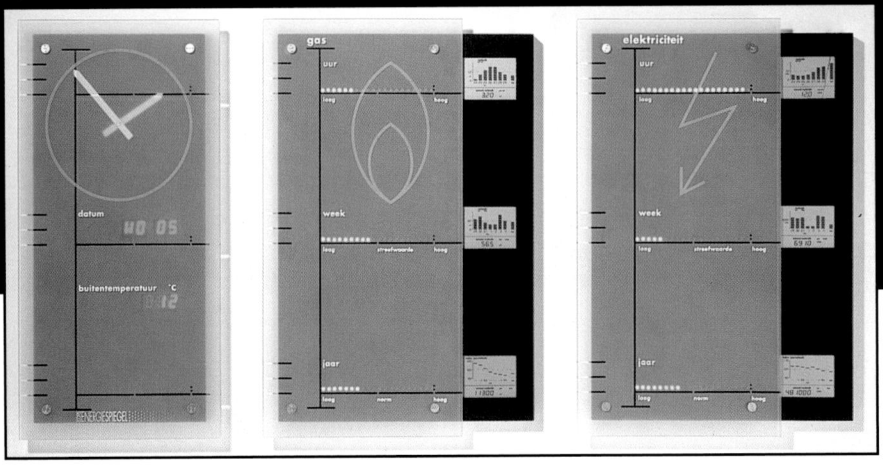

20

The Toshiba building, located in the Shibaura waterfront, overlooking the world.
1 2 3
4 5 6
7 8 9
* 0 #
Enter
Rupo
12

21

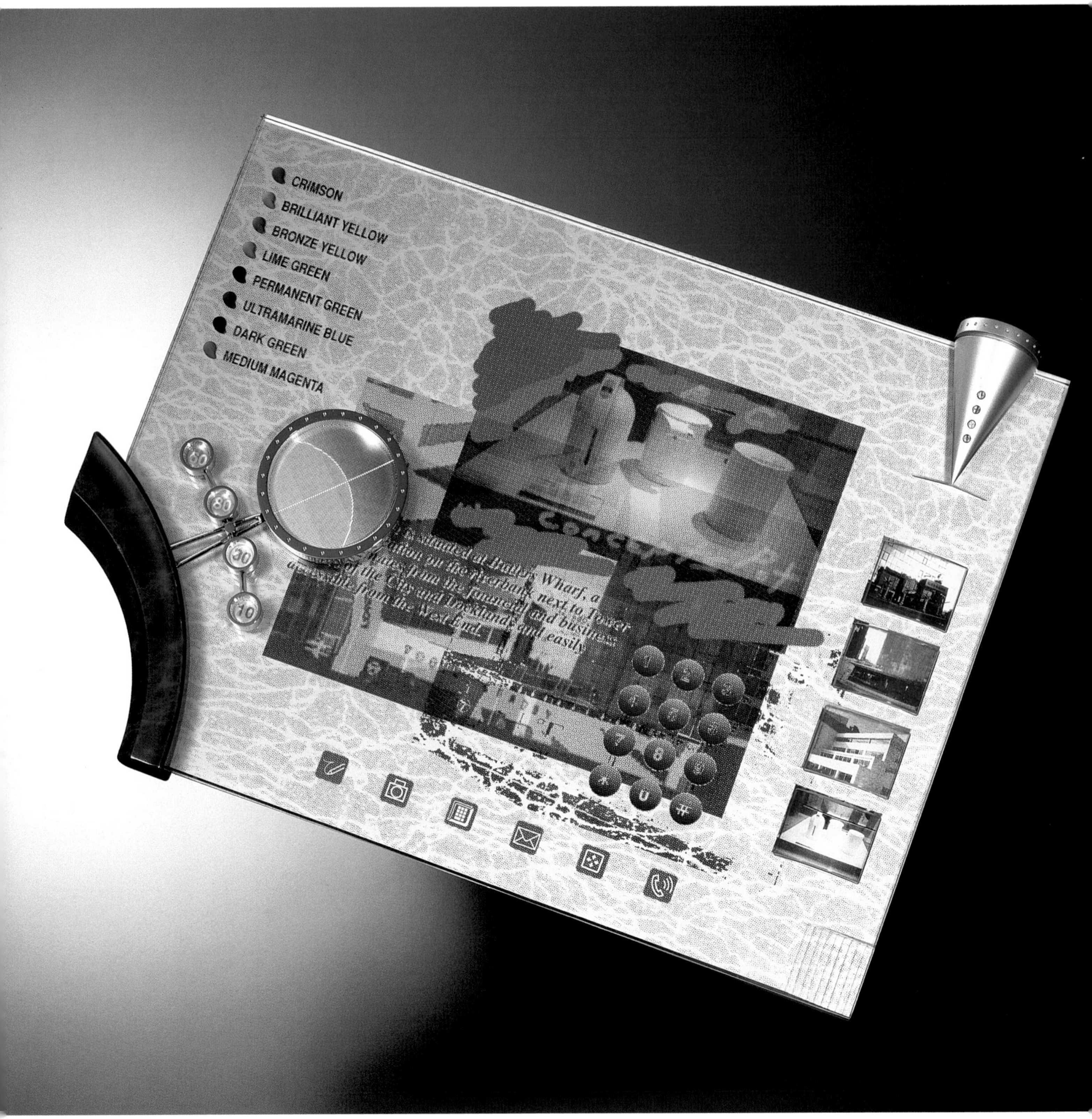
CRIMSON
BRILLIANT YELLOW
BRONZE YELLOW
LIME GREEN
PERMANENT GREEN
ULTRAMARINE BLUE
DARK GREEN
MEDIUM MAGENTA

22

Two new products from the Toshiba Corporation's Design Centre show how quickly the design of the computer input device is moving away from the rigid hierarchy of fixed keyboard and screen in favour of pen input. They also show the industry moving away from general products with structured uses to more flexible ones. The *Image Instrument*, (page 183) has a transparent LCD screen so that it can be used to input data or create images in the field, using the visible real image as a backdrop or template. The keyboard is on the reverse sides: learning to handle it may take slightly longer, but, as with a musical instrument, once it is mastered the user's potential is much enhanced. The *Multi-function Sketch Pad* shows new technology learning from older cultures. It is based directly on the traditional Chinese writing or sketch pad, with paper and ink stick, inkstone and brush. The input pen is, like a brush, pressure sensitive, the colours are laid out in a tool window, lettering can be added via an IC card, and the LCD screen can be coloured or tinted. The machine is portable, and images created on it can be downloaded on to a PC. By giving the user flexibility of expression, the sketch pad allows for more natural and direct communication.

23

22 **Toshiba Corporation Design Centre**
Multi-function sketch pad
h 19.8cm w 26cm d 2.5cm
h 7¾in w 10¼in d 1in
Toshiba Corporation, Japan

23 **Le Corbusier**
Globe
Plastic, chromium-plated metal
Anthologie Quartett, Germany

Product design is often about the re-interpretation of simple objects: Droog Design's tap is minimal plumbing with exquisite form, while Tadao Ando's transparent cigarette lighter, or Kenneth Grange's travel iron (page 194) are exacting exercises in a known vocabulary. Simplicity is not a limit, however, more a starting point: what may begin as a reductive process becomes a springboard. The Swatch Watch is a good example of this (page 190): formally there is a strict set of shapes and dimensions to follow. This brief confines the designer in one sense, and at the same time pushes the creative impulse in a fixed direction. Traditional objects, such as curtain rails or spectacles, provide just such a restrained opportunity for Riccardo Dalisi and Toshiyuki Kita (pages 192–3).

24

24 **Pol Quadens**
Keyholder
Magnetic stainless steel, epoxy, magnets
h 46cm w 18cm d 1cm
h 18⅛in w 7⅛in d ⅜in
Pol International Design, Belgium

25 **Dick van Hoff**
Tap, *Stop DD32*
Copper
h 28cm w 17cm d 17cm
h 11in w 6¾in d 6¾in
Droog Design, The Netherlands
(Prototype)

25

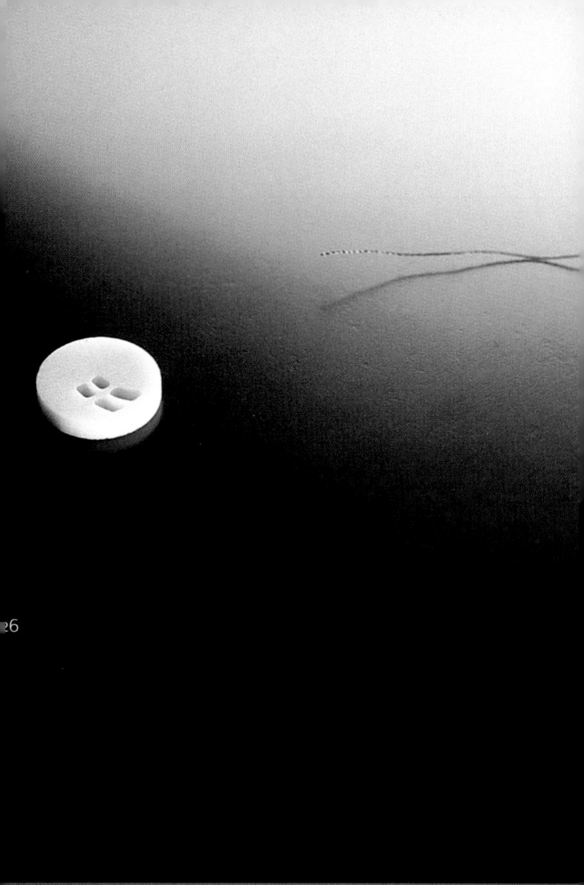

28

26 **Siggi Fischer**
Button
Mother-of-Pearl
di 1–2cm
di ⅜–¾in
Best Friends, Germany

27 **Robert Wettstein**
Rocking horse, *Naseweiss*
Wood, paper
h 76cm w 26cm l 80cm
h 29⅞in w 10¼in l 31½in
Structure Design, Switzerland
(Limited batch production)

28 **Philippe Starck**
Toy, *The Face*
PE, ABS
h 18, 20cm l 80cm d 36, 20cm
h 7⅛, 7⅞in l 31½in d 14⅛, 7⅞in
Big-Spielwarenfabrik, Germany
(Prototype)

29 **Marc Newson**
Watch, *Seaslug Collection*
Stainless steel, natural rubber
h 1cm w 3.9cm l 24cm di 3.9cm
h ⅜in w 1½in l 9½in di 1½in
Ikepod Watch Company, Switzerland
(Limited batch production)

30 **James Smith**
Swatch Watch, *Scuba*
Plastic
l 23.2cm di 3.6cm
l 9⅛in di 1⅜in
(SMH) Swatch AG, Switzerland

29

29

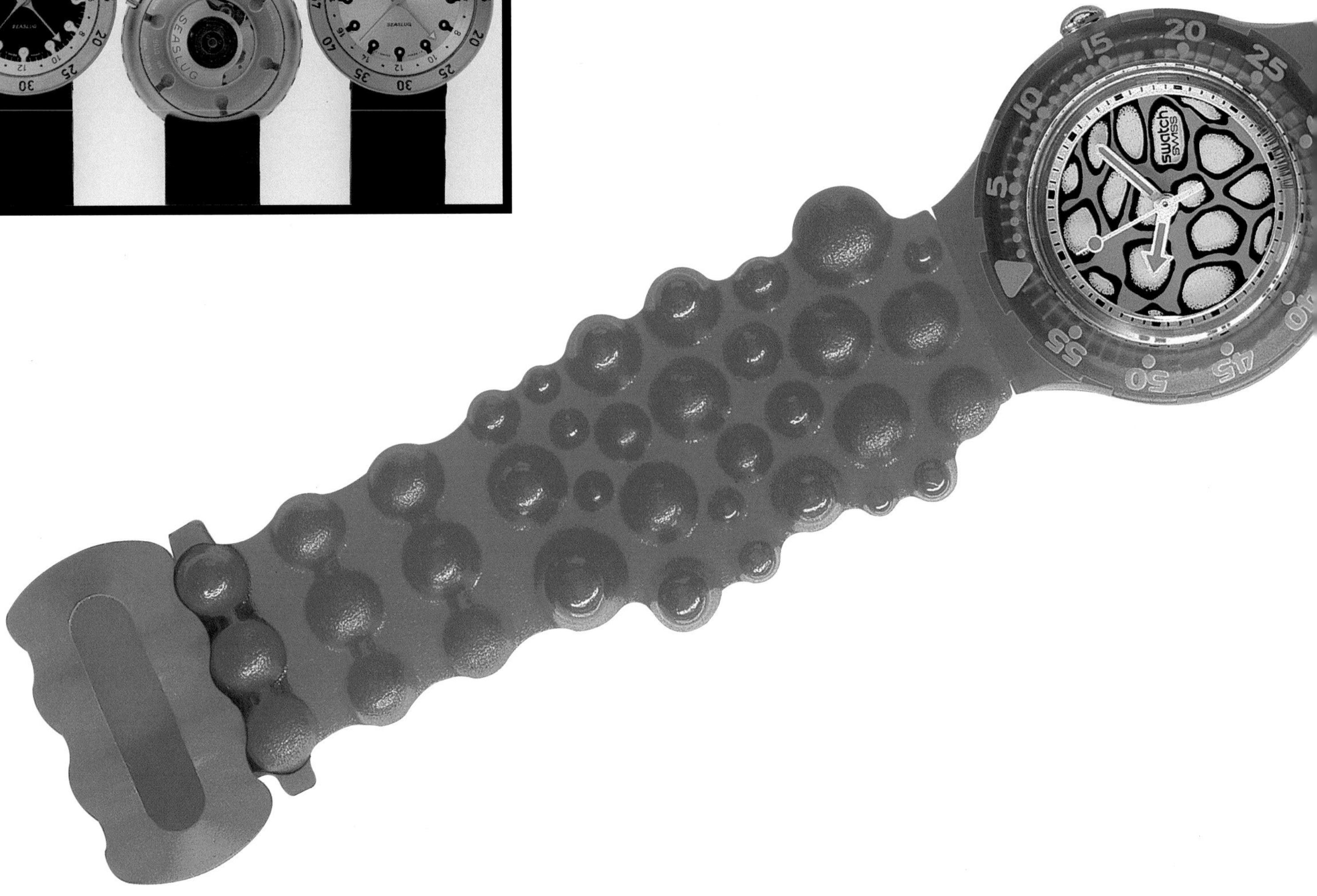

30

31 **Robert Altman**
Swatch Watch
Plastic, metal
l 23.2cm di 3.6cm
l 9⅛in di 1⅜in
(SMH) Swatch AG, Switzerland

32 **Akira Kurosawa**
Swatch Watch
Plastic, metal
l 23.2cm di 3.6cm
l 9⅛in di 1⅜in
(SMH) Swatch AG, Switzerland

33 **Pedro Almodovar**
Swatch Watch
Plastic, leather, pearls, metal
l 23.2cm di 3.6cm
l 9⅛in di 1⅜in
(SMH) Swatch AG, Switzerland

31

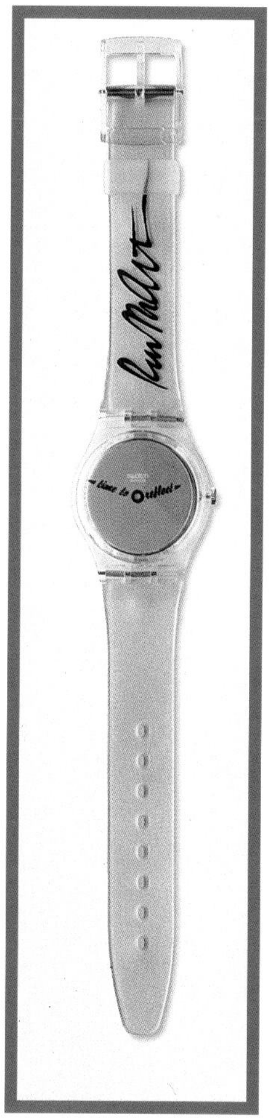

32

33

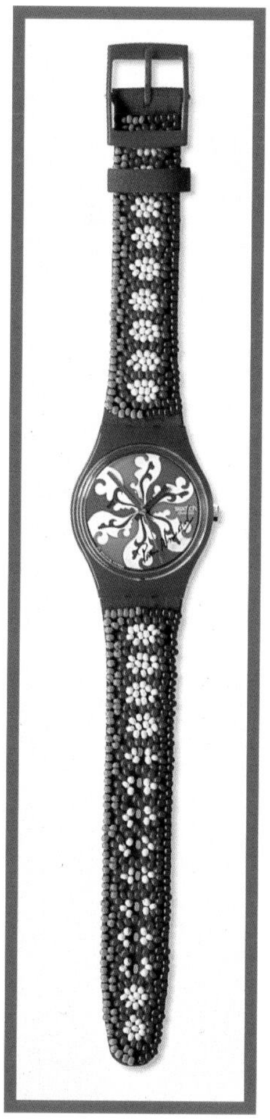

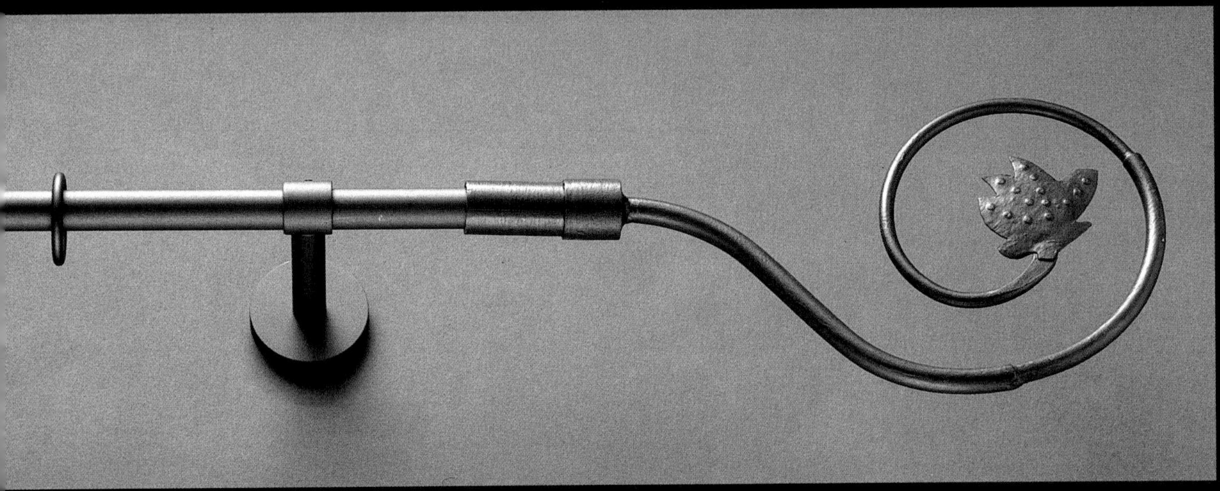

34

34 **Riccardo Dalisi**
Curtain-wire set, *Leaf*
Copper, solid brass
l up to 500cm di 1.6cm
l up to 196⅞in di ⅝in
Hubert Blome GmbH, Germany

35 **Toshiyuki Kita**
Spectacles
Titanium
h 4.7, 4.2, 3.8cm w 12.8, 12.7, 12.3cm
l 13.6, 11.5, 11cm
h 1¾, 1⅛, 1⅜in w 5, 4⅞, 4¾in
l 5¼, 4½, 4¼in
Mizushima Optical Co. Ltd, Japan
(Limited batch production)

35

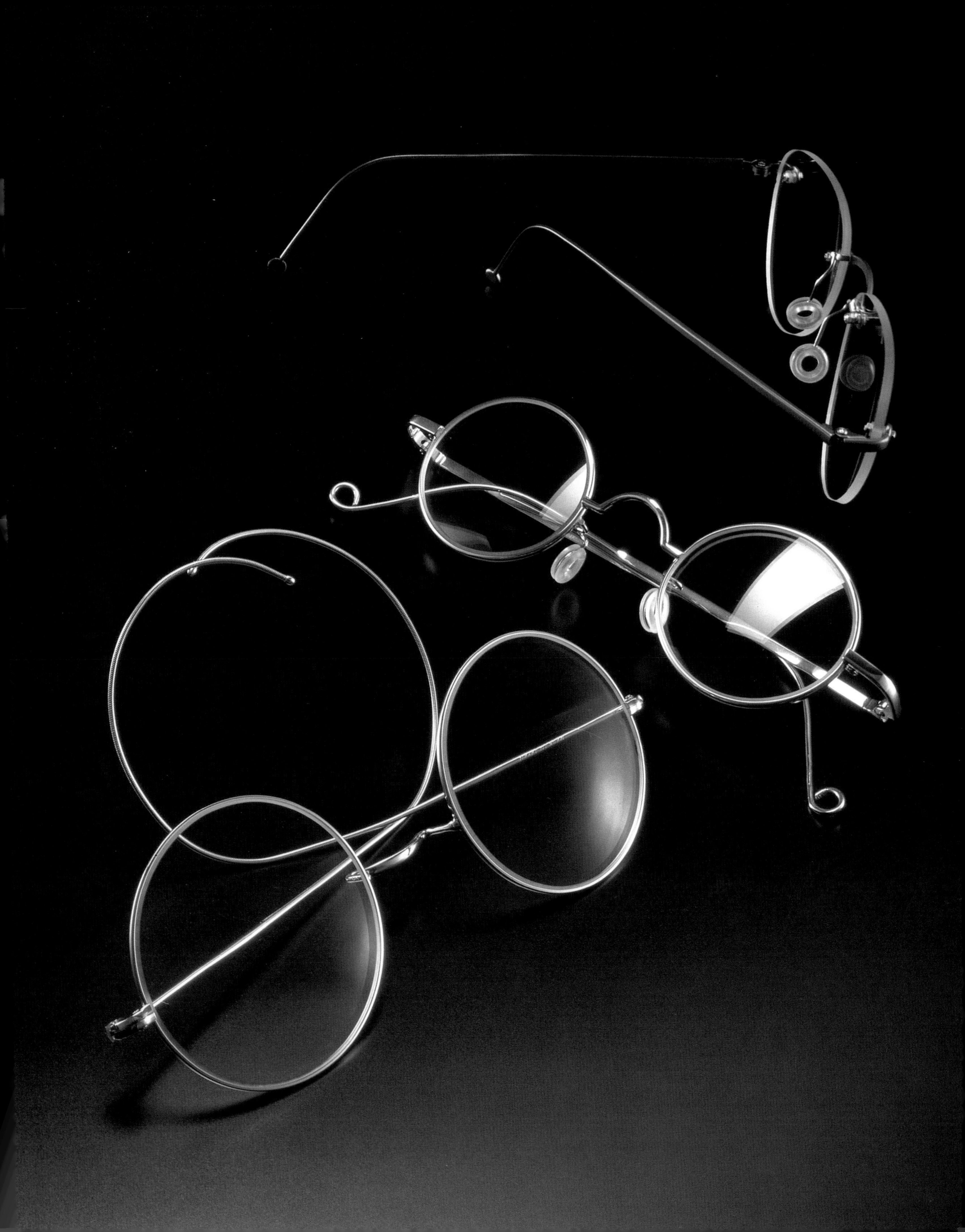

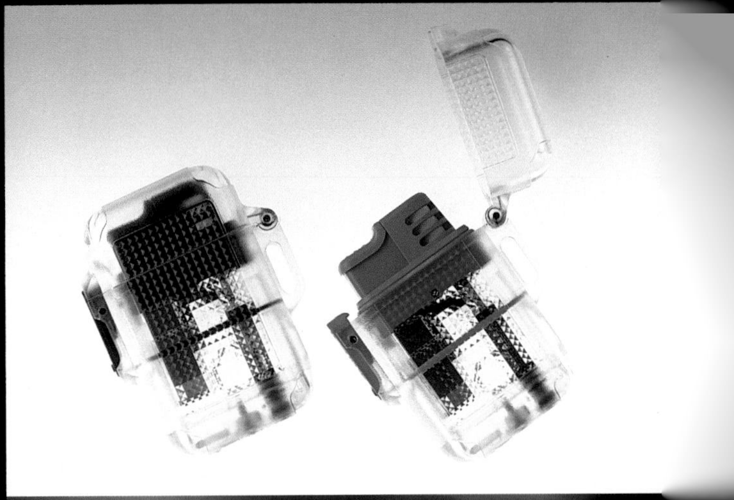

39

40

41

36 **Setsu Ito**
Ashtray, *Doso*
Crystal
h 10cm w 10cm
h 3⅞in w 3⅞in
(Limited batch production)

37 **Kenneth Grange and Gavin Thomson**
Compact travel iron, *ST50*
Moulded plastic, die-cast metal
h 9cm w 18.3cm
h 3½in w 7⅛in
Kenwood Ltd, UK

38 **Konstantin Grcic**
Shelves/container
Polypropylene
h 9, 9, 21cm w 11cm l 12, 12.5, 43cm
h 3½, 3½, 8¼in w 4⅜in l 4¾, 4⅞, 16⅞in
Authentics artipresent GmbH, Germany

39 **Shinkichi Tanaka**
All-weather lighter
Plastic
h 5.3cm w 4.2cm d 1.6cm
h 2⅛in w 1⅝in d ⅝in
Windmill Co. Ltd, Japan

40 **Kenneth Grange and Johan Santer**
Cool wall deep-fryer, *DF450*
Moulded plastic, die-cast alloy
h 25.5cm w 27cm d 35cm
h 10in w 10⅝in d 13¾in
Kenwood Ltd, UK

41 **Gaetano Pesce**
Photograph frame, *My Frame*
Cast resin, glass, steel
h 24cm w 29cm d 3cm
h 9½in w 11⅜in d 1⅛in
Fish Design, The Netherlands
(Limited batch production)

42 **Nazanin Kamali**
Kitchen rack
Stainless steel, zinc-plated wire
h 5cm l 75cm d 30cm
h 2in l 29½in d 11¾in
Aero, UK

43 **Angela Carvalho and Alexander Neumeister**
Ceiling fan
Recyclable polypropylene, metal
h 7.2cm di 108cm
h 2⅞in di 42½in
Singer do Brasil SA, Brazil

SONY
MINIDISC!
SONY
SONY
VOLUME
MD EJECT
MD
CD
RADIO
BAND
FM/AM
PERSONAL MINIDISC SYSTEM
PMC-M2
CD OPEN/CLOSE
SONY
SONY
MD WALKMAN
SONY
MD WALKMAN
MZ-E3

44

The progress of contemporary architecture has provided a valuable source of visual inspiration for product design. This can be seen in the development of an independent semantic for electronic products such as cameras and audio equipment, which have often sought to share the Modern Movement's fascination with black and white, and with materials such as plastic and steel. This relationship is freeing up, however, just as architecture has shed the shackles of Modernism. Sony's *MiniDisk System* recalls a Renaissance cathedral, and Herman Wittocx's washstands (page 200) the fashion for deconstructed buildings. The same values have influenced door furniture and taps, cameras and loudspeakers, though these objects retain the familiar monochrome approach.

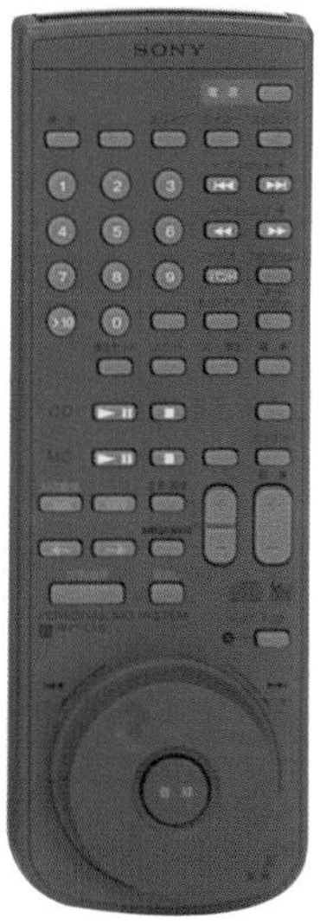

44 **Sony**
MiniDisc System PMC-M2,
MD Recorder MZ-B3,
MD Walkmen MZ-E3 and *MZ-R3*
Aluminium
System (without speakers):
h 25.3cm w 18cm d 29.2cm
h 9⅞in w 7in d 11½in
Speakers:
h 30.9cm w 17.5cm d 25cm
h 12in w 6⅞in d 9¾in
MZ-B3: h 3cm w 13.5cm d 8cm
h 1⅛in w 5⅜in d 3⅛in
MZ-E3: h 2cm w 11.6cm d 7.4cm
h ¾in w 4½in d 2⅞in
MZ-R3: h 3cm w 11.6cm d 8.1cm
h 1⅛in w 4½in d 3¼in
Sony Corporation, Japan

45

45 **GK Incorporated**
Hi-Fi mini component system, *CC-90*
Aluminium, wood, ABS
h 43cm w 92cm d 25cm
h 16⅞in w 36¼in d 9⅞in
Yamaha Corporation, Japan

46 **Dieter Sieger**
Shower, *BetteOmega*
Enamelled steel
h 215cm w 90cm d 95cm
h 84⅝in w 35⅜in d 37⅜in
Bette GmbH & Co. KG, Germany

47 **Ninaber, Peters, Krouwel Industrial Design**
Cycle stand for Tacx Tools
Steel, polyamide
h 115cm w 75cm d 54cm
h 45¼in w 29½in d 21¼in
Technische Industrie Tacx, The Netherlands

48 **Yoshitaka Sumimoto**
Satellite lens antenna, *Satela Ball DSA 221*
Plastic
h 22.1cm w 22cm d 27cm di 27cm
h 8¾in w 8⅝in d 10⅝in di 10⅝in
DX Antenna Co. Ltd, Japan

49 **Michele de Lucchi, Alessandro Chiarato**
Portable typewriter, *ETP Linea 101*
Plastic
h 13.7cm w 38cm l 25.5cm
h 5⅜in w 15in l 10in
Ing. C. Olivetti & Co. SpA, Italy

45

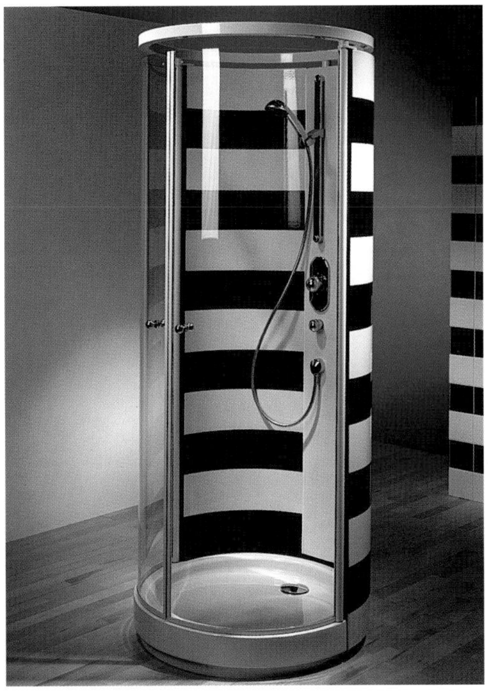
46

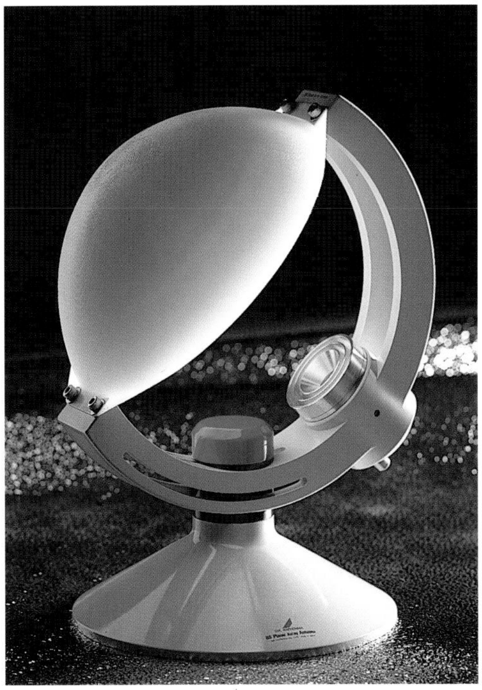
48

47

49

50 **Herman Wittocx**
Washstand, *Spalk*
Formica
h 90cm w 159cm d 45cm
h 35⅜in w 62½in d 17¾in
Herman Wittocx Meubelontwerper, Belgium
(One-off)

51 **Yoshiaki Iida**
CD Stack
Heat resistant plastic, ABS
h 12.9cm w 12.7cm d 0.5cm (unit)
h 5⅛in w 5in d ¼in
Excel, Japan
(Prototype)

50

51

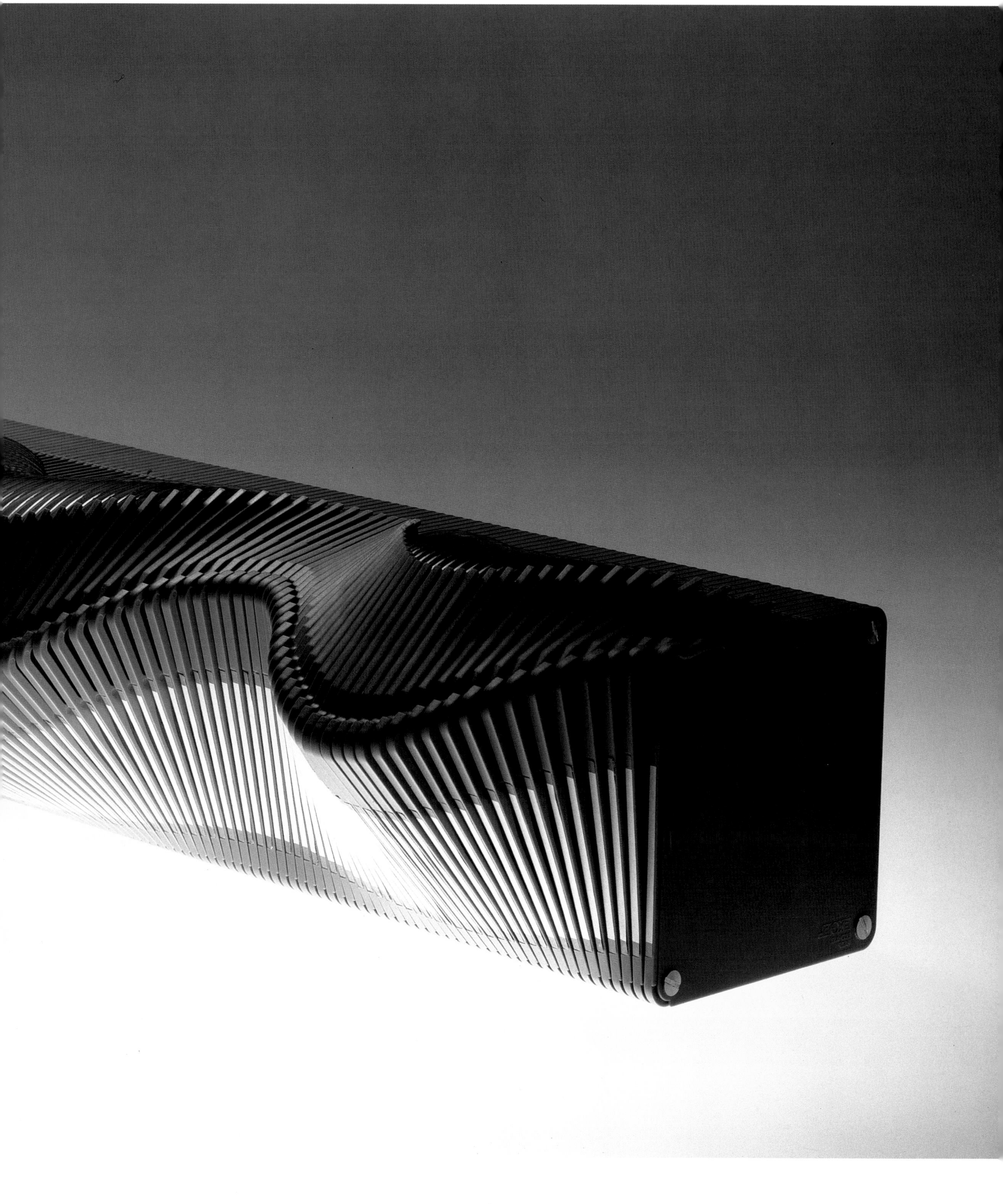

24X
Hi-Fi STEREO
Movieboy E1
Canon

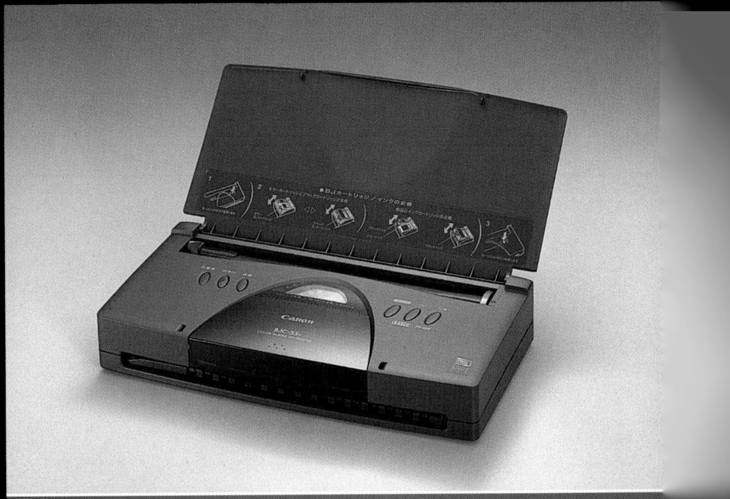
Canon

55

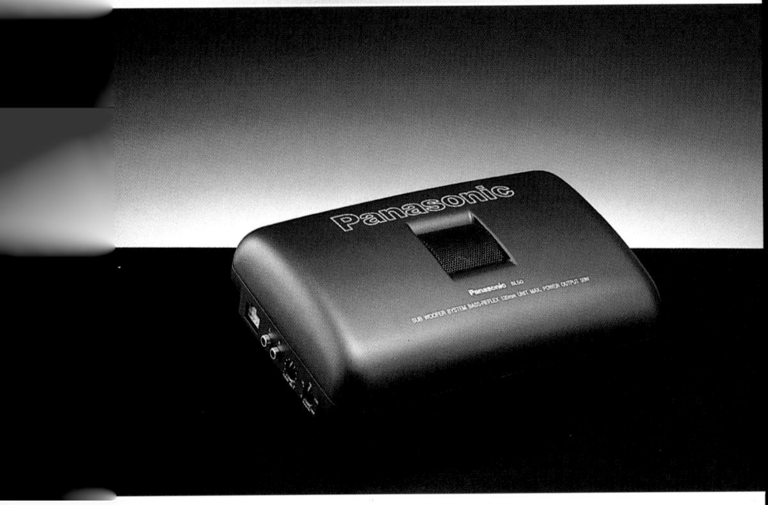
Panasonic
Panasonic

Panasonic
Panasonic

56

Canon
Autoboy
Luna
PANORAMA
AiAF

Nikon
FUJIX
Nikon
FUJIX
Nikon

57

58

52 **Canon Inc.**
Video camera, *UGX 1Hi*
ABS, rubber-coated paint
h 10.1cm w 10cm d 18.8cm
h 4in w 3⅞in d 7⅜in
Canon Inc., Japan

53 **Corporate Design Centre**
Car speaker, *CJ-BL50D*
Plastic, metal
h 7.5cm w 28.1cm d 18.1cm
h 2⅞in w 11in d 7⅛in
Matsushita Communication Industrial Co. Ltd, Japan

54 **Canon Inc.**
Camera, *Prima Super 28V*
Aluminium, polycarbonate
h 6.4cm w 12.3cm d 4.4cm
h 2½in w 4⅞in d 1¾in
Canon Inc., Japan

55 **Canon Inc.**
Colour bubble jet printer, *BJC-35v*
ABS
h 5.7cm w 30cm d 15.3cm
h 2¼in w 11¾in d 6in
Canon Inc., Japan

56 **Corporate Design Centre**
Car speaker, *CJ-SA70D*
Plastic, metal
h 8.7cm w 31.8cm d 19.1cm
h 3⅜in w 12½in d 7½in
Matsushita Communication Industrial Co. Ltd, Japan

57 **Jun Akabane, Nobuya Kawahata and Jun Konno**
Digital still camera, *E2/E2s*
Polycarbonate, aluminium
h 14cm w 16.4cm d 12cm
h 5½in w 6½in d 4¾in
Nikon Corporation, Japan

58 **Clare Brass (with graphics by Dolcini Associati)**
Pastry tins, *Tia*
Non-stick coated aluminium
di 10–30cm
di 3⅞–11¾in
T.V.S. SpA, Italy

59

60

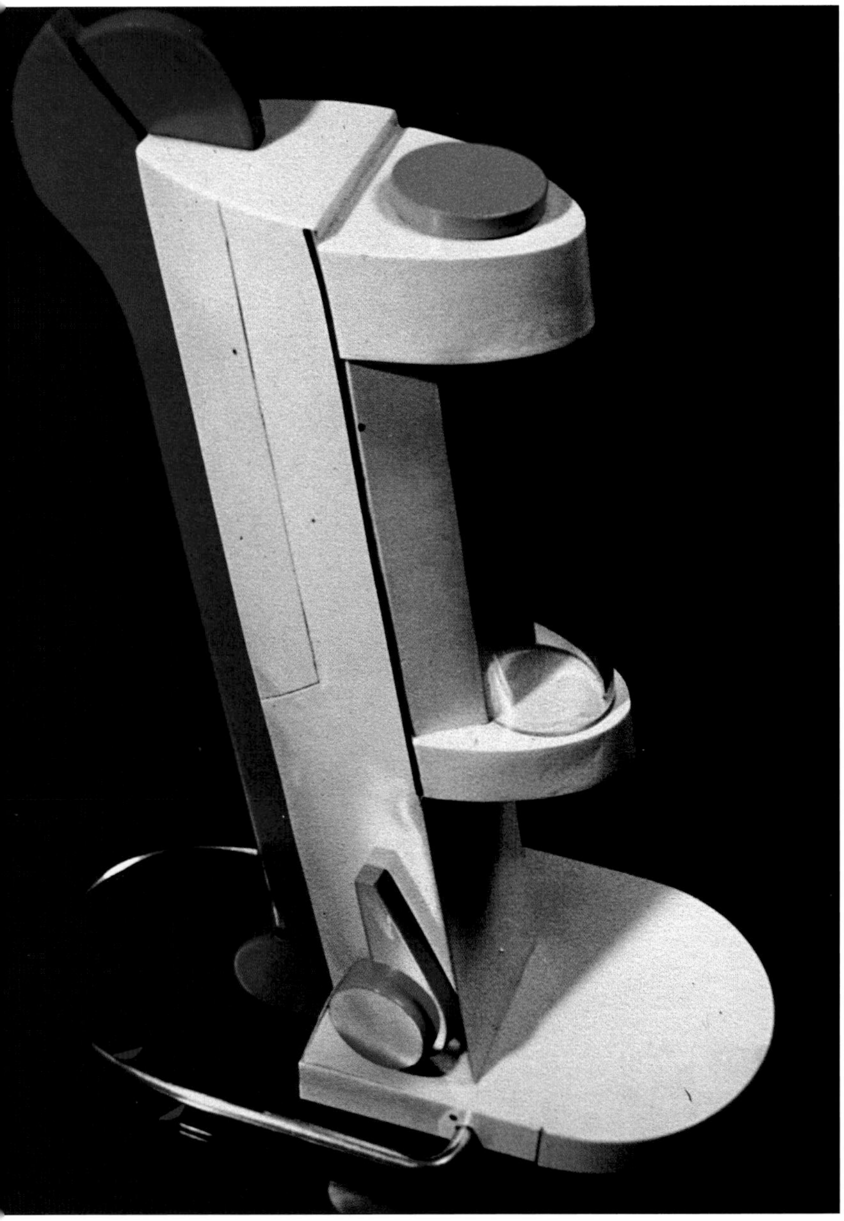

61

59 **Hartmut Weise**
Handle collection, *1028, 1029*
Aluminium
1028 (top): l 13.5cm d 6cm
l 5¼in d 2⅜in
1029: l 13.3cm d 6.7cm
l 5¼in d 2⅝in
FSB Franz Schneider Brakel GmbH & Co., Germany

60 **Susanne Ewert for Team Buchin Design**
Tap, *Aquamix*
Brass
h 14.4cm w 5.6cm d 9.5cm
h 5⅝in w 2¼in d 3¾in
Aqua Butze-Werke AG, Germany

61 **Iyer Swaminathan**
Soda maker/water aerating unit
ABS, transparent P.E.T.
h 34cm w 20cm l 25cm
h 13⅜in w 7⅞in l 9⅞in
(Prototype)

Fizzy drinks are fun, but most of the machines for making soda have more of the hospital than the home about them. In Indian designer Iyer Swaminathan's redesign for a soda maker for the Indian market,the functional verticality of the machine is broken by the inclined, transparent aerating container in reinforced polythene.

If some product design is tied to a monochrome, quasi-industrial approach, in plenty of other cases both taste and wit demand colour. The Yamaha metronome or Marco Zanuso's bottle opener (page 211) use colour to reposition the products involved, moving them outside the framework of the purely utilitarian, while Rainer Lehn's *Sharky* clothes pegs or Josep Lluscà's tricycles (page 210) are simple, cheerful exercises in colour. Authentics' wastepaper bins (page 209) create a sea of coloured shapes, like the kaleidoscope image often used by Mendini to describe the open-ended nature and colourful diversity of his own design projects.

62

62 **Yoshitaka Sumimoto**
Handsaw and case, *Gomboy and Gomcase II*
Steel, synthetic rubber
h 3.5cm w 7cm l 25cm
h 1⅜in w 2¾in l 9⅞in
UM:Kogyo Inc., Japan

63 **Yamaha Product Design Laboratory**
Quartz metronome, *Yamaha QT-1*
h 4.4cm di 9.5cm
h 1¾in di 3¾in
Yamaha Corporation, Japan

64 **Roberto Pezzetta**
Electric oven, *Softech BMS 441*
Glass, steel, enamel, thermoplastic rubber
h 60cm w 60cm d 55cm
h 23⅝in w 23⅝in d 21⅝in
Zanussi Elettrodomestici SpA, Italy

63

64

65 **Hans Maier-Aichen**
Wastepaper basket, *LIP*
Polypropylene
h 18, 33.5, 43cm
w 17, 29, 36.5cm
d 9.5, 17, 21cm
h 7⅛, 13⅛, 16⅞in
w 6¾, 11⅜, 14⅜in
d 3¾, 6¾, 8¼in
Authentics artipresent GmbH,
Germany

66 **Konstantin Grcic**
Wastepaper basket, *Square*
Polypropylene
h 40cm w 26cm l 31cm
h 15¾in w 10¼in l 12¼in
Authentics artipresent GmbH,
Germany

67 **Marc Newson**
Paperweight, *Pod*
Polyurethane, lead
w 6cm l 10cm d 3.5cm
w 2⅜in l 3⅞in d 1⅜in
(Limited batch production)

68 **Kartell**
Wastepaper basket
Thermoplastic technopolymer
h 38cm di 25cm
h 15in di 9⅞in
Kartell, Italy

The paperweight should be an anachronism in the electronic office, but we all know that in Parkinsonian fashion, the more desk space we have, the more paper gets on to it. In commissioning a new series of paperweight designs from a group of international designers, Lippert and Wilkens offer a resolutely witty answer to this problem. Newson's tactile solution to this challenge is a subtle echo of his concerns in furniture, while acting also as a sufficiently exciting object to make even the pending pile look interesting.

65

66

65

67

68

69

70

69

71

72

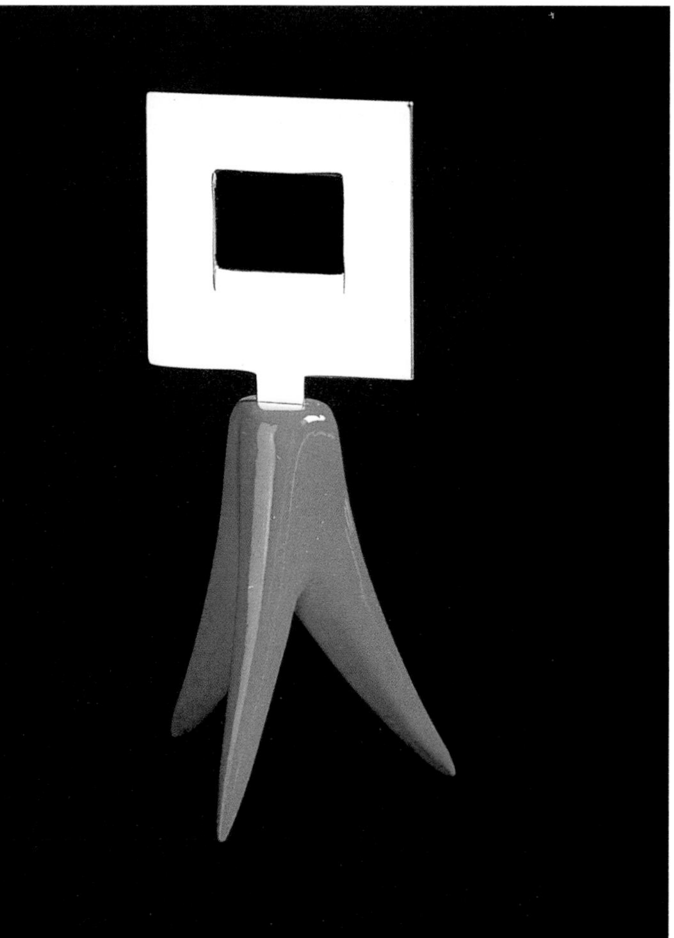

Stefano Giovannoni's *Girotondo* photograph frame joins a series of similar objects in the Alessi range, beginning with the *Girotondo* tray in 1989. Alberto Alessi sees the series as prototypical of the affective codes the company's best designs have generated. Its "apparently over-elementary decoration", he writes, is "in actual fact highly meaningful to memory." The cut-out figures piercing the edges of these objects are only superficially abstract: they retain enough figurative power to evoke an independent memory in each of us, whether of a children's game, a dance, or a crowd. Many of Alessi's other objects make an even more direct appeal to the figurative, seeking to place themselves in a nexus of sense, memory and imagination.

69 **Josep Lluscà**
Children's tricycles
Steel, ABS, PE
h 50cm l 70cm d 37cm
h 19¾in l 27½in d 14½in
Famosa, Spain

70 **Rainer Lehn**
Clothes peg, *Sharky*
Polypropylene
h 3.5cm w 11cm d 0.7cm
h 1⅜in w 4⅜in d ¼in
Koziol GmbH, Germany

71 **Stefano Giovanonni and Guido Venturini**
Photograph frame, *Girotondo KK22*
Stainless steel
h 24.1cm w 19.2cm d 7.1cm
h 9½in w 7½in d 2¾in
Alessi, Italy

72 **Marco Zanuso Jr**
Bottle opener, *MZ-1*
Steel, aluminium
h 13.3cm w 5.4cm l 5.7cm
h 5¼in w 2⅛in l 2¼in
Giotto Green Design Ltd, Hong Kong

73 **Philips Corporate Design**
Ladyshave Aqua HP 2760
ABS
h 14.6cm w 4.5cm l 4cm
h 5¾in w 1¾in l 1⅝in
Philips International BV, The Netherlands

74 **Antonio Cagianelli**
Mirrors
Transparent resin
h 35cm w 18cm d 18cm
h 13¾in w 7⅛in d 7⅛in
(Limited batch production)

75 **Leonid Yentus**
Wall clock, *Shadow*
Plastic, adhesive films
h 50.8cm w 43.1cm di 11.4cm
h 20in w 17in di 4½in
(Prototype)

76 **Gaetano Pesce**
Table mirror, *Kalos*
Mirror, resin
h 50.2cm w 29.8cm d 5cm
h 19¾in w 11¾in d 2in
Fish Design, The Netherlands
(Limited batch production)

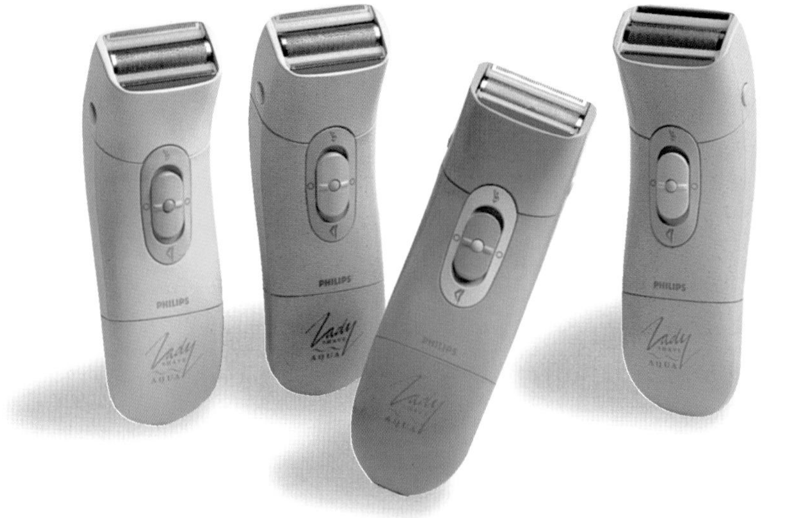

73

74

75

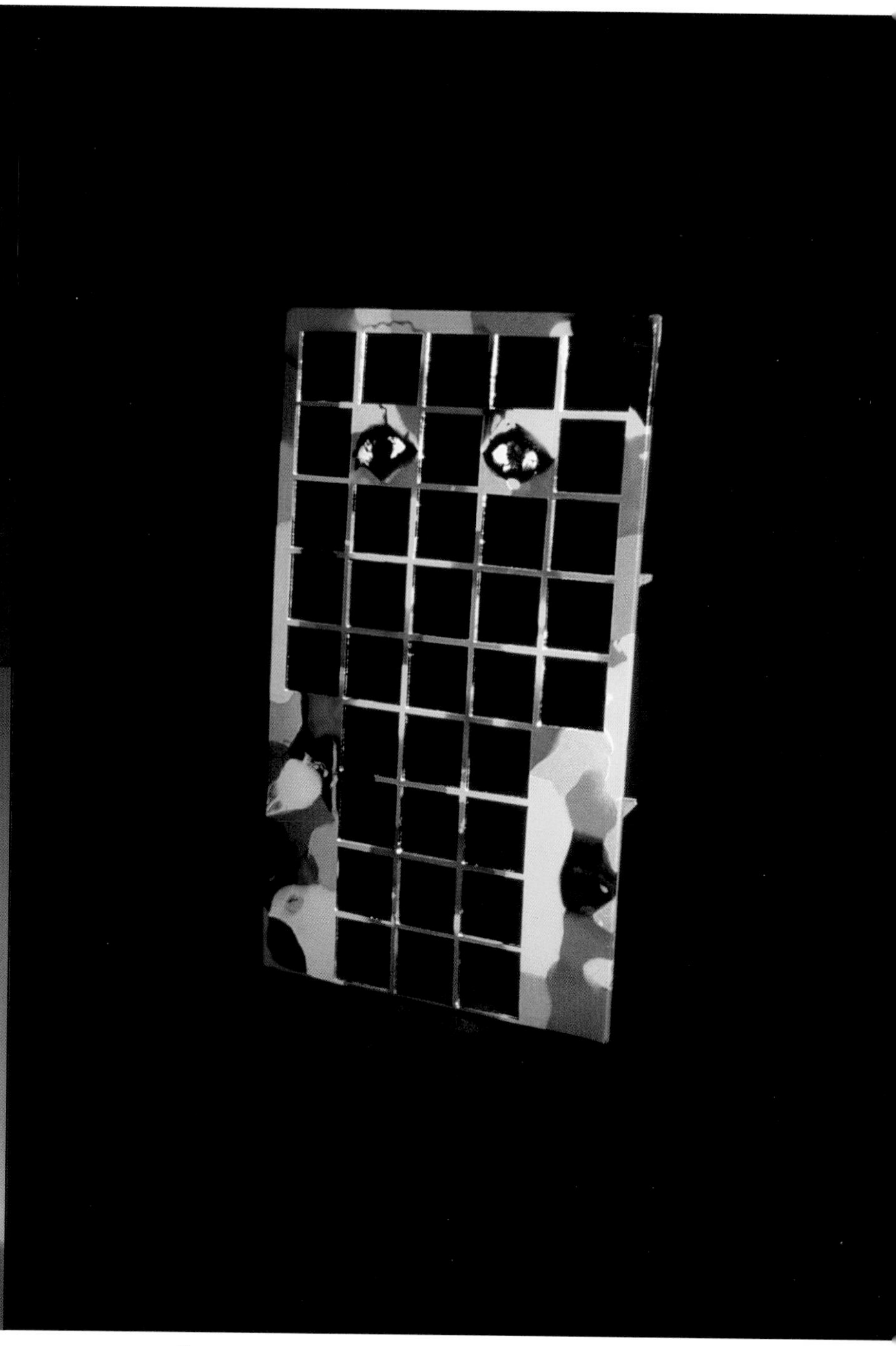

76

innovation in product design not only creates new forms and new activities (the Walkman being a key example), it can also create new cultures. Rollerblading is closer to riding a motorbike than driving a car, not only through the disposition of the wheels but also through the social attitudes and rituals of the riders. So it is with snowboarding. Skiing is about performance, technology and mastery; snowboarding is about self-expression, dynamics and fun. Skis are abstract, snowboards figurative. Snowboards have created a separate culture, a separate ceremony of expression.

Some technologies support human activities, others extend them. A karaoke machine, an extensible video arm, a distress signal – all these products celebrate the endless purpose of design in empowering and enriching its users, by creating new opportunities, whether the objects, in Mendini's words, "be beautiful or ugly, strange or reassuringly familiar, enjoyable or austere, magical or psychological, ironical or classical, imaginative or functional, fairy-tale or high-tech. Every piece in this kaleidoscope has the same right to exist."

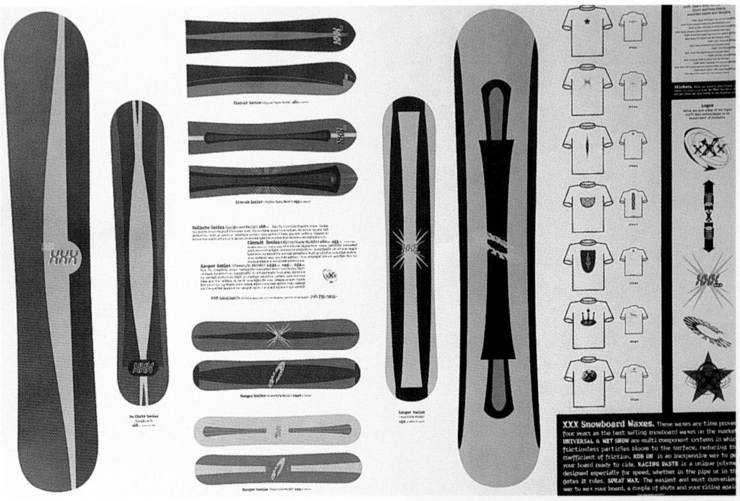

77

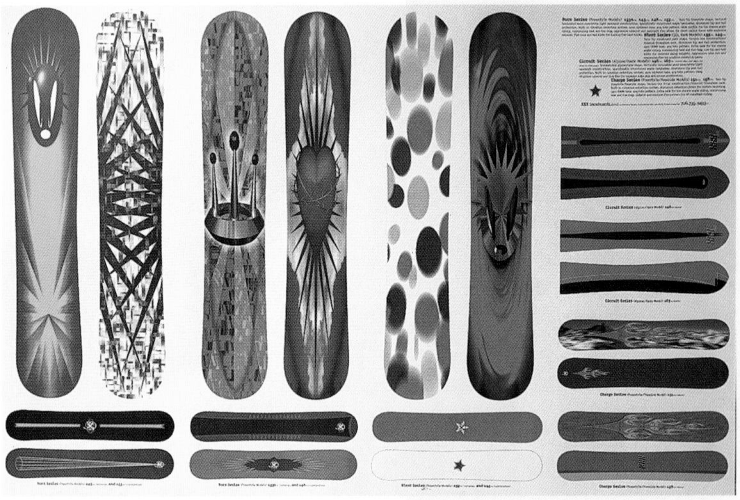

78

77 **Carlos Segura**
Snowboards
Left: *De Chute Series*
Fibreglass, carbon, aluminium
l 168cm
l 66⅛in
Top centre: *Circuit Series*
Laminated wood core,
maple laminates, aluminium
l 160, 153cm
l 63, 60¼in
Bottom centre, right: *Ranger Series*
Laminated wood core,
maple laminates, aluminium
l 154, 149, 144cm
l 60⅝, 58⅝, 56¾in
XXX Snowboards [B.T.B.], USA

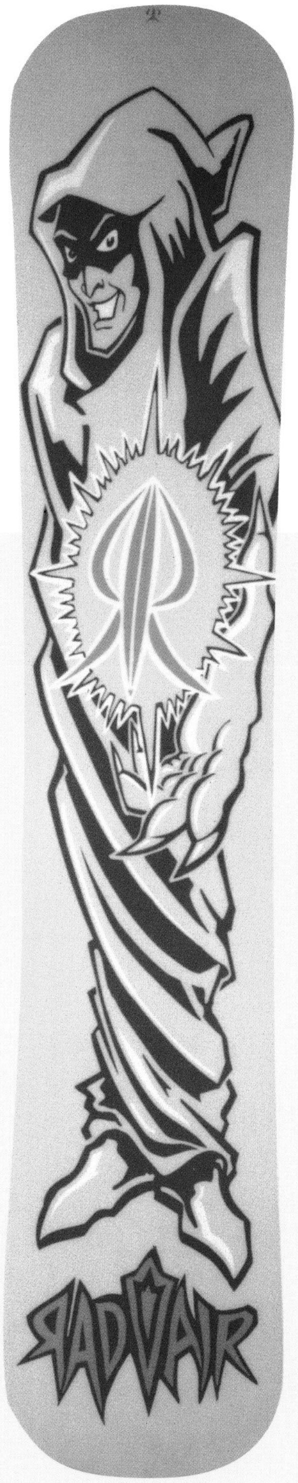

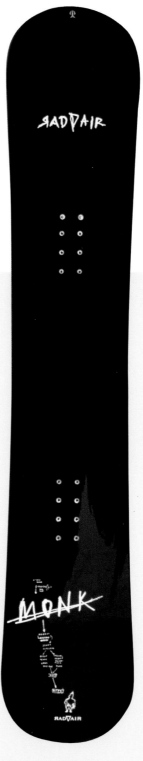

79

79

78 **Carlos Segura**
Snowboards
Left and centre: *Burn Series*
Laminated wood core,
maple laminates, aluminium
l 153, 148, 143, 133cm
l 60¼, 58¼, 56¼, 52⅜in
Centre: *Blunt Series*
Fibreglass, aluminium
l 145, 135cm
l 57, 53⅛in
Top right: *Circuit Series*
Laminated wood core,
maple laminates, aluminium
l 167, 146cm
l 65¾, 57½in
Bottom right: *Charge Series*
Fibreglass, aluminium
l 158, 151cm
l 62¼, 59½in
XXX Snowboards [B.T.B.], USA

79 **Marcel Langenegger**
Snowboard, *Monk*
UV gloss, reinforced fibreglass,
ABS, laminated woodcore, reinforced
polyethylene
w 26.6–30cm l 154cm d 1cm
w 10½–11¾in l 60⅝in d ⅜in
Rad/air, Switzerland

80

81

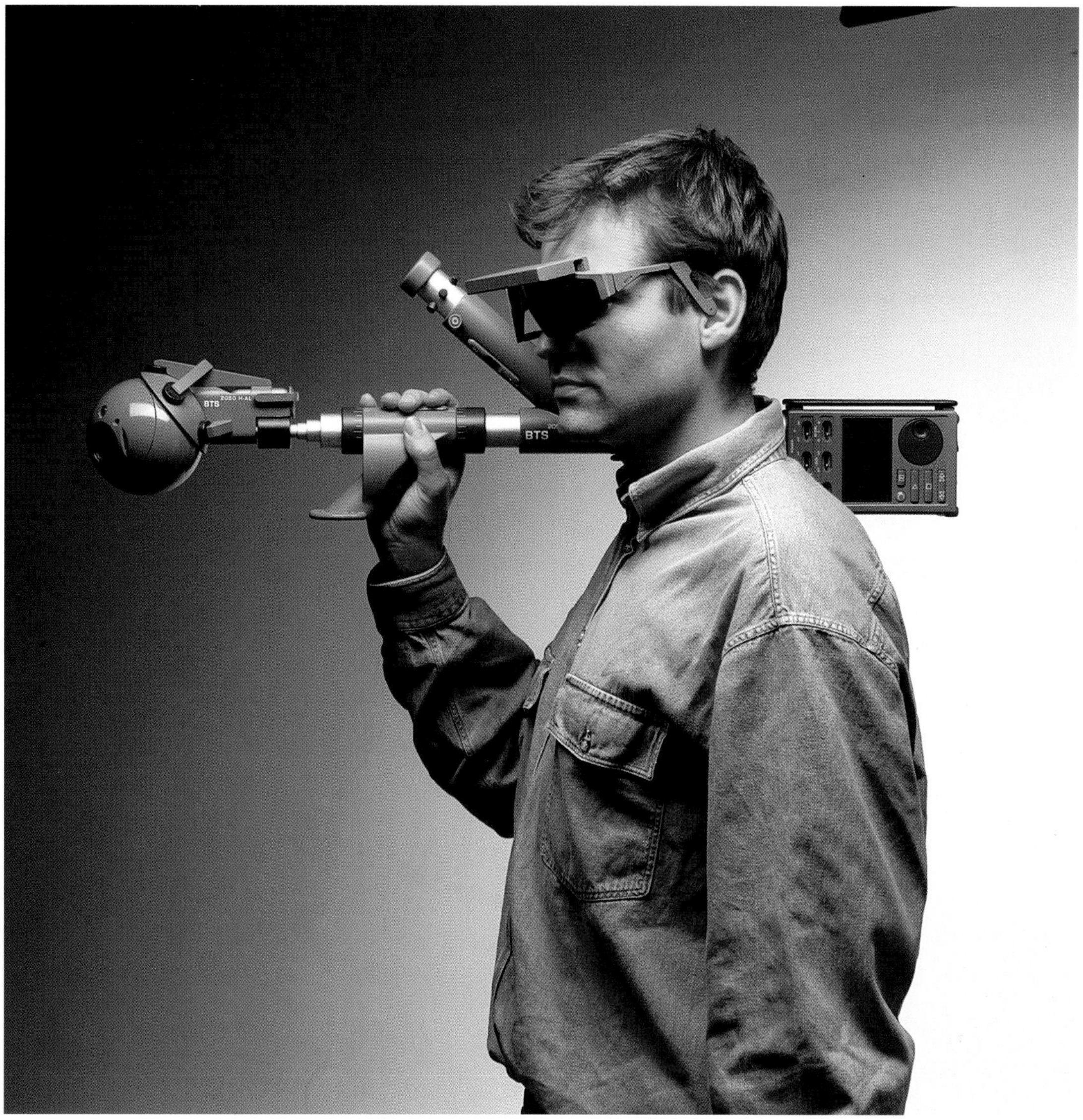

The next best thing to being hardwired into cyberspace could be Matthias Bohner's TV camera. Superficially an extension arm to allow a distant camera to be manipulated and its images to be seen by the operator, its android form makes it a cybernetic extension of the body, a metaphor emphasized by the robotic semantics of the object itself.

80 **An Reto Furrer for**
DNR Sportsystem Ltd
Snowboards, *Santa Cruz*
Rubber, fibreglass, wood core, stainless steel, ABS, steel, polyethelene
l 154, 152, 146cm
l 60⅝, 59⅞, 57½in
DNR Sportsystem Ltd, Switzerland

81 **Matthias Bohner**
TV-camera, *H-AL 2050*
Aluminium, Keflar, plastic
h 25cm w 12cm l 80–200cm
h 9⅞in w 4¾in l 31½–78¾in
(Prototype)

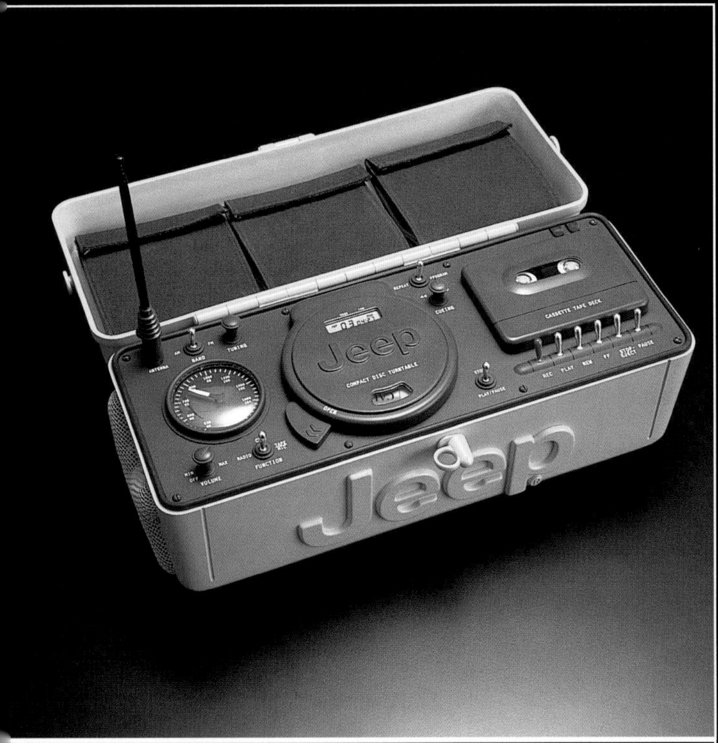
Jeep
COMPACT DISC TURNTABLE
CASSETTE TAPE DECK
Jeep

Polaroid

84

85

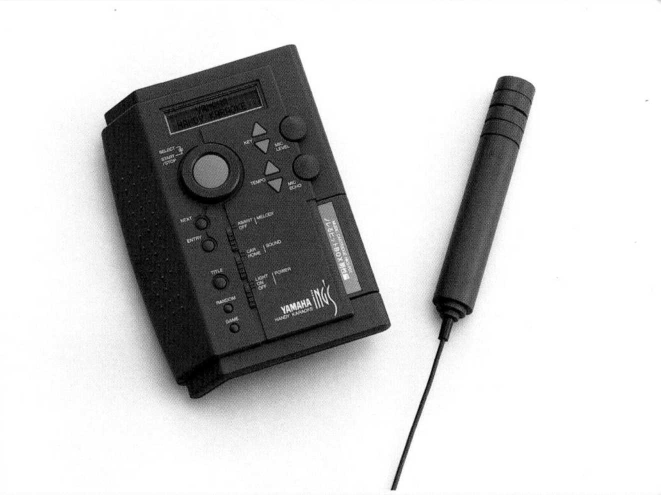
YAMAHA

86

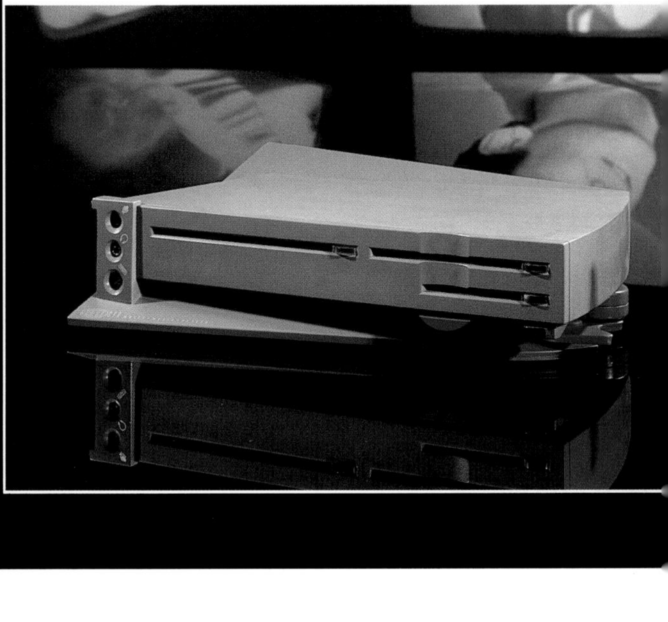

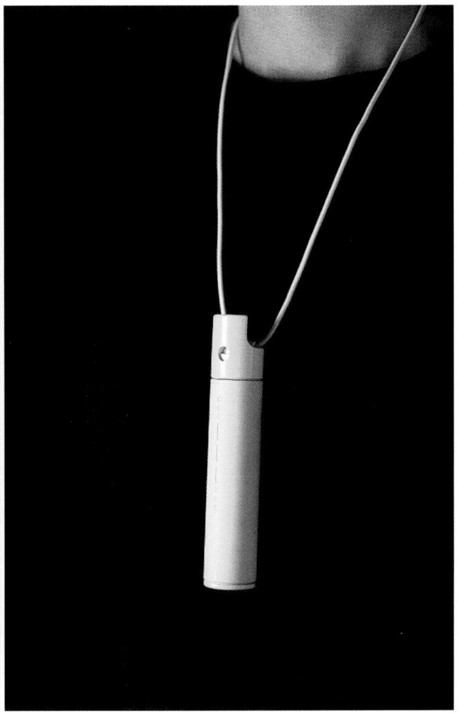

87

82 **Skip Kirk, Paul Lacotta, Walter Stoeckmann**
Portable stereo, *Jeep*
Injection-moulded ABS, polypropylene, silicon
h 26.6cm w 45.7cm d 20.3cm
h 10½in w 18in d 8in
Kash 'n Gold, USA

83 **John Betts of Dreyfuss Associates**
Camera, *Spectra*
ABS, Hytrel
h 7.8cm w 17.2cm d 15.5cm
h 3⅛in w 6¾in d 6⅛in
Polaroid Corp., USA,
in collaboration with Parkhurst Design and Development, UK

84 **Scott Henderson for Smart Design**
Star Trek Mouse
Injection-moulded ABS
h 4cm w 8cm l 12cm
h 1⅝in w 3⅛in l 4¾in
Brainworks, USA

85 **Yamaha Product Design Laboratory**
Handy Karaoke
Acrylic, ABS plastic
h 5.3cm w 19.8cm d 14.1cm
h 2⅛in w 7¾in d 5⅝in
Yamaha Corporation, Japan

86 **Andrew Serbinski of Machineart**
Multimedia player, *SynapSys*
ABS
h 8.2cm w 30.5cm l 22.3cm
h 3¼in w 12in l 8¾in
Fujitsu Ltd, Japan
(One-off)

87 **Kazuo Kawasaki**
Emergency radio, *Tokyo Lalia*
Engineering resin
l 12.7cm di 2.5cm
l 5in di 1in
Ouzak Enterprise Ltd, Japan
(Prototype)

88

89

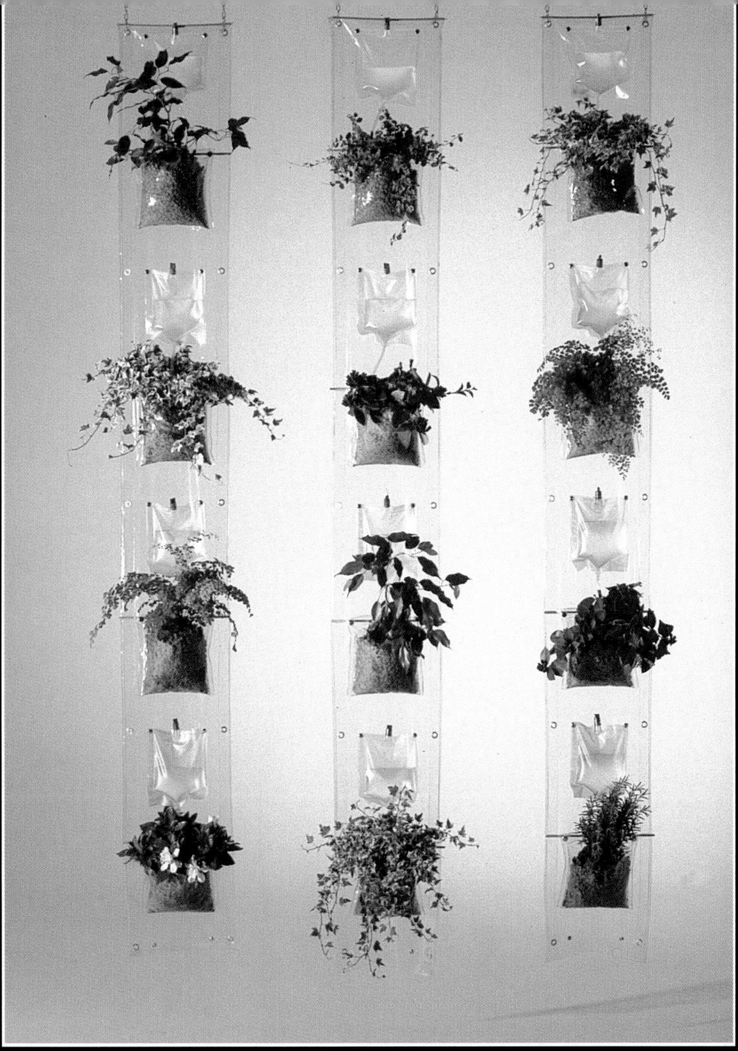

90

91

88 **Terri Pecora**
Spectacle frames, *Past and Present*
Acetate, metal
h 5cm l 14cm
h 2in l 5½in
Silhouette, Austria

89 **Walter Garro**
Swatch Watch
Leather, metal
l 23.2cm di 3.4cm
l 9⅛in di 1⅜in
(SMH) Swatch AG, Switzerland

90 **Bortolani/Becchelli**
Plantholder, *Erbale*
Transparent plastic
h 240cm l 30cm d 10cm
h 94⅞in l 11¾in d 3¾in
Aleph/Driade, Italy

91 **Philips Corporate Design**
Kettle from the Philips-Alessi Line, *HD 2001*
Enhanced polypropylene, stainless steel
h 26.6cm w 24.6cm d 10.3cm
h 10¾in w 9¾in d 4in
Philips International BV, The Netherlands

Biographies

Every effort has been made to obtain details about the designers whose work is featured in this book, but in some cases information was not available. The figures following each entry refer to the illustrations of that designer's work (the number before the full point indicates the chapter number).

Eero Aarnio studied industrial and interior design at the Institute of Industrial Arts of Helsinki between 1954 and1957 before setting up his own studio in Helsinki in 1962. His innovative use of shape and materials for the Ball chair (1963) and the Pastill chair (1967) launched him on the international market. His works today are found in numerous collections and museums including, among others, the Museum of Modern Art, New York; the Vitra Design Museum, Weil am Rhein; the Centre Georges Pompidou, Paris and the Victoria and Albert Museum, London. 1.53

Abdi Abdelkader was born in 1959 in Algiers where he obtained a diploma in Fine Arts. After moving to Paris he completed a two-year research course on contemporary furniture and received a second diploma from the Ecole Nationale Supérieure des Arts Décoratifs. Abdelkader numbers Bénotteau, Bisazza, Glas, Néotù and the Institut du Monde Arabe amongst his clients and has received the SM d'Argent and the Nombre d'Or prizes. He currently teaches at the Ecole des Beaux-Arts, Paris, the Institut d'Arts Visuels in Orléans and at the Ecole Supérieure de Mobilier in Paris. 1.39

Helle Abild was born in Copenhagen in 1964 and graduated with a degree in textile design in 1989. A freelance textile designer, she has also designed furniture, including among her pieces a sales counter for the Royal Theatre in Copenhagen. She is currently working in New York. 4.61, 62, 64

Jun Akabane was born in 1955 and graduated from Chiba University in Japan in 1979. Since then he has worked for the Nikon Corporation. 5.57

Nick Allen is a Fine Arts graduate from Epsom College of Art, Surrey, UK. He is interested in designing furniture using fine woods with intricate veneers, inlay and marquetry as well as metal patinations. He has begun working in glass and is developing a range of glassware items. He has exhibited in Europe, America and Hong Kong and his pieces can be found in the permanent collection of the Victoria and Albert Museum, London. 1.31; 2.28

Pedro Almodovar was born in La Mancha in the 1950s. Since moving to Madrid when he was 17, he has become one of the foremost independent film-makers of international reknown with films such as *Matador*, *Women on the Verge of a Nervous Breakdown* and *Tie Me Up! Tie Me Down!* He has been the recipient of various national and international awards. In 1995 he designed a watch for Swatch as one of a special series dedicated to the cinema. 5.33

Robert Altman began his career in 1969 with the film *M*A*S*H*, which received the Palme d'Or at the Cannes Film Festival of that year. He was born in 1925 in Kansas City, Missouri, USA, and studied engineering at the University of Missouri. In 1955 he made his first feature film, *The Delinquents*. His second feature was *The James Dean Story*, a documentary that was noticed by Alfred Hitchcock who then offered Altman a chance to direct films for television programmes like "Alfred Hitchcock Presents". He came to movie-making in 1963 when he founded his own production company, Lion's Gate Films. Since then he has directed films such as *Nashville*, *Popeye*, *Come Back to the 5 & Dime Jimmy Dean, Jimmy Dean*, *The Player* and *Short Cuts* and has become a producer. In 1995 Altman designed a watch for Swatch as one of a special series dedicated to the cinema. 5.31

Ron Arad was born in Tel Aviv in 1951 and studied at the Jerusalem Academy of Art and the Architectural Association, London (from 1974 to 1979). In 1981 he founded One Off Ltd with Dennis Groves and Caroline Thorman and in 1983 designed One Off's first showroom in Neal Street, Covent Garden. He started to exhibit both nationally and internationally, and hosted shows for other designers, notably Danny Lane, Tom Dixon and Jon Mills in 1986. In 1988 he won the Tel Aviv Opera Foyer Interior Competition with C. Norton and S. McAdam, and the next year formed Ron Arad Associates in order to realize the project, moving the firm's premises to Chalk Farm, London. As well as the design and construction of the new One Off Design Studio, furniture gallery and workshop in 1990, recent projects have included furniture design for Poltronova, Vitra, Moroso and Driade, and the design of various interior installations and domestic architectural projects, such as a house in Schopfheim for a German publisher. Ron Arad was the editor of the 1994 *International Design Yearbook* and is a guest professor at the University of Applied Arts in Vienna. Recent exhibitions include "Breeding in Captivity", a one-man show at the Edward Totah Gallery, London; joint shows with Ingo Maurer at the Galleria Internos and the Galleria Facsimile, Milan; and "Gaz Naturel, L'Energie Créative" at the Grand Palais, Paris. 1.67, 126

Junichi Arai was born in Kiryu City, Gunma Prefecture, Japan in 1932. Since the mid-1950s he has developed new techniques for weaving with metallic fibres and was given the International Trade Industry Minister's award in the Grand Fair of Synthetic Fibres in Japan in 1961. Arai works with both Japanese and international fashion designers and has exhibited internationally, most recently in the "Textiles of the World" show at the Saint Louis Art Museum, USA. His work can be seen in the permanent collections of the Fashion Institute of Technology, USA; the Victoria and Albert Museum, London; the Museum of Art, Rhode Island School of Design, USA; the Cooper-Hewitt Museum, New York and the Okawa Museum, Kiryu, Gunma Prefecture, Japan. In 1987 Arai was awarded an honorary membership to the Royal Designers for Industry, UK. 4.31–35

Jan Armgardt was born in 1947. He trained initially as a cabinet-maker and later in interior design. After gaining practical experience in a firm involved in furniture design, he opened his own furniture studio in Bensheim, Germany, in 1974. He collaborates with companies such as de Padova, de Sede, Knoll and Wittman, and besides furniture also designs kitchen and table accessories, office equipment and lamps. He has been the recipient of numerous awards and prizes. 1.23, 85, 86

Gertrud Arndt was born in Ratibor, Upper Silesia in 1903. She studied at the Erfurt School of Arts and Crafts and at the Bauhaus weaving workshop in Weimar under Georg Muche and in Dessau under Gunta Stölzl. She also took basic courses with Lászlö Moholy-Nagy, Paul Klee, Wassily Kandinsky and Adolf Meyer. She was awarded a diploma on completion of her studies in 1927. 4.8

Florian Asche was born in Germany in 1963. He studied at Central Saint Martin's College of Art and Design, London, receiving a BA (Hons) in Product Design. He has designed furniture for Lucci and Orlandini, electronic instruments for Bauer Computer GmbH and furniture for Victorian Woodwork. 1.114

Sergio Asti set up his own studio in 1953 and was one of the founding members of the ADI (Associazione per Il Disegno Industriale). He designs furniture, lighting, glassware, wooden products, ceramics, electrical appliances, interiors, stores and exhibitions. He has received numerous awards including the gold medal at the XI Milan Triennale and a Compasso d'Oro (1962), and his work has been exhibited internationally. 3.18

Jane Atfield trained in architecture before completing an MA in furniture design at the Royal College of Art, London in 1992. Since graduating she has worked as a freelance furniture designer for companies such as Formica, Habitat and Katherine Hamnett Ltd. Some commissions involving collaborations with architects are the University of Westminster Student Bar and designs for Live TV, based in Canary Wharf Tower, London. Recent exhibitions include the Contemporary Arts Society "Every Angle" at the ITN Building, London (1994); ECO Design in Brussels (1994); and "Not so Simple" in Barcelona (1995). During the last year Jane Atfield has concentrated on researching and setting up Made of Waste, a new agency for recycled materials; their first product is recycled plastic sheets which originate from post-consumer high-density polyethylene bottles. 1.101; 2.21, 54

Gae Aulenti graduated in architecture from Milan Polytechnic in 1954. As well as carrying out architectural projects, she has designed stage sets and costumes for opera and drama, lectured extensively on architecture, held exhibitions throughout the world and received many awards. She was responsible for the design of the Musée National d'Art Moderne at the Centre Georges Pompidou and for the interior architecture of the Musée d'Orsay, Paris. In 1977 President Mitterrand conferred on her the title of Chevalier de la Légion d'Honneur. 3.60, 61

Masayo Ave was born in Tokyo in 1962 and graduated from the architectural department at Hosei University. After working in the architectural office of Ichiro Ebihara, she moved to Milan and completed her master's degree in industrial design at the Domus Academy, establishing her own design studio, Ave Design Co., in 1992. Since then she has received international acclaim for her works in the fields of industrial, furniture and textile design, theatre sets and architecture. She is particularly interested in the potential of such new materials as the Shibori textile, and in the fusion of traditional Japanese tie-dyeing techniques with modern technology. 1.105; 2.46; 4.49

Hiroshi Awatsuji (1929–1995) was born in Kyoto, Japan, and graduated from the Kyoto City University of Art. In 1964 he began his collaboration with the Fujie Textile Co. Ltd. In 1988 he became a professor at the Tama Art University, Tokyo. He participated in exhibitions worldwide and was internationally recognized for his work. He received an Outstanding Award at the 3rd International Textile Competition in Kyoto in 1992 and later that year a Gold Award at the 38th ID Annual Design Review in the USA. 4.30

Jochen Backs, senior industrial designer for IDEO, holds a degree from the Fachhochschule für Gestaltung Schwäbisch Gmünd and Munich. He has designed numerous computer, medical and consumer products. Whilst in Germany he specialized in tool and consumer product design. At IDEO since 1991, Backs has focused on medical and computer products for companies like Apple, Samsung and Cisco Systems. He has received many design awards, including the "Best Design Concept of Europe" at the International Biennial in Kortrijk, Belgium. 2.29

Gijs Bakker was born in Amersfoort, The Netherlands in 1942. He studied at the College of Arts and Crafts (now the Rietveld Academy), Amsterdam in the Department of Jewellery Design, and later at the Konstfackskolan, Department of Industrial Design in Stockholm. From 1962 to 1963 he worked as a designer at Van Kempen & Begeer in Zeist; he then founded a studio with his wife in Utrecht. Until 1986 Bakker was a freelance designer for companies such as Bussum and Artifort Maastricht. He also taught (1971–78) at the Akademie van Beeldende Kunsten at Arnhem in the Department of Metal and Plastic Design. From 1987 to 1989 he was a partner in the design studio BRS Premsela Vonk in Amsterdam. Today he is head of the "Man and Living" Department of the Akademie Industriële Vormgeving in Eindhoven, and design advisor for the Keramische Industrie Cor Unum. In 1993 Bakker established Keizersgracht 518 in Amsterdam. His work can be seen in major design collections at the Stedelijk Museum, Amsterdam; the Power House Museum, Sydney; the Denver Museum of Art, Colorado; the Cooper-Hewitt Museum, New York; and the Victoria and Albert Museum, London. 1.26, 117; 4.24

Bang Design was founded in Sydney in 1989 by Bryan Marshall and David Granger. Both are graduates of industrial design, with degrees from the School of Environmental Design at the University of Canberra. Before forming their own company, they spent six years working for manufacturers and design consultants. Bang Design's work has been exhibited and published widely in Australia. 1.54

Bär and Knell Design is the design studio of Hartmut Knell and Beata and Gerhard Bär. Hartmut Knell trained as a carpenter and has taken part in exhibitions in Germany, Belgium and Japan. Beata Bär was born in 1959 and studied interior design and architecture. In 1987 she founded her own design studio, BÄR – Design, before undertaking a study period in Rome. Bär and Knell was founded in 1991, and since then they have worked with such clients as Thonet, Steelcase and Artifort. 1.7–9

Vincent Beaurin was born in 1960 and graduated from the Ecole Boulle in Paris with a specialization in bronze engraving. He designed his first series of furniture in 1981–88 and in 1989 formed and co-ordinated the manufacturing of the EGO line designed by Shiro Kuramata. Recent works include furniture and lights for Néotù and VIA, and the lay-out and creation of furniture for the Théâtre du Merlan, Marseilles. Until 1994 he was Professor at the Ecole Camondo in Paris. 1.123

Yves Béhar, born in Switzerland in 1967, is a senior industrial designer at Lunar Design. He received his BSc in industrial design from the Art Center College of Design, Pasadena, and worked for Steelcase before moving to San Francisco. He practised exhibit and furniture design with Bruce Burdick and is now lead designer for the Lunar Design team that creates designs for Hewlett-Packard's home products division. 5.17, 18

Annette Berliner is self-taught and makes decorative objects in paper. She has designed for Gabbia Proggetti (Trieste, Italy), Rosalie Pompom (Brussels, Belgium) and the University of Parma (Italy). 3.71

Circe Bernardes and **Iris di Ciommo** both studied architecture at the São Paulo University, Brazil. Today Circe Bernades specializes in graphic, interior and textile design as well as fine art. Iris di Ciommo is involved in visual communication, building signs and exhibition and textile design. 4.51

John Betts joined Henry Dreyfuss Associates as Senior Designer in 1984, and since that time was promoted to Senior Project Manager in 1988, and Associate in 1989. He graduated in 1978 from the University of Illinois, Urbana, with a BFA in Industrial Design and worked for several design consultancies in the USA before joining Henry Dreyfuss Associates. Today he provides design and project management for various clients, including Polaroid cameras, and is a member of the Industrial Designers Society of America. 5.83

Matthias Bohner was born in 1966. He studied industrial design under Richard Sapper at the Kunstakademie in Stuttgart and received a diploma in 1994. Since 1992 he has worked in the design studio Industrial Design Bachmayer, Bohner and Lippert. 5.81

Renata Bonfanti was educated at the Istituto Statale d'Arte in Venice and at the Kvinnelige Industriskole in Oslo in the early 1950s. She produces hand-woven rugs and tapestries as well as machine-woven material. She has taken part in various exhibitions and competitions, including the Milan Triennale (1954, '57, '60, '64), the Venice Biennale (1956–60), the Biennale de la Tapisserie of Lausanne (1975–77) and the "Design since 1945" exhibition at the Philadelphia Museum of Art (1983). In 1962 she received the Compasso d'Oro for her designs. 4.4

Fabio Bortolani and **Walter Becchelli** have been working together since 1991, having studied at the University of Florence and the Bologna Academy of Arts, respectively. Their clients include Alessi/Twergi and Ravanni & Castoldi, and their work has been published in such design periodicals as *Abitare* and *Gap Casa*, among others. 5.90

Claude Bouchard was born in 1957 and studied in the interior design department of the François-Xavier Garneau College in Quebec. He has been Assistant Professor of free-hand drawing at the Columbia University New York-Paris Program since 1991. His design work includes a refurbishment of Artemide's showrooms in Montreal, exhibition design for the Musée des Arts Décoratifs, Montreal, and various fit outs in Paris, including a restaurant at La Grande Arche de la Défense executed in collaboration with Christian Liaigre. He has also exhibited drawings and ceramics in Paris. 1.12

Constantin Boym as born in Moscow in 1955. He graduated from the Moscow Architectural Institute in 1978 and from 1984 to 1985 studied for a master's degree in design at the Domus Academy in Milan. He became a registered architect in the USA in 1988 and today has his own design consultancy in New York. He has designed award-winning products for many international companies including Morphos, Néotù and the Formica Corporation. Since 1986 he has taught at the Parsons School of Design, New York, where he currently serves as a director of Product Studies in the Department of Product Design. Recent awards include the ID Annual Design award (1988 and 1990). His work is included in the permanent collection of the Cooper-Hewitt Museum, New York, and in the Musée des Arts Décoratifs in Montreal. 3.53

Andreas Brandolini was born in Taucha, Leipzig in 1951. He studied architecture at the Technische Universität, Berlin and after graduation worked as an industrial designer until 1981 when he joined Block-Bran-Dolini-Rolfes Architects. From 1982 to 1986 he was a partner in Bellefast, an experimental workshop, after which he taught industrial design in Berlin. Since 1989 he has been Professor of Industrial Design at the Hochschule der Bildenden Künste in Saarbrücken. In 1993 he moved to France where he lives and works today. 1.28; 5.7

Clare Brass graduated with a BA Honours degree in design from Middlesex University, UK in 1985, and in the same year moved to Milan, where she worked for Andrea Branzi. In 1988 she opened her own design studio and six years later created Fuorischema, an associated office for design and architecture. She is a founding member of O2 Italy, an international collaboration of designers carrying out research into design and the environment for industry and for the international design community. Clare Brass lectures in Britain and the United States and has taught on a regular basis at the Istituto Europeo di Disegno in Milan. 5.58

Monica Bella-Broner (1911–1993) was born in Nuremberg as Monica Ullmann. She studied under Gunta Stölzl at the Bauhaus weaving workshop in Dessau (preparatory course with Josef Albers; colour theory and analytical drawing with Paul Klee and Wassily Kandinsky). In 1937 she emigrated to Palestine and opened her own workshop with Arieh Sharon, and the following year she moved to Los Angeles, where she had her own studio for production design and set decoration. In the late 1940s she spent a couple of years in Paris before returning to the US to work as a textile stylist in the industrial sector. From 1968 until her death she lived and worked in Stuttgart. 4.7

Team Buchin was founded by Karl Buchin in Berlin in 1969. They specialize in product development for consumer and investment companies from Bosch to IBM. 5.60

Gary Bukovnik was born and educated in Cleveland, Ohio, and moved to San Francisco where he has his studio today. His work can be found in collections and museums throughout the USA: the Metropolitan Museum of Art, New York; the Brooklyn Museum; the Museum of Fine Arts, Boston; the Smithsonian Institution, Washington, DC; the Art Institute of Chicago; and the Fine Arts Museum of San Francisco. 4.54, 55

Antonio Cagianelli was born in Pisa in 1964. After studying architecture at the University of Florence he moved to Paris, where he lives and works today. In 1991 he took part in an international exhibition at the Galleria Clara Scremini in Paris. He works in coloured transparent resin. 5.74

Sergio Calatroni was born in San Guiletta, Italy, in 1951 and studied at the Accademia di Belle Arti in Milan. He is presently involved in architecture, design and interior design, sculpture and journalism. He is the founder of the design group Zeus and of the Gallery Zeus Arte Milano in New York, as well as the publishing company Editions Marrakech, which specializes in books on design, architecture and art theory. His principal projects include offices in Osaka and Shizuoka, the Kashiyama boutique in Paris, the Fujitaka restaurant in Milan, the Seiren showroom, also in Milan, and the Copy Centre in Shizuoka. He has taught interior design at the Istituto Europeo di Disegno in Milan and product design at the Futurarium in Ravenna. Calatroni is consultant editor on the design magazine *Interni* and has collaborated on design articles for most of the leading international design periodicals. 2.58

Pierangelo Caramia was born in 1957 in Cisternino, Italy. He studied architecture under Professor Remo Buti and graduated in 1984. In 1986 he received a master's degree in urban design from the Domus Academy, Milan, where he was taught by Professor Andrea Branzi. He has designed products for numerous manufacturers including XO, Sawaya and Moroni, Arredaesse, Cassina and Alessi, and has also designed the interior of Doublet, a flag factory in Lille, and the Bond Street Café, with Alex Locadia, in New York. He is currently Professor of Design at the Ecole des Beaux Arts in Rennes and has exhibited his work widely both nationally and internationally, most notably at the 3rd International Architecture Exhibition organized by Aldo Rossi at the Venice Biennale, and at a solo show for XO during Designers' Week in Milan. 3.52

Angela Carvalho graduated with a degree in industrial design in 1977 and continued her studies at the Milan Polytechnic, specializing in product design. She then moved to Germany and trained in furniture design at the Institut für Möbel Design, Stuttgart. Today she works with Alexander Neumeister's company Axis/NCS Design Studio. Neumeister studied in Ulm, Germany and at the Tokyo University of Arts. From 1985 to 1987 he was vice president of ICSID (International Council of Societies of Industrial Designers). His work, shown at the Hanover Furniture Fair, has received many awards. 5.43

Chérif was born in 1962 and studied at the Ecole des Beaux Arts in Algeria, and at the Ecole Nationale Supérieure des Arts Décoratifs in Paris. Since graduation he has exhibited for VIA in France and abroad, and in 1994 created a collection of furniture, objects and jewellery. 1.72

Alessandro Chiarato graduated with a degree in architecture from Rome University, after which he worked for Autonautica Sport and International Boat Italia. In 1983 he studied for a master's degree in design at the Domus Academy under Mario Bellini. He then worked with Olivetti SpA in their consumer products division. Today he is a consultant for Studio de Lucchi. 5.49

Studio Cibic is active in architecture and in graphic and interior design in Italy and abroad, and has recently become involved in city management and art direction. The company was set up in 1989 by Aldo Cibic, who was previously a founding member of both Sottsass Associati and Memphis. 1.102

Biagio Cisotti and **Sandra Laube** have been working together since 1993. Cisotti was born in Aradeo, Italy, in 1955 and graduated in 1980 from the architecture programme of Florence University, where he also taught from 1981 to 1992. In 1982 he started his collaboration with Poltronova and became art director. Since 1989 he has lectured at ISIA (the Istituto Superiore delle Industrie Artistiche) and has worked with Aurea, a design and architecture studio in Munich. He was also responsible for the conception and development of B.R.F. He has exhibited his work throughout Europe. Sandra Laube studied at ISIA and graduated in 1983. In 1992 she was awarded a scholarship from the College of Art and Design, Minneapolis, Minnesota, and for several years worked in communication and graphic design. 1.73

Antonio Citterio was born in Meda, Italy in 1950. He studied at Milan Polytechnic, and has been involved in industrial and furniture design since 1967. In 1973 he opened a studio with Paolo Nava, and the two have worked jointly and individually for B & B Italia and Flexform, among other clients. In 1979 they were awarded the Compasso d'Oro. In 1987 Terry Dwan became a partner in Studio Citterio Dwan, and the company has undertaken many interior design projects, including a range of schemes for Esprit and offices and showrooms for Vitra. Among the work realized in Japan, in partnership with Toshiyuki Kita, is the headquarters in Kobe for World Company, the Corrente Building in Tokyo and, in 1992, the Daigo headquarters in Tokyo. Citterio has taught at the Domus Academy in Milan and has participated in many exhibitions, including independent shows in Hanover, Rome, Amsterdam, Paris and Weil. In 1993 he designed the layout of the exhibition "Antonio Citterio and Terry Dwan" promoted by Arc en Rêve in Bordeaux, which travelled to both Osaka and Tokyo in 1994. 1.19

Marzio Rusconi Clerici and **Laura Agnoletto** were born in Milan in 1960 and 1963, respectively. Clerici graduated from the Milan Polytechnic in 1987; Agnoletto attended the Classical Lyceum in Milan and is currently finishing a degree in philosophy. They have worked together for several years for companies such as Glas, Nemo, Fiorucci and are currently designing for Swatch. Other involvements include designs for television productions and interiors and architecture. They have participated in several exhibitions in Italy and abroad including the "Light" show organized by Memphis (1988); the Alessandro Mendini exhibition "Existens Maximum", Florence (1990); and "La Fabbrica Estetica" at the Grand Palais, Paris (1993). 2.22

Franco Clivio was born in 1942 and studied design in Ulm, Germany from 1963 to 1968. Since graduating he has been a product designer for Gardena, Ulm and has carried out freelance commissions for other companies such as ERCO, Siemens and the International Building Exhibition Emscherpark. Today he is a lecturer in product design at the College for Design, Zurich and is a frequent guest lecturer at colleges in the United States, Finland and Germany. 2.20

Nigel Coates was born in 1949 in Malvern, England. He studied at the University of Nottingham and at the Architectural Association, where he has lectured since his graduation in 1974. In 1985 he co-founded Branson Coates with Douglas Branson. He is known for his belief that architecture can be odd and amusing as well as extremely well-built and durable, and his projects include work for Jasper Conran and Katherine Hamnett. He has also designed restaurants in Japan, including the Nishi Acabu Wall in Tokyo, and the Sea Hotel restaurant in Otaru. His most recent projects include two restaurants at Schiphol Airport, Amsterdam. 1.42

John Coleman was born in London in 1953. He studied furniture design at Kingston Polytechnic and the Royal College of Art before establishing his own company in 1981. He now designs for a studio workshop at London Bridge specializing in limited editions of furniture for retail through such outlets as The Conran Shop. He has sold and exhibited his work widely both in the UK and abroad. 1.45, 48

Denis Colomb was born in Milan in 1957 and studied at the Istituto Superiore di Architettura e Disegno. He has his own studio in Paris and collaborates with leading fashion designers, creating shops and offices. In 1994 he went to New York to participate in the French Show House and in the same year started to design furniture. His Push Me chair has been selected by the French Embassy for the Cultural Counsellor's office. 1.107

Le Corbusier, born Charles-Edouard Jeanneret, (1887–1965) studied metal engraving at the Arts and Craft school La Chaux-de-Fonds under Charles L'Eplattenier. He worked with Josef Hoffmann at the Wiener Werkstätte, with Tony Garnier in Lyons and Henri Sauvage in Paris. He was an apprentice in the Perret Brothers' architecture office where he experimented in the use of concrete as a building material, before joining the staff of Peter Behrens's office in Berlin. It was at this time that he met Mies van der Rohe and Walter Gropius. In 1918 he returned to Paris and met Amédée Ozenfant with whom he developed a style of painting, Purism. He wrote several manifestos under the pseudonym "Le Corbusier" which he later adopted for all facets of his career. From 1925 he worked with his cousin Pierre Jeanneret in their architectural practice in Paris. The white concrete houses of this period were later dubbed "The International Style of Architecture". In 1927 he started to design tubular steel furniture with Jeanneret and Charlotte Perriand. From the 1930s, Le Corbusier concentrated on architecture and planning. 5.23

Creadesign was founded in 1981 by Hannu Kähönen. Kähönen studied graphic and industrial design at the University of Industrial Arts, Helsinki, where he now teaches. He is a visiting lecturer on industrial design in Oslo, Amsterdam, Madrid, Singapore, Hong Kong, Tokyo and Kyoto, chairman of the National Council of Crafts and Design and a Member of the Arts Council, Finland. Since 1975 Kähönen has created over fifty product designs, exhibitions and corporate identities, as well as designing local trains (colour and interiors) for the Finnish State Railway. He has exhibited in Europe and the USA, most recently at the Chicago Athenaeum – "Designed in Finland" (1994) and examples of his work can be seen in the permanent collections of the Taideteollisuusmuseo Konstindustrimuseet, Helsinki; Die Neue Sammlung, Staatliches Museum für Angewandte Kunst, Munich; the Design Centre, Stuttgart; and the Israel Museum, Jerusalem. In 1992 he was given a Certificate/Honourable Mention as the Industrial Designer of the Year, Finland. 5.11

Rondell Crier is an art student working as a Guild Member at YA/YA, Inc. He has designed back-drops for Black Entertainment TV and the cover and interior graphics for the book *Part of the Solution: Creative Alternatives for Youth*. He has exhibited through YA/YA in The Netherlands, Japan and France, and has created watches for Swatch and a chair, Line Creator, which was purchased by Alessandro Mendini and displayed at the exhibition "Piccolo Mercato", the Piccola Scuola, Milan. 1.14

Hermann Czech was born in 1936 and studied architecture at the College of Technology and the Academy of Fine Arts in Vienna, where he attended the Master Class of E. A. Plischke. From 1954 to 1956 he trained at the School of Film-making at the Academy of Music and Performing Arts. He has taught at the Academy of Applied Arts where he was visiting professor from 1985 to 1986, and was also visiting professor at Harvard University until 1989. Since then he has worked as a freelance architect primarily on retail, domestic and leisure facilities in his native Austria. He has exhibited his designs in Vienna. 2.16

Riccardo Dalisi, the Italian avant-garde designer, was a member of the experimental design group Global Tools throughout the 1970s. He has written several books on architecture and animation, and teaches architectural composition at the University of Naples. He was awarded the Compasso d'Oro in 1981 for a coffee-maker produced by Alessi. He has also collaborated with Baleri Italia, Oluce, Play Line and Zanotta. He has participated in many exhibitions, including the Venice Biennale and the Milan Triennale. 1.104; 3.33; 5.34

Antonio Da Motta Leal graduated from the University of Pennsylvania and continued his studies at the Barnes Foundation and Fine Arts Academy, also in Pennsylvania. He is involved in painting, theatre design, illustration and video production as well as interior design, and in 1993 founded Da Motta Studio with businessman Rolando Niella. 1.111

Jean-Charles de Castelbajac trained as a fashion designer and is now involved in interior, furniture and object design. 2.38, 39

Delo Lindo was created in 1985 by Fabien Cagani and Laurent Matras who were both born in France and received diplomas from the Ecole Nationale Supérieure des Arts Décoratifs, Paris. Their expertise covers interior design, exhibition design and furniture design for clients such as Soca Line and Cinna, as well as tableware for Algorithme. 1.32, 33

Michele de Lucchi was born in Ferrara, Italy, in 1951 and graduated from Florence University in 1975. During his student years he founded the "Gruppo Cavat", a group concerned with avant-garde and conceptual architecture. He worked and designed for Alchimia until the establishment of Memphis in 1981. Today he produces exclusive art-orientated handmade products, industrial consumer items and furniture in wood, metal, stone and other materials for companies serving specialized markets. His architectural activities range from shop design to office buildings and private apartment blocks. De Lucchi's work has received many awards and he has published and exhibited widely both nationally and internationally. He has taught at design schools and universities such as the Domus Academy, Milan, and the University of Detroit. 2.56; 5.49

Laura de Santillana was born in Venice in 1955. She has been graphic designer at Vignelli Associates, New York; Art Director and designer for Benini Murano, Italy; co-founder, Art Director and designer for EOS, Murano; and today is designer for both Rosenthal, Germany and for Ivan Baj, Bolzano, Italy. She has held solo and group exhibitions internationally, among them "Laura de Santillana" at the Osiris Gallery, Brussels (1994); "Italia Italia – Masterworks of Italian Design 1960–94", the Denver Art Museum, USA (1994); and "Murano – I Vetri di Laura de Santillana", Blanchaert & Arosio, Milan. Her work can be found in permanent design collections in Italy, America, Germany and Brazil and has been widely published. 3.5

Thibault Desombre was born in 1958 and trained as a cabinet-maker. He studied furniture design at the Ecole Supérieure Nationale des Arts Décoratifs, with J. C. Maugirard and M. Pigeon, and graduated in 1983. He has designed for the Palais de l'Elysée and has also taken part in "Le Groupe des Halles" at the Salon du Prêt à Porter in 1992. Clients include Soca Line, Ligne Roset, Maugrion and Ercuis. Desombre has received considerable recognition in France for his work: he was awarded the Designer of the Year title at the Salon du Meuble in Paris in 1994. 1.58

Matthias Dietz was born in Frankfurt in 1957 and from 1976 to 1980 studied ecology at the Free University and the Technical University, Berlin. In 1980 he studied industrial design at the Academy of Fine Arts, Berlin and the Academy of Visual Arts, Hamburg, and worked as a freelance designer. From 1985 to 1989 he was the Design Manager at Deutsche Leasing AG, Bad Homburg. During this time he worked with Borek Sipek and David Palterer. Dietz Design Management GmbH was founded in 1989 and offers a full range of design strategy, research, analysis and consultancy. Clients include Artemide, Belux, Silhouette International, the Vitra Museum, Moormann, and Deutsche Lufthansa. Dietz has organized numerous design exhibitions and has published a book on design. 5.13

David D'Imperio was born in Pennsylvania in 1960. He graduated from Kutztown University with a Bachelor of Fine Arts degree in 1982. Today he designs and produces lighting, furniture and exhibition systems and has participated in numerous shows including the International Furniture Fair in Frankfurt. He currently lives and works in Miami, Florida. 2.45, 47

Nanna Ditzel was born in 1923 in Copenhagen and graduated from the Kunsthåndvaerkerskolen, Copenhagen in 1946. Also in that year she established an industrial design studio in Copenhagen with Jorgen Ditzel and since then has founded several practices in London and Copenhagen. She is active in the fields of furniture, textile, jewellery and tableware design, and has belonged to numerous professional institutions, most recently acting as chairwoman of the Danish State Arts Foundations' Committee for Industrial Arts and Design. She has received international acclaim for her work, winning the Gold Medal (with Jorgen Ditzel) at the Milan Triennale in 1960 and the Gold Medal at the International Furniture Design Competition, Asahikawa, Japan in 1990. In 1991 a film on the life and work of Nanna Ditzel was made by the Danish Ministry of Education. Examples of her work can be seen in the permanent collections of the Louisiana Museum of Modern Art, Humlebaek, Denmark; the Museum of Decorative Art, Copenhagen; the Museum of Applied Art, Trondheim, Norway; and Goldsmiths' Hall, London. 1.121

Tom Dixon was born in Sfax, Tunisia, in 1959 and moved to the UK when he was four. From 1981 to 1984 he was involved in nightclub promotion and event organization, and formed Creative Salvage with Nick Jones and Mark Brazier-Jones in 1985. His studio, SPACE, is where his prototypes and commissioned works – including stage sets, furniture, sculpture, illuminated sculpture, architectural installations, chandeliers and numerous other objects – are made. His clients include Cappellini, Comme des Garçons, Nigel Coates, Ralph Lauren, Vivienne Westwood and Terence Conran. Dixon is visiting tutor at the Royal College of Art, the Architectural Association and Kingston Polytechnic. He has exhibited his work both nationally and internationally, most recently in "A New Century in Design" at the National Museum of Modern Arts, Tokyo. Examples of his designs can be found in the permanent collections of the Victoria and Albert Museum, London; the Musée des Arts Décoratifs and the Centre Georges Pompidou, Paris; the Vitra Chair Museum, Basle; the Crafts Council and the Design Museum, London; and the Brooklyn Museum, New York. In 1994 Dixon opened the SPACE shop. 1.25, 79, 110

Frédérick Du Chayla is the chief designer and founding member of the three-man strong, Lyons-based architectural, scenographic and interior design office, Studio Totem. Major projects include the scenography and interiors of the Ville de Vitralles, a stadium and 5,000-seat theatre designed in collaboration with the architect Rudy Riccolti (1994); the re-design of various communal exterior spaces such as the seafront at Ville de Saint Hilaire-de-Riez; the reception area of the Bibliothèque Municipale de la Port-Dieu, Lyons (1994); and numerous offices and private houses, bars and restaurants. Since 1981 Studio Totem have also designed limited series of furniture, objects, lights and accessories which can be found in many private and public collections, including the Musée des Arts Décoratifs in Paris, the Fondation Cartier, the Musée d'Art Moderne de Saint-Etienne and the Musée de Grenoble. They have exhibited their designs widely throughout France. 1.76

Nathalie du Pasquier was born in Bordeaux in 1957 and is self-taught. Her work has been inspired by her extensive trips to Africa, Australia and India. In 1980 she set up a studio with George Sowden and in 1981 became a founding member of the Memphis Group, working with Ettore Sottsass. Today she has her own studio which is more intensively oriented towards painting. 3.38, 39

Hartmut Engel was born in Stuttgart in 1939. He studied electrical engineering in Stuttgart and Darmstadt, then industrial design in Pfirzheim. After qualifying as an industrial designer in 1968, he set up his own studio in Ludwigsburg. He has received numerous awards in Germany, including the Industry Forum Design, Hanover "Top Ten of the Year" Gold Award. 2.32, 33

Anna Eoclidi was born in Alseno, Italy, in 1965 but today lives and works in New South Wales, Australia. She completed a Bachelor of Fine Arts in jewellery and object design at the Sydney College of the Arts whilst at the same time working as a freelance designer. Since 1993 she has worked at the Jam Factory Craft and Design Centre, first as Associate Designer in the Metal Design Studio, then since 1995 as a Designer/Maker for Studio 7. 2.26

André Feldmann and **Arne Jacob Schultchen**, born in 1964 and 1965, respectively, have worked as a team since they met at the Hochschule für Bildende Künste, Hamburg from which they graduated in industrial design in 1992/93. In 1994 they established their own studio in Hamburg. The range of their work runs from product design, furniture, lighting and interior design to graphics, packaging, exhibition design and experimental works. 2.35

Kitty Fischer was born in 1908 as Catherine Louise van der Mijll Dekker. From 1929 to 1932 she studied under Gunta Stölzl in the weaving workshop of the Dessau Bauhaus (basic course with Josef Albers; theory of forms and analytical drawings with Wassily Kandinsky; courses with Joost Schmidt and Paul Klee) and she received a diploma signed by Mies van der Rohe. She moved to Nunspeet in Holland and founded her own studio, later working with Greten Köhler and Hermann Fischer. In 1933 she took part in the Milan Triennale where she received a silver medal for two cellophane materials. She worked on commissions for public buildings and museums and designs for the Dutch Textile Industry and later the Dutch royal family. In 1935 she participated in the Dutch entry for the World Exhibition in Brussels, where she was awarded the Gold Medal in 1937; and in the World's Fair in Paris, where she received the Diplome d'Honneur. From 1934 to 1979 Kitty Fischer was the weaving instructor at Amsterdam's College of Arts and Crafts, now the Rietveld Academy. 4.6

Siggi Fischer was born in Cologne in 1954 and studied industrial design in Wuppertal. Since 1990 he has worked independently and has a list of clients that includes Thomas Schulte Designmanufaktur, Vericom GmbH and Best Friends Collection. He has exhibited his work in Germany, Italy and Japan. 5.26

Martijn Fransen is a student at the Akademie Industriële Vormgeving in Eindhoven, due to graduate in 1996. 1.74

Michal Fronek and **Jan Nemecek** were born in 1966 and 1963, respectively. Both studied at the Academy of Applied Arts in Prague under Borek Sipek. They began their first collaboration as the design group Olgoj Chorchoj shortly after having attended a summer workshop at the Vitra Design Museum, and since then they have completed numerous interior design projects in Prague. Artel II was founded in 1993 and exhibited at the Milan Furniture Fair; at the International Conference of Arts and Crafts, London; at the International Design Exhibition, Turin, and at the Gallery Genia Loci, Prague. Currently Fronek and Nemecek teach alongside Sipek at the Academy of Applied Arts in Prague and are designing the interior fittings in Vaclav Havel's Prague house. Their work has been published in magazines such as *Abitare*, *Ambiente*, *Elle*, *Modo* and *Arena*. 1.127; 3.28

Kazuko Fujie established her own studio in 1977. In 1982 she created the bench Kujira (Whale), constructed from panels of plywood. There followed the Mangekyo (Kaleidoscope) series in 1990 and the Morphe series in 1992. 1.75

An Reto Furrer was born in Zurich in 1967 and studied interior design, specializing in restaurant and hotel design. From 1988 to 1989 she worked as a freelance illustrator for newspapers and advertising agencies as well as designing clothes and furniture. In 1990 she started her collaboration with Santacruz and Sims Snowboards designing boards, boots and outfits. 5.80

Piero Gaeta was born in Matera in 1961 and took a degree in architecture in Florence. In 1991 he was commissioned to design street furniture for the first Japan Expo in Toyama by Country Co. Ltd, Tokyo, and in 1994 he worked on a collection of Swatch telephones. As well as designing products and furniture for industrial production, he also designs exhibitions and interiors and has worked for clients that include Arflex, Glas, Steel and YKK. 1.84; 2.42

Olivier Gagnere was born in 1952 in Paris. From 1980 to 1981 he collaborated with Memphis and since then has worked for VIA, Néotù and Ecart. His furniture designs and his work in glass and terracotta have been widely exhibited internationally and he has received several awards. His work can be seen in the permanent collections of the Musée des Arts Décoratifs in Paris and Bordeaux and in the Museum of Modern Art in San Francisco. 2.18

Walter Garro was born in Milan in 1961. After completing graphic design courses, he collaborated with advertising and packaging companies. While partner of the design studio Alchimia, he developed graphic and communications projects. He is currently working for Swatch on the creation of new watches, and with S. Parker on a collection of lamps. He lives and works in Milan. 5.89

Massimo Giacon was born in Padua in 1961. He started his career as a cartoonist for Mondadori Publications working on magazines such as *Dolce Vita*, *Cyborg* and *Comic Art*. He is also active in art-rock music, as founder of the band I Nipoti del Faraone. Since 1985 Giacon has been working as a consultant for architects Sottsass Associati developing several projects for the studio. He has also been producing designs for Memphis Textile Design, Design Gallery (fabrics), Swatch, Interflex (tapestries), Alessi (porcelain) and Artemide (graphics and packaging for the Gilda lamp). In 1987 he designed an audiovisual aid in computer graphics for Olivetti France and La Villette Museum in Paris, and in 1993 he collaborated with Matteo Thun on the Philips Fantasy World project creating the character of "Captain Isy" as well as the corresponding graphics, merchandising and murals. He has exhibited his art and design work internationally. Giacon is currently working on a computer-animated exhibition sponsored by Olivetti and frescoes for the Malpensa airport, Milan. 3.6, 7; 4.60

Gabriella Giandelli was born in 1963 and lives and works in Milan. She has worked as an illustrator for magazines and in advertising. Her design work includes carpets for Alchimia, textile designs for Memphis, watches for Swatch and a vase for Sottsass Associati. She has exhibited work in group shows in Italy, Spain and the United States. 4.58

Louise Gibb was born in Edinburgh in 1957 and studied art at Lancaster University. From 1986 to 1993 she lived and worked in Milan designing fabrics for the fashion industry whilst at the same time making animal sculptures and experimenting in product design. She returned to live in London in 1993 and is currently working on a master's degree in Design Studies at Central Saint Martin's College of Art and Design in London. She has worked for companies such as Alessi, Silhouette, Swatch, Ritzenhoff and Memphis and has exhibited her work in Italy and Great Britain. 3.70; 4.59

Anna Gili was born in Orvieto in 1960 and studied at the Istituto Superiore delle Industrie Artistiche, Florence, graduating in 1984 with a "Sound Dress" project which has since been shown at the Padiglione di Arte Contemporanea in Milan, the Seibu Department Stores in Tokyo and the Kunstmuseum in Düsseldorf. She has designed objects for Alessi; tiles for Inax, Tokyo; ceramic pots for Richard Ginori; carpets, tapestries and furniture for Cassina; glass vases for Salviati and Bisazza; furniture and textiles for Cappellini; and furniture for Interflex and Play Line. In 1992 she was the cultural co-ordinator of the exhibition "Nuovo Bel Design", and in 1994 the curator of the exhibition and conference "Primordi", which was held in the Triennale Building in Milan and dealt with the transformation and problems of the latest generation of designers. Gili is the curator of the exhibition "Mutamenti" under the patronage of the Milan City Council (1995) and since 1990 has taught industrial design at the Accademia di Belle Arti in Milan. 1.81, 103; 3.11, 27

Ginbande was founded in Frankfurt by Uwe Fischer and Laus Achim Heine in 1985. Uwe Fischer studied design at the Hochschule für Gestaltung, Offenbach, specializing in industrial design; Heine studied mathematics and physics at the Johann Wolfgang Goethe Universität, Frankfurt, and then design at the Offenbach Hochschule specializing in visual communication. Ginbande works on corporate identities for public and private companies, and their experimental two- and three-dimensional pieces are regularly shown and published. 1.93

Paolo Giordano was born in Naples in 1954 and studied architecture in Milan. Today he lives in Milan and India and works as a designer and a photographer, producing his own collection of furniture in limited edition in India. 1.119, 129

Stefano Giovannoni was born in La Spezia, Italy in 1954 and graduated from the Faculty of Architecture at the University of Florence in 1978. From 1978 to 1990 he lectured and carried out research at Florence University and also taught at the Domus Academy in Milan and at the Institute of Design in Reggio Emilia. He is the founding member of King-Kong Production, which is concerned with avant-garde research in design, interiors, fashion and architecture. Clients include Alessi, Cappellini, Arredaesse and Tisca France. In 1991 he designed the Italian Pavilion at "Les Capitales Européennes de Nouveau Design" exhibition which was held at the Centre Georges Pompidou in Paris. His work has been displayed in exhibitions in Italy and abroad. 3.37, 42, 43; 5.71

Claudio Giunnelli founded the design and consultancy practice Studio Minimo with Marcello Panza in 1983. They have worked on the corporate image of Driade and in 1989 organized "Design Connection", a series of exhibitions in Italy and abroad with the aim of promoting the importance of design. Giunnelli teaches at the Istituto Superiore di Disegno in Naples. He has exhibited his work in Italy and in the "Zeit Wände" show organized by Rasch at the carpet museum in Kassel. 5.8

Natanel Gluska was born in Israel in 1957 but now lives and works in Zurich. He has studied in Israel, The Hague and at the Rietveld Academy, Amsterdam (1985–89). He has exhibited work in The Netherlands and Switzerland. 1.5, 6

Kevin Goehring studied at Florida State University and founded Square One, a Tampa-based company specializing in handmade ceramics, six years ago. He has been selected by the Estates of Salvador Dali, Walt Disney and Elvis Presley to create limited series of tableware. 3.9

Nuala Goodman was born in Dublin, Ireland in 1962. She studied at the National College of Art and Design and received a diploma in 1984. She travelled to Milan with a scholarship from the Italian Cultural Institute and worked for a short period with Sottsass Associati. Today she lives and works in Milan designing fabrics, window displays and objets d'art. On occasion she collaborates with Marianna Kennedy and James Howett in London working on small furniture and product commissions for private clients. Her main interest is in Fine Art, and she is currently producing a series of sculptural paintings, part of which formed the subject of an exhibition that travelled to Dublin and Milan. 1.11; 3.2

Kenneth Grange was educated at the Willesden School of Art, London and served in the Royal Engineers as a technical illustrator. He then worked for eight years in various architectural and design offices before establishing his own industrial design practice in 1959. He was a founding partner of Pentagram in 1972 and his work includes mass-production items ranging from small appliances to the Intercity 125 train. In 1969 he was appointed Royal Designer for Industry and in 1984 was awarded the CBE. He holds Honorary Doctorates from the Royal College of Art, London (1985) and Heriot-Watt University, Edinburgh (1986) and has served as Master of the Faculty of Royal Designers for Industry (1985–87), as well as being the President of the Chartered Society of Designers (1987). He has been the recipient of major design prizes including ten annual Design Council Awards. 5.37, 40

Tobias Grau was born in Hamburg in 1957. He studied design in New York at the Parsons School of Design, after which he worked in the Design and Development office of Knoll International in Pennsylvania. He founded Tobias Grau KG in Hamburg in 1984, producing light designs for his own collection. Graudesign was set up four years later and under this name he redesigns hotels and showrooms and was responsible for the corporate identity of forty branches of the jeans shop Werdin. He also produces series of furniture and product designs for various clients. He received the ID Magazine Award, New York, in 1993. 2.27

Michael Graves received his architectural training at the University of Cincinnati and Harvard University. In 1960 he won the Rome Prize and studied at the American Academy in Rome of which he is now a trustee. Graves is Schirmer Professor of Architecture at Princeton University, where he has taught since 1962, and a Fellow of the American Institute of Architects. His works, which have won numerous awards, include the Newark Museum, New Jersey; the Whitney Museum, New York; Emory University Museum of Art and Archaeology, Atlanta; the master plan for the Detroit Institute of Arts; the Denver Public Library and the Clark County Library in Las Vegas. Graves is also well known for his design of furniture and decorative accessories which he produces for manufacturers including Memphis, Sawaya and Moroni, Alessi and Swid Powell. His projects appear in many periodicals and several monographs have been dedicated to his life and work. 2.12; 3.32, 59

Johanna Grawunder was born in 1961 in San Diego and received a Bachelor of Architecture in 1984 from the California Polytechnic State University, San Luis Obispo. She is an architect with Sottsass Associati in Milan, where she has worked since 1985 and where she became a partner in 1989. In addition to her architectural design activity, she has participated in several design exhibitions including "Memphis Lights" (Milan, 1988); "Women in Design" (Museum of Contemporary Design, Ravenna, 1990); and "Chairs" (Milan, 1989) among others. In 1992 she presented a personal exhibition called "Trucks" at Gallery Jannone (Milan) and at the Argentaurum Gallery (Belgium). She has designed objects for the Collection Cleto Munari, lamps for Saviati, a collection of objects for Gioto Hong Kong, and marble pieces for Ultima Edizione (Massa). 1.83, 98, 99; 2.34

Konstantin Grcic is a German furniture designer who is at present working freelance in London and Munich. He was born in 1965, trained as a cabinet-maker and continued his education at the John Makepeace School for Craftsmen and the Royal College of Art, London. 1.24, 27, 34, 95; 4.9; 5.38, 66

Giorgio Gregori was a design member of the Alchimia Group from 1978 to 1990, designing for Alessi, Philips, Toshiba and I.C.E. Los Angeles. He participated in the Groninger Museum project with Alessandro Mendini, and has produced furniture for Design Gallery, watches for Swatch, a bus stop for the city of Hanover and is currently working with some Italian companies on product and interior design. 3.62

Marno Gudiksen is Associate Professor at the Royal Academy of Fine Arts, Furniture Design Department, Copenhagen. His work can be found in the Museum of Decorative Arts, Copenhagen. 1.41

Alessandro Guerriero was born in 1943. He set up his own design group, Alchimia, in 1976 with his sister Adriana. They were later joined by Alessandro Mendini and Giorgio Gregori. Guerriero is known as one of the creators of the postmodernist school because of the clear forms, gaudy colours and playful details of his designs. He lives and works as an architect and designer in Milan. 3.29

Johanna Gunkel was born in Düsseldorf, Germany, and received a diploma in object design in 1991. She opened her own design office in Cologne and since 1993 has worked as a set artist for television and theatre. 1.13

Zaha Hadid was born in Baghdad. Today her London-based architectural firm encompasses all fields of design, ranging from the urban scale through to products, interiors and furniture. Hadid studied architecture at the Architectural Association from 1972 and was awarded the Diploma Prize in 1977. She then became a member of the Office for Metropolitan Architecture, began teaching at the AA with Rem Koolhaas and Elia Zenghelis and led her own studio at the AA until 1987. Since the formation of her independent company, projects have included furniture and interiors for Bitar, London (1985), designs for several buildings in Japan, the Exhibition Pavilion for Video Art in Groningen (1992), and the Vitra Fire Station (1993). Since 1989 various large-scale studies have been completed for harbour developments in Hamburg, Bordeaux and Cologne leading to the prize-winning Düsseldorf art and media centre project. Hadid's paintings and drawings have been widely exhibited, notably in "Deconstructivist Architecture" (Museum of Modern Art, New York, 1988) and at the Graduate School of Design at Harvard University (1993), and her work is in the permanent collections of various institutions such as MOMA and the Deutsches Architektur Museum in Frankfurt. Hadid has been visiting professor at Columbia and Harvard universities and has given a series of master classes and lectures at venues around the world. Current work includes the Cardiff Bay Opera House, which is due to open in the year 2000. 3.25

Annaleena Hakatie was born in Helsinki in 1965. She studied at the Sheridan College of Art and Design in Toronto, specializing in glass design, before moving to the University of Art and Design, Helsinki, where she is currently working on an MA diploma in glass design. She has exhibited work in joint shows in Finland, Canada, Sweden and Iceland as well as in the solo exhibitions "XXY" at the Museum of Applied Arts, Finland, and "Kliniska Svulstigheter" at the Pro Persona Gallery, Stockholm. 3.14

Ashley Hall was born in Cardiff, Wales, in 1967. He studied furniture design at the University of Trent, Nottingham, and the Royal College of Art, graduating in 1992. He has exhibited internationally and has continued to develop his skills on a range of products, from lighting and furniture to small accessories, for both his own production and for other manufacturers. 1.97; 2.49

Koji Hamai was born in Japan in 1964 and graduated from the Bunka Fashion College. He believes strongly in the importance of the textile in fashion design and is well known for producing highly fashionable fabrics. He initially joined Miyashin Corporation in Hachioji, where he acquired his knowledge of textile production. In 1986 he moved to the Issey Miyake Design Studio, staying there until 1991, when he left to work as a freelance fashion designer. He has received many awards in Japan, such as the Grand-Prix at the International Textile Design Contest (1991). 4.25–29

Maria Christina Hamel was born in New Delhi in 1958 but today lives and works in Milan. In 1981 she began a collaboration with Alchimia and later with the Atelier Mendini. She is involved in domestic product design using ceramics, glass, silver and enamel, and also in the practice of applying chromatics to architectural structures. Since 1989 she has taken part in numerous exhibitions in Europe and has held solo shows in Milan and Verona. Hamel has taught at the University of Vienna, at the Art Schools of Faenza and Limoges, and in India. She was mentioned in the XVII Premio Compasso d'Oro for her saxophone design, Alessofono, which she created with Alessandro Mendini. 1.35; 3.34, 51; 5.9

Marc Harrison started his career as a builder and manufacturer of boats. He studied at the Queensland College of Art, after which he established his own design and manufacturing business. He is currently mass-producing four designs and continuing to produce one-off pieces of furniture. 1.120; 2.41

Greg Healey is a freelance designer. He received a Bachelor of Arts in jewellery design from the Sydney College of Arts in 1985 and a graduate diploma the following year. Until 1994 he was principal designer at the metal and design studio the Jam Factory in Adelaide. 2.23

Piet Hein Eek is a Dutch furniture and product designer. He works with Nob Roygrok producing series of furniture as well as one-off commissions. In recent years he has concentrated on his "door project", recycling old windows and doors and creating a collection of varied cupboards, working at times with Jeanine Keizer. He has exhibited his work widely, most recently at the Stedelijk Museum, Amsterdam (1994), the Museum Für Angewandte Kunst, Cologne (1994), at the Holland Expo in Japan (1995) and at the Groninger Museum. 1.96

Scott Henderson was born in Virginia in 1966 and currently works in New York City as a senior industrial designer for Smart Design. He graduated from the University of the Arts in Philadelphia in 1988. While Henderson was a senior designer at Teague Associates, his work on head-mounted displays for the emerging virtual reality revolution was featured in an exhibition at the Guggenheim Museum and was noted in NASA "Tech Briefs" for excellence in technology transfers. His design work in the areas of consumer electronics, housewares, furniture and lighting has been widely published. 5.84

Yoshiki Hishinuma is a fashion and textile designer who was born in Sendai, Japan in 1958. He has presented collections since 1984, showing in both Japan and Europe. In 1992 he became the subject of a monograph, *Here and There*, and exhibited his work at Expo '92 Seville. Since 1993 he has been costume director of Universiade '95, Fukuoka. Recent exhibitions include "Japanese Design 80" at the Seoul Museum of Modern Art, and "The History of Jeans" at the Musée de la Mode du Costume, Paris. 4.12–23

Vlastislav Hofman (1884–1964) studied with J. Fanta, J. E. Koula and J. Schiltz at the Czech Technical University from 1902 to 1907. He worked in the building department of the Prague Magistrate before becoming a member of the Artel Co-operative and the Mánes Association of Plastic Artists. He wrote many theoretical essays and was considered one of the founders of the Czech modern movement. In 1912 he left Artel and returned to Mánes, participating in the competition for Zizka's monument at Vítkov Hill. He won a gold medal at the International Exhibition of Decorative Art in Paris in 1913, the Grand Prix at the Exhibition of Arts and Technology in Paris in 1937 and the Grand Prize at the Milan Triennale in 1940. Hofman's wide-ranging activities included architecture, applied arts, painting and, from 1919, scenography, primarily in collaboration with Karel Hilar. 1.109

Geoff Hollington studied in London at Central Saint Martin's College, and graduated in 1971 with a BA in industrial design (engineering). He gained an MA in environmental design from the Royal College of Art in 1974. While at Central Saint Martin's he exhibited a large environmental art installation at the Institute of Contemporary Art in London (1970), and at the Royal College of Art he designed two fashion shows and a new student bar for the college (1974), both in collaboration with Ben Kelly. From 1976 until 1978 he worked on the design team at the new city of Milton Keynes and became a visiting tutor in product and interior design at Kingston Polytechnic, Surrey (1975–82). In 1980 he formed Hollington Associates with the aim of concentrating on industrial design, and today it has become one of the world's leading creative consultancies, listing among its clients Herman Miller, Parker Pen, Matsushita, NEC, Gordon Russell, Filofax, Lloyd Loom and SCP. Products designed by Hollington Associates have won many international awards and are in several museum collections. A monograph, *Hollington Industrial Design*, was published in 1990. In addition to his design work, Hollington is an occasional visiting tutor at the Royal College of Art and has lectured worldwide. He has written many articles and reviews for magazines including *Blueprint*, for which he has been a regular contributor. He is a Fellow of the Royal Society of Arts, an international member of the Industrial Design Society of America and a Fellow of the Chartered Society of Designers. 1.90

Bohuslav Horak was born in Pardubice in the Czech Republic in 1954 and attended both the Zizkov Art School of Prague and the Academy of Applied Arts. In 1987 he became a member of the design group Atika, also in Prague. He has recently designed a range of furniture and tableware for Anthologie Quartett. 1.30, 128; 2.53; 3.1, 12

Isao Hosoe was born in Tokyo in 1942. He received a Bachelor of Science in 1965 and a Master of Science (1967) in aerospace engineering from the Nihon University in Tokyo. He is currently a professor of design at the Domus Academy in Milan, at Milan Polytechnic and at the Istituto Superiore delle Industrie Artistiche, Florence, as well as at the University of Siena. He has received international acclaim for his design work and awards such as the Compasso d'Oro and a Gold Medal at the Milan Triennale. He has had one-man shows in Japan and the United States and his works can be seen in the permanent collections of the Victoria and Albert Museum, London, and the Centre Georges Pompidou, Paris. 2.31

Dwight Huffman and **John Rantanen III**, born in 1967 and 1961, respectively, together founded Haute House. They specialize in "reconstruction furniture design" which combines new perceptions of form and space with the use of low-impact materials such as locally harvested wood. Their work is widely available in the United States. 1.43

Richard Hutten was born in 1967 in Zwollerkerspel, The Netherlands. He studied at the Akademie Industriële Vormgeving in Eindhoven and trained under Frans Van Praet, Antwerp; Peer de Bruyn, Breda; and Ziv Potampa Architects, San Francisco. In 1991 he started his own design studio working on a range of furniture, No Sign of Design. He also received a grant from the Dutch Ministry of Culture to develop his table concept. His work can be seen in the collection of the Stedelijk Museum, Amsterdam. 1.44, 69, 70

Yoshiaki Iida was born in 1947 in Aichi Prefecture, Japan. Before founding the I.C.I. Design Institute in 1985 he worked for Matsushita Electric Industrial Co. Ltd. He has been awarded numerous design prizes including the Gold Prize from Design Forum, Korea, and the Gold Medal from the 14th Biennial of Industrial Design, Ljubljana. He is technical advisor for Osaka Prefecture Government and an advisor for the Korean Design and Packaging Centre, as well as lecturer in Industrial Product Design at the College of Design, Osaka. His sewing kit design, Plateon, is on show in the permanent collection of the Museum of Modern Art, New York. 5.51

James Irvine was born in London in 1958 and graduated from the Royal College of Art in 1984. He then moved to Italy and worked as a consultant designer at Olivetti with Ettore Sottsass and Michele de Lucchi. He participated in "12 New Memphis 86" and became a member of the group Solid. In 1987 Olivetti arranged a cultural exchange for him with Toshiba in Tokyo, where he carried out research in industrial design. On his return to Milan he designed industrial products for Olivetti with Michele de Lucchi and eventually became responsible for a new range of mini-computers and work-stations. In 1988 he opened his own studio in Milan designing interiors, furniture and industrial products and collaborating with various companies including Alessi, Cappellini and Fantini. In 1990 Irvine taught as a visiting lecturer at the Domus Academy, Milan. In 1993 he held his first personal exhibition at the Royal College of Art, Stockholm. 1.51

Setsu Ito was born in Yamaguchi, Japan, in 1964. He obtained his master's degree in product design at the University of Tsukuba and has since published studies on product semantics and design valuations for the Japanese Society for the Science of Design. He has undertaken design research projects for the TDK Corporation, NEC Electric Co. and Nissan Motor Co., and in 1989 worked for Studio Alchimia in Milan. Since 1989 he has collaborated with Angelo Mangiarotti and has also become consultant designer for the TDK Corporation, with Bruno Gregory. 5.36

Hella Jongerius studied at the Akademie Industriële Vormgeving in Eindhoven and spent periods as an apprentice with Xinta Tinta fashion fabrics in Barcelona and with Catherine Laget in Paris training in styling. She has exhibited at Le Vent du Nord in Paris, at Droog Design in Milan and in the show "Mutant Materials in Contemporary Design" at the Museum of Modern Art, New York. 3.46, 47

Carsten Jorgensen was born in Denmark in 1948. From 1965 to 1969 he studied at the School of Art, Copenhagen after which he became a designer at Royal Copenhagen. After a period as lecturer at the School of Art, he co-founded the Experimental School of Fine Arts "Atelier 12" in Copenhagen and taught there until 1978, whilst at the same time starting to work for Bodum. In 1983 he moved to Switzerland. Several of his products have been selected by museums in Europe and the USA. In 1986 he became a member of the Danish Design Board (IDD). 3.41

Eric Jourdan was born in 1961. He is a professor at the Ecole des Beaux-Arts de Saint-Etienne and guest lecturer at the Ecole Nationale Supérieure des Beaux-Arts, Paris. He has worked for clients such as VIA, Zeus and Algorithme. 1.21

Nazanin Kamali is a Persian refugee and a graduate of the Royal College of Art, London. Her intricate work has gained her much acclaim. She is based in London and works in the partnership "Non-Specific Creativity". 5.42

Masafumi Katsukawa is a young Japanese designer currently living and working in Milan. He graduated from the Kyoto Institute of Technology in 1983 and since moving to Italy has collaborated with Studio Arosio, Studiodada and Sottsass Associati. He is currently a freelance designer and consultant for Lumen Center Italia. 2.6

Nobuya Kawahata was born in 1963. He graduated from Chiba University in 1982 and has received recognition for his designs in the form of national prizes such as the Good Design Award (Japan) in 1990 and the Machine Design Award, 1991 from the Business and Technology Daily News. He is a designer for Nikon Corporation. 5.57

Kazuo Kawasaki, one of Japan's leading industrial designers, was born in Fukui in 1949. Following his graduation from Kanazawa University in 1972, he joined Toshiba and contributed to the design and development of hi-fi audio products. In 1980 he founded eX-DESIGN, INC., where he participated in design theory and practice, working in areas ranging from business strategies and community revitalizations to traditional crafts, interior design and computers. He is currently the director of Kazuo Kawasaki Design Formation. He is also known for being an early pioneer of the Macintosh Computer in Japan. He has received numerous awards, including the 1992 I.C.S.I.D. Excellence Award. He was also given the Mainichi Design Award, one of Japan's most esteemed honours for products designed for the physically handicapped. His work is in the permanent collections of the Cooper-Hewitt Museum, New York, and the Musée des Arts Décoratifs, Paris. 5.87

Eleanor Kearney was educated at Camberwell College of Arts, London. She received a First Class Honours Award from the Worshipful Company of Pewterers in 1993. She has exhibited in Jeddah, Vienna, Dublin, London and New York and lectures on product design at Evesham College and on art and design at Kingsway College, London. 3.55

Michael Kindler is part of the design group metz.schlett.kindler produktdesign. He also works on the design team for the public transport companies of Bremen and Hanover. 3.3

Skip Kirk is the Senior Design Director of Human Factors Industrial Design Inc. He was educated at the Carnegie Mellon University, Pittsburgh where he studied physics, mechanical engineering and architecture. He joined HFID in 1981 and has been involved in a wide range of successful products from surgical skin staplers and medical lasers to industrial measuring equipment and consumer electronics. His credits include over fifty products and eight US patents for inventions. With Paul Lacotta and Walter Stoeckmann he was awarded the IDEA 95 Gold Award for the design of a portable stereo system. 5.82

Toshiyuki Kita was born in Osaka in 1942. He has been working in the field of environmental product design in Milan and Japan since 1969, and is also involved in traditional Japanese craft design. In 1987 he took part in the celebration of the tenth anniversary of the Centre Georges Pompidou, and in 1990 was awarded the Delta de Oro in Spain. In 1991 Kita designed the interiors and a chair for the revolving theatre for Seville Expo '92. His work is in the permanent collections of the Museum of Modern Art, New York (Wink chair, Kick table) and the Design Museum, London. 3.26, 69; 5.35

Makoto Komatsu was born in 1943 in Tokyo and from 1970 to 1973 was assistant to Professor Stig Lindberg at Gustavsberg Porcelain in Sweden. He has achieved national acclaim through various design awards and his work can be seen in the permanent collections of the Museum of Modern Art, New York and the Victoria and Albert Museum, London. He has also held numerous exhibitions including "91 Objects by 91 Designers" Gallery 91 (New York, 1991); "A Perspective on Design" (Montreal, 1993); and an exhibition of Japanese tableware at the Sitama Modern Art Museum (Japan, 1994). 1.124

Kazuyo Komoda was born in Tokyo and studied at the Musashino University of Art. She started her career in industrial and interior design in 1982 and since 1989 has worked in Milan. She is currently a freelance designer and has been working for Denis Santachiara. Her work has been exhibited throughout Europe and Japan as well as being published widely. Clients include Domodinamica, Proggetti and Bernini. 2.40

Jun Konno was born in 1967 and graduated from Chiba University in 1990. He works for Nikon Corporation. 5.57

Defne Koz was born in Ankara, Turkey in 1964. She is a freelance industrial and interior designer based in Istanbul and Milan. She studied Italian literature and language in Ankara, participated in workshops in industrial design at the Middle East Technical University, Ankara, and received a master's degree in Industrial Design from the Domus Academy, Milan. Clients include Steel, Foscarini, Alparda, Progetto-Oggetto, Pesaro and Ala Rossa; she has also undertaken domestic and retail interior design projects in Ankara. On first moving to Milan she spent two years at Sottsass Associati working on projects involving door handles, bathroom accessories, windows and solar cars. 1.56; 3.45

Stephan Koziol was born in 1952. He studies at the Design Academy Hanau, Germany and has his own design studio. 3.66

Randi Kristensen was born in Denmark in 1959. After studying literature and textile design, he moved in 1984 to Milan, where he collaborated with Studio Sowden until 1994. He now works in Milan as a surface designer and has designed for Alessi, Glas, Assia and Talam. 3.31; 4.2

Erik Krogh was born in 1942 and trained as a cabinet-maker and furniture designer at the Danish School of Art and Design and at the Royal Danish Academy. He is currently head of Industrial Design at Danmarks Designskole, has his own workshop and is a freelance journalist for Danish design magazines. He has exhibited his work and been awarded numerous prizes within Denmark. 1.17, 18

Akira Kurosawa represents the Japanese cinema throughout the world. In 1950 with *Rashomon* he brought Japan's film industry to the attention of the international public and since then, with over twenty-six films to his credit, he has become a cultural icon who is recognized throughout the world as a master of his craft. Kurosawa was born in Tokyo at the end of the Meiji Period to a family that held Samurai rank. He began his career as a painter and became involved with film-making in 1936. He has maintained a great love for traditional Japanese art forms whilst achieving a co-existence and dialogue between Eastern and Western art, most notably with his Shakespeare adaptations. His films include *Seven Samurai*, *Yojimbo*, *Dersu Uzala* and *Ran*. In 1995 Kurosawa designed a watch for Swatch as one of a special series dedicated to the cinema. 5.32

Paul Lacotta is Senior Industrial Designer for Human Factors Industrial Design, Inc. He received a BS in industrial science from the Pratt Institute, New York, and has ten years of experience at HFID with over thirty-five product-design and development programs to his credit. He was the winner of Business Week's "Best Products of 1990" and in 1995 was awarded the IDEA Gold Award with Skip Kirk and Walter Stoeckmann for a portable stereo system. 5.82

Danny Lane was born in Urbana, Illinois, in 1955. Largely self-taught, he moved to England in 1975 to work with the stained-glass artist Patrick Reyntiens, then attended Central Saint Martin's College of Art and Design in London, studying painting with a strong emphasis on the esoteric tradition in art and design. In 1983 he co-founded Glassworks with John Creighton and began a three-year association with Ron Arad. He has extended his designs to include work with metal and wood, and has participated in numerous museum and gallery exhibitions and international furniture shows. In 1988 he held three one-man shows in Milan, London and Paris and started producing work for Fiam Italia. Since then he has participated in more individual exhibitions, and in 1990 he received commissions for architectural artworks in Tokyo and Osaka. In 1994 he was commissioned by the Victoria and Albert Museum to install a balustrade of stacked glass in the Museum's new Glass Gallery and also held a one-man show at the Röhss Museum of Arts and Crafts in Göteborg, Sweden. 1.100, 106; 2.1, 10

Marcel Langenegger graduated with a degree in communication design from the Art Centre College of Design, Zurich, in 1992. The following year in Zurich he founded Redhouse, an international agency for design advertising which today also has an office in Los Angeles. Langenegger currently lives and works as a designer and film-maker in Los Angeles. 5.79

Jack Lenor Larsen was born in 1927 in Seattle, Washington. He studied architecture, furniture design and weaving at the University of Washington and elsewhere, and founded his international fabric company in 1953. In 1959 he produced the first printed velvets and in 1961 the first stretch upholsteries. From 1957 to 1959 he was the consultant to the State Department for a grass-weaving project in Taiwan and Vietnam, after which he became Co-director of the Fabric Design Department at the Philadelphia College of Art in Pennsylvania. He has been Artist in Residence at the Royal College of Art, London, and curator of "Wall Hangings" at the Museum of Modern Art, New York. From 1981 to 1989 Larsen was President of the American Craft Council and he became President Emeritus in 1990. In 1992 he founded the LongHouse Foundation in East Hampton, New York. Jack Lenor Larsen is affiliated with most of the leading American design institutions, including the American Institute of Architects and the American Society of Interior Designers, and his work can be seen in the permanent collections of leading design museums worldwide. His latest award was the Brooklyn Museum Design Award for Lifetime Achievement (1993). 4.50, 65

Pietro Ferruccio Laviani was born in Cremona, Italy, in 1960. He studied at Milan Polytechnic, graduating from the Faculty of Architecture in 1985, and undertook further training at the Polytechnic of Design. From 1986 to 1991 he worked in the de Lucchi Studio, and since then he has been a consultant for exhibitions and events at Kartell. He also works as a freelance designer for such companies as Foscarini, Busnelli, Moroso and Mito. 2.48

LCD Design Consultants was founded in 1989 and is active in the fields of product design, packaging, graphics and multimedia. They export extensively to Germany, Italy and Belgium, and their clients include France Télécom, Sagem, Matra Communication, Aris, Legrand and UV Control. In 1995 they were awarded the Janus d'Industrie and the Industry Forum Design, Hanover. Members of their design staff teach at the Ecole Supérieure de Design Industriel (ESDI) in Paris. 5.15

Olivier Leblois was born in 1947 in Paris and studied in Washington, D.C. and in Paris at the Ecole des Beaux-Arts. Today he is a practising architect involved in urban projects and a theoretician lecturing at ESA and CAMONDO, private schools of architecture in Paris. The Cardboard Armchair is his first edited furniture design; his intention is to develop a collection of cardboard furniture. 1.57

Jennifer Lee was born in 1956 in Aberdeenshire, Scotland and attended the Edinburgh College of Art and the Royal College of Art, London. She has held one-person exhibitions at venues including the Victoria and Albert Museum and the Crafts Council, London, and has shown her work at numerous group exhibitions, most recently at the Gallery Koyanagi, Tokyo. Examples of her work can be seen in many permanent UK collections and in the Los Angeles County Museum of Art and the Röhss Museum of Arts and Crafts, Göteborg, Sweden. 3.4

Rainer Lehn was born in 1961. He studied at the University of Darmstadt and received practical training at the Pakistan Design Institute in Karachi. In 1988 he received 2nd Prize in the Laffon Package Design competition and in 1990 won an honourable mention at the Design Centre Nordrhein Westfalen for his Coat Hanger No. 1. 5.70

Anders and **Christina Leideman** were born in Örebro and Skövde, Sweden in 1958 and 1962, respectively. They graduated from the Chalmers University of Technology and started their own company, DesignHuset in 1991, moving to Milan in 1992. They have exhibited designs at the Milan Furniture Fair and also at the Triennale in Milan. The Leidemans currently live and work in Stockholm where they have their own showroom and in 1994 started a collaboration with Collage & Co., also in Stockholm. 1.59

Giovanni Levanti was born in Palermo in 1956. He graduated with a degree in architecture from the University of Palermo in 1983 and later obtained a Master of Industrial Design from the Domus Academy. He collaborated with Andrea Branzi until 1986 and since then has been working as a freelance designer with such clients as Bernini, Cassina, Campeggi, Domodinamica, Foscarini, Memphis, Pallucco, Proggetti and Twergi/Alessi. He is also a teacher at the University of Palermo. Levanti's work has been widely exhibited, most recently at "Nuovo Bel Design" in Milan (1992), and at La Fabbrica Estetica at the Gran Palais, Paris. 2.43

Stefan Lindfors was born in 1962 and studied interior architecture and furniture design at the University of Art and Design, Helsinki. He is a member of the Association of Finnish Interior Architects (SIO) and of the Association of Finnish Sculptors. He has offices in Finland and the USA and works with lighting and furniture companies in Germany, Switzerland, Italy and Finland. Currently he is the Joyce C. Hall Distinguished Professor of Design and Chair of the Design Department at the Kansas City Art Institute, and is internationally recognized for his work in industrial design, sculpture, graphic design, interior architecture, furniture design and scenography. Recent work includes a TV chair for Asko Furniture, Finland; a permanent outdoor sculpture for Ostrobothnian Museum, Vasa, Finland; a design for tableware for First Co., Kansas, and an exhibition of new sculpture, Kansas City (1995). He has also been commissioned by Swatch to create a sculptural clock tower for the 1996 Olympics in Atlanta, Georgia, USA. Lindfors holds a number of major international awards including the Väinö Tanner Trailblazer Award (1992) and the Medal of Honour, Italy's Cup Competition at the Milan Triennale (1986). 1.92

Mary Little trained at the Royal College of Art, London and graduated in 1985. Before founding her own studio in London she worked as a freelance designer in Milan. She makes furniture to commission and for exhibition. 1.77, 78

Josep Lluscà was born in Barcelona in 1948. He studied industrial design at the Escola Eina where he is now professor, and at the Ecole des Arts et Métiers, Montreal. He was vice-president of ADI-FAD (Industrial Designers' Association) from 1985 to 1987, and was one of the founding members of the ADP (Association of Professional Designers). He is also a member of the Design Council of the Catalonian Government. He has been the recipient of several major awards, including the 1990 National Design Award and two prizes from the "ID Design Award in Furniture" presented by *ID* magazine, New York (1993). He frequently attends international exhibitions and conferences, most recently "Catalonia 90's" in New York and "International Design" at the Design Museum, London. 2.30; 5.69

Chi Wing Lo was born in Hong Kong in 1954. He studied architecture at the University of Toronto, where he received his Bachelor of Architecture with honours in 1986, and then at Harvard University, where he gained a Master of Architecture and won the best thesis prize in 1988. He has taught architectural design at Syracuse University in New York and in 1991 was awarded a scholarship and became a member of the Akademie Schloss Solitude in Stuttgart where he also held a solo exhibition of his works, "To Kardizu and Non-secular Landscape". In 1989 he established an Athens-based practice with Panagiota Davladi. Projects include the Crete War Memorial (1990); "Ideas for the Greek Pavilion", presented at the Venice Biennale (1991); "The Alphabet of a Silent Language" (1992); the New German Parliament (1992); the Copenhagen Concert Hall (1993); and the Library of Athens (1994). Chi Wing Lo has won numerous awards for his designs and has exhibited throughout Europe and in America and the Soviet Union. 1.61, 62

Brett Loveday works for the Lunar Design Team creating products for Hewlett-Packard's home products division. 5.18

Vico Magistretti was born in Milan in 1920 and graduated with a degree in architecture in 1945. Since 1967 he has been a member of the Academy of San Luca in Rome. As well as teaching at the Domus Academy in Milan, he is an honorary member of the Royal College of Art in London, where he is a visiting professor. He has been the recipient of numerous major awards including the Gold Medal at the Milan Triennale in 1951, the Compasso d'Oro in 1967 and 1979 and the Gold Medal of the Society of International Artists and Designers in 1986. Magistretti's buildings are primarily found in Italy, but his furniture, lamps and other designs are known internationally. He has worked for numerous companies such as Alias, Artemide, Cassina, de Padova, Fiat, Knoll International, and Rosenthal. He has exhibited widely in Europe, the USA and Japan, and his work can be seen in the most important design collections worldwide. 1.50; 2.19

Hans Maier-Aichen was born in Stuttgart in 1940. He studied interior design at the Academy of Applied Arts in Wuppertal and fine art at the State University of Fine Arts, Munich. He has taught at the Art Institute of Chicago, The Academy of Fine Arts, Münster, and the National Academy of Fine Arts, Karlsruhe. He joined Artipresent GmbH in 1974 as Managing Director and created the Authentics trademark in 1980. From 1978 to 1985 Maier-Aichen was the consultant for cultural affairs in the European Community, Brussels. 5.65

Philipp Mainzer was born in Mainz, Germany in 1969. In 1991 he opened an alternative exhibition space, "Galerie für Eisenwaren" in Hamburg whilst at the same time graduating from Central Saint Martin's College of Art and Design, London where he specialized in product design. He continued his training at the Architectural Association where he is presently undertaking a diploma course. He has exhibited in Germany and the UK. 1.114

Chiaki Maki was born in Toyama, Japan in 1960. She was educated at the Musashino University of Art and the Rhode Island School of Design, and received a Bachelor of Fine Arts in Textile Design in 1985. Before creating Maki Textile Studio in 1990, she worked for various clothing companies in New York and Tokyo, including Toray Co. with Junichi Arai, and trained with Indian weavers in New Delhi. She was a finalist in the International Textile Design Contest sponsored by the Japanese Fashion Foundation in 1986, 1987 and 1990, and has exhibited her work widely in Japan. Today she is a lecturer at the Musashino University of Art and at the Wild Silk Association. 4.36, 37

Kaori Maki was educated at the Rhode Island School of Design and received a Bachelor of Fine Arts in Textile Design in 1988. She then began a professional internship with Jack Lenor Larsen in New York. Before joining her sister Chiaki Maki in the Maki Textile Studio in 1992, she worked as a freelance textile designer in New York, Thailand and Japan. In 1987 she was nominated for the Grand Prix in the American section of the International Textile Design Contest and was again a finalist in that section in 1988. 4.38, 39

Alain Manoha studied social sciences at the University of Pointe à Pitre, Nanterre and at La Sorbonne. He continued his training with an additional course at La Sorbonne in Furniture Design, a subject he studied further at l'ENSCI. He has worked for VIA, who have regularly exhibited his furniture designs. He is also involved in ceramic and lighting design, working for Néotù and ARDI. 3.65

Thierry Manoha was born in Tain l'Hermitage, Drôme, France in 1959. He trained as a potter, specializing in enamel-work, and was awarded the CAP in pottery in 1978. He established his own studio in 1981 whilst also gaining experience in numerous workshops in France and through extensive travel abroad. Two years later he moved to shop/studio premises in Pouzilhac. He has held several solo and group exhibitions in France and has worked many times with Alain Manoha creating items of tableware and ceramics, most notably the Odyssées collection (1993). In 1990 Manoha produced a collection of furniture in volcanic lava and beaten iron. 3.65

Ugo Marano was born in 1943. He studied mosaic in the Vatican and at the Ravenna Academy. He held his first exhibition of sculpture in 1968, at which time he also began his involvement with ceramic design working for the RIFA factory and creating his own studio, Living Museum. In 1975 he founded the Salerno '75 Group. In the 1980s he took part in the Milan Furniture Fair showing one-off pieces of furniture and works of art made from terracotta, mosaic, rusty iron, stone, wood, herbs and trees. He has written several manifestos on his radical and anarchistic style as well as a treatise on a new utopian scheme for town planning. In 1992 he trained 27 potters from Cetara on the Amalfi Coast, choosing ordinary people who were not artists to be his students. He now lives and works in Cetara. 1.80; 3.67, 68

Enzo Mari was born in Novara in 1932 and studied at the Accademia di Belle Arti in Milan. In 1963 he co-ordinated the Italian group Nuove Tendenze and in 1965 was responsible for the exhibition of optical, kinetic and programmed art at the Biennale in Zagreb. He has also taken part in several Biennali in Venice and in the Milan Triennale. In 1972 he participated in "Italy: The New Domestic Landscape" at the Museum of Modern Art, New York. Mari is involved in graphic and industrial design, publishing and the preparation of exhibitions. He has recently been occupied with town planning and teaching and has organized courses for the History of Arts faculty at Milan Polytechnic. He has been awarded the Compasso d'Oro on three occasions and was President of the Association for Industrial Design from 1976 to 1979. His work can be found in the collections of various contemporary art museums including the Stedelijk Museum, Amsterdam, the Musée des Arts Décoratifs, Paris, and the Kunstmuseum, Düsseldorf. 1.82; 3.54

Javier Mariscal was born in Valencia in 1950. He trained as an artist and graphic designer at the Elisava School, Barcelona and collaborated on the Memphis collection in 1981. Early works include an illustrated primer and the "Bar Cel Ona" logo which became one of the symbols for the city. He has designed lights, with Pepe Cortès, for the Barcelona firm Bd Ediciones de Diseño, textiles for Marieta and carpets for Nani Marquina as well as collections of furniture and china-ware for companies such as Alessi, Akaba and Rosenthal. More recently he has produced a cartoon series on "Cobi", the mascot for the Barcelona '92 Olympic Games, which he designed in 1988, and he has worked with Alfredo Arribas on the interior of the Torres de Avila bar in Barcelona. In 1994 he invented and co-ordinated the corporate identity for the post-production company Frame Store (UK). Studio Mariscal is currently collaborating with Canal Plus (Spain) and Colossal Pictures (San Francisco) in the development of an animated cartoon project, Mondo Loco, based on Mariscal's early cartoon characters "Los Garris". 1.126; 4.1

Geoffrey Mason is currently studying at the Sydney College of the Arts, specializing in glass design. He has a Fine Art Diploma in Painting and Print-making, and has exhibited his work at the Jam Factory Craft and Design Centre, Adelaide. 3.15

Ingo Maurer was born in 1932 on the Island of Reichenau, Lake Constance, Germany and trained in typography and graphic design. In 1960 he emigrated to the United States and worked as a freelance designer in New York and San Francisco before returning to Europe in 1963. He founded Design M in Munich in 1966, and since then his lighting designs have achieved world recognition. He has exhibited widely, in shows that include "Ingo Maurer: Making Light", at the Museum Villa Stuck, Munich, and "Licht Licht" at the Stedelijk Museum in Amsterdam, and his work is in the permanent collections of many museums, including the Museum of Modern Art, New York. 2.3, 4

Hilton McConnico was born in Memphis, Tennessee in 1943 and worked initially as a stylist for companies that included Ted Lapidus, Jacques Heim and Yves Saint-Laurent before moving into show business and designing the decor in films such as *La Lune dans le Caniveau* and *Diva*. In the late 1980s he expanded his interests to include textiles, tableware and lighting design as well as painting and photography. Since 1991 his rugs for Toulemonde Bochart have been included in the permanent collections of museums in New York and Lausanne and in the Musées des Arts Décoratifs in Oslo and in Paris. In 1994 he completed his first architecture and interior design project, a restaurant and sandwich bar in the Parisian superstore La Samaritaine. 4.43

Alberto Meda was born in Como, Italy in 1945 and graduated with a degree in mechanical engineering from Milan Polytechnic in 1969. He worked at Magneti Marelli as assistant to the production manager, and at Kartell as executive producer before starting a freelance practice collaborating with a number of clients including Gaggia, Kartell, Centrokappa, Lucifero, Cinelli, FontanaArte, Luceplan, Anslado, Mondedison, Mandarina Duck and Carlo Erba. He has been awarded numerous international prizes including the Compasso d'Oro in 1989 for his Lola lamp and in 1994 for the Metropoli lamp, and the Design Plus in 1992 for his Titania lamp. 2.17

Mette Mikkelsen was educated at the School of Arts and Crafts in Kolding, Denmark, and graduated in 1990. She designs both one-off and mass-produced fabrics collaborating with furniture designers, architects and textile manufacturers nationally and internationally. 4.53

Howard Montgomery is a British industrial designer who was born in Glasgow, Scotland. He studied furniture and product design at Kingston University, Surrey, and graduated from Cranbrook Academy of Art, Michigan, with a degree in design. He practised for several years in lighting design and engineering with Shiu-Kay Kan and architect José Cruzat and is now living and working in the USA. 2.59

Massimo Morozzi was born in Florence in 1941. Today he is an Associate of the CDM Group (Consulenti Design Milano) and develops co-ordinated image projects and product lines. Clients include Alessi, Cassina, Driade, Fiam, Georgetti, Edra and Mazzei and he is currently developing designs for IRJ Corporate Image in Japan. Morozzi is art director of Edra and Mazzei and in 1990 he set up Morozzi & Partners together with Silvia Centeleghe, Giovanni Lauda and Cristina Dosio Morozzi. He lectures in Amsterdam, San Paolo, Melbourne and at the Domus Academy and the Istituto Europeo di Disegno in Milan. 1.89

Jasper Morrison was born in London in 1959. He studied at the Kingston School of Art, Surrey and the Royal College of Art, and won a Berlin scholarship in 1984. In 1986 he established his own design office in London. He designs for SCP, Cappellini, Alias and Vitra, amongst others, and lectures at the Hochschule der Künste, Berlin and Saarbrücken, the Istituto Europeo di Disegno, Milan and the Royal College of Art, London. He has exhibited widely in Europe and the UK, most notably for Vitra in Milan, at the Kunstmuseum in Düsseldorf and at Galerie Néotù, Paris. 1.51, 94; 5.13

Heike Mühlhaus was born in 1954 in Wiesbaden-Sonnenberg, Germany and studied design and ceramics in the Fachhochschule at Wiesbaden where she graduated with a Design Diploma. She founded Cocktail in 1992 since which time she has exhibited her work extensively in Germany. Examples can be found in the permanent collections of the Kestner-Museum in Hanover, the Berliner Kunstgewerbe Museum and the Magdeburger Museen. 3.63, 64

Katsushi Nagumo was born in the Nigata prefecture of Japan in 1956 and graduated from the Tokyo Zokei University of Art and Design in 1979. He started his career in the studio of Jo Nagahara & Associates, and left in 1987 to open his own workshop. He was made a member of the Japan Urban Design Institute in 1992 and has produced work for Daitsu. He has been the recipient of many design awards in Japan. 1.46

Alexander Neumeister see **Angela Carvalho**

Carlos Neville is an art student specializing in cartoons. He attended the School of Visual Arts, New York and is currently living in New Orleans and working with YA/YA, Inc. During his time as a guild member with YA/YA he has designed for Swatch, Alessi and MTV. He has been featured on "MTV House of Styles" and "Sesame Street". 1.1

Marc Newson was born in Sydney in 1963 and graduated from the Sydney College of Art in 1984. In 1985 the Powerhouse Museum, Sydney acquired some of his designs for their permanent collection, and at the same time offered him a Craft Council Grant to devise new work. Since 1987 he has worked periodically in Japan for Idée, creating, amongst other designs, the Rattan and Felt series. Newson lives in Paris and is currently working on new designs and forthcoming exhibitions in New York and Los Angeles. 5.29, 67

Adriane Nicolaisen studied anthropology at the University of California, Berkeley, and graduated with a BA in 1972. Throughout the 1970s and 1980s she studied at both the Mendocino Art Center and Berkeley. She is the founder of Handwoven Webworks which, since 1987, has been producing original designs of handwoven fabrics and apparel. She has exhibited her work at the American Crafts Council in Baltimore and San Francisco each year since 1991, and other recent shows include "Adriane Nicolaisen Handwovens and Mark Sutton Jewellery" at the Mind's Eye in Scottscale, Arizona (1994) and the Flying Shuttle in Seattle, Washington, also in 1994. Adriane has taught textile design at the Mendocino Art Center, where she was Artist in Residence in 1990, and at the College of the Redwoods, Fort Bragg, California. 4.63

Ninaber/Peters/Krouwel Industrial Design was established in 1985 by Bruno Ninaber van Eyben, Wolfram Peters and Peter Krouwel with the aim of producing a wide variety of line-assembly and mass-produced products for the consumer and professional market. Ninaber graduated from Maastricht Art Academy in 1971, Peters and Krouwel from the Delft Technical University in 1978. Their work covers all stages from design through development to pre-production management. They have won recognition both within The Netherlands and abroad, and their designs can be seen in the permanent collections of the Museum of Modern Art, New York, the Stedelijk Museum, Amsterdam and the Design Museum, London, among others. In 1990 nine of their products received a Gute Industrieform recognition. 5.20, 47

Katsuhiko Ogino was born in 1944 and graduated from the Musashino University of Art in 1966. From then until 1969 he was a lecturer at the Japan Design School after which he established various practices – Mono-Pro Kogei (1972), Humpty Dumpty Ltd (1976) and Time Studio Ltd (1978). He has received national recognition for his work and in 1986 was made a member of the Craft Centre Japan, of which he is now director. 3.24

Sinya Okayama was born in 1941 in Osaka where he is now a freelance architect and interior designer. Since 1981 he has also started production of a series of original design furniture and lighting appliances under the Sinya brand name. He has shown in the USA, Italy and Japan and in 1986 collaborated with Alessandro Mendini in the exhibition "Sei Mobiletti" at the Museo Alchimia. His work can be seen in the permanent collections of the Musée des Arts Décoratifs, Montreal; the Philadelphia Museum of Art; the Cooper-Hewitt Museum, the Museum of Modern Art and the Metropolitan Museum of Art, New York. 1.65, 68

Paola Palma and **Carlo Vannicola** are architects and designers, but spend most of their time teaching furniture, interior and industrial design in Florence. They are the founding members of the "Made Useful Art and Design" group which is involved in design research, and are also consultants for the fashion exhibition "Firenze Pronto Moda" for which they design exhibition stands and advertising. Their expertise covers furniture design, with clients such as Zeritalia, BRF and Oliko; jewellery design for Flavio Mancini; carpets (Sisal Collezioni); and industrial design. Palma and Vannicola also collaborated with Gae Aulenti and B. Ballestrero in the design of the entrance and reception areas of the Florence Railway Station for which they created the Gap and Novella lamps. Their work has been exhibited widely both in Italy and abroad and has received numerous international awards. 3.16

Verner Panton is a Danish architect, born in 1926 in Gamtofts. He trained at the Copenhagen Royal Academy of Fine Arts and continued his studies in various European countries between 1953 and 1955. His innovative early designs include a series of architectural projects built between 1957 and 1960 such as the "Cardboard House" (Denmark, 1957) and the "Plastic House" (Denmark, 1960). He continued with numerous interior design schemes including the Junior Casino (Germany, 1973) and the Gruner and Jahr Publishing House (Hamburg, 1974). He is recognized as a leading design figure in Denmark and Germany and is a Fellow of the Royal Society of Arts, London. He was a visiting professor for industrial design at the Hochschule für Gestaltung in Offenbach until 1984. 1.87

Guinter Parschalk has a degree in architecture and a Master of Industrial Design. In 1983 he was commissioned by the architect Ricardo Ohtake to supervise the audio-visual department of the Centro Cultural São Paulo. Today he works in his own studio developing projects in architecture, lighting and product design. 2.55

Terri Pecora was born in 1958 in Idaho, USA, and grew up in California. She studied fashion illustration at the Art Center College of Design in Pasadena, and then moved to Milan in 1989 to take a course in product design at the Domus Academy. She established her own studio in 1991. Clients include Authentics, Edra, Esprit, Silhouette, Swatch and Sech Ratan. 1.36; 2.15; 5.88

Jirí Pelcl was born in the Czech Republic. He studied architecture at the Academy of Applied Arts in Prague and furniture design at the Royal College of Art in London. He is a founding member of the group Allka and since 1990 has run his own architectural/design studio. Commissions include Vaclav Havel's study in Prague Castle (1990); the interior of St Lawrence Church, Prague (1994); the interiors of the Czech Embassy in Rome (1995); the interiors of the Ministry of Foreign Affairs, Prague (1995) and Cernin's Palace in Prague (1995). He has exhibited in Prague, Brno, Vienna, Berlin, Munich, Amsterdam and Paris. 1.116

Nestor Perkal is an Argentinian architect and designer. Born in Buenos Aires in 1951, he now lives and works in Paris. He opened a gallery to promote new design (1982–94) and has been the Artistic Director of Algorithme since 1987. He was also commissioned by the Ministry of Culture to found and direct the Centre for Research into Craft at the Ecole Nationale des Arts Décoratifs, Limoges. His work includes furniture for the Musée des Arts Décoratifs, Paris, and for the Fonds National d'Art Contemporain; lamps for Drimmer and Algorithme; and a series of interior architecture projects, most recently the seminar centre, conservation department and communal areas of the Fondation Cartier, Paris. He has exhibited his work in France, Prague and Italy. 2.44

Gaetano Pesce was born in 1939 in La Spezia, Italy and studied in the architecture department of the University of Venice between 1959 and 1965. He is currently Professor at the Institut d'Architecture et Etudes Urbaines in Strasbourg, although he lives and works in New York and has an office in Paris. Pesce is known for his multi-disciplinary approach, and his work ranges from architecture to industrial design, exhibition design, drawing, sculpture, music, fashion and urban planning. He has worked for companies internationally such as Cassina, Italy; Knoll International, USA; and Vitra, Switzerland. Many of his works are in the permanent collection of major design museums including the Metropolitan Museum of Art, New York; the Musée des Arts Décoratifs and the Centre Georges Pompidou, Paris; and the Musée des Arts Décoratifs, Montreal. Major works include the "Organic Building", Osaka (1990–93), and the Chiat/Day office, New York. 1.66; 2.7; 3.8, 44; 5.41, 76

Roberto Pezzetta was born in Treviso, Italy, in 1946. He began his career as a product designer in 1969 and has been head of Zanussi Elettrodomestici Industrial Design Centre since 1982. His designs have been exhibited in several museums within Europe and he has been awarded many European design awards including the Compasso d'Oro in 1981 together with the Zanussi Industrial Design Centre. Five of his products were also selected at the Compasso d'Oro in 1987, 1989 and 1991. Pezzetta is currently the Director of Design for the Electrolux European Design Management. 5.5, 64

Andrea Ponsi was born in 1949 in Viareggio, Italy, and holds degrees in architecture from the University of Florence, the Architectural Association in London and the University of Pennsylvania. In the early 1970s he focused on the relationship between architecture and ecology and participated in the design of experimental communities in California. Upon his return to Italy in 1988, he concentrated on interior architecture and product design, establishing Andrea Ponsi Design, a studio dedicated to the production of interior furnishings. In 1995 *Design Elementaire* was published, a monograph on his design theory and recent work. He has taught at the University of California at Berkeley, the California College of Arts and Crafts, the University of Toronto and since 1990 has been a visiting professor at Syracuse University. 2.14

Gregory Prade has worked in lighting design for the last four years. He was born in America and studied in San Antonio, Texas and in Milan. He has worked in the oil fields of Alaska, with F. Hundertwasser on the illumination of the Spittlauer Tower in Vienna and with the Ingo Maurer team in Munich. He currently lives and works in Sulzberg, Germany. 2.50

Andrée Putman, the Parisian interior designer, initially studied music at the Paris Conservatoire with François Pulenc. After several years as a stylist and journalist, she founded the design company Créateurs et Industriels, working with fashion designers such as Issey Miyake and Jean-Charles de Castelbajac. Today her own enterprise, Ecart International, focuses on the production and revival of classic furniture design and modernist accessories. She has worked with deSede, Charles Jourdan, Sasaki and Toulemonde Bochart, among other companies, and her interior design projects have brought her world fame. These include Morgans Hotel, New York; the Wasserturm Hotel, Cologne; Le Lac, Japan; villas and shops for the clock and watch company Ebel; offices for the French Minister of Culture; an art museum in Rouen; and the Museum of Modern Art in Bordeaux. Work carried out in 1993–94 includes the headquarters of Air France; the Hotel Sheraton, Paris-Roissy, and the concept for the chain of Bally shoe shops worldwide. 4.5

Pol Quadens is a freelance furniture designer who lives and works in Brussels. He has recently started working for Italian companies as a consultant; he also produces work by other Belgian designers. 5.24

Karim Rashid received a Bachelor of Industrial Design degree in 1982 from Carleton University in Ottawa, Canada. He completed his graduate studies in Italy under Ettore Sottsass and Gaetano Pesce, then moved to Milan on a one-year scholarship at the studio of Rodolfo Bonetto. On his return to Canada he worked for seven years with KAN Industrial Designers in Toronto as head designer on projects ranging from hi-tech products to furniture. He also co-founded and designed the Babel Collection (a clothing range for men and women) before setting up North Studio, a conceptual-based studio producing objects for exhibitions and galleries worldwide. Since 1991 he has been principal designer for Karim Rashid Industrial Design. Projects include furniture, lighting, houseware and product designs. Rashid has been a faculty member at the Ontario College of Art and a full-time assistant professor at the Rhode Island School of Design and today is assistant professor of industrial design at the Pratt Institute, New York and at the University of the Arts, Philadelphia. His work has received international recognition. 2.25

Ravage is a Paris-based design company that produces ceramics and textiles for manufacturers such as Sasaki, Swatch, Italseta and Pawson. 3.30; 4.52

Heinz Röntgen is a self-taught designer. In the 1950s he worked independently and also as a consultant for textile and embroidery manufacturers specializing in fashion fabrics. In 1964 he began to market his work through his own company, nya nordiska, and has since diversified into furnishing fabrics. He has been awarded numerous design prizes in Germany and Switzerland. 4.44, 56

Aldo Rossi was born in Milan in 1931 and studied architecture at Milan Polytechnic. In 1960 he became Director of the magazine *Casabella* and a year later founded his own studio. In 1965 Rossi became Professor at the Milan Polytechnic and subsequently at the Architectural Institute of Venice. He has lectured in Zurich and at Harvard and Yale Universities. In 1988 he received the first prize in the design competition for the National Museum of Berlin History and in 1990 the Pritzker Prize. His most important works include the Modena Cemetery, a residential housing scheme in the Gallaterese district of Milan, the Theatre of the World and the Lighthouse Theatre in Lake Ontario, the Architecture School of Miami University and the hotel Il Palazzo in Fukuoka. Rossi has designed furniture for Molteni and Unifor and products for Alessi. 1.52

Michael Rowe was born in 1948 in High Wycombe, England. He graduated from the Royal College of Art, London, in 1972 and set up his own metalworking studio. He became head of the Department of Metalwork and Jewellery at the RCA in 1984. Rowe's work is in the British Crafts Council, the municipal galleries of Birmingham and Leeds, the Victoria and Albert Museum in London, the Karlsruhe Museum in Germany, the Art Gallery of Western Australia, the Stedelijk Museum in Amsterdam and the Vestlandske Kunstindustrimuseum, Bergen, Norway. 3.17

Cheryl Stuart-Ruine and **Paul Ruine** were born in New York in 1951 and 1947 respectively. Cheryl received a master's degree in art, with a speciality in sculpture and photography from the Pratt Institute in New York. Paul studied jewellery design in the 1960s before opening a shop in New York specializing in twentieth-century design. Ruine Design Associates, founded in 1987, produces furniture, lighting, accessories, fabrics and jewellery, often signed and in limited editions. 1.37

Rolf Sachs studied business administration in London and San Francisco but his interest in art, design and film has resulted in his career as a furniture designer specializing in one-off and limited-edition sculptural pieces. He has held one-man shows in Germany and exhibited in Germany, Austria and Paris. 1.15, 125

Gunnel Sahlin was born in 1954 in Umel, Sweden. He studied textile art and design and has worked for Kosta Boda since 1986. He has held solo shows of his work throughout Sweden and in Japan and the USA. His work is represented in numerous design museums including the National Museum of Stockholm, the Tel Aviv Museum in Israel and the Museum of Glass in Corning, New York. 3.10, 13

Jeffrey Salazar graduated from the Art Center College of Design, Pasadena, California in 1994 with a bachelor's degree in industrial design. He joined Lunar Design following his graduation. 5.17

Thomas Sandell was born in Jakobstad, Finland, and started his architectural training at the KTH in Stockholm. Since 1985 he has been employed by the architectural office of Professor Jan Henriksson and has worked on several projects within Sweden, including the Café for the National Museum of Cultural History in Stockholm and the Eden Hotel, also in Stockholm. 1.55

Denis Santachiara was born in Reggio-Emilia, Italy, and now lives and works in Milan. He collaborates with major European manufacturers such as Oceano Oltreluce, Artemide, Kartell, Vitra, Yamagiwa, Domodinamica and Zerodisegno. His work has been exhibited in private and public galleries, and he has taken part in the Venice Biennale and Documenta Kassel, as well as the Milan Triennale in 1982, 1984, 1986 and 1988. 1.40

Johan Santer studied at the Central Saint Martin's School of Art and Design, London, and taught industrial design before joining Pentagram, where in 1989 he became an associate. He has worked on a wide range of consumer and industrial products, including Kenwood food-mixers and kitchen appliances, Reuters monitors and keyboards, Thorn lighting and Wilkinson Sword razors. He has also been involved in the development of a range of bathroom fittings for Inax, one of Japan's largest tile manufacturers. He has received a number of awards including the "G-Mark" for Good Product Design from Japan's Ministry of Trade and Industry. His product designs are on permanent display at the Design Museum in London. 5.40

Peter Schmitz was born in 1959 in Duisburg, Germany. He was trained in window-display design but from 1982 to 1986 studied product design and metalwork in Hildesheim setting up his own studio there in 1982. Since 1995 he has been Professor of Design at the Fachhochschule in Düsseldorf and has exhibited his work widely in Germany. He has been the recipient of several awards, most recently the Peter Joseph Krahe prize for Architecture in Braunschweig (1994). 3.58

Wulf Schneider was born in 1943 and studied furniture construction and interior design at the Free College of Art and the State Academy of Visual Arts in Stuttgart. He has held management positions with a number of architectural firms and in 1976 he founded the Office for Design Concepts. His activities include environmental design, interior design, consultancy for industrial and furniture companies, design and development of buildings and furniture, and writing. He has received national and international awards and since 1991 has been Professor of Design at Munich Technical College. 1.113

Frank Schreiner was born in 1959. Since 1981 he has worked in experimental graphics for broadcasting, art and product design, collaborating with both Kershin Quitsch (from 1988) and Stiletto Studio (from 1991). He has held solo exhibitions internationally in Vienna, New York, Ljublijana and Stuttgart. 2.11

Christian Schwamkrug was born in Düsseldorf, Germany, in 1957. He received a diploma in industrial design from the University of Wuppertal after which he worked on a freelance basis for several design studios. He has been a designer for Porsche Design, Zell am See, Austria since 1987. 5.16

Carlos Segura was born in Cuba but moved to the United States in 1965. He lived first in Miami, where he was involved in the pop music industry working as drummer and public relations manager for his own band. On leaving the group he compiled all the graphic design work he had used for promotions into a book and on its strength was employed in a production agency in New Orleans. He relocated to Chicago in 1980 and worked for advertising agencies such as Masteller, Foote Cone & Belding and DDB Needham. In 1991 he founded Segura Inc. so that he could pursue his interest in design and created [T-26], a new digital type foundry, in order to diversify into typographical and graphic design. 5.77, 78

Andrew Serbinski is the principal of Machineart Industrial Design. He is a graduate of the Pratt Institute, New York. From 1973 to 1975 he worked in Tokyo designing office automation products for export markets. He established Machineart in 1988 and consults regularly with Japanese corporations. 5.86

Zeukyau Shichida was born in Yokohama in 1964. She studied architecture at the Musashino University of Art from 1988 to 1991 and edited the design magazine *Icon*. Since 1991 she has been a freelance editor and has worked for various design and architecture periodicals. In 1994 Shichida established her own brand name, Kwau Shau An, manufacturing lighting, furniture and accessories for the home and office. 2.57

Kotaro Shimogori was born in Tokyo in 1960 but since 1979 has lived and worked in Los Angeles. He is an internationally recognized product designer and has worked on various pieces of office equipment including desktop calendars, writing instruments and other accessories. He is also involved in industrial design and has worked on numerous consumer items, including computer peripheral devices, mass-market media dispensers, food dispensers and a series of patented chopsticks in holders. As a furniture designer, he founded IDT, which manufactures and distributes his patented table designs and chairs worldwide. 1.115

Dieter Sieger established his own architect's office in Münster-Albachten, Germany, following his graduation from the Dortmund School of Arts and Crafts in 1964. From 1965 to 1976 he was occupied with the design and construction of terraced houses and single-family houses in Greece, Spain, France, the USA and Saudi Arabia. An interest in sailing led to his interior design for sailing and motor yachts, which in turn has resulted in a collaboration with Dornbracht, and designs for modern equipment for private bathrooms. In recent years he has also ventured into ceramic design. Sieger has been awarded state prizes in Japan, Northern Westphalia and The Netherlands and his work has been exhibited worldwide. In 1994 a solo show, "Dieter Sieger – Architect, Shipbuilder, Designer", was held at the Stadtmuseum Münster. 3.40; 5.46

Borek Sípek was born in Prague in 1949. After taking a furniture design course at the School for Arts and Crafts in Prague he moved to Germany in 1968 where he studied architecture in Hamburg and took a philosophy course in Stuttgart. Before moving to Amsterdam in 1983 he taught design theory at the University of Essen and was the scientific assistant at the Institute for Industrial Design at the University of Hanover. Since starting his own architecture and design studio in 1983 he has held numerous solo exhibitions including shows at the Musée des Arts Décoratifs, Paris; the Stedelijk Museum, Amsterdam; the Vitra Design Museum, Weil am Rhein; and the Umeleckoprumyslové Muzeum, Prague. His work can be seen in the permanent collections of major design museums worldwide and he has been honoured internationally, receiving La Croix Chevalier dans l'Ordre des Arts et des Lettres from the French government in 1991 and the Prins Bernard Fonds Prize for Architecture and Applied Arts in 1993. Recent works include interior design projects such as the offices for Art Factory, a computer animation company in Prague (1995) and the conversion of a warehouse to showroom/art gallery in Amsterdam for the Steltman Gallery (1995). Sípek is currently senior lecturer in

Architecture at the Prague Academy of Applied Arts. 1.29, 38; 3.57

James Smith was born in Wales, UK in 1970 and received a master's degree in industrial design from Leicester University in 1992. He then moved to Milan and worked as apprentice to Alessandro Mendini and later for Swatch. In 1995 he set up his own studio in Amsterdam working on products and graphics. 5.30

Ayala Sperling-Serfaty was born in Israel in 1962. Following early education and military service in Israel, she studied fine art at Middlesex Polytechnic, UK and art history and philosophy at Tel-Aviv University. She was awarded a scholarship from the Sharet Fund, Israel, in 1984 and presented with first prize in the Annual Furniture Design Competition in Israel in 1993. Her work has been exhibited in Israel and published in Israel, Japan and Italy. 1.108; 2.36, 37

Philippe Starck was born in Paris in 1949. After a period of activity in New York, he returned to France where he has since built up an international reputation. He has been responsible for major interior design schemes, including François Mitterrand's apartment at the Elysée Palace, the Café Costes, and the Royalton and Paramount hotels in New York. He has also created domestic and public multi-purpose buildings such as the headquarters of Asahi Beer in Tokyo. As a product designer he works for companies throughout the world, collaborating with Alessi, Baleri, Baum, Disform, Driade, Flos, Kartell, Rapsel, Up & Up, Vitra and Vuitton. His many awards include the Grand Prix National de la Création Industrielle. His work can be seen in the permanent collections of all the major design museums. 1.63, 64; 5.1–4, 28

Walter Stoeckmann is a mechanical engineer at Human Factors Industrial Design, Inc. He received a B.E.T. from the University of New Hampshire and has an associate degree in design and drafting. He has worked for HFID for eight years and with Skip Kirk and Paul Lacotta received the IDEA 95 Gold Award for a portable stereo system. 5.82

Reiko Sudo was born in Ibaraki Prefecture, Japan, and educated at the Musashino University of Art. From 1975 to 1977 she assisted Professor Tanaka in the Textile Department. Before co-founding Nuno Corporation in 1984, she worked as a freelance textile designer and has since designed for the International Wool Secretariat, Paris, and the clothing company Threads, Tokyo. She is currently the Director of Nuno Corporation and a lecturer at the Musashino University of Art. She has exhibited both nationally and internationally, and her work can be seen in the permanent collections of the Museum of Modern Art and the Cooper-Hewitt Museum, New York; the Museum of Art, Rhode Island School of Design; the Philadelphia Museum of Art; the Museum of Applied Arts, Helsinki; and the Musée des Arts Décoratifs, Montreal. She has received many prizes for her work including the Roscoe Award in 1993 and 1994, and is a member of the Japan Interior Designers Association. 4.40–42

Yoshitaka Sumimoto was born in Ono City, Hyogo in 1953 and graduated from Kobe University Department of Civil Engineering in 1978. He established Design EMI Associates in 1980 and became the Managing Director in 1985 when he was awarded the Good Design Prize for products used in light industry. He has designed for Silky and Mitsubishi, Japan. 5.48, 62

Svitalia Design was founded in 1986 by Susann Guempel and Urs Kamber. They have studios in Agra, Switzerland and Milan. Susann Guempel was born in 1956 in Germany and studied textile design in Basel. Urs Kamber was born in 1948 in Switzerland. He studied architecture in Zurich, interior design in Basel and industrial design in Milan. The practice is involved in product design, interior decoration, interior architecture for industrial projects and private commissions. Since 1989 Svitalia have manufactured under their own name. Guempel and Kamber have exhibited both nationally and internationally and lecture in experimental design at the Istituto Europeo di Disegno, Milan, and Cagliari. 2.52

Iyer Swaminathan took a bachelor's degree in mechanical engineering, then joined an industrial centre in Bombay. In 1992, after a master's programme in design, he worked with several firms in Bombay before setting up his own design studio, Shell Design. 5.61

Shinkichi Tanaka was born in 1950. In 1972 he graduated from the Kuwasawa Design School and entered Aiwa Co., Ltd. Since 1978 he has been working for Zero-one Design Establishment. 5.39

David Trubridge is a designer and cabinet-maker working in the UK and New Zealand. His works can be found in the permanent collections of the Victoria and Albert Museum, London, and the Auckland Museum, New Zealand. He has received various New Zealand design awards and has exhibited in New Zealand, Tokyo, San Francisco, Chicago and Munich. 1.47

Jan Truman is a professional textile artist who studied at the Royal College of Art, London for a master's degree in Textile Design. She has been working as a full-time designer since 1980 and now runs her own small business, called Wireworks, specializing in three-dimensional structures. She is the Publicity Officer for the Textile Society and has recently held exhibitions in the UK and Japan. 4.48

Oscar Tusquets Blanca was born in Barcelona in 1941. He attended the Escuela Técnica Superior de Arquitectura, Barcelona, and in 1964 established Studio Per with Lluis Clotet, collaborating on nearly all their projects until 1984. He has been a guest professor and lecturer at universities in Germany, France and the USA, and his work has been exhibited worldwide. Both his architecture and his design projects have received many awards. 1.20

Paul Tuttle is an American designer who was born in Springfield, Missouri, in 1918. He has been associated with Alvin Lustig, Knoll Associates, Welton Becket and Associates, architect Thornton Ladd, Doetsch and Grether, Strässle International and Atelier International. His work can be found in many of the leading permanent collections within the USA and he has exhibited widely both nationally and internationally in shows such as "Innovative Furniture in America 1800 to the Present", at the Cooper-Hewitt Museum, New York (1981) and "21 Tools for Relaxing", a travelling exhibition organized by the Copenhagen Fair (1986). Several books have been published on his work. 1.88

Shigeru Uchida was born in Yokohama, Japan, in 1943 and graduated from the Kuwasawa Design School in Tokyo in 1966. In 1970 he established the Uchida Design Studio, which was followed in 1981 by Studio 80, founded with Toru Nishioka. He has lectured at universities and design schools in Japan, the USA and Italy and at IDEA '93 in Melbourne. Currently he is a lecturer at Milan Polytechnic. Uchida is best known for his interior design projects which include the Wave Building in Roppongo, Tokyo, Il Palazzo hotel in Fukuoka and La Ranarita in Azumabashi, Tokyo. His most recent schemes are the lobby at the Kyoto Hotel (1994) and the bar lounge Bar Roose and restaurants Mira Mar, and Bahia Blanca at the Osaka World Trade Centre Building. Product design clients include Alessi, Esprit and Chairs. He has exhibited internationally, and his work can be found in the permanent collections of the Metropolitan Museum of Art, New York, the Denver Art Museum, the San Francisco Museum of Modern Art, and the Musée des Arts Décoratifs, Montreal. In 1995 he held the Shigeru Uchida Tearoom Exhibition "Method Remembered" at the Spazio Krizia in Milan. 3.19–23

Sofia Uddén was born in 1964. She attended the Gorkesborgs Art School, Stockholm, and had further training at the National College of Arts and Crafts, Stockholm, where she studied painting and interior design. She has also spent time at Middlesex Polytechnic, UK, and at the Royal Institute of Technology, Stockholm, where she studied architecture. 3.49, 50

Masanori Umeda was born in Kanagawa, Japan, in 1941 and graduated from Kuwasawa Design School in Tokyo in 1962. In 1967 he moved to Italy to work for the studio of Achille and Piero Giacomo Castiglioni in Milan, and for Ettore Sottsass, participating in the design of the Memphis collection. In 1986 he established U-Meta Design Inc. in Tokyo. Major projects include the interior design for the restaurant and bar Ginza MG Planet, the Mutsugoro cup and saucer, the Xspace office toilet system for INAX corporation, the interior design for Tomato Bank in Okayama, and the Getsuen chair, Ros chair, Sishun chair and Antherium table for Edra. He has exhibited widely and his designs can be seen in the permanent collections of the Museum of Modern Art, Kyoto; the Metropolitan Museum of Art, New York; the Musée des Arts Décoratifs, Montreal; and the Denver Art Museum. 1.118; 2.60

Jaap van Arkel was born in Utrecht in 1967. After military service he joined the Akademie Industriële Vormgeving in Eindhoven where he is currently a student. 1.60

Christine Van der Hurd is principal and creative director of her own New York-based textile design studio where she works on a range of fabrics from limited-edition carpets to decorative tapestries, cushions, home fashion accessories and glassware; her specialization is in couture floor coverings commissioned to the specifications of architects and designers. She was born in London and trained at the Winchester College of Art. After graduation she designed textiles on a freelance basis for names such as Kenzo, Cacherel, Mary Quant and Biba. She moved to the United States in 1976 and worked for Donghia and for Jack Lenor Larsen before launching her own studio in 1980 and her Greenwich Village showroom in 1992. In 1993 she began to offer custom machine-made broadlooms in wool and nylon for larger residential and specialized contract use. 4.3

Marc van Hoe is a Belgian textile designer. He studied industrial design, fine art and textile history and opened his own workshop in 1975. He is involved in technical research into industrial textiles and fibre art and his work can be seen in the permanent collections of several museums. 4.45

Dick van Hoff was born in 1971 in Amsterdam and studied at the College of Arts in Arnhem. He designs for Droog Design in The Netherlands. 5.25

Katrien Van Liefferinge originally trained as a cabinet-maker in Belgium, her native country. She completed her studies in the UK at the Leeds Metropolitan University and the Glasgow School of Art, gaining a BA Hons in three-dimensional design and an MA in art and design. Ranging from one-off commissions through to product design and theatre design, her work has received critical acclaim in Paris and New York. 2.5

Guido Venturini was born in Alfonsine, Italy in 1957. He graduated as an architect in Florence, where he still collaborates with Professor R. Buri on the interior decoration course. Together with Stefano Giovannoni he took second prize in the Shinkenchiku Residential Design Competition and founded the King-Kong Production Company. In 1988 he was the winner of the competition to restructure the town centre of Castel di Sangro. In the same year he taught at the Domus Academy and designed the Casa Martini in Alfonsine. In 1989 he designed the Maddalena bar in Prato, with King-Kong. He designs for a number of companies including Alessi, Ultima Edizione and Bianchi & Bruni. His works have been displayed in exhibitions in Italy and abroad. 5.71

Arnout Visser was born in 1962 in Middelburg, The Netherlands and studied at the College of Arts in Arnhem (1984–89) and at the Domus Academy in Milan (1990–91). Since graduation he has been working freelance, designing in glass, metal and recycled materials. His work can be found in several museums including the Boymans-Van Beuningen in Rotterdam, the Museum für Angewandte Kunst in Cologne and the Design Museum in London. 3.56

Norbert Wangen was born in Prüm, Germany, and served his apprenticeship as a carpenter from 1981 to 1983 after which he studied architecture in Aachen and Munich. 1.71

Hartmut Weise was born in 1953 in Halle, Germany. He graduated with honours from the Burg Giebichenstein, the highest ranking design college in what used to be East Germany. Since 1991 he has been a house designer for FSB. 5.59

Carol Westfall studied at the Rhode Island School of Design and at the Maryland Institute College of Art. She has exhibited her work in various museums throughout the United States including the Museum of Art, Carnegie Institute, Pittsburgh; the Textile Museum, Washington; and the Baltimore Art Museum, Maryland. She is also known in Japan and India and has participated in shows in France, Mexico, Canada and Switzerland. Westfall has received recognition for her work in awards such as the Artpark Residency, an Indo-American Fellowship and the Governor of New Jersey Purchase Award. Her designs can be found in permanent collections in both the USA and Japan. 4.57

Robert A. Wettstein was born in Zurich in 1960 and is a self-taught furniture designer. He founded his own studio, Structure Design, in 1985 and today works for clients such as Anthologie Quartett, Authentics artipresent and Noto Zeus. He has held solo exhibitions in Italy and Germany and his clothes stand Herz and lamp Spunk form part of the permanent collection of the Kunstmuseum, Düsseldorf. 1.91; 2.51; 5.10, 27

Weyers and Borms are self-taught designers. They were born in the 1960s. 2.2, 8, 9, 13

Rupert Williamson studied at the Royal College of Art, London and formed his own studio/workshop in 1976. He works as a designer and maker of one-off pieces of furniture, usually to commission, using wood as his primary material. His work is represented in several national museum collections. 1.112

Herman Wittocx was born in 1949 and has been working as a freelance designer since 1979. He is a member of the Flemish Designers Association and has exhibited in Belgium, Switzerland, Germany, The Netherlands, France and, most recently, at the International Contemporary Furniture Fair in New York. His work has been published in many of the leading design periodicals. 5.50

Helmut Wolf is a designer of objects in precious stones. He was born in Idar-Oberstein, Germany, in 1940 and studied at the Weiherschleife Institute. He set up his own studio in 1968, and his designs have won numerous prizes such as the State Prize of the Palatinate in 1972, and the first prize at the International Gemstone Competition at Idar-Oberstein in 1984. He currently collaborates with Eva-Maria Melchers. 3.48

Gil Wong, an industrial designer, joined Lunar Design in 1987 and has worked on projects ranging from computers to medical products for such clients as Hewlett-Packard, Apple Computer, Coherent Medical and Zenith Data Systems. Wong has received numerous national and international design awards and patents, and his work has appeared in various design books and publications. He was born in Hong Kong and graduated with a BSID degree from San Jose State University in California. 5.17

Terence Woodgate was born in London in 1953. He studied at Westminster and Middlesex Colleges and in the mid 1980s he spent two years at what is now known as the London Guildhall University. His present work consists mainly of furniture, lighting and product design. His clients include Cappellini, Casas, Concord Lighting, Punt Mobles, SCP, Teunen and Teunen and Victoria Design. He has won two major design awards; the British Design Award 1992, and the German Design Award "Die Besten der Besten Design Innovationen 1992". His work is exhibited in the collection of the Museo de las Artes Decorativas, Barcelona, and in the review collection of the Design Museum, London. In 1994 he set up a studio in Portugal where he now lives and works. 1.22

YA/YA or Young Aspirations/Young Artists, is a collective of individual artists, founded in 1988. Located in New Orleans, Louisiana, it consists of a group of thirty high school and college students. The students work with Jana Napoli, the founder of YA/YA, and four other professional artists to develop technical skills whilst producing works that reflect their culture and community. YA/YA's Guild System, Mural Project, Outreach Programme and appearances on television shows such as "Sesame Street" also ensure that their teaching reaches as wide an audience as possible. 1.1, 14

Yamo graduated from the National Arts School of Algiers in 1982 and from the Ecole National Supérieure des Arts Décoratifs (ENSAD), Paris in 1988, where he studied interior and industrial design, respectively. Since 1988 he has been in charge of the prototype workshop of the furniture section of ENSAD and has received numerous French design awards. He has recently expanded his interests to cover exhibition design and is responsible for the conception and realization of the "Tribute to Orpheus" space at the Decorative Arts Exhibition. He has started a collaboration with Corinne Metrah, interior designer, and in 1994 completed a reconstruction of a villa in Ibiza, Spain. He has received many awards for his designs and his work has appeared in both joint and solo exhibitions in France. 2.61

Leonid Yentus is an exhibition, interior and furniture designer who founded his own company, Y Design, in New York in 1995. He was born in Odessa, USSR, in 1945 and attended the Muckina Industrial Art Institute in 1974 as an industrial designer. In 1990 he emigrated to New York where he joined the studio of Gaetano Pesce. He has participated in several group shows in the USA and Canada, and his works have been published in Italy and the USA. In 1990 he took part in the project research for "100% Make-Up" for Officina Alessi. A number of his furniture objects are in Rutgers University Art Museum and the Musée des Arts Décoratifs, Montreal. 5.75

Max Yoshimoto, Studio Manager/Vice President of Lunar Design, holds a bachelor's degree in industrial design from the San Jose State University in California. Before joining Lunar Design he was principal of his own firm where he specialized in industrial design for electronics and medical technology companies. From 1984 to 1986 he was a designer with Steinhilber, Deutsch and Gard, a San Francisco exhibition and product-design firm. Yoshimoto has received a number of awards from the Industrial Designers Society of America and his work has been widely published. 5.17

Marco Zanuso was born in 1954 in Milan and studied architecture at the University of Florence. He became assistant to the Professor of Industrial Design at Milan Polytechnic in 1980, and in the same year set up his own practice which specializes in architectural, industrial and exhibition design. In 1981 he became one of the founding members of the lighting trademark Oceano Oltreluce. His clients include de Padova, Néotù, Artelano, Ultima Edizione, Memphis and Giotto International Ltd; he has also realized various architectural projects throughout Europe and interior design schemes in Milan. Zanuso's work has been seen nationally and internationally; recent exhibitions include the "Design Miroir du Siècle", Gran Palais, Paris (1993) and "Fantasy Objects", Galleria Frau, New York (1993). 5.72

Suppliers

Abdi Abdelkader, 44 Avenue de Paris, Châtillon 02320, France.

Adelta Finlandcontact GmbH, Friedrich-Ebert-Strasse 96, D-46535 Dinslaken, Germany.

Aero Ltd, Unit 4, Glenville Mews, Kimber Road, London SW18, UK.

Afro City, 24 via Molemello, 20121 Milan, Italy.

Ajeto, Lindava 167, 47158 Czech Republic.

Ala Rossa, 20 via Calastri, Cesano Maderno, 20031 Milan, Italy.

Alessi SpA, via Privata Alessi 6, 28023 Crusinallo, Novara, Italy. *Outlets* Denmark: Gense AS, 17 Maglebjergvejm, 1800 Lyngby. Finland: Casabella OY, 24 Yliopistonakatu, 20100 Turku. France: Société Métallurgique Lagostina, 62 rue Blaise Pascal, 93600 Aulnay-sous-Bois. Germany: Van der Borg GmbH, Sandbahn 6, 4240 Emmerich. Japan: Italia Shoji Co. Ltd, 5-4 Kojimachi, 1-chome, Chiyoda-ku, Tokyo 102. The Netherlands: Interhal BV, 8 Zoutverkoperstraat, 3330 CA Zwijndrecht. Sweden: Espresso Import, 10E Furasen, 42177V Frolunda. Switzerland: Guido Mayer SA, 9 rue du Port Franc,1003 Lausanne. UK: Penhallow Marketing Ltd, 3 Vicarage Road, Sheffield S9 3RH. USA: The Markuse Corporation, 10 Wheeling Avenue, Woburn, Massachusetts 01801.

Nick Allen, 1-3 Shelgate Road, London SW1 1BD, UK.

Alparda, 99/a GMK Bulvari, Maltepe 06570, Ankara, Turkey.

Amedei Tre Snc, 3 Amedei, Milan, Italy.

A.M.O.S., Jezuitska 11, 60200 Brno, Czech Republic.

ANA - Arte Nativa Aplicada, Rua Mario Ferraz, 351 São Paulo SP, Brazil.

Anibou Pty Ltd, 726 Bourke Street, 2016 Redfern, NSW, Australia.

Anthologie Quartett, Schloss Hünnefeld, Bad Essen 49152, Germany. *Outlets* Austria: Wolfgang Schatzl, Traunsee, 4801 Traunkirchen. Belgium: Surplus, Zwarte Zusterstraat 7-9, 9000 Ghent. Bosnia: Intermeuble sarl, Kaslik-face atci, 601 Corniche du Fleuve, Beyrouth. France: Altras, 24 rue Lafitte, 75009 Paris. Hong Kong: Le Cadre Gallery, 8 Sunning Road, Causeway Bay. Italy: various including Telos, via Giusti 28, 20154 Milan. Japan: Takayuki Harada Alphax Inc., Canal Tower 9-3, Nohonbashi Koami-cho, Chuo-ku, Tokyo. The Netherlands: Binnen, Keizergracht 82, 1015 Amsterdam.

ANTworks, 81 Vale Street, Moorooka 4105, Queensland, Australia.

Ron Arad Studio, 62 Chalk Farm Road, London NW1 8AN, UK.

Junichi Arai,1-1228 Sakaino-cho, Kiryu-city 376, Japan.

Architektur & Wohnen, Redaktion, Possmoorweg 5, D-22301 Hamburg, Germany.

Jan Armgardt, 45 Grieselstrasse, 64601 Bensheim, Germany.

Asia Edition, 7 Cagnola, Milan, Italy.

Jane Atfield, Made of Waste, 19 Calthorpe Street, London WC1X OJP, UK.

Authentics artipresent GmbH, 30 Max-Eyth-Strasse, Holzgerlingen 71088, Germany. *Outlets* Denmark: Niels Blom-Andersen, 28 Dyrehavevej, Klampenborg 2930. France: Jean-Marie Ritterbeck, 1 Allée Taine, Pontault-Combault 77380. Italy: Modo & Modo srl, 21 via Bressan, 20126 Milan. Japan: Fujii Corp. Ltd, 8 Ichibancho, Chiyoda-ku, Tokyo 102. The Netherlands: Steve Top, 5 Welgelegen Staat, Brussels 1050, Belgium. Spain: Fisura SA, Carretera Leon Astorg Trobajo del Camino, Leon 24198.

Masayo Ave, via Olmetto 10, 20133 Milan, Italy.

Gijs Bakker, 518 Keizersgracht, Amsterdam 1017 EK, The Netherlands.

Baldinger, 19-02 Steinway Street, Astoria, New York 11105, USA. *Outlets* Germany/Austria/Switzerland: Brendel Leuchten GmbH & Co. KG, BE28 Mecklenburgische Strasse, Berlin D-14197. Japan: Yamagiwa Lighting Centre, 4F Higashi-Nippori, Arakawa ku, 4-5-18, Tokyo 116.

Baleri Italia, via S. Bernardino 39, Lallio 24040, Bergamo, Italy. *Outlets* France: Francis Helven, 21 Côte des Chapeliers, Valence 2000. Germany: Walter Schiedermeier, Marienbergerweg 12, Cologne 5000. Japan. Casatec Ltd, 9-6 Higashi, 2-chome Shibuya-ku, Tokyo 150. The Netherlands: Kreymborg, 66 avenue Molière, Brussels 1180, Belgium. Scandinavia: Lysygn, 1 Horseager, Greve 2670, Denmark. UK: Viaduct Furniture, 10 Spring Place, London, NW5 3BH. USA: I.C.F. Inc., 305 East 63rd Street, New York, NY 10021.

Bär & Knell Design, 30 Hauptstrasse, D-74206, Bad Wimpen, Germany. *Outlets* Cyprus: Cocoon Furniture, PO Box 1126, Limasol. Italy: Delafabro SNC, Mobili di Casa, via dei Ponti 7, 330967 Spilimbergo; AGF Srl, via Madonna Dena Neve, 24 Bergamo; Marmi & Graniti, Zantedeschi, via A. de Gaspari, 37015 Domegliara; Dilmos s.a.s, Piazza San Marco, 20121 Milan. South Africa: Innovation Furniture Contracts, 179 Loop St., Cape Town 8001. Switzerland: Interni, Emmentalstrasse 240, 3414 Oberburg; Kluge AG, Dufourstrasse 138, 8008 Zurich. UK: Galerie Space, 28 All Saints Road, London W11 1HG.

B.C. Kôbô Co. Ltd, 3-3-4 Aobadai, Meguroku 153, Tokyo, Japan.

Annette Berliner, Av. Reboucas 151, ap 43, São Paulo, SP Brazil.

Best Friends, Schloss Hünnefeld Haus Sorgenfrei, Bad Essen 4514, Germany.

Bette GmbH & Co., KG, 1 Heinrich-Bette-Strasse, Delbrück 33129, Germany. *Outlets* Belgium: Gils & Gils B.V.B.A., 11 Sterrenborgstraat, B-2140 Antwerp. France: J. Calmels, rue de Joinville, F, 94120 Fontneay s/Bois. The Netherlands: Van Staveren Agenturen, 11 Spoorakkenweg, NL-AL 5070 Udenhout. UK: Alan Head Marketing, Park View, Lower Clopton, Upper Quinton, Stratford-upon-Avon.

Big-Spielwarenfabrik, Dipl.-Ing Ernst A. Bettag, Alfred Nobel-Strasse 55-59, 90765 Fürth, Bayern, Germany.

Bisazza SpA, 36041 Alte-Vicenza, Italy.

BJ-Metal, 24 Mefalbuen, Ballerup 2750, Denmark.

Hubert Blome GmbH, 3 Im Karweg, Sundern 59846, Germany. *Outlets* Austria: Gustav Schörner & Co., 56 E. Kittenbergergasse, Vienna. France: André Houlès & cie SA, 18 rue St. Nicolas, Paris Cedex 12 75579. Italy:

Gabastro Corporation srl., 29 via Melzi d'Eril, Milan 20154. Japan: Toso Company Ltd, Shinkawa I & L Bldg., 22-13 1-chome 10FL, Shinkawa, Schuo-ku, Tokyo 104. The Netherlands: Wijnants BV, 19 Randweg, Emmeloord 8300. Scandinavia: Sisustus Nalle OY, 32 Yrjönkatu, Helsinki 00100, Finland. Spain: Alsonso Mercader SA, 43 Caspe, Barcelona 08010. UK: Planet International, Tong Hall, Tong Lane, Bradford, BD4 ORR. USA: Blome Corp., 74 Henry Street, Secaucus, New Jersey 07094.

Bodum (Schweiz) AG, Kantonsstrasse CH-6234, Triengen, Switzerland. *Outlets* Australia: Gibsons & Paterson (WA) Pty, Gibpat House, Herdsman Business Park, 40 Hasler Road, Osborne Park, WA 6017. Austria: Bodum (Österreich), Franz Quantsschnig, A-9072 Ludmannsdorf 38. Canada: Danesco Inc., 18111 Trans-Canada Highway, Kirkland (Montreal), Quebec H9J 3K1. Denmark: Bodum (Danmark) A/S, Vibe Allé 4, DK-2980 Kokkedal. France: Bodum (France) SA. Z.A. de Courtaboeuf, 18 Avenue du Québec, Bât N3 – B.P. 703, F-91961 Les Ulis Cedex. Germany: Peter Bodum GmbH, Postfach 1164, D-24559 Kaltenkirchen. Israel: Hemick Ltd, Bezalel Street 6, Ramat Gan. Italy: Bodum (Italia) srl, via Perugino 13, I-20093 Cologno Monzese, Milan. The Netherlands: Bodum (Nederland) BV, Satijnbloem 14, NL-3068 JP Rotterdam. New Zealand: Peter Gower Ltd, PO Box 37-411, 7 Windsor Street, NZ-Parnell, Auckland. Portugal: Bodum (Portuguesa) SA, Apartado 8/Fojo, P-3460 Tondela. Singapore: Lexim (Singapore) Pte Ltd, 112 Killiney Road, Singapore 0923. South Africa: Louis Smiedt (Wholesalers) (Pty) Ltd, PO Box 6700, Johannesburg 2000. Spain: Bodum España SA, P.A.E. Neisa Norte, Avenida Valdelaparra, 27 Nave 15, Edf. III, E-28100 Alcobendas, Madrid. Sweden: Bodum Stenius AB, Box 748, S-13124 Nacka. UK: Bodum (UK) Ltd, Bourton Industrial Park, Bourton-on-the-Water, Cheltenham, Gloucestershire, GL54 2LZ. USA: Bodum Inc., 2920 Wolff Street, Racine, Wisconsin 53404.

Bohner, Bachmayer, Lippert, 71 Falkerstrasse, Stuttgart 70176, Germany.

Bolgheri Franchise for Memphis, via Olivetti 9, Pregnana Milanese 20010, Milan, Italy.

Renata Bonfanti SNC, 52 via Piana d'Oriente, Mussolente 36065, Vicenza, Italy.

Brainbox, 60-62 Alte Garten, Leverkusen, Nordrhein-Westfalen 51371, Germany.

Brainworks, 20 Seaview Blvd., Port Washington, New York 11050, USA.

B.R.F., snc, Loc S. Marziale, I-53034 Colle Val d'Elsa, Siena, Italy. *Outlets* Belgium: UBIK, Thierry Hens, Avenue Brugmann 11, B-1060 Brussels. Canada: Triede Design, 460 rue Mac Gill, Montreal, Quebec H2Y 2H2. Denmark: GUNI Design, Ostergade 24c, DK 1100 Copenhagen. France: Artefact, 20 rue du Chateau, F-21000 Dijon. Germany: Arredo Ralf Nadolski, Riellngshäuser-strasse 74, D-71711 Steinheim/Murr. Hong Kong: Morelington, Nuovo Collection, 12-18 Blue Pool Road, Happy Valley, Hong Kong. Korea: DAE-AH Trading Co. Ltd, 96-15 Dong Yang Building B1F, Chong Dam Dong, Kang Nam KI, Seoul. The Netherlands: Visio BV, Zuid Willemsvaart 19, NL-5211 5B 's Hertogenbosch. Portugal: DOMO, Largo de Santos 1G/1, P-1200 Lisbon. Spain: Forum International Avda. de Salavert 25,5, E-46018 Valencia. Sweden/Norway/ Finland: Anders Wahlstedt, Manhemsvägen 7, S-19145 Sollentuna, Sweden. Switzerland: Ben'arreda, Markus Haefull, Bündtwenweg 497, Ch-5732 Zetzwil. Taiwan: Anivant International Co. Ltd, 107-1 Section 4, HSIN Y1 Road, 10657 Talpei/Taiwan ROC. USA: Ernst Stoecklin, 135 Fort Lee Road, Leonia, New Jersey 7605.

Brosier-Saderne, 16 rue du Port de L'Anire, Angers 49100, France.

Campeggi srl, 22040 Anzano del Parco (Como), Italy.

Canon Inc., 3-30-2, Shimomaniko 146, Tokyo, Japan. *Outlets* Australia: 1 Thomas Holt Drive, North Ryde, Sydney NSW 2113. Belgium: Bessenveldstraat 7, 1831 Diegem. Finland: Kornetintie 3, 00380 Helsinki. France: Centre d'Affaires Paris-Nord, 93154 Le Blanc-Mesnil Cedex. Germany: Hellersbergstrasse 2-4, W-4040 Neuss. Italy: via Mecenate 90, 20138 Milan. Japan: 11-28, Mita 3-chome, Minato-ku, Tokyo 108. Latin America: Apartado 7022, Panama 5, Republic of Panama. The Netherlands: Bovenkerkerweg 59-61, 1185 Je Amstelveen. Spain: Calle Joaquin Costa, No. 41, 28002 Madrid. Sweden: Stensätravägen 13, S-127 88 Skärholmen. Switzerland: Industriestrasse 9, 5432 Neuenhof/AG. UK: Canon House, Manor Road, Wallington, Surrey SM6 OAJ. USA: One Canon Plaza, Lake Success, New York, NY 11042.

Cappellini Arte, via Marconi 35, 22060 Arosio, Italy. *Outlets* Austria: Wolfgang Bischof OHG, Judenplatz 6, 1010 Vienna. Belgium: Rika Andries, Turnhoutsebaan 144b, 2200 Borgerhout. France: Cerutti Giuseppe, Loc. Gran Chemin 1, 11020 Saint Christophe. Germany: Novus, Gartenstrasse 26, 7959 Achstetten Bronnen 3. Greece: Aveope SA, 40 M. Botsari, G-151-21 Pefki. The Netherlands: Hansje Kalff Meubelagenturen, Puttensestraat 8, 1181 Je Amstelveen. Portugal: Galante Interior Design, Rua Borges, Carneiro 49/55, P-1200, Lisbon. Spain: Santa & Cole, Blames 71, E-8440 Cardedeu, Barcelona. Sweden: Mobile Box AB, Nybrogatan 11, 11439 Stockholm. Switzerland: Yves Humbrecht Diffusion, Mon Repos 3, 1066 Epalinges. UK: SCP Ltd 135-139 Curtain Road, London EC2. USA/ Canada: I.L. Euro Inc., 9000 Broadway 902, New York, NY.

Angela Carvalho and **Alexander Neumeister**, NCS Design Rio Ltd, Av. Pasteur, 405 Rio de Janeiro, Brazil.

C.E.M. Cantù, 20 Fossano, Cantu 22063, Como, Italy.

Ceramic Japan Inc., Shinjuku-ku, Shinjuku, Tokyo, Japan.

Chérif, 2 Square Paul Bert, 96260 Asnierès, France.

Classicon GmbH, 8 Perchtinger Strasse, Munich 81379, Germany. *Outlets* Italy: Sign. Galimberti, 44 via Ponchielli, Monza 20052. Japan: Yamada Shomei Lighting, 3-16-12 Sotokanda, Chiyoda-ku 101, Tokyo. The Netherlands: Topic BV Agencies Cees de Hoop, 71 Graaf Floris Weg, AH Gouda 2805. UK: Aram Designs, 3 Kean Street, London WC2B 4AT.

John Coleman, A-Z Studios, Hardwige Street, London SE1 3SY, UK.

Denis Colomb Créations, 1 avenue Pasteur, Aix-en-Provence 13100, France.

Antonio Da Motta Leal, Da Motta Studio Inc., 12 East 22nd Street, Suite 11D, New York, NY 10010, USA.

Michele de Lucchi, 31 via Pallavicino, 20145 Milan, Italy.

Laura de Santillana, San Marco 2914, 20124 Venice, Italy.

Design Gallery Milano, via Manzoni 46, 20121 Milan, Italy.

Iris Di Ciommo e Circe Bernardes, rua Sampaio Vidal, 564 São Paulo, SP Brazil.

DMD-Developing Manufacturing Distribution, Partweg 14, 2271 AJ Voorburg, The Netherlands. *Outlets* Italy: Dovetusai, 24 via Sannio, 20137 Milan. The Netherlands: Mobach, 5 Portengen, Kockengen 3628. Scandinavia: Dawson, 158 Postboks, Copenhagen 1005. UK: Space, 28 All Saints' Road, London W11 1HG. USA: Moss Ltd, 146 Greene Street, New York, NY 10012.

DNR Sportsystem, Ruessenstrasse 6, CH-6340 Baar, Zurich, Switzerland.

Domodinamica srl, 118 Alzaia Naviglio Pavese, Milan, Italy.

Dr. Trading, 1444 Atlasova, Uvaly 20800, Czech Republic.

Driade SpA, (Aleph) 12 via Padana Inferiore, 29012 Fossadello di Caorso, Piacenza, Italy. *Outlets* France: Arturo Del Punta, 7 rue Simon Le France, 75004 Paris. Germany: Stefan Müller, Bereiteranger 7, 8000 Munich 90. Japan: Ambiente International Inc., Sumitomo Semei Bldg, 3-1-30 Minami-Aoyama, Minato-ku, Tokyo. The Netherlands: Espaces & Lignes, Nassaulaan 2A, 2514 The Hague. Scandinavia: Design Distribution, Doebelnsgatan 38A 1, 11352 Stockholm, Sweden. Spain: Bd Ediciones de Diseño, 291 Mallorca, 08037 Barcelona. UK: Viaduct Furniture Ltd, Spring House, 10 Spring Place, London NW5 3BH.

Droog Design, 518 Keizersgracht, Amsterdam 1017 ER, The Netherlands.

DX Antenna Co. Ltd, 2-15 Hamazaki Dovri, Hyogoku 652, Kobe, Japan.

E15, 118 Carpenters Road, London E15 2DY, UK.

Ecart, 111 rue St Antoine, 75004 Paris, France.

Ecofys, Kanaalweg 95, 3533 HH Utrecht, The Netherlands.

Edition Asplund, Nybrogatan 34, 114 39 Stockholm, Sweden.

Les Editions Marchal, 13 Chaligny, Paris 75012, France.

Piet Hein Eek, Molenstraat 9a, 56 64 HV Geldrop, The Netherlands.

Emaux d'Art de Longwy, 2 bis Place Giraud, Longwy 54400, France.

Anna Eoclidi, 2 Carlisle St., Leichhardt, Sydney 2040 NSW, Australia.

Erco Leuchten GmbH, 80-82 Brockhauser Weg, 58507 Lüdenscheid, Germany. *Outlets* Australia: Spectra Lighting Pty., Ltd, 15 Industrial Avenue, Wacol, Queensland 4076. Austria: Erco Leuchten GmbH, Zweigniederlassung Wien, Modecenter Strasse 14/4, OG/BC A-1030, Vienna. Belgium: Erco Lighting Belgium Bvda/SPRL, avenue Molière 211, B-1060 Brussels. Cyprus: J. N. Christofides Trading Ltd, PO Box 1093, 29a Michalakopoulou Str., Nicosia. Denmark: Lightmakers AS, Indiavej 1, Sondre Frihavn 2100 Copenhagen O. Finland: OY Hedengren AB, Lauttasaarentie 50, SF-oo 200 Helsinki, Postilokero 190. France: ERCO Lumières, SARL, 6ter rue des Saints Pères, 75007 Paris; Succursale Lyons, 4 rue V. Lagrange, 69007 Lyons. Germany: ERCO Leuchten GmbH, Postfach 2460, 58505 Lüdenscheid. Greece: Christos Vakirtzis (Ltd), Rizari 17, Athinai 11634. Hong Kong: Architectural Lighting (HK) Ltd, 3/F Shing Dao Industrial Building, 232 Aberdeen Main Road, Aberdeen, Hong Kong. Iceland: Segull Ltd, Eyjaslod 7, 101 Reykjavik. Ireland: ERCO Lighting Ireland Ltd, 289 Harolds Cross Road, Dublin 6. Italy: ERCO Illuminazione srl, via Cassanese 224, Palazzo Leonardo, 20090 Segrate, Milan; ERCO Illuminazione srl., via Dei Colli Portuensi 345, 00151 Rome. Japan: ERCO TOTO Ltd, 3-44-1 Mukoujima, Sumida-ku, 131 Tokyo. Korea: Al-Omar Electrical Lights Est, PO Box 6512, 32040 Hawalli, Kuwait. Malaysia: Seng Hup Electric Co., Snd Bhd., 44-2 et 44-3 Jalan Sultan Ismail, 50250 Kuala Lumpur. The Netherlands: ERCO Lighting Nederland BV, Gooimeer 13, NL-1411 DE Naarden. Norway: ERCO Belysning AS, Industriveien 8B, N-1473 Skarer, Postboks 83, Ellingsrudåsen, 1006 Oslo 10. Oman: Delta Ltd, PO Box 4537, Ruwi. Portugal: Omnicel Técnicas de Illuminação SA, rua Castilho, 57-5 Dto. 1200 Lisbon. Qatar: Rafco, PO Box 831, Old Rayyan Road, Doha. Saudi Arabia: Technolight, PO Box 12679, Jeddah 21483. Singapore: De.De Ce Design Centre c/o Kliktube Electrical Systems, Pty Ltd,11 Keppel Road, Singapore 0409. Spain: Erco Illuminacion SA, Poligono El Plà, c/ El Plà s/n (Parcela 28), 08750 Molins de Rei. Sweden: Aneta Belysning AB, Box 3064, 35033 Växjö. Switzerland: Neuco AG, Würzgrabenstrasse 5, 8048 Zurich. Thailand: Palicon Pro-Art Lighting Ltd, 4th Floor, 29-4 Sukhumvit 31, Phrakanong, Bangkok 10110. Turkey: Total Aydinlatma Mümessillik, Sanayi ve Ticaret AS, Tevukiye Caddesi No. 73/3 , 80200 Istanbul. United Arab Emirates: Scientechnic, PO Box 325, Dubai. UK: ERCO Lighting Ltd, 38 Dover Street, London W1X 3RB.

Excel, 2-8 Yoko Kojimachi 6-chome, Higashi Osaka City, Osaka 579, Japan.

Lou Fagotin Editions, Les Moulins, 23290 St Pierre de Fursac, France.

Famosa, 8 San Antonio, Onil 03430, Alicante, Spain. *Outlets* Germany: ECO-Spielwaren GmbH, Bahnhofstrasse 20, D-92360 Mülhausen. Belgium: Inexa Sprl., Chausée de Ninove 1120, Boite 1, 1050 Brussels. Brazil: Manufactura de Brinquedos Estrela SA, Caixa Postal 441401051, São Paulo. Denmark: Jorgen K. Hansen Aps, Finsensvej 82, DK-2000 Frederiksberg. Finland: Oy Norstar AB, Bruksmastarv 11, SF 02320 Espo. France: Jalec SA, 21 Impasse François Ayral, 31200 Toulouse. Holland: International Bon Ton Toys BV, Touwbaan 26, Industrieterrein de Baanderij, 2352 CZ Leiderdorp. Hong Kong: Famosa Internacional Ltd, 16/F.Li Fung Tower, 33 Canton Road, Kowloon. Israel: Moran Toys Ltd, 7 Lishanski St., Rishon Le Zion 75650. Italy: Linea G.I.G. SpA, via Volturno 3/12, 50019 Osmannoro, Sesto Fiorentino. Kuwait: Kuwait Babies Est., Al-Hillali Street, Al Assfoor Building, 2nd Floor Office, 7 Murgab, 20422 Safat. Norway: Norstar AS, Postboks 398, N-3201 Sandefjord. Portugal: Bonecas E Brinquedos Profamosa Ltda, Casal Do Miranda - Estrada da Paia Apartamento 173, 2675 Odivelas. Russia: New Toys City, The Central Pavilion VVC, Prospect Mira 129 223, Moscow. Sweden: Magtoys Swedberg AB, Upplagsvagen 10, S-11743 Stockholm. UK: Famosa Toys Ltd, 66 High Street, Hucknall, Nottingham NG15 7AX. USA: International Bon Ton Toys Inc., 182 Route 522, Suite 1, Dayton, New Jersey 08810.

Fine Factory srl, via Liguria 4, 20040 Bellusco, Milan, Italy. *Outlets* Belgium: UBIK, Brussels. Germany: Sievert AG, Hamburg.

First Products, 9903 Pflumm, Lenexa, Kansas 66215, USA.

Fish Design, c/o Gallery Mourmans, Keizer Karelplein 8B, 6211 TC Maastricht, The Netherlands.

Flavia Srl, via A. Gramsci 16, 50056 Montelupo Fiorentino, Florence, Italy. *Outlets* Hong Kong/ Singapore/China/Taiwan/Macau: 4/F Unit Q, Lladro Building, 72-80 Hoi Yuen Road, Kwun Tong, Kowloon, Hong Kong. Saudi Arabia/Kuwait/Oman/UAE: Mr Massimo Bert, PO Box 996, PC 13010, Safat, Kuwait.

Flos SpA, via Angelo Faini 2, Bovezzo 25073 Brescia, Italy. *Outlets* Belgium: Flos SA, Gossetlaan 50, 1702 Groot Bijgaarden. France: Flos SARL, 23 rue de Bourgogne, 75007 Paris. Germany: Flos GmbH, Am Probsthof 94, 5300

Bonn 1. Spain: Flos SA, c/Bovedillas 16, San Just Desvern, 08960 Barcelona. UK: Flos Ltd, The Studio, 120 High Street, South Milford, Leeds LS25 5AQ. USA: Flos Inc., 200 McKay Road, Huntingdon Station, New York, NY 11746.

FontanaArte, Alzaia Trieste 49, 20094 Corsica, Italy. *Outlets* Austria: Kilga Markus, Seilergasse 15, 6020 Innsbruck. Belgium/Luxembourg: Dalcan Sprl, 36 Avenue Beau Séjour, 1410 Waterloo. France: Rousselin & Pecnard, 42 rue des Poissonniers, 92200 Neuilly sur Seine. Germany: Sabine Rick, Leo Statz Strasse 14a, 40474 Düsseldorf. The Netherlands: Andrea Kok, Pilatus 4, EK 1186 Amstelveen. Spain: Fabio Ballabio, Calle Remei 37/41 1o2o, 08028 Barcelona. Switzerland: Karl Kasper, Loewengraben 24, 6000 Lucerne 5. UK: Clemente Cavigioli, 86 Ladbroke Grove, London W11 2HE. USA: Ivan Cuini, I.L. Euro Inc., 900 Broadway 902, New York, NY 10003.

Fredericia Stolefabrik A/S, Treldevej 183, DK-7000 Fredericia, Denmark. *Outlets* France: Bivex, 65 rue Pascal, F-75013 Paris. Germany: Gert Klockgether, Völckersstrasse 14–20, D-22765, Hamburg. Iceland: Epal h/f Faxafen 7, IS-108 Reykjavik. Italy: Inge With Intern, 143 Monté de la Colle de René, F-83150 Bandol, France. Luxembourg/Belgium/Holland: Fa. Morin, Amsteldijk Noord 40, Ouderkerk A/D Amstel, The Netherlands 1148 TD. Norway: Robert Tandberg, Parkveien 51, N-0256 Oslo. USA: DSI, PO Box D, 30, E Mount Airy Road, Croton on Hudson, New York 10520.

Michal Fronek and Jan Nemecek, Libensky Ostrov 7555, Prague 8, Czech Republic 18000.

FSB Franz Schneider Brakel GmbH & Co., Nieheimer Strasse 38, D-33034 Brakel, Germany. *Outlets* France: FSB by DOM/FSB France, 2 ave des Roses, ZA des Petits Carreaux, 94386 Bonneuil-Sur-Marne. Japan: FSB by Yamagiwa Corporation, c/o Ryoko Sohko, 1–8–18 Shinden, Adachi-ku, Tokyo 123. UK: FSB by Allgood Hardware Ltd, Carterville House, 297 Euston Road, London NW1 3AQ. USA: FSB by Edward R. Butler Co., Inc., 75 Spring Street, New York, NY 10012.

Fujie Textile Co. Ltd, 4–7–12 Sendagaya, Shibuya-ku, Tokyo 150, Japan.

Fujitsu Ltd, 1015 Kamikodanaka, Kawasaki, 211 Nakahara-KV, Japan.

Paolo Giordano, via Cagnola 7, Milan 20154, Italy.

Giorgetti SpA, via Manzoni 20, 20036 Meda, Milan, Italy. *Outlets* Benelux: Giorgetti Benelux BV, Smidswater 20, 2514 BW Den Haag, Holland. Germany: Giorgetti GmbH Deutschland, Murrer Strasse 16, D-71711 Steinheim/Murr.

Giotto Green Design Ltd, 4R On Hing Building, 1 On Hing Terrace, Hong Kong.

Natanel Gluska, Renggerstrasse 85, 8038 Zurich, Switzerland.

Kevin Goehring, Square One, Box 184, Parrish, Florida 34219, USA.

Nuala Goodman, via Cagnola 7, Milan 20154, Italy.

T. Grau KG GmbH & Co., 18 Borselstrasse, Hamburg 22765, Germany.

Marno Gudiksen, 10 Laerkebakken, Copenhagen 2400, Denmark.

Johanna Gunkel, 0 Horbeller Strasse, 50858 Cologne, Germany.

Ashley Hall, 9 Legard Road, London N5 1DE, UK.

Koji Hamai, 303 1–15–6 Kamitenjaku, Mitaka City, Tokyo 181, Japan.

Maria Christina Hamel, 15 via Tadino, Milan 20124, Italy.

Fritz Hansen A/S, Allerodvej 8, 3450 Allerod, Denmark. *Outlet* USA: Hughes Network Systems (subsidiary of General Motors), 10450 Pacific Center Court, San Diego, California 92191.

Haute House, 1428 Danby Rd, Ithaca, New York 14850, USA. *Outlets* France: Néotù Gallery, 25 rue du Renard, 75004 Paris. Japan: N. Vision, 29–16 Midori, Gaoka, 6–chome, 228 Zama-shi. USA: Néotù Gallery, 84 Wooster, New York, NY 10012.

Greg Healey, 33 Snows Road, Stirling, South Australia 5035, Australia.

Hewlett Packard Company, 3000 Hanover, Palo Alto, California 94304, USA.

Hironen, 502 Seiho Residence, Osaki 2–7–18, Shwagawa-ku, Tokyo 141, Japan.

Hishinuma Institute Co. Ltd, 5–41–2 Jingumae, Shibuya-ku 150, Japan.

Hitch/Mylius Ltd, Alma House, 301 Alma Road, Enfield, Middlesex EN3 7BB, UK. *Outlets* France: Jeremy Edwards, 25 rue des Trois Frères, Paris 75018. Germany: Sabine Wesemann, Konig Konzept, Hermann Lons Strasse 1, 31275 Lehrte. Ireland: Tom Caldwell Galleries, 40–42 Bradbury Place, Belfast BT7 1RT.

Human Factors Industrial Design Inc., 575 Eighth Avenue, New York, NY 10018–3011, USA.

IDT, 1854 West 169th Street, Gardena, California, 90247, USA. *Outlets* UK: Aram Designs Ltd, 3 Kean Street, Covent Garden, London WC2B 4AT. USA: Modern Age, 121 Greene Street, New York, NY 10012; Diva, 8801 Beverley Boulevard, Los Angeles, California 90048; Limn, 290 Townsend Street, San Francisco, California 94107.

IKEA of Sweden, Box 702, 34381 Älmhult, Sweden.

Ikepod Watch Co., Krönleinstrasse 31, PO Box 674, CH–8044, Zurich, Switzerland. *Outlets* France: Antoine de Macedo, 46 rue Madame, 75006 Paris. Germany: Teunen & Teunen, Postfach 36, D–65362 Geisenheim. Italy: Roberto Cella, via Carlo Osma 2, I–20151, Milan. Japan: World Commerce Co. Ltd, Hong MF Bldg, 3F, 1–24–1 Hongo, Bunkyo-ku, Tokyo 113. The Netherlands: Kreymborg, Minervalaan 63, NL–1077 NR Amsterdam. UK: The Watch Gallery, 129 Fulham Road, London SW3 6RT. USA: Douglas Biro, 30 West 15th St. 3-s, New York, NY 10011.

David D'Imperio, 2961 Aviation Avenue, Miami, Florida 33133, USA.

Interier Maly, Marakova 6, Prague 6, Dejvice 16000, Czech Republic.

Interior Object Inc., 2–4–2 Ueshio, Chuo-ku 542, Osaka, Japan.

Ishikawaseishi, 11-13 Otaki, Imadate-cho, Imadate-gun, Hukui-ken, 915–02, Japan.

Ishimaru Co. Ltd, 202 Maison Akashi, 7–3–24 Roppongi, Minato-ku, Tokyo 107, Japan.

Iyobe, 23–13 Senda Koto-ku, Tokyo 135, Japan.

Kaleidositalia srl, trada Provinciale Ridolfina, Loc Pian di Rose, S. Ippolito 61040, Pesaro, Italy.

Karhu-Titan Oy, PO Box 242, Porvoo 06101, Finland.

Kartell SpA,, via dell Industrie 1, 20082 Noviglio, Milan, Italy. *Outlets* Australia: Plastex, 85 Fairbank Road, 3168 Clayton, Victoria. Austria: Eugen Leopold, Fielderstrasse 2–4, 4020 Linz. Belgium: Tradix SA, 90–02 rue du Mail, 1050 Brussels. Denmark: Collection Creative Danas Plads 15, 2000 Frederiksberg. France: C & D Diffusion SARL, 3 avenue du Bois Vert, 77240 Vert-Saint-Denis. Germany: Gotthilf Riexinger, Vorstadt 7, 7034 Gärtringen. Hong Kong: William Artists International Ltd, 232 Aberdeen Main Road, 3/F Shing Dao, Aberdeen. Israel: Goldberg and Co., 21–10 Haorgim Street, 58857 Holon. Japan: Interdecor Inc., 2–9–6 Higashi, Shibuya-ku, Tokyo 150. Lebanon: Vent Nouveau SARL, PO Box 233, Jal El Dib, Beirut. The Netherlands: Modular Systems, Bosboom Toussaintstraat 24, 1054 Amsterdam. Portugal: Grup Dimensao SA, Av. Eng. Arantes E Oliveira 5, 1900 Lisbon. Spain: Jordi Rotger, Zaragoza 62, 8008 Barcelona. Sweden: Claes Brechensbauer, Möbelagentur, Kyrkoköpinge Pl. 26, 23191 Trelleborg. Switzerland: Gatto Diffusion, 30 rue des Chavannes, 2016 Cortaillod. Turkey: Mood, Akkavak Sok. 47/2 Nisantasi, 80220 Istanbul. UK: Environment, The Studio, 120 High Street, South Milford, Leeds LS25 5AQ, Yorks. USA: I.L. Euro Inc., 900 Broadway 902, New York, NY 10003.

Kash 'n Gold Ltd, One Trade Zone Court, Ronkonkoma, New York 11779, USA. *Outlets* Australia: ABA Telecommunications Pty Ltd, 18–35 Foundry Road, Seven Hills, NSW 2147. Canada: Carr-Tech Distributing Inc., 2706 Slough Street, Unit No. 2, Mississauga, Ontario, L4T 1G3. Germany: Herweck GmbH, 1m Drescher 10, D–66459 Kirkel-Neuhausel. Greece: Yiannakopoulos Bros Ltd, Sarantaporoy Str 1, 143 42 Filadelfia. Hong Kong: American Canyon Ltd, Room 2021–2027 Metro Centre, 32 Lam Hing Street, Kowloon Bay, Kowloon. Italy: Master Verophone Italia srl, Piazza Dante 19–20, 57121 Livorno. The Netherlands: Superfone Telecom Ltd, Achter Clarenburg 23, 3511 Utrecht. Singapore: Kash 'N Gold Pte Ltd, 111 North Bridge Road, 4–33 Peninsula Plaza, Singapore 0617. UK: United Technologies Limited, 6 Bath Street, London EC1V 9DX.

Masafumi Katsukawa, via Marchesi de Taddei 18, 20146 Milan, Italy.

Kenwood Ltd, New Lane, Havant, Hampshire PO9 2NH, UK. *Outlets* France: Société Kenwood France, Immeuble Strategic Orly, 13 rue du Pont des Halles, 94150 Rungis Cedex. Germany: Kenwood Elektro Gerate GmbH, Dornhos Strasse 18, 63263 Neu-Isenburg. Hong Kong: Kenwood Appliances Hong Kong, Ltd, 6D HK Spinners Industrial Building Phase 5, 760 Cheung Sha Wan Road, Kowloon. Italy: Singer Italia SpA, via Trento 59, 20021 Ospiate di Bollote, Milan. Japan: Aikosha Manufacturing Co. Ltd, 7–10–8 Chuo, Warabi-shi, Saitama 335. The Netherlands: Beska Nederland BV, PO Box 2009, Moeskampweg 20, 5202 CA, 's Hertogenbosch. Scandinavia: Kenwood AS, Brogrenen 8, 2635 Ishoj, Copenhagen, Denmark. Spain: River International SA, Beethoven 15, Atico 7A, 08021 Barcelona. USA: The Rival Co., 800 East 101 Terrace, Kansas City, Missouri 64131.

King Kong, 4 Guili, 20147 Milan, Italy.

The Knoll Group, 105 Wooster Street, New York, NY 10012, USA.

Knoll Textiles, (Suzin Steerman), 105 Wooster Street, New York, NY 10012, USA.

Kokusaikako Co. Ltd, 4–11–17 Minamisenba, Chuô-ku, Osaka 542, Japan.

Kazuyo Komoda, 7 Fabio Filzi, 20124 Milan, Italy.

Koziol GmbH, 90 W.V. Siemens Strasse, Erbach 64711, Germany. *Outlets* Belgium: Zet BVBA, 98 Noorderlaan, Antwerp 2030. France: Vesa, 14 Allée des Fongeres, Paris 93340. Italy: Anteprima srl, 11/7 via Fonseca Pimentel, 20127 Milan. Japan: Shimada Internati Ing., 15F Canal Tower, Tokyo 103. The Netherlands: Copi, 24B Stadhouderskade, Amsterdam 1054 ES. Scandinavia: Lisbeth Dahl, 8B Harmsdorthsvej, Frederiksberg 1874, Denmark. Spain: Pilma Disseny SA, 20 Valencia, Barcelona 08015. Switzerland: Samei AG, 16 Oberdorf Strasse, Wädenswil 8820. UK: Environment, 120 High Street, Leeds LS25 5AG. USA: Robert Greenfield Ltd, 225 Fifth Avenue, New York, NY 10010.

Randi Kristensen Design, via Fiori Oscuri 7, 20121 Milan, Italy.

Kvadrat Boligtextiler A/S, 0 Lundbergsvej, Ebeltoft 8400, Denmark. *Outlets* Italy: Rapsel SpA, 13 via Alessandro Volta, Settimo Milanese 20019. The Netherlands: Danskina, 14 Hettenheuvelweg, Amsterdam 1101. UK: Kvadrat Ltd, 62 Princedale Road, London W11 4NL.

Kwau Shau An, 8–13–3 Horikiri Katsushika, Tokyo 124, Japan.

Danny Lane, Studio 19, Hythe Road, London NW10 6RT, UK.

Jack Lenor Larsen, 41 East 11th Street, New York, NY 10003, USA. *Outlets* Argentina: Bozart srl, Paraguay 1140,1057 Buenos Aires. Australia: Arkitex Fabrics Pty Ltd, 162 Queen Street/PO Box 61, Woollahra, NSW 2025. Austria: Zimmer & Rohde, Schottengasse 1, 3, Halbstock, 1010 Vienna 1. Bahrain: Leif Pederson Assoc., PO Box 5648 Manama. Belgium: L. Kreymborg NV, avenue Molière Laan 66, 1180 Brussels. Denmark: Atmosphere Interior Textiles of Denmark, Tjaereborgvej 39, DK–2760 Maalov. Finland: Oy Naccanil AB, Kyklanevantie 2b, pl. 6, 00321 Helsinki. France: Zimmer & Rohde, Galerie Véro Dodat, 2 rue du Bouloi, 75001 Paris. Greece: Cripe, 48 P. Mela Str., Thessaloniki. Hong Kong: Altfield Interiors, 45 Graham Street. Israel: Arig Ltd. 59 Frishman St., Tel Aviv. Italy: Concetto srl, Corso Venezia 36, 20121 Milan, Italy. Japan: Fujie Textile Co. Ltd, No. 7–12, 4 chome, Sendagaya, Shibuya-ku, Tokyo 151. Mexico: Grupo Estravangan Del Noreste SA, Pino Suarez 753 NTE, Monterrey NL.; Stravaganza, Anatole France, 129 Col. Polanco, 115550 Mexico City. Norway: Peter Sveen A/S, Gabelsgate 8, PO Box 7561 Skillebekk, 0205 Oslo. Portugal: Casamia LDA, rua Marechal Saldanha 378, 4100 Porto. Singapore: Aftex Fabrics, 9 Penang Road, No. 06–01 Park Mall, Singapore 0923. Spain: Pepe Arcos, Apdo. Correos No. 7, 28760 Tres Cantos, Madrid. Sweden: Hakans agentur HB, PL 2735 Zimsdal, S–76192, Norrälje. Switzerland: Palazzo M., Hofackerstrasse 11, Postfach 56, 8032 Zurich. The Netherlands: Gerard Ernst, Weteringschans 126, 1017 XV Amsterdam, Holland. UK: Zimmer & Rhode UK Ltd, 15 Chelsea, Garden Market, Chelsea Harbour, London SW10 OXE.

Le Cose Nostre srl, 47 via dei Mille, La Spezia 19121, Italy. *Outlet* The Netherlands: Indoor, 22 P. Potterstrart, Amsterdam 1071.

Jennifer Lee, 16 Talfourd Road, London SE15 5NY, UK. *Outlets* Germany: Marianne Heller, Allmendstrasse 31, Sandhausen 6902, bei Heidelberg. Japan: Gallery Koyanagi, 1–7–5 Ginza, Chuo-ku, Tokyo. USA: James Graham & Sons, 1014 Madison Avenue, New York, NY 10021.

Christina and Anders Leideman, 42 Torsgatan, Stockholm 11362, Sweden.

Giovanni Levanti Architetto, via A. Rosmini 6, 20154 Milan, Italy.

Mary Little, 37 Henty Close, London SW11 4AH, UK.

Luceplan SpA, 44/46 via E. T. Moneta, 20161 Milan, Italy. *Outlets* Austria: Lindmaier Möbel & Leuchten, Silbergasse 6, 1190 Vienna. Australia/Singapore: Ke-Zu Pty Ltd, 95 Beattie St., Balmain NSW 2041. Belgium: Sisterco SA/NV, Altenaken 11, 3320 Hoegaarden. Brazil: Broadway Ind Coms S, Rua des Crisandalias 104, Jardim das Acacias, São Paulo, CEP 04704-020. Denmark: Finn Sloth APS, Heilsmindevej 1 2920 Charlottenlund. France: Arelux, Zac Paris Nord II, 13 rue de la Perdrix, 93290 Tremblay-en-France. Germany: Agentur Holger Werner GmbH, Nachtigallenweg 1c, D-61462 Koenigstein/TS (postal districts 1,4,5,6); Doris Schmidt Agentur für Licht und Möbeldesign, Johannesweg 1, D-33803 Steinhagen (postal districts 2,3); Robert Karl Karo, Amalienstrasse 69, D-80799 Munich. Hong Kong: Artemide Ltd, 102–103 Ruttonjee Centre, 11 Duddell Str., Central Hong Kong. Israel: D. I. Lighting Fixtures Ltd, Heh B'lyar 22, PO Box 21330, II-61213 Tel Aviv. Japan: Casa Luce Inc., 3–16–12 Sotokanda Chiyoda-ku, Tokyo 101. Mexico: Grupo D.I. S. de R.L., Altavista 119, Col San Angel, Mexico DF 010160. The Netherlands: Simon Eikelenboom BV., Keomembergweg 54, 1101 GC Amsterdam ZO. Spain: Rotger, C/Nou 8, 00870 Garraf, Barcelona. Sweden: Annell Lluis & Forum AB, Surbrunnsgatan 14, 11421 Stockholm. Switzerland: Andome Engros, Eigentalstrasse 17, 8425 Oberembrach. USA: Luceplan, 900 Broadway No. 902, New York, NY 10003.

Luxo Italiana SpA, 1 via della More, 24030 Presezzo, Bergamo, Italy. *Outlets* Austria: Ing. Manfred Prunnbauer, Selzergasse 10, Vienna 1150. Belgium: Elma Obreg, Avenue Carton de Wiartlaan 74, Brussels 1090. Denmark: Luxo Danmark, 27–29 Tempovej, 2750 Ballerup. Finland: Sahkokonsultti Oy, 44B Vihertie, Vantaa 01620. France: Luxo France, 96 Blvd Auguste Blanqui, Paris 75013. Germany: Luci Leuchten, 16 Burglen, Immenstaad 68087. Japan: Yamagiwa Corporation, 1–8–18 Shinden, Adachi Ku, Tokyo 123. The Netherlands: Ansems Industrial Design, 10A Dorpsstraat, Ledeacker 5816. Norway: Luxo Norway, 17 Enebakkvn, Manglerud, Oslo. Portugal: Casa das Lampadas Ltda, 894 rua do Arroteia, Leca do Balio 4465. Spain: Luxo Espanola, 39–41, Sugranyles, Barcelona 0812. Sweden: Luxo Sweden, 10/A Kraketorpsgatan 431, 53 Mölndal. UK: Luxo UK Ltd, 4 Barmeston Road, Catford, London SE3 6BN. USA: Zelco Industries Inc., 630, S. Columbus Ave., Mt Vernon, New York 10550; Luxo Lamp Corporation, 36 Midland Avenue, Port Chester, New York.

Maki Textile Studio, 899–7 Totohara, Itsukaichi-Machi 190–01, Nishitama-gun, Tokyo, Japan.

Marsberger Glaswerke Ritzenhoff, Paulienstrasse 84, 34431 Marsberg, Germany. *Outlets* Australia/New Zealand: Ventura Design, 60 Justin Street, Lilyfield NSW 2040. Austria: Emiliano, Viktorgasse 12/6, A-1040 Vienna. Brazil: via Acrca, rua Dias Ferreira 214, Rio de Janeiro 22431. Canada: Mr Jean Michel Laberge, 1247 Susex, Montreal H3H 2A1, Quebec. Cyprus: Three S Trading Ltd, Hermes Building Office 101, 31 Chr Sozos Street, PO Box 2104 Nicosia. Denmark: Oenskemoebler, Klostertorvet, 8000 Aarhus. France: Quartz Diffusion, 12 rue des Vents, F-75006 Paris. Hong Kong: Lane Crawford Ltd, 8/F Somerset House, 28 Tong Chong Street, Quarry Bay. Israel: Tollman's, Medinat Hayehudim 87, Herzliya Pituah 46766. Italy: Viceversa, via Ricasoli 53/R, 50122 Florence. Japan: Nippon Yo-Ko Boeki K.K., 2–6–5 Ginza, Chuo-ku, Tokyo 104. Mexico: Mexico Importadora N.I.S.A. de C.V., 103 Av. Sonora, Col Roma, 06700 Mexico, DF. The Netherlands: Interhal Select BV, 8 Zoutverkopersstraat, 3334 KJ Zwijndrecht. Norway: Howard Cuisine, Skovveien 6, 0257 Oslo. Spain: M. Echevarría SL, 159 Entenza, 08929 Barcelona. Sweden: Toftenow i Lund AB, Fabriksgatan 2, S-22237 Lund. Switzerland: Mayer & Bosshardt, Schwarzwaldallee 200, CH-4016 Basel. UK: Penhallow Marketing Ltd, 3 Vicarage Road, Sheffield S9 3RH. USA: Sorelli Imports, 900 Park Avenue, 28th Floor, New York, NY 10021.

Martin Cunel SA, rue André Dunouchez, BP 078, Amiens Cedex 2 80082, France.

Geoffrey Bjorn Mason, 27 Sunnyside Crescent, Castlecroig 2068, NSW, Australia.

Matsushita Communication Industrial Co. Ltd, 600 Yokohama 226, Kanagawa, Japan.

Matsushita Electric Industrial Co., Ltd, 1–4 Matsuo-cho, Kadoma City 571, Osaka, Japan. *Outlets* Canada: Matsushita Electric of Canada Ltd, 1475 The Queensway, Toronto M8Z IT3, Ontario. France: Panasonic France SA, 932/8 Avenue de Président Wilson, 1a Plaine Saint Denis 270, Cedex. Germany: Panasonic Deutschland, 22525 Winsbergring, Hamburg 54. Hong Kong: Shun Hing Electronic Trading Co. Ltd, New East Ocean Centre 14th–15th Floor, 9 Science Museum, Kowloon. Italy: Panasonic Italia SpA, No. 19 via Lucini, 20125 Milan. Scandinavia: Panasonic Svenska AB, Fitta Backe 3, Norsborg 145, 84 Stockholm. Spain: Panasonic Sales Spain SA, 20–30 Plantas 4, Josep Taradellas, 5Y608029 Barcelona. UK: Panasonic House, Willoughby Road, Bracknell, Berkshire RG12 8FP. USA: Matsushita Electric Corporation of America, One Panasonic Way, Secaucus, New Jersey 07094.

Matsushita-Kotobuki Electronics Industries Ltd, Office Equipment Division, 247 Fukutake, Saijo City 793, Ehime, Japan. *Outlet* USA: Panasonic Company, Division of Matsushita Electric Company, One Panasonic Way, Secaucus, New Jersey 07094.

Ingo Maurer GmbH, 47 Kaiserstrasse, 80801 Munich, Germany. *Outlets* France: Altras SARL, 24 rue Lafitte, 75009 Paris. Japan: Studio Noi Co., Ltd, Rangee Aoyama Bldg, No 710, 1–4–1 Kita-Aoyama, Minato-ku, Tokyo 107. The Netherlands: inter collections b.v., 2 Bosrand Schiedam 3121 XA. Scandinavia: Mr Finn Sloth, 1 Heilsmindevej, Charlottenlund, Denmark 2920. Spain: Santa & Cole, 71 Balmes, 08440 Carcedeu, Barcelona.

Mazzei SpA, via Livornese-Est 108, 56030 Perignano, Pisa, Italy.

Eva-Maria Melchers, 3 Domsheide, Bremen 28195, Germany.

Memphis srl, via Olivetti 9, Pregnana Milanese 20010, Milan, Italy.

Memphis Milano, via Olivetti 9, Pregnana Milanese 20010, Milan, Italy.

Metall & Gestaltung, Güntherstrasse 40, D-31134 Hildesheim, Germany.

Mette Mikkelsen, 44 Studsgade, Aarhus 8000, Denmark.

Minerva Co. Ltd, 1–10–7 Hiratsuka, Tokyo 142, Japan.

Mito, via Lamia, S.S. 18, Nocera Superiore 84015, Salerno, Italy. *Outlets* Australia: Studio Italia Pty Ltd, 176 Coventry Street, 3205 Victoria, South Melbourne. Austria/Germany: SRS Design Marketing, Steiweg 14, 88299 Leutkirch-Unterzeil. Belux: Carla Doesburg BVBA, Langerstraat 20, 9150 Kruibeke, Belgium. France: New Model SARL, Lou Calendal 12, 13580 la Fare les Oliviers. Greece: Business Design Group, 4/10 Patmou Street, 15123 Maroussi, Athens. Korea: Daewon Cable Ltd, Mito Trading, 2 Dong, Songpa-ku, Seoul. The Netherlands: Trampoluce, Archterstraat 12, AZ Den Hout. Orient: Atalia, Via Disbino 4, 22063 Cantù, Como. Portugal: Arquitectonica LDA, rua Escola Politecnica 94, 1200 Lisbon. Spain: Hustadt Illuminacion SA, C. Bolivia, 340 Local 60 Barcelona. Switzerland: Riediffusion, Avenue Temple 19/c, 1010 Lausanne 10. UK: Eurolights, 655 Finchley Road, London NW2 2HN. USA: Ernest Stoecklin, PO Box 208, 135 Fort Lee Road, Leonia, New Jersey 07605.

Mizushima Optical Co. Ltd, 43–71 Ochii-cho, Sabae City 916-11, Fukui, Japan.

Howard Murray Montgomery, 1221 Woodward Ave, Bloomfield Hills, Michigan 48303–0801, USA.

Moroso SpA, 60 via Nazionale, 33010 Cavalicco/UD, Italy. *Outlets* Australia: Canberra Flaor Pty Ltd, 8 Ipswick Street, Fyshwick Act. 2609. Austria: Michel Pilte, via dei Colli 24, 33019 Tricesimo, Udine, Italy. Asia: Italmobil (Asia) Pte Ltd, 20 Kramat Lane, 04–06 United House, Singapore 0922. Belgium: Tradix SA, rue du Mail 90–92, 1050 Brussels. Denmark and Sweden: Interstudio A/S, Luedersvej 4, Frlhavnen, 2100 Copenhagen, Denmark. Finland: Stanza OY, Annankatu 24, 00100, Helsinki. France: Chennouf Gilles, 15 rue de Petit Musc, 75004 Paris. Germany (postal codes 1–3): Thomas Graeper, Enzianstrasse 8, 4902 Bad Salzufluen; (postal codes 4–5): Walter J. Schiedermeier, Marienbergerweg 12, 5000 Cologne 71; (postal codes 6–8): Hubert Essenko, Maxim-Wetzgerstrasse, 8000 Munich 19. Greece: Avel srl, 190 Klfsias Ave, 121 Athens 36. Hong Kong: Le Cadre Gallery Ltd, 4B Sunning Road G/F, Causeway Bay. Hungary: Comester, Aranykez u 8, 1052 Budapest. Ireland: O'Hagan Contract, 101 Chapel Street, Dublin 1. Japan: Corrente Corporation, 3–2–chome, Kanda-Isukasa-cho, Chiyoda-ku, Tokyo. The Netherlands: Ivo Verbeek Meubelimport, Johan Huizinhgalaan 288, 1065 JN Amsterdam. Singapore: Abraxas Design Pte Ltd, 4 Shenton Way, 01–01 Shing Kwan House, Singapore. Spain: Roger Sin Roca, Ronda Gral. Mitre 174–176, 08006 Barcelona. Switzerland: Oliver Ike, Kroenleinstrasse 31/a, 8044 Zurich. Turkey: Atelye Derin, Apdj Ipekci Caddesl 14/1, 80220 Nisantasl, Istanbul. UK: Atrium Ltd, Centrepoint 22–24, St Giles High Street, London WC2H 8LN. USA: Ernest Stoecklin, PO Box 208, 135 Fort Lee Road, Leonia, New Jersey 07605.

Nani Marquina, Diseño y Promocion SL, Bonavista 3, Barcelona, Spain. *Outlets* Benelux: Quattro, Altenaken 11, Hoegaarden B-3320. France: Marialuz, 10 Passage Dudony, Paris, 75011. Germany & Switzerland: Inter Marketing Distribution, Eebrunnestrasse, 26 Haussen, CH-5212, Switzerland. Italy: Dessie srl, via di Moriano 831, Lucca, 55100. Taiwan: Euro Taiwan Co. Ltd, 97–3 Si-Tun Rd sec. 2, Taichung, Taiwan, R.O.C.

Néotù, 25 rue du Renard, 75004 Paris, France. *Outlet* USA: 409 West 44th Street No. 2, New York, NY 10036.

Adriane Nicolaisen, Handwoven Webworks, Box 1027, Mendocino, California 95460, USA.

Nikon Corporation, Fuji Bldg., 2–3 Marunouchi, 3-chome, Chiyoda-ku, Tokyo 100, Japan. *Outlets* France: Nikon France SA, 191 rue du Marché Rollay, 94504 Champigny-sur-Marne, Cedex. Germany: Nikon GmbH, Tiefenbroicher Weg 25, 40472 Düsseldorf 30, Germany. Japan: Nikon Optical Co., Ltd, 10–8 Ryogoku 2-chome, Sumida-ku, Tokyo 130. The Netherlands: Nikon Europe BU, Schipholweg 321, 1171 PL Badhoevedorp. UK: Nikon UK Ltd, 380 Richmond Road, Kingston, Surrey KT2 5PR.

Ninaber, Peters, Krouwel Industrial Design, De Witte Poort, Noordeinde 2d, 2311 CD Leiden, The Netherlands.

Noto-Zeus, via Vigevano 8, 20144 Milan, Italy. *Outlets* France: Giles Chennou, 15 Rue du Petit Musc, 75004 Paris. Germany: Sabine Hainlen, Hermann Kurz Strasse 14, 7000 Stuttgart. Italy: Noto-Zeus, 21/9 Corso San Gottardo, 20136 Milan. Japan: Ambiente Int., Minami Aoyama, 4–11–1 Minato-ku, Tokyo 107. The Netherlands: Miracles, 218 Prinsengracht, 1016 HD, Amsterdam. Scandinavia: Casalab, 19 Mosebakken, Virumy, 2836 Copenhagen. UK: Viaduct, 1–10 Summer's Street, London EC1R 5BD. USA: Luminaire, 7300 S.W. 45th Street, Miami, Florida 33155.

Nuno Corporation, Axis B1 5–17–1 Roppongi, Minato-ku 106, Tokyo, Japan. *Outlet* USA: Nuno N.Y., D & D Building 2nd Floor, 979 Third Avenue, New York, NY 10022.

Nya Nordiska, An den Ratswiesen, Dannenberg D-29451, Germany. *Outlets* Austria: Theodor Jandl, Boltzmanngasse 12, A-1090 Vienna. Belgium: Etienne u. Didier Peeters, Kapucinessenstraat 37, B-2000 Antwerp. Canada: Primavera, Interior Access, 160 Pears Avenue No. 111, Toronto, Ontario M5R 1T2. Finland: Runar Hagen, Ståhlbergsvägen 6 D 37, SF 00570 Helsinki. France: nya nordiska – france i.s., 86 rue du Cherche-Midi, F-75006 Paris. Italy: nya nordiska italia srl, Piazza San Alessandro 4, I-20123 Milan. The Netherlands: G.J.M. de Rie, Dirck van Deelenstraat 1, NL-5246 HC Rosmalen. Norway: Anette Holmen, Josefines Gt. 37, N-0351 Oslo. Sweden: Erik M. Andersen, Grev Tureg 57, S-11438 Stockholm. Switzerland: H.P. Gehri, Sägegasse 2, CH-3110 Münsingen. USA: Randolph & Hein, 1 Arkansas Street, San Francisco, California 94107.

Ing. C. Olivetti & Co. SpA, 77 G. Jervis, Ivrea 10015, Turin, Italy.

Ouzak Enterprise Ltd, 2–40–10 Nittazuka, Fukuishi 910, Fukui, Japan.

Pallucco Italia SAS, via Treviso 99, 30037 Scorze, Italy. *Outlet* UK: Viaduct Furniture, 1–10 Summer's Street, London EC1R 58D.

Guinter Parschalk, rua Rio de Janeiro, 316 ap 201 São Paulo, SP Brazil.

Philips International BV, Building SX, PO Box 518, 1 Glaslaan, Eindhoven 5600 MD, The Netherlands. *Outlets* France: SA Philips Industrielle et Commerciale, 51 rue Carnot, PO Box 306, 92156 Suresnes Cedex. Germany: Philips GmbH – U.B. Elektro-Hausgerate, Hammerbrookstrasse 69, 20097 Hamburg; Postfach 10 48 49, 20033 Hamburg. Italy: Philips SpA, Piazza IV Novembre 3, PO Box 3992, 20124 Milan. Japan: Philips K.K. Kaden Division, Philips Building, 13–37 Kohnan, 2-chome Minato-ku, Tokyo 108. The Netherlands: Philips Nederland BV, Boschdijk 525, Gebouw VB-10, 5621 JG Eindhoven. Spain: Philips Iberica S.A.E., Martinez Villergas 2, Apartado 2065, Madrid 28027. Sweden: Philips Hushallsapparater AB, Kottbygatan 7, 16485 Stockholm. UK: Philips Electronics, PO Box 298, City House, 420–430 London Road, Croydon CR9 3QR.

Pol International Design Company SPRL, Av R. Vander Bruggen 85–87, 1070 Brussels, Belgium. *Outlets* Belgium: Tradix SA, 90–92 rue du Mail, 1050 Brussels. France: Edifice, 27 bis Blvd Raspail, 75007 Paris; Conran Shop, 117 rue de Bac, 75007 Paris. Germany: D-Tec, Telleringstrasse 5, 40597 Düsseldorf. Hong Kong: Ratio Mobili Ltd, Shops 318, 319 Prince's Building, Chater Road Central. The Netherlands: Bjart Design Group, De Smalle Zijde 4, 3903 Veenendaal. Taiwan: H.N. Lin, 1F, 32 Chin Shan S, Road Sec. 1, Taipei. UK: The Conran Shop Ltd, Michelin House, 81 Fulham Road, London SW3 6RD. USA: Linea, 8843–49 Beverley Blvd, Los Angeles, California 90048; Cumberland Furniture 30–20 Thomson Avenue, Long Island City, NY 11101, New York.

Polaroid Corp., 575 Technology Square, Cambridge, Massachusetts 02139, USA.

Polythema GmbH, Oettingenstrasse 22, 80538 Munich, Germany. *Outlets* Belgium: UBIK Designfurnitures, Avenue Brugmann 11, B-1060 Brussels. Denmark: Habeck & Ravn Agencies, PO Box 93, DK-5700 Svendborg. France: Artefact, Difussion de Mobilier, 20 rue du Château, F-21000 Dijon. Germany: Doreen Schotte, Topplerweg 9, D-91541 Rothenburg. The Netherlands: BKA Agenturen, J. Wagenstraat 25, NL-9728 VP Groningen. UK: Double Three Double Four Ltd, "Maylands" Bryne Lane, Padbury, Buckingham MK18 2AL.

Andrea Ponsi, via Laura 18R, 50121 Florence, Italy.

Gregory Prade, Primavera Light, Am Fichtenholz 5, D-87477 Suizberg, Germany.

Quart de Poil, 27 rue de Bièvre, 75005 Paris, France. *Outlets* Japan: Guichet M, 3-12-17 Naka-Ochici, Shinjuku-ku, Tokyo. USA/Canada: Kiosk Design Incorporated, 115 Dupont Street, Toronto M5R 1V4, Ontario, Canada.

rad/air Snowboards Research & Development, Hauptstrasse 41, CH-9436 Balgach/SG, Switzerland.

Radix Comercial Ltda, Rua Fernado Falcao, 121 São Paulo SP, Brazil.

Karim Rashid, 145w 27th Street, 4e, New York, NY 10001, USA.

Ravage, 36 rue de Fontaine, Au Roi/Paris 75011, France.

Requisitenbau Franke & Winkler, Erhardtstrasse 10, D-80469, Munich, Germany.

Richard-Ginori Corporation of America, 41 Madison Avenue, New York, NY 10010, USA. *Outlet* Japan: R.G. Far East Co. Ltd, Ebisu CS Building, 9-6 Ebisu Minami 1-chome, Shibuya-ku, Tokyo.

Michael Rowe, 24 Holyport Road, Fulham, London SW6 6LZ, UK.

The Royal College of Art, Kensington Gore, London SW7 2EU, UK.

Ruine Design Associates, 250 West 27th Street, Suite 6A, New York, NY 10001, USA. *Outlets* Canada: Telio & Cie, 1047 rue de la Montagne, Montreal, Canada H3G 1Z3. Japan: The Port Authority of New York/New Jersey XPORT/JETRO, One World Trade Centre - 34N, New York, NY 10048.

R.W.F., 5 New Bradwell Works, St James Street, Milton Keynes MK13 0BW, UK.

Rolf Sachs Furniture, Tower House, 2 Fulham Park Road, London SW6, UK. *Outlet* Europe: Designer's Agency, Prinzregentenstrasse 2, 83022 Rosenheim, Germany.

Samsung Aerospace Ind. Ltd, 24th Floor, Samsung Life Building, 150, 2-Ka Taepyung-Ro, Chung-Ku, Seoul, Korea 100-176 C.P.O. Box 9762. *Outlets* Australia: Camera House, 2 Villiers Place, Dee Why, NSW 2099. Bahrain: Gulf Colour Laboratories W.L.L., PO Box 62, Manama. Canada: Tegra Photo Inc., 750 Millway Ave, Unit 8 Concord, Ontario L4K 3TZ. Dubai: Ashraf & Partners Co. L.L.C., PO Box 1677, Riga. Finland: Foka Oy, PO Box 165, 20101 Turku. France: Samsung Image et Media, BP 146 Tour Maine Montparnasse 33, ave du Maine, 75755 Paris Cedex 15. Germany: Samsung Deutschland GmbH, Mergenthaler Allee 38-40, 65760 Eschborn. Italy: Giliberto Fotoimportex srl., via Ticino, 12-50019 Sesto. Japan: Takesue Kousakusho, 3-19-16 Aoba, Sagamihara-Shi, Kanagawa-Ken 229. Malaysia: O'connor's Engineering and Trading (Malaysia) Bhd., Wisma O'connor, 1 Jalan 219, PO Box 91, 46710 Petaling Jaya, Selangor. Portugal: Fotorvo LDA, rua José Acúrcio das Neves 8-B, 1900 Lisbon. Qatar: Ali Bin Ali Est, PO Box 75, Doha. Saudi Arabia: Samir Photographic Supplies, Medina Road, Kilo 14, PO Box 599 Jeddah 21421. Singapore: O'connor's Singapore Pte Ltd, O'connor House, 98 Pasir Panjang Road. South Africa: Camcor Photographic Agencies Pty, Ltd, 43-13th Road, Kew, PO Box 592, Johannesburg 2000. Spain: Visanta SL, C/29 de Abril 58, Las Palmas de Gran Canarias. Switzerland: Zuppinger AG, Letzigraben 176, CH-8047 Zurich. Thailand: Rank PT O'connor's Co. Ltd, 318/6-7 Sukhumivit (Soi 22), Prakanong Bangkok 10100. UK: Samsung UK Ltd, Samsung House, 3 Riverbank Way, Great West Road, Brentford, Middlesex TW8 9RE. USA: Samsung Optical America Inc., 40 Seaview Drive, Secaucus, New Jersey 07094.

Thomas Sandell, c/o CBI, 34 Birger Jarlsgatan, Box 26126, S10041 Stockholm, Sweden.

Sannelli e Volpi, 7 Melzo, 20129, Milan, Italy.

Sawaya & Moroni SpA, 11 via Manzoni, 20121 Milan, Italy. *Outlets* Belgium: Top Mouton, Obterrestraat 67-69, 8994 Poperinge, Proven. France: Dominique Devoto, 11 rue Azais Barthes, 34500 Beziers. Germany: Gisela Grimm, 20 Rosengartenstrasse, 70184 Stuttgart. Switzerland: Mr Gehri, c/o Mobilform, 2 Saegegasse, 3110 Muensingen.

SCP Ltd, 135-139 Curtain Road, London EC2A 3BX. *Outlets* Germany: Jorg Franzbecker, Postfach 1367, 31865 Lavenan. Ireland: O'Hagan Contract, 99-101 Chapel Street, Dublin 2. The Netherlands: Amende Argenturen, Dr. J. G. Mazgenestraat 50, 2041 H.C. Zandvoort. Spain: Pilma Disseny, Valencia 20, Barcelona 08015. Sweden: C & B1, Burgerjarlsgatan 34, Box 26126, Stockholm 10041. USA: Palazzetti Inc., 515 Madison Avenue, New York, NY 10022.

Carlos Segura, 361 West Chestnut Street, Chicago, Illinois 60610, USA.

Sharp Corporation, 22-22 Nagaike-cho, Abeno-ku, Osaka 545, Japan.

Silhouette International Schmied GmbH & Co., KG, Postfach 538, Elibognerstrasse 24, A-4021 Linz, Austria. *Outlets* Australia: Silhouette Fashion Eyewear, Australia Pty Ltd, PO Box 100, Edgecliff, NSW 2027. Belgium: Silhouette Benelux BVBA, Desquinlei 6, B-2018 Antwerp. Canada: Canadian Optical Supply Co. Ltd, 8360 Mayrand, Montreal, Quebec H4P 2C9. Czech Republic: Merkuria Aussenhandels GmbH, Argentinska 38, Prague 7. Denmark: A. Schmied Danmark A/S, Hasselvej 15a, DK-5591 Gelsted. Finland: Kaukomarkkinat Oy, Optical Department, PO Box 54, SF-01721 Vantaa. France: New Charmes, SARL, 7 and 9 rue du Bois Sauvage, F-91055 Evry Cedex. Germany: ADM Silhouette, Dünnwald-Metzler GmbH & Co., D-70731 Fellbach. Greece: Hatziargiris Bros SA, 56 Panepistimiou Str., 10678 Athens. Hong Kong: Artist Optical Co., Room 906, Car Po Commercial Bldg., 18-20 Lyndhurst Terrace, Central District. Iceland: NYA Gleraugnasalan, Laugavegi 65, Reykjavik. Israel: Romulus Ltd, PO Box 18161, Tel Aviv. Italy: Silhouette Italia srl, via del Lavoro 8, I-22100 Como. Japan: Sinsei Shoji Co., Ltd, PO Box 51, 100-91 Tokyo. Korea: Eye Fashion Korea, C.P.O. Box 964, Seoul. Mexico: Optica Lux SA, Pino 307-3, Col Sta. Ma. Insurgentes, Deleg Cuauhtémoc, 06430 Mexico DF. New Zealand: Elegance in Eyewear Ltd, 19 Prosford Street, Ponsonby, Auckland. Norway: Silhouette Norge A/S, Haavard Martinsens Vei 19, PO Box 18 Haugenstua, 0978 Oslo 9. Portugal: Modavisao Lda, rua Santa Catarina, 1500-2 Dto., 4000 Porto. Singapore: SKY Bright Opticals Pte Ltd, 35 Tannery Road, No. 03-10 Tannery Block, Ruby Industrial Complex, Singapore 1334. South Africa: Moscon Optics International, Pty Ltd, PO Box 46073, Orange Grove 2119. Spain: A. Schmied España SA, Ausias March 74 Entlo, E-08013 Barcelona. Sweden: Kauko Time AB/Silhouette Department, Albygatan 109 D/Box 1385, S-171 27 Solna. Switzerland: Von Hoff AG, Rütistrasse 16, CH 8952 Schlieren, Zurich. Thailand: Sorn Thai Co. Ltd, 89-16-17 Bangkok Bazaar, Rajdamri Road, Bangkok 5. UK: A. Schmied UK Ltd, 333 High Road, Wood Green, London N22 4LE. USA: Silhouette Optical Ltd, PO Box 246, Northvale, New Jersey 07647.

Singer do Brasil SA, Rod Santos Dumont KM 68, Campinas, SP Brazil.

Soca Line, 7 rue Vega, 2A La Belle Etoile, 44470 Carquefou, France. *Outlets* Australia: Ke Zu Pty Ltd, 95 Beattie Street, Balmain NSW 2041. Belgium/ Luxembourg/ The Netherlands: Quattro Benelux SA NV, Altenaken 11, 3322 Hoegaarden. Canada: Kiosk Mobilia, 115 Dupont Street, Toronto, Ontario M5R 1V4.Finland/Sweden/ Norway: Design Distribution, Dobelnsgatan 38A, 1 TR S, 11352 Stockholm, Sweden. USA: IDA Stein and Associates, 1337 Merchandise Mart, PO Box 3342, Chicago, Illinois 60654.

Sony Corporation, 6-7-35 Kitashinagawa, Shinagawa-ku, Tokyo, Japan. *Outlets* France: Sony France SA, 15 Floréal, 75017 Paris. Germany: Sony Europa GmbH, Hugo Eckemer-Strasse 20, 50829 Cologne. Italy: Sony Italia SpA, via Fratelli Gracchi 30, 20092 Cinisello Balsamo, Milan. Spain: Sony Espāna SA, Calle Sabinoide Arana 42-44, 08228 Barcelona. UK: Sony UK Ltd, The Heights, Brooklands, Weybridge, Surrey KT13 0XW. USA: Sony Corporation of America, 9 West 57th Street, 43rd Floor, New York, NY 10019.

Space, 28 All Saints' Road, London W11 1HG, UK.

Ayala Sperling-Serfaty, 69 Maze'h St., 65789 Tel Aviv, Israel. *Outlet* Germany, Switzerland & Austria: Gabriele Ammann, Designer's Agency, Prinzregentenstrasse 2, 83022 Rosenheim, Germany.

Staff GmbH & co., KG, Grevenmarschstrasse 74-78, 32657 Lemgo, Germany. *Outlets* Austria: Zumtobel Licht Ges. mbh, Schweizerstrasse 30, 6851 Dornbirn. Belgium: Elma Obreg n.v., Oude Gentweg 100, 2070 Zwijndrecht-Burcht. Denmark: Louis Poulsen & Co. A/S, Sluseholmen SV, 2450 Copenhagen. Finland: Louis Poulsen Oy, Kanavaranta 3D, 00 160 Helsinki. France: Zumtobel-STAFF (France) SARL, B.P. 4, 67127 Molsheim Cedex; Avenue de la Gare, 67120 Duttlenheim. Iceland: Reykjafell GmbH, Skipholti 35, 125 Reykjavik. Ireland: Bob Bushell Ltd, 2 Sir John Rogersons Quay, Dublin 2. Italy: Zumtobel STAFF, Illuminazione srl, Viale Berbera 49, 20162 Milan. Luxembourg: ELCO ME SA, 9 rue de la Déportation, 1415 Luxembourg. The Netherlands: Dieter Kuenen, Veronaplein 16, 5237 EH 's Hertogenbosch. Norway: STAFF Belyssning a.s., Postboks 20 44, Hasle, 3239 Sandefjord. Portugal: Lledo Iluminacao, Portugals Lda, Pua Vitorino Nemésio, 10-C, 1700 Lisbon. Spain: Lledo Iluminacion SA, Apartado de Correos 50331, 28080 Madrid. Sweden: Annell Ljus Och Form AB, Surbrunnsgatan 14, 11421 Stockholm. Switzerland: Zumtobel Licht AG, Riedackerstrasse 7, 8153 Rümlang, Zurich. Turkey: Cedetas, Ciragan Cad. No. 46, 80700 Besiktas, Istanbul. UK: STAFF Lighting Ltd, Unit 5 - The Argent Centre, Pump Lane, Hayes, Middlesex UB3 3BL.

Steltman Editions, 30 Spuistraat, Amsterdam 1012 VX, The Netherlands.

Stiletto Studios, 2 Peterburger Platz, Berlin 10249, Germany. *Outlet* Austria: Di[sain] Hagn & Kubala OEG, 69 Zieglergasse, Vienna 1070.

Strässle Söhne AG, 11 Hargenbergstrasse Kirchberg 9533, St Gallen SG, Switzerland. *Outlets* France: La Boutique Danoise, 42 ave de Friedland, Paris 75008. Germany: Wilhelm Schilcher, 22 Goethestrasse, Mötzingen 71159. Italy: Faram SpA, Arredamenti Razionali, 71 via Schiavonesca, Giavera di Montello 31040. Japan: Köln Aim Co., Ltd, 27-25 Tsutsui, 3-chome, Higashi-ku, Tokyo 105. The Netherlands: Axent, 12 Uilkensstraat, Reeuwijk 2810 EA. Scandinavia: Don Batchelor SpA, 25 Vidnaesdal, 2840 Holte, Denmark. Spain: Ibersit SA, 10 Avda de Barcelona, S. Coloma d. Cerve 08690. UK: R.H.K., 207 Hampden Way, London N14. USA: ICF Int. Contract Furnishings Inc., 305 East 63rd Street, New York, NY 10021. Singapore: Diethelm Industries Pte., Ltd, Furniture Division, 8 Shenton Way, 01-02 Treasury Building, Singapore 0106.

Studio 80, 1-17-14 Minami-Aoyama, Minato-ku, Tokyo 107, Japan.

Studio Totem, 51 rue du Bon Pasteur, Lyons 69001, France.

Suzuhan Co. Ltd, 3-6-9 Minamikumoji-cho, Chuo-ku, Osaka 541.

Svitalia Design SA, Piazzetta, Agra, CH-6927 Ticino, Switzerland.

Iyer Swaminathan N., Flat 42, Bldg 79-B, Brindaban, Thane 400601, Maharashtra, India.

Swatch SA, Jakob-Stämpflistrasse 94, Biel-Bienne 2504, Switzerland. *Outlets* Argentina: Framont SA, Sarmiento 183, 5 Piso, 1041 Buenos Aires. Australia: SMH Australia Ltd, 47 Wellington Street, Windsor Vic. 3181, PO Box 456 Prahran Victoria 3181. Belgium: SMH Belgium, rue de la Venerie 44, B-1070 Brussels 7. Bulgaria: Sahara Trading Ltd, 51 Parvy May Str., 4700 Smolian. Canada: SMH, 555 Richmond Street West, Suite 1105, M5V 3B1 Toronto, Ontario. Chile: Briones SA, Av. Las Americas 585, Casilla 13510 Correo 21, Santiago. Cuba: Planning 2000 SA, Calle 16 No. 108, Apart. 6, Entre 1oY 3o, Miramar - Havana. Cyprus: Michael P. Michaelides Ltd, 11 Dighenis Akritas Avenue, Nicosia. Czech Republic: Hibernia Spol S.R.O., Karmelitska 28/269, CR 118 00 Prague 1. Denmark: Henning Staehr A/S, Grusbakken 14, DK-2820 Gentofte. Finland: Oy Perkko, Valimotie 13, PO Box 29, SF-00381 Helsinki. France: SMH France, 168 ave Charles de Gaulle, F-92522 Neuilly-sur-Seine. Germany: SMH Uhren und Mikroelektronik GmbH, Postfach 1520, 65800 Bad Soden. Hong Kong: SMH (Hong Kong) Ltd, Swatch Division, 40/F Manulife Tower, 169 Electric Road, North Point. Indonesia: PT Inti Fashindo International, Jalan H. Agus Sakim, No. 44 3rd Floor, Jakarta 10340. Ireland: B . J. Fitzpatrick and Co. Ltd, Grafton Gouse, Ballymoss Road, Sandyford Industrial Estate, Dublin 18. Israel: CLAL Marketing & Commerce Ltd, 4 Yirmiyahv Street, Tel Aviv 63507. Italy: SMH Italia SpA, Centro Direzionale, Milanofiori, Strada 7, Palazzo R1, I-20089 Rozzano, Milan. Japan: SMH Japan K.K., Swatch Division, Dai-Ni Marutaka Building 9F, 13-8 Ginza 7-chome, Chuo-ku, Tokyo 104. Malaysia: Silvaroyal Pte Ltd, 10th Floor Letter Box 11, Bangunan Hong Kong Bank Building, No. 2 Leboh Ampang, 50100 Kuala Lumpur. Mexico: La Locura Suiza SA de CV, av. Ejercito Nacional, 499 - 1er Piso, Col Granada, 11520 Mexico DF. Middle East: SMC Startime Middle East, Arbit Tower, Floor 17, Creek Road, PO Box 15912, Deira - Dubai/U.A E. The Netherlands: Ed Maassen CV, Postbus 1250, Lage Barakken 45, NL 6221 CH Maastricht. New Zealand: Olympic Swiss Ltd, 3 Olive Road, PO Box 12-346, Penrose, Auckland. Norway: A. Hausammann A/S, Stalfjaera 26, PO Box 143, Kalbakken, N-0902 Oslo 9. Portugal: Tempus Internacional LDA, rua Dos Douradores 83-10, P-1100 Lisbon. Saudi Arabia: Al Zouman General Trading, PO Box 2069, 21451 Jeddah. Singapore: Timestar Marketing Pte Ltd, 250 North Bridge Road, 15-01/02 Raffles City Tower, Singapore. South Africa: Goodman Bros Pty Ltd, PO Box 17002, Johannesburg 2000. Spain: SMH España SA, Avenida de Aragon 334, Poligono de Las Mercedes, E-28022

Madrid. Sweden: SMH Sweden AB, Swatch Division, Arstaängswägen 1B, Box 47325, S-100 74 Stockholm. Taiwan: SMH Taiwan, 24F 510 Chung-Hsiao East Road, Section 5, Taipei, R.O.C. Thailand: C. Thong Panich, 447-451 Jawaraj Road, Bangkok 10100. Turkey: Vakko Tekstil VE, Londra Asfalti, Meter-Topkapi, 34010 Istanbul. UK: Swatch UK, Empress Road, Bevois Valley, Southampton, Hants SO9 7BW. USA: Swatch Watch USA, 35 East 21st Street, New York, NY 10010.

Taihan Electric Wire Co., 194-15, 1-Ka, Hoehyun-Dong, Chung-ku, Seoul 100-500 Korea. *Outlet* USA: Sang Yong (USA) Inc., 12101 Western Avenue, Garden Grove, California 92641.

Team Buchin Design, c/o Aqua Butzke-Werke AG, Ritterstrasse 21-27, D-10969 Berlin, Germany. *Outlets* Australasia: RBA Group, PO Box 30, Suite 5, 32 Frederick Street, Oatley, NSW 2223. Austria: Klepp & Co., Perfektastrasse 63, 1230 Vienna. Belgium/Luxembourg: SERVICO NV, Kontichsesteenweg 17, 2630 Aartselaar. Canada: Dieter Rock, 209 Clonmore Drive, Scarborough, Ontario M1N 1Y3. Croatia: Aqua-Teh, Z. Petranovica 1, 51000 Rijeka. Denmark: Hans Teller A/S, Formervangen 6, 2600 Glostrup. Finland: Rafu Lönnström Oy, Pulttitie 2, PO Box 66, 00881 Helsinki. France: Eurosanit SA, ZA de la Croix des Hormes, 69250 Montanay. Greece: Kallergis SA, 50 3rd Septemvriou St., 104 33 Athens. Hungary: Buda Flat Invest Kft, Radnoti Miklos u 41, III.2, 1137 Budapest. Israel: Pools Equipment (1988) Ltd, Hebron Street 3, PO Box 401, 51418 Bnei Braq. Italy: Ernst Innerhofer AG, Postfach 190, Dantestrasse 1, 390031 Bruneck. Kuwait: Bahman Trading Corporation, Department 2, PO Box 327, 13004 Safat. The Netherlands: Van Hoeflaken BV, Postbus 324, 1200 AH Hilversum. Norway: Rade Teknikk A/S, Kanalgata 7, Postboks 1241, 3254 Larvik. Singapore: Labquit Industries Pte Ltd, Block 55, Ayer Bajah Crescent No. 07-01, Singapore 0513. Sweden: Abramatic AB, PO Box 5110, 141 05 Huddinge. Switzerland: Belinox AG, Im Sterrerfeld 1, 5608 Stetten. Turkey: Ideal Dis Ticaret Insaat Sanayi AS, Oymaci Sokak No. 15, Altunizade 81190, Istanbul. UK: Lochinvar Heating Equipment Ltd, Units D-F Acorn Way, Wildmere Industrial Estate, Banbury, Oxon, OX16 7XS.

Technische Industrie Tacx, Rijksstraatweg 52, 2241 BW Wassenaar, The Netherlands. *Outlets* Germany: various including Stier, Johannesstrasse 11, D-70176 Stuttgart 1. UK: various including Townsend Cycles, Horizon Park, Green Fold Way, Leigh Business Park, Leigh. USA: Quantum Bicycles & Fitness Inc., 26 West 515th St., Charles Road., Unit B, Carol Stream, Illinois 60188.

Thomson Multimedia, 9 Place des Vosges, 92050 Paris la Défense, Cedex, France.

Gebrüder Thonet GmbH, 1 Michael-Thonet-Strasse, Frankenberg 35066, Hessen, Germany.

Toshiba Corporation Design Centre, 1-1 Shibaura 1-chome, Minato-ku, Tokyo 105-1, Japan.

Toulemonde Bochart, 7 Impasse Branly, 91320 Wissous, 2.1. de Villemilan, France. *Outlets* Austria: Designers Details, Judengasse 7, A 1010 Vienna. Belgium: Créadis, Obterrestraat 67, B 8972 Proven, Poperinge. Germany: Andreas Jaek (postal districts 0,1,2,3) Neue Strasse 3, 26122 Oldenburg; Andreas Franoschek (postal districts 4,5,6), Wiedersbacherstrasse 11, D 90449 Nürnberg; Gotthilf Riexinger (postal districts 7,8,9), Vorstadt 7, D 71116 Gärtringen. Italy: Pierre Frey Italia, via Vela 18, 10128 Turin. Middle East: SORFRACE, PO Box 1326, Dubai. The Netherlands: Topolino, Postbus 70, 1260 AB Blaricurm. Scandinavia: Skanno, Aleksanteriulscetu 40, 00100 Helsinki, Finland. Singapore: Abraxas, 5 Temasek Bldg., No. 04-02/03 Suntec City Tower, Singapore 0103. South Korea: Inter C.R. Inc. (Cassina), 587-14, 15 Shisa-Dong Gangnam-Ku, Seoul. Spain: Camino de la Ereuita S/N, 08430 Santa Ines la Roca. Turkey: Artepe, Noramin Is Merkez 407, Büyükdere Cad. Uç Yol Mevkii, Maslak, 80670 Istanbul. UK: The Conran Shop, Michelin House, 81 Fulham Road, London SW3 6RD. USA: Luminaire, 310 West Superior, Chicago, Illinois 6810.

David Trubridge Ltd, 44 Margaret Ave., Havelock North, Hawkes Bay 4201, New Zealand.

Jan Truman, 35 The Folly, Chewton Mendip, Bath BA3 4LG, UK.

T.V.S. SpA, via Gaucei 2, Fermigniano, Italy. *Outlets* Belgium: IMPEX, 28 Boulevard St Michel No. 1, 00140 Brussels. Finland: Helena Helenius Oy, Vesannontie 7 Bio, 00510 Helsinki. France: 7 rue Taine, 75012 Paris. Germany: Linea GmbH, Venloer Strasse 1503, 5024 Pulheim. Japan: Kai Corporation, C & K Building, 1-17-6 Higashi Kanda, Chiyoda-ku, Tokyo. Spain: Pinti España SA., Avenida de Barcelona 24, Sant Joan Despi, 08970 Barcelona. Sweden: Kamph Agenturer As, Slottsgatan 10, S-72211 Vaesteraae. Switzerland: Hagro H. Untersee & Chr Gerber, Industriestrasse 14, Wangen B/Olten CH4612. UK: TVS Cookware, Keepers Cottage, Farm Manor House Lane, Higher Heath, Whitchurch, Shropshire SY13 2HS. USA: PBA Corp. Inc., 124 Water Street, Quincy, Massachusetts 02169.

Twergi, Pza Battista srl, 18 via don Bosco, Crusinallo 28023, Novara, Italy.

UM:Kogyo, 1051-1 Kishi-cho, Ono City 675-13, Hyogo, Japan. *Outlet* The Netherlands: De Wild, 54 DeMeeten, 4700 BD Roosendaal.

Unifor SpA, 1 via Isonzo, 22078 Turate, Como, Italy. *Outlets* Australia: Unifor Office Systems Pty Ltd, 276 Devonshire Street, Surry Hills, Sydney, NSW 2010. Austria: Pfau, A.M. Gestade, A-1010 Vienna. Belgium: Luc Vincent, 39 rue du Château d'Eau, 11080 Uccle. Denmark: Engelbrecht, Skindergade 38, DK-1159 Copenhagen. France: Unifor France SA, 6 rue des Saints Pères, 75007 Paris. Germany: Unifor Vertrieb, 32 Barer Strasse, 80333 Munich. Hong Kong: Salotto Ltd, 17/F Cheung-Lee Industrial Building, 9 Cheung-Lee Street, Chai Wan. Ireland: Inside Contracts Furniture Ltd, 12 Dame Court, Dublin 2. Japan: Shukoh Co. Ltd, 2-10 2-chome Yaguchi, Ohta-ku, 146 Tokyo. The Netherlands: SV Design Office Systems BV, 137 Terbregse Recther Rottekade, 3055 XC Rotterdam. Norway: Martens Interior A.S., Bygdoy Alle 58B, 0265 Oslo. Singapore: Unifor Regional Office, 54 Genting Lane, 07-04, Hiang Kie Complex 2, Singapore 1334. Spain: Ciento Quince SL, 115 Paseo de la Castellana, 28046 Madrid. Sweden: AB Nordiska Galleriet, Nybrogatan 11, 11439 Stockholm. Switzerland: Unitrend, Riedstrasse 1, CH 6343, Rotkreuz. Taiwan: Eter Group, 2Fl-1, No. 62, Fu Shing N. Rd., Taipei, R.O.C. UK: Ergonom Ltd, Langley Business Centre, Station Road, Langley, Berks., SL3 8YN. USA: Unifor Inc/I.D.C./Center Two, 30-20 Thomson Ave, Suite 706, Long Island City, New York 11101.

Christine Van der Hurd, 99 University Place, New York, NY 10003, USA.

Katrien Van Liefferinge, 3rd Floor Design Studios, Unit 6 - Carr Mills, 322 Meanwood Road, Leeds, LS7 2HY, UK.

Venini SpA, 50 Fondata Vetrai, Murano, Venice 30141, Italy. *Outlets* France: Collectania, 168 rue de Rivoli, Paris 75001. Germany: Graf Bethusy - Huc Vertriebs, 1 Hans-Sachs-Strasse, Krailling 8033. Hong Kong/Singapore: Lane Crawford Ltd, 28 Tong Chong Street, 8/F Somerset House, Quarry Bay, Hong Kong. Japan: Kitaichi Glass Co. Ltd, 1-6-10 Hanazono, Otaru, Hokkaido 047. Monaco: L'Art Venitien, 4 avenue de la Madone, Monaco 98000. The Netherlands: Desideri, 50 Gossetlaan, Groot-Bijgaarden 1702, Belgium. Saudi Arabia: Khair M. Al-Khadra Trading Estate, PO Box 1376, Jeddah 21431. UK: Liberty Retail Ltd, Regent Street, London W1R 6AH. USA: Hampstead Lighting & Accessories, 1150 Alpha Drive, Suite 100, Alpharetta, Georgia 30201.

Verwo Projecten, PB 415, Alphen A/D Rijn 2400 AK, The Netherlands.

VIA, 4-6 Cours du Commerce St André, 75006 Paris, France.

Vitra (International) AG, 15 Henric, 4010 Basle, Switzerland. *Outlets* Austria: Vitra GmbH, Pfeilgasse 35, 1080 Vienna. Belgium: N.V. Vitra Belgium SA, Woluwelaan 140A, 1831 Diegem. France: Vitra SARL, 40 rue Violet, 75015 Paris. Germany: Vitra GmbH, Charles-Eames-Strasse 2, 7858 Weil am Rhein. Italy: Vitra Italia srl, Corso di Porta Romana 6, 20122 Milan. Japan: Haller Japan Ltd, Canal Tower, 9-3 Koamicho Nihonbashi, Chuo-ku, Tokyo 103. The Netherlands: Vitra Nederland BV, Assumburg 73, 1081 GB, Amsterdam. Saudi Arabia: Vitra Middle East Ltd, PO Box 64 80, Dammam 31442. Spain: Vitra Hispania SA, Serrano No. 5, 4o, 4a, 28001 Madrid. UK: Vitra Ltd, 13 Grosvenor Street, London W1X 9FB. USA: Vitra Seating Inc., 30-20 Thomson Avenue, Long Island City, New York, NY 11101.

Vorwerk & Co., Teppichwerke GmbH & Co. KG., Kuhlmannstrasse 11, D-31785 Hameln, Germany. *Outlets* Austria: Vorwerk Austria GmbH, Postfach 361, A-60901 Bregenz. Belgium: Decortex SPRL, PVBA, rue Fr. Stroobantstraat 33, B-1060 Brussels. Denmark: K. E. Berggren, Refshedevej 6, St Darum, DK-6740. Finland: Travico Oy, Mantytie 23, SF-00270 Helsinki. France: Vorwerk France SA Textil, 30 Ave. Admiral Lemonnier, 78160 Marly-le-Roi. Iceland: Vidir Finnbogason hf., Grensasvegi 13, IS-00128 Reykjavik. Italy: Eurocarpet Snc., via Volturno 84/86, I-24100 Brescia. The Netherlands: A. Mommersteeg BV, Dockterskampstraat 1, NL-5222 AM 's Hertogenbosch. Norway: Interioragenturer, Jan F. Sveen A/S, Prinsessealleen 2, N-0275 Oslo. Spain: Decotek, Plaza Lasala 5 Bajo, E-20003 San Sebastian. Sweden: Paul Ogeborg AB, Flygfaltsgatan 4B, S-12821 Skarpnack. Switzerland: Vorwerk Textil Schweiz, Weinbergstrasse 146, CH-8042 Zurich. UK: P.J.E. International, 41 Ledbury Road, London W11 2AA.

Waesland NV, 22 Kempstraat, Waregem 8790, Belgium.

Norbert Wangen, 44 Isabella Strasse, Munich 80796, Germany.

A. R. Wentworth (Sheffield) Ltd, Tankard House, 25 Leadmill Road, Sheffield S1 3JA, UK.

Carol Westfall, 162 Whitford Avenue, Nutley, New Jersey 07110, USA.

Robert A. Wettstein, 188 Josefstrasse, Zurich 8005, Switzerland.

Weyers and Borms, Antwerpse Steenweg 48/5, 9410 Tielrode, Belgium.

Windmill Co. Ltd, 1-7-2 Higash Ueno 110, Taito-ku, Tokyo, Japan.

Herman Wittocx, 262 Gallifortlei, Antwerp 2100, Belgium.

WMF, Eberhardstrasse, Geislingen/ST 73312, Germany.

Woka Lamps Vienna, 16 Singerstrasse, Vienna 1010, Austria. *Outlets* France: Altras, 24 rue Lafitte, Paris 75009. Germany: H. H. Buennagel, 2A Robert Koch, Cologne 5. Italy: Gabriele Galimberti, 44 via Ponchielli, Monza 20052. Japan: AIDEC, Mori Bldg., Nishiazabu 4, 28 Minato-ku, Tokyo 106. The Netherlands: Art Collection, 63 Weilland, Nieuwenburg 2415. Spain: B.d. Ediciones de Diseño, 291 Mallorca, Barcelona. UK: M.D. United, 3 Willow Way, London SE26 4PQ. Switzerland: Vitrine Ag, 73 Gerechtigkeitsgasse, Bern CH-3011. USA: George Kovacs, Deiano, Glendale, New York 11385.

XO, Cide 4-Servon, Brie Comte Robert 77170, France.

Yamaha Corporation, 10-1, Nakazawa-cho, Shizuoka 430, Japan.

Yamamoto Metal Manufacturing Co. Ltd, 2-5-22 Shiba, Minato-ku, Tokyo 105, Japan.

Yamo, 192 Diderot No. 9, Champigny 94500, France.

Leonid Yentus, 130 72nd Street No. 3C, Brooklyn, New York 11209, USA.

Young Aspirations/Young Artists (YA/YA) Inc., 628 Baronne Street, New Orleans, Louisiana 70113, USA.

Zanettin Tappeti, via Vigazzolo 104/1, 36054 Montebello Vicentino (VI), Italy.

Zani & Zani, 51 via Porto, Toscolano 25088, Brescia, Italy.

Zanotta SpA, via Vittorio Veneto 57, 20054, Nova Milanese, Milan, Italy; Giovanni Marelli, via Guglielmo Oberdan 5, PO Box 148, I-20036 Meda, Milan, Italy. *Outlets* Australia: Arredorama International Pty Ltd, 1 Ross Street, Glebe, NSW No. 2037. Austria: Prodomo, 35-37 Flachgasse, 1060, Vienna. Belgium: Zaira Mis, 35 Boulevard Saint Michel,1040 Brussels. France: Giuseppe Cerutti, Località Grand Chemin 1, I-11020 St Christophe (AO), Italy. Germany: Fulvio Folci,14 Dahlienweg, 4000 Düsseldorf 30. Japan: Nova Oshima Co. Ltd, Sakakura Bldg, Akasaka, Minato-ku, Tokyo. The Netherlands: Hansje Kalff, 8 Puttensestraat, 1181 Je Amstelveen. Norway/Denmark/ Sweden: Poul Vigsø, Bagøvaenget 20, Skaerbaek, Fredericia 7000, Denmark. Spain: Angel Pujol, Av. República Argentina 218, 08023 Barcelona; Fernandez Casimiro, Urbanizacion Soto de Llanera, Casa No.5, 33192 Pruvia, Oviedo. Switzerland: Peter Kaufmann, 123 Rychenbergstrasse, 400 Winterthur. UK: The Architectural Trading Co. Ltd, 219-29 Shaftesbury Avenue, London WC2H 8AR. USA: International Contract Furnishings, 305 East 63rd Street, New York, NY 10021.

Zanussi Elettrodomestici SpA, 3 via G. Cattaneo, Pordenone 33170, Italy. *Outlets* France: Cofradem, 43 Felix Louat, Senlis 60307. Germany: Zanussi Elektrogerate GmbH, 72/74 Rennbahnstrasse, Frankfurt 60528. Japan: Electrolux Japan Ltd, 1-8 Arai Bldg, Onoe-cho, Naku-ku. The Netherlands: Electrolux Nederland B.V., 1 Vennootsweg, Alphen A.D. Rijn 2400. Scandinavia: AB Elektro Helios, 23 Luxgatan, Lilla Essingen, Stockholm 105 45, Sweden. Spain: Albilux SA, 20 Mendez Alvaro, Madrid 28045. UK: Zanussi Ltd, Hambridge Road, Newbury RG14 5EP.

Acquisitions

Acquisitions by design collections in 1995. Dates given in parentheses refer to the dates of the designs (from 1960 to the present day).

Australia

Wagga Wagga City Art Gallery Collection

Ben Edols/Kathy Elliott clear vase and bowl (1994)
Ben Edols/Kathy Elliott vase, Murrini (1994)
Ben Edols/Kathy Elliott Black bottle (1994)
John Elsegood platter (1994)
Gerry King Cicatrix Shield (1994)

Canada

Musée des Arts Décoratifs de Montreal

Joe Colombo alarm-clock, Optic (1970)
Morison S. Cousins colander (1984)
Morison S. Cousins bowl, Thasta (1992)
Morison S. Cousins canisters, One Touch (1992)
Morison S. Cousins bowl, Zuppa a Noci (1994)
Wendell Castle table, Cookie Cutter (1969)
De Pas, D'Urbino & Lomazzi armchair, Joe (1970)
Carlo Diearli hat stand (c. 1965)
Massimo Iosa Ghini armchair, Getto (1989)
Massimo Iosa Ghini bench, Vertigine (1989)
Gruppo Architetti Urbanisti Citta Nova lamp, Nesso (1965)
King and Miranda Arnaldi standing lamp, Jill (1978)
Shiro Kuramata vase (1990)
Masayuki Kurokawa table lamp, Lavinia (c. 1989)
Albert Leclerc clock, Arcobaleno (1972)
Erik Magnussen jug, Thermo (1977)
Eleanora Peduzzi Riva/Klaus Vogt/Ueli Berger and Hans Ulrich seating unit (1968)
Jan Roth table lamp, Grasl (1973)
Lino Sabattini ice bucket, Eskimo (1978)
Emma Schweinberger umbrella stand, Dedalo (1967)
Ettore Sottsass rug, Pilastro (1990)
Ettore Sottsass case (1988)
Ettore Sottsass chest of drawers, Mobile Giallo (1988)
Ettore Sottsass jug (1985)
Ettore Sottsass vase, Ringhiera Rossa (1985)
Ettore Sottsass vase (1985)
Philippe Starck cheese grater, Mr Meumeu (1992)
Studio Tetrach table, Tovaglia (1969)
Superstudio table lamp, Gherpe (1967)
Matteo Thun tray, Manitoba (1982)
Oscar Tusquets Blanca chair, Gaulino (c. 1987)

Denmark

Museum of Decorative Art, Copenhagen

Toshiharu Arai spoon and fork, Taste (1991)
Nanna Ditzel Dynamo chair, In Charge (1994), manufactured by Dynamo Stol/Claus Lundsgaard
Nanna Ditzel chair, Trinidad and table, Tobago (1993), manufactured by Fredericia Stolefabrik
Marno Gudiksen chair (1993)
Andreas Hansen chair, Minimal Monument (1989)
Le Klint suspension light, Sinusline (1971)
Komplot Design chair, Joy (1987)
Verner Panton lamp, Moon (1960)
Torben Skov rocking chair, Chair (1989–90)

France

Musée des Arts Décoratifs, Paris

Pierre Alechinsky plate from the Diane service
Jean-Louis Avril child's table and chair (1967)
Jean-Louis Avril table lamp (1967)
Vincent Beaurin adjustable lamps (1993)
Pierre Buraglio two plates (1993)
Pierre Buraglio several pieces from the Diane service (1990)
Sydney Cash objet d'art (1994)
Pierre Charpin adjustable lamp (1993)
Sylvain Dubuisson lamp (1993)
Britte Flander four glasses (1994)
Etienne Hajdu dessert bowl (1970)
Eric Jourdan adjustable lamp (1993)
Jean Marcel chest of drawers (1987)
Sebastian Matta plate (1993)
Richard Meltner bedroom candlestick (1994)
Verner Panton chair, Cantilever (1960)
Nestor Perkal adjustable lamp (1994)
Christophe Pillet adjustable lamp (1993)
Borek Sípek teacup and saucer (1990)
Ettore Sottsass vase, Moneciga (1977)
Vera Szekely seven assemblages (1977)
Roger Tallon collection comprising chairs, screen, seats, etc. (1960–78)
Matteo Thun vases, Volga and Danube (1982)
Emmanuelle Torck/Emmanuelle Noirot adjustable lamp (1993)

Germany

Kunstmuseum Düsseldorf im Ehrenhof

Luigi Colani chair (1970), manufactured by Fritz Hansen
Raymond Loewy container furniture (1967)
Sergio Mazza chair, Toga (1968), manufactured by Artemide
Dieter Rams sofa, Modell 620 (1962), manufactured by Wiese Vitsoe
Dieter Rams chair, Modell 620 (1962), manufactured by Wiese Vitsoe
Philippe Starck armchair, Lord Yo (1993), manufactured by Aleph
Philippe Starck table, Miss Balu (1993), manufactured by Aleph
Philippe Starck (1992) **Franco Clivio** (1994)
Jasper Morrison (1991) doorhandles, manufactured by FSB Franz Schneider

Vitra Design Museum, Weil am Rhein

Helmut Bätzner three Bofinger chairs (1964–66)
G. Belotti chair, Spaghetti
Mario Botta chair, Seconda
Scott Burton two metal chairs
Luigi Colani two chairs and two Zocker stools
Joe Colombo armchair, Birillo
Joe Colombo armchair, Elda
Frank O. Gehry bar stool and table, High Wiggle (c. 1972)
Frank O. Gehry table, Experimental Edges
Enzo Mari ten box chairs
Ingo Maurer six lamps
Alberto Meda chair, LightLight
Jasper Morrison, Ply-Table
Dieter Rams armchair, Vitsoe
P. Rizzatto armchair, Young Lady
Ettore Sottsass lamp, Asteroide
Philippe Starck stool, W.W.
Philippe Starck armchair, Louis 20
Philippe Starck armchair, Yo, manufactured by Aleph
Martin van Severen ten objects

Japan

There are no public design museums in Japan at the present time. However, there are approximately 15 in the planning stage. There are a few permanent collections of graphic design in museums and galleries but none for products. There are no concrete plans for permanent collections for other items, but there is a possibility that such collections could be founded within the next three years.

The Netherlands

Museum Boymans-van Beuningen, Rotterdam

Frank O. Gehry side chair, Wiggle (1970), manufactured by Vitra Design
Friso Kramer two-seater bench (1965), manufactured by Wilkhahn
Rafael Marquina i Audoard oil and vinegar set (1961)
Floris Meydam various glassware (1960s), manufactured by Leerdum
Jasper Morrison chair, Ply, manufactured by Vitra Design
Borek Sípek vases for the city of Rotterdam (1988)
Borek Sípek desk made for the municipality of Rotterdam (1988)
Martin Visser five chairs (1985–95), prototypes and manufactured by 't Spectrum

Stedelijk Museum, Amsterdam

Gijs Bakker vase, Duet (1994)
Justus Kolberg chair, P.08 R.V.S. (1993)
Benno Premsela vase, Passepartout (1994)
Borek Sípek service, Semaine (1990)
George Sowden teapot, Teirera No. 5 (1994)
Philippe Starck chair, Dr Sonderbar (1983)
Jan van der Vaart two vases (1994)

Norway

Nordenfjeldske Kunstindustrimuseum, Trondheim

Olympus camera, XA2 (1979)
Minolta camera, Hi-matic (1960s)

Poland

National Museum, Warsaw

Franciskek Aplewicz chair (1960s), manufactured by Lad
Wieslaw Sawczuk decanter (1960s), manufactured by Hortensja Glass Factory

Sweden

Nationalmuseum, Stockholm

Åke Axelsson chair, Cello, manufactured by Formfaner
Karin Björquist teacup (1993)
Ulla Christiansson chair and stool, Barbar (1993), manufactured by JIO-Mobler
Joe Colombo chair (1965), manufactured by Kartell
Kerstin Danielsson bowl (1994)
Mattias Ljunggren chair, Cobra (1991), manufactured by Kallemo AB
Vico Magistretti table, Demetrio 70, manufactured by Artemide
Ursula Munch-Petersen service, Ursula (1992), manufactured by Royal Copenhagen A/S
Alev Siesbye service, Sirius (1992), manufactured by Royal Copenhagen A/S

Röhsska Konstslöjdmuseet, Gothenburg

Junichi Arai double woven fabric (1990)
Karin Björquist tea cup and coffee cup for the Royal Palace (1990)
Ingrid Dessau for Klassbol linen napkin, Nobel (1992)
Pelle Frenning chair, Rocking chair (1983)
Gosta Grahs three teapots (1990s)
Ingela Karlsson earthenware jugs (1995)
Markku Kosonen basket (1995)
Malin Lager machine embroidered picture, Stone Letter (1994)
Danny Lane screen, Manna from Heaven (1994)
Britta Lincoln embroidered picture (1994)
Mattias Ljunggren two laminated stools (1994)
David Persson chair (1994), manufactured by Möbelakrobaterna/The Furniture Acrobats
David Persson set of cutlery (1994), manufactured by Möbelakrobaterna/The Furniture Acrobats
Mats Sjöberg painted box, The Flight (1994)
Jimmy Söderholm candleholder (1994), manufactured by Möbelakrobaterna/The Furniture Acrobats
Bertil Vallien glass object, Mummy (1994)

Switzerland

Museum für Gestaltung, Zurich

Anna Castelli-Ferrieri round modular unit, manufactured by Kartell
Joe Colombo chair, Mod 4868 (1968), manufactured by Kartell
Alfredo Walter Häberli and Christophe Marchand lamp, Foli (1994), manufactured by Birchler Siebdruck AG
Christoph Hefti different fabrics (c. 1991), manufactured by Fabric Frontline
Enzo Mari chair, Sof-Sof (1971), manufactured by Driade
Giancarlo Piretti chair, Plia (1970), manufactured by Castelli
Dieter Rams TV-set, FS 80/1 (1965/66), manufactured by Braun
P. Schneider sound camera, Nizzo 2056 (1976), manufactured by Braun
Wristwatch Atmos Classic (1974), manufactured by Jaeger-Le Voultre

UK

The Conran Collection, selected by Jasper Morrison

Paul Barbieri shopping trolley, Caddie
Andrea Branzi divisional furniture, Grand Spina, manufactured by Design Gallery
Braun vacuum cleaner, Multiquick
Achille Castiglioni suspension lamp, Brera, manufactured by Flos
Antonio Citterio storage system (1994), manufactured by Kartell
Coolike-Regerny Lufthansa refreshment towel
Michele de Lucchi table lamp, Tolomeo (1989), manufactured by Artemide
Fujichrome Provia slide film pack
Gillette Sensor Excel Shaver (1993)
Stefano Giovannoni/Guido Venturini tray (1990), manufactured by Alessi
Stefano Giovannoni toilet brush, Merdolino, manufactured by Alessi
Ideal Standard basin, Michelangelo
Massimo Iosa Ghini two-seater sofa, Leggero, manufactured by Cassina
Massimo Iosa Ghini laundry basket, manufactured by Cappellini
Massimo Iosa Ghini binoculars, manufactured by Chinon
Massimo Iosa Ghini transistor radio, manufactured by Sony
Massimo Iosa Ghini ashtray on stand, manufactured by Cappellini
Massimo Iosa Ghini small ashtray, manufactured by Cappellini
Kleen-e-ze interchangeable broom (1994)
Willie Landels sofa, Throwaway (1965), manufactured by Zanotta
Lovegrove and Brown thermos, Alfi
Vico Magistretti armchair and chair, Silver, manufactured by De Padova
Alberto Meda/Paolo Rizzatto light, Titania D13 (1989), manufactured by Luce Plan
Alberto Meda/Paolo Rizzatto light, Metropoli (1992), manufactured by Luce Plan
Michelin Map Series (1994)
Jasper Morrison bottle racks (1994), manufactured by Magis
Jasper Morrison door handles (1993), manufactured by FSB
Jasper Morrison various pieces from the Atlas range (1993), manufactured by Alias
Jasper Morrison bookcase, Alpha (1993), manufactured by Alias
Jasper Morrison chair, Quatro Gambe (1992), manufactured by Montina
Jasper Morrison TV/video stand (1994), manufactured by Alias
Jasper Morrison ashtray (1994), manufactured by Alias
Lugi Mosdu Grip 6181 (1969), manufactured by Valextra
Muji business card file; propelling pencil; display book
Marc Newson light, Helice (1993), manufactured by Flos
Nilfisk vacuum cleaner, GM80
Norika paper clip
Pace mountain bike
Paolo Rizzatto light, Costanza D13 (1989), manufactured by Luce Plan
Sagar water pitcher
Sakari takeaway cup, NewCup
Seibu paper bag
Sigg Fuel water bottle
Clive Sinclair Zike, manufactured by Sinclair Research
Sony portable telephone
Sony transistor radio, ICF48OL (1992)
Valextra attache case, 4530 Premier
Andries Hiroko Van Onck vegetable rack, Dove (1990), manufactured by Magis
Westminster cardboard coffin (1993)
Yankee bird feeder

The Design Museum, London

James Dyson vacuum cleaner, Dyson Duel Cyclone (1993), manufactured by Dyson Appliances

Victoria and Albert Museum, London

Furniture and woodwork collection
Mary Little chair, Margrét (1993)
Jasper Morrison two chairs (1989), manufactured by Vitra in 1994
Jasper Morrison two chairs (1994), manufactured by Montina
Ernest Race Bottleship (1963), manufactured by Isokon
Roberts Radio portable radio, model RT1 (1958–60)
Roberts Radio portable radio, model R200 (1960–64)
H. W. Wood sofa, Oberon (1964)
Terence Woodgate storage system, River (1995), manufactured by Punt Mobles, Spain

Ceramics and glass collection
Margaret Alston pâte de verre bowl
Karin Björquist coffee pot, bowl and serving plate from the Nobel Service (1995), manufactured by Hackman Rörstrand
Brian Blanthorn laminated glass dish
Tessa Clegg glass form (1994)
Contrex glass carafe, L'Ocybelle (1994)
Bob Crooks glass candlestick and wine glass from the Coloured Ball range (1994), manufactured by First Glass
Gunnar Cyren glass vase, Dolby (1992), manufactured by Orrefors
Emsa Design plastic mug printed with blue and white "Meissen" pattern (1990)
Peter Furlonger engraved glass bowl, Tree of Life
Haxby mugs printed with designs by Terry Frost (1970s)
Diana Hobson pâte de verre bowl
Erika Lagerbielke glass vase, The Lion Heart (1992), manufactured by Orrefors
Marie-Claude Lalique glass vase, Tanega (1988)
Sharmian Mocatta sandblasted glass bowl, Best Fruits Ripen Slowly
Keiko Mukaido glass bowl (1994)
David Pilkington engraved glass vase, Filigree Form (Sonnets)
Pyrex carafe, Glass Tender from the Creative Glass collection (1970–80)
Karlin Rushbrooke glass bowl (1990)
Christina Sheppard tiles (1970s)
Troika Pottery vase and vessels (1970s)
Emma Woffenden glass form, Breath (1994)
Tony Zuccheri glass carafe and tumblers (1964), manufactured by Venini

Textile collection
Robert Allen furnishing fabric (1975–80)
Nigel Atkinson furnishing fabric (1990)
Cambridge Consultants Ltd samples (1980–81)
Nina Campbell sample books (1989–91)
Manuel Canovas sample book, printed furnishings (1975–80)
Polly Courtin tapestry, Jazz Singer (1989)
Marguerite De Nice for Bassett McNab Co. furnishing fabrics (1975–80)
Designers Guild various pattern books (1993–94)
Donghia Textiles various sample swatches and sample books (1994)
Donghia Textiles furnishing fabrics, Boboli, Big Wiggle (1994)
Sev Gence tapestries (1974)
Romeo Gigli for Donghia Textiles sample swatches (1993–94)
Juliet Glynn-Smith furnishing fabrics (1965)
Brigitta Hahn furnishing fabric for Svenskyt Team (1989)
Patsy Hely tapestry, Bottlebrush (1989)
Nicholas Herbert Ltd furnishing fabrics (1992)
IKEA furnishing fabrics (1992)
Kawashima Italia srl furnishing fabrics (1993–4)
Sarah Knill Jones for Liberty furnishing fabrics (1992)
Lee/Joffa various furnishing fabrics (1975–80)
Andrew Martin International Ltd furnishing fabrics (1994)
Murfil sample book of textile wallcoverings (1975–80)
Osborne & Little sample books and furnishing fabrics (1980–90s)
Parker Knoll various sample books (1975–80)
H. A. Percheron sample book (1975–80)
Jimmy Pike tapestry, Two Men Sitting at a Waterhole
Lorenzo Rubelli sample book (1975–80)
Arline Sunnida for Bassett McNab Co. various furnishing fabrics (1975–80)
Timney Fowler sample books (1990s)
Murray Walker Victorian Tapestry Workshop tapestry, Mark (1992)
Winfield Design Associates sample book of foil wallcoverings (1975–80)

USA

Museum of Fine Arts, Boston, Massachusetts

Ron Arad chair, London Papardelle, and crate (1992), manufactured 1993
Ron Arad chair, Schizzo (1989), manufactured by Vitra (International) AG in 1994
Bennet Bean earthenware untitled work from the Wing Series (1992)
Wim Borst stoneware, Reflections VIIa (1992)
Mark Brazier-Jones chair, Lyre (1989), manufactured 1993
Erik de Graaff chair, Cross (1976), manufactured 1993
Tom Dixon chair, Crown (1988), manufactured 1994
Tom Dixon chair, Jester (1988), manufactured 1994
Bengt Edenflak vase (1960), manufactured by Skruf Glass
Lisa Gralnick locket No. 7 (1993)
Myra Mimlitsch Gray candlesticks (1991)
Chris Hawthorne vessel from the Painted Vessel Series (1993)
Geert Lap vase (1992)
Mark Lindquist puzzle jar, Totem (1980)
Mark Lindquist Ascending Bowl No. 11 (1980)
Alessandro Mendini chair, Poltrona di Proust (1978), manufactured by Studio Alchimia in 1991
Barbara Nanning three vessel forms from the Terra Series (1994)
Jim Partridge bowl (1993)
Ed Rosbach basket, The Red and the Black
Reiko Sudo furnishing fabric, Tiger Stripes/Leopard Spots (1993), manufactured by Nuno Corporation
Jen Tarantino bench, Bend (1991)
United States Zenith turned wood funerary urn (1980–84)
Netty van del Heuvel porcelain object (1989)
Jan van der Vaart vase (1989)

The Brooklyn Museum, New York

Boris Bally various pieces of tableware; x-panded flatware (prototypes) (1980s–90s)
Andries Dirk Copier drinking glass (1965) manufactured by Leerdam
Vivika Heino/Otto Heino vase (1955–60)
Nik Mills stool, Eiffel Tower (1994)
Robert Schellin glazed stoneware (1960)
Randy Shull South Cabinet (1992)
Paul Stankard paperweight (1994–95)
Russel Wright cream pitcher (1963), manufactured by Yamato Porcelain Co.
Russel Wright coffee pot and lid (1963), manufactured by Yamato Porcelain Co.
Russel Wright glass (1963), manufactured by Schmidt International

The Chicago Athenaeum, Chicago, Illinois

Tiina-Liisa Aalto doorhandles, Manda (1993), manufactured by Primo
Earo Aarnio chair, Liisa (1993), manufactured by Asko Furniture Ltd
Kari Asikainen chair, Pajezzo (1993), manufactured by P.O. Korhonen Oy
Karl-Axel Andersson and Morgan Ferm vacuum jug Art (1972), manufactured by Hammarplast AB
Atelier Mendini various appliances for Alessi, Philips, Daniel Swarovski Corporation AG, Olivari B. SpA, Artemide, Swatch
Atelier Mendini (Michael Graves, Arata Isozaki, Yuri Soloviev, Philippe Starck) plastic knobs for Falstaff pots (1989), manufactured by Alessi SpA
Cini Boeri chair, Ghost (1991), manufactured by Fiam Italia
Max Caspani chair, Ole (1994), manufactured by Enrico Pellizzoni
Peer Clahsen toy, Cella (1978), manufactured by Naef
Xavier de Clippeleir toy, Zita (1984), manufactured by Naef
Cousins Design hair dryer, Max 1000, manufactured by Gilletti Co.
Pietro del Vaglio chair, Grace (1994), manufactured by Arcon
Henry Dreyfuss Associates razor, Flicker (1972), manufactured by American Safety Razor
Henry Dreyfuss Associates instant camera, Model 100 (1964), manufactured by Polaroid
Mauro Fadel chair, Duoxa (1994), manufactured by Emme I
Brita Flander bowl, Stormskal (1993), manufactured by Skanno Ltd
Brita Flander lamp, Snacka 9621 Suspension Lamp (1992), manufactured by Skanno Ltd
Brita Flander candlesticks, Northern White Lights (1992), manufactured by Marimekko
Brita Flander glasses, Women Glasses (1993), manufactured by Marimekko
Brita Flander goblets, Seven Brothers (1994), manufactured by Marimekko
Massimo Iosa Ghini chair, Bom-Bay (1994), manufactured by Moroso
Penetti Hakala chair, W. Chair (1987), manufactured by Martela Oy
Penetti Hakala chair, OR (1993), manufactured by Lilyriver
Keith Haring puzzle (1985)
Simo Heikkila chair, ETC (1990), manufactured by Isku Oy
Tapani Holma lockable window escutcheon (1993), manufactured by Primo (Abloy Oy)
Karle Holmberg chair, Paletti (1992), manufactured by Lepo Product
Fujiowo Ishimoto textiles, various designs, manufactured by Marimekko
Kristina Isola textiles, Stone and Sand Collection (1993), manufactured by Marimekko
Maijo Isola textiles, various designs, manufactured by Marimekko
Pasi Jarvinen ski pole, Avanti (1988), manufactured by Excel Ltd
Jouko Jarvisalo chair, Lippi (1992), manufactured by Yosoy Ltd
Jouko Jarvisalo bar stool, Sola (1988), manufactured by Inno Finland SA
Hannu Kähönen padlocks, AVA (1990), PL241 (1993), Abloy Control Key (1993), manufactured by Abloy Oy
Heikki Kiisi telephone, Teleste PC 2000 Sickroom Phone System (1991), manufactured by Teleste Communications
Harri Korhonen chair, Oscar (1990), manufactured by Inno Finland SA
Yrjo Kukkapuro chair, Alnus (1993), manufactured by Averte Oy
Olavi Linden (with **Svante Ronnholm** and **Kenneth Wickstrom**) various tool designs, manufactured by Fiskars Oy AB
Stefan Lindfors sofa, BOOA3 (1992), manufactured by Skanno Ltd
Stefan Lindfors chair, Draco (1993), manufactured by Asko Furniture
Vico Magistretti chair, Mauna-Kea (1994), manufactured by Montina International
Heikki Metsä-Ketelä compass, Suunto Design Line 115 Series Marine Compass (1990), manufactured by Suunto Oy
Jasper Morrison chair, Quattrogambe (1994), manufactured by Montina International
Martti Muranen doorpulls, Oniga (1993), manufactured by Primo (Abloy Oy)
Ulrich Namislow toy, Kaskado (1985); Topolino (1987), manufactured by Naef
Jo Niemeyer toy, Modulon (1984), manufactured by Naef
Nokia Footwear Design Group various footwear designs
Tuomo Nousiainen compass, Suunto M9 Wrist Compass (1989), manufactured by Suunto Oy
Luigi Origlia chair, Aria (1994), manufactured by Origlia
Pasi Pankakainen chair and table, Arena (1993), (1994), manufactured by Arvo Piiroinen Oy
Werner Panton chair, Swinging (1994), manufactured by Ycami Edizioni
Eljas Perheentupa computer, Suunto Companion Drive Computer (1992), manufactured by Suunto Oy
Ingvar Persson carton opener (1976), manufactured by Samhall Rehab
Markku Piri textiles, The European Championships in Helsinki series (1994), manufactured by Finlayson
Ferdinand A. Porsche chair, Boulevard (1994), manufactured by Ycami Edizioni
Kuno Prey cement clock (1986), manufactured by Danese
Paavo Räsänen tool, Handy 650 Camping Axe (1987), manufactured by Fiskars Oy
Ristomatti Ratia candleholders, Ilta (1993), Lighthouse Tripod (1993), manufactured by Design Ideas (USA)
William Sawaya chair, Wienerin (1994), manufactured by Sawaya & Moroni
Luca Scacchetti chair, Sabik 3-seater (1994), manufactured by Poltrona Frau
Heikkila Simo chair, Flok (1992), manufactured by Klaessons AB (Sweden)
Davor Spoljaric compass, Suunto Design Line 95 Series Marine Compass (1990), manufactured by Suunto Oy
Philippe Starck chair, Lord Yo (1994), manufactured by Driade
Philippe Starck chair, Olly Tango (1994), manufactured by Driade
Timo Sunla tool, Handy 650 Camping Axe (1987), manufactured by Fiskars Oy AB
Jouni Teittinen safety respirator, Air Ace (1987), manufactured by Air-Ace Oy
Enrico Tonucci chair, Nido (1994), manufactured by Triagolo
Jorma Vennola doorhandles, Line Series (1993), manufactured by Primo (Abloy Oy)
Lella and Massimo Vignelli chair, Pitagora (1994), manufactured by Poltrona Frau
Marjaane Vitra textiles, Media Text (1993), manufactured by Marimekko Oy
Reinhold Weiss personal fan (1971), manufactured by Braun
Yrjo Wiherheimo chair, Bird (1991), manufactured by Vivero Oy
Yrjo Wiherheimo chair, Flok (1992), manufactured by Klassons AB (Sweden)

Cooper-Hewitt Museum, New York

Donald Carr videophone, Sign Post 101 (1994), manufactured by AT&T Global Information Systems
George Carwardine lamp, Anglepoise Model 1227.01 (1993), manufactured by Anglepoise Ltd
Stephen Copeland lamp, IOS (1992), manufactured by Details
Timothy de Fiebre The Layered Wood Chair (1993)
Walter Dorwin Teague Associates Inc. audio tele-conferencing system, Conference Master (1993), manufactured by Coherent Communications Systems Corporation
Henry Dreyfuss thermostat, T87 Round (1990), manufactured by Honeywell Inc.
frogdesign inc. personal communicator, EO 440 (1990), manufactured by EO Computer Inc. for AT&T Global Information Systems
frogdesign inc. computer and monitor, NeXT (1985–87), manufactured by NeXT Inc.
frogdesign cordless telephone, Angelo (1990), manufactured by G-Tel Telecommunications
Kobeou Associates set of cutlery, Liisa (1993), manufactured by Dansk International Designs Ltd
Lisa Krohn telephone prototype, Phone Book (1980s)
Enzo Mari desk calendar (1967), manufactured by Danese Milano
Richard Sapper and Marco Zanuso portable radio, Brionvega LS502 (1964)
Takeshi Tsuruta, Siji Wade, Takanoby Fujimoto of Mitsubishi Electronic Co.; **Greg Breiding, Keith Kresge, Deane Richardson** of Fitch Co., cellular telephone (prototype), Talisman (1994)
David Tompkins, Deane Richardson, Keith Kresge, Don Rebele facsimile transceiver, Qwip 1200 (1976), manufactured by Qwip Systems

The Denver Art Museum, Denver, Colorado

Franco Albini/Franca Helg bowl, Panocchia (1971), manufactured by San Lorenzo srl
Franco Albini/Franca Helg vase, Fresic (1971), manufactured by San Lorenzo srl
Emilio Ambasz flashlight (prototype), (1985)
Emilio Ambasz television, Handkerchief (prototype), (1992), manufactured by Briovega SpA
Emilio Ambasz office chair, Qualis (1989), manufactured by Tecno SpA
Andrea Anastasio vase, Anna (1991), manufactured by Memphis Extra
Archizoom and Paolo Deganello chair, AEO (1973), manufactured by Cassina SpA
Archizoom seating, Superonda (1966–67), manufactured by Poltronova srl
Gae Aulenti table (1965), manufactured by Knoll International
Gae Aulenti lamp Patrocolo (1975), manufactured by Artemide SpA
Gae Aulenti lamp, Pipistrello (1965–66), manufactured by Martinelli Luce SpA
Luigi Baroli folding screen, Cartoons (1992), manufactured by Baleri Italia
Mario Bellini lamp, Area 50 (1974), manufactured by Artemide SpA
Mario Bellini armchair, Break (1976), manufactured by Cassina SpA
Mario Bellini typewriter, ETP 55 (1985–86), manufactured by Ing. C. Olivetti SpA
Mario Bellini settee, Le Bambole (1972), manufactured by B & B Italia SpA
Mario Bellini typewriter Lexikon 82 (1972–73), manufactured by Ing. C. Olivetti & C., SpA
Mario Bellini computer, Programma 101 (1965), manufactured by Ing. C. Olivetti SpA
Mario Bellini television, Sider 20 (1972), manufactured by Brionvega SpA
Cini Boeri seating, Serpentone (1971), manufactured by Arflex
Cini Boeri/Tomu Katayanagi armchair, Ghost (1987), manufactured by Fiam Italia SpA
Andrea Branzi armchair (prototype), Domestic Animals, manufactured by Zabro
Anna Castelli-Ferrieri stacking units (1969), manufactured by Kartell SpA
Achille Castiglioni tumblers and carafe, Ovio (1983)
Achille Castiglioni/Pier Giacomo Castiglioni lamp, Arco (1962), manufactured by Flos Inc.
Achille Castiglioni/Pier Giacomo Castiglioni armchair, Sanluca (1961), manufactured by Bernini SpA
Livio Castiglioni/Gianfranco Frattini lamp, Boalum (1969-70), manufactured by Artemide
Antonio Citterio office chair, Famiglia AC2 (1988), manufactured by Vitra Inc.
Joe Colombo lamp, Alogena (1970), manufactured by O-Luce Srl
Joe Colombo storage trolley, Boby (1970), manufactured by Bieffeplast SpA
Joe Colombo side chair, Universale (1965–67), manufactured by Kartell SpA
Tony Cordero lamp, Ecate (1990), manufactured by Artemide SpA
Riccardo Dalisi centrepeice, Coppa Reale (1993–94), manufactured by Edizioni Galleria Colombari
Constantino Dardi teapot for the Turandot service, Principessa (1990–91), manufactured by Cleto Munari Design Associati srl.
Antonio Da Ros vase (1964–65), manufactured by Gino Cenedese e Figlio
Paolo Deganello vases, Trivaso (1986), manufactured by Tribu
Laura de Santillana platter, Ninfee (1989), manufactured by EOS Design Nel Vetro srl
Gabriele De Vecchi teapot, Emisfera (1985), manufactured by Argenteria Gabriele De Vecchi
Egidio Di Rosa/Alessandro Giusti round vase (1968), manufactured by Up & Up srl
Guido Drocco/Franco Mello coat rack, Cactus (1972), manufactured by Gufram Industria Arredamento srl
D'Urbino, De Pas, Lomazzi armchair, Blow, manufactured by Zanotta SpA
D'Urbino, De Pas, Lomazzi seating, Joe (1970–71), manufactured by Poltronova srl
Alison Filippo samovar, Vesevo (1985), manufactured by Sabattini Argenteria SpA
Gianfranco Frattini tableware items (1981), manufactured by Progetti srl
Piero Gatti/Cesare Paolini/Franco Teodoro seating, Sacco (1969), manufactured by Zanotta SpA
Frank O. Gehry goblet (1990), manufactured by Swid Powell
Giandomenico Belotti side chair, Spaghetti (1979–80), manufactured by Alias srl
Piero Gilardi seating, I Sassi (1967), manufactured

by Gufram Industria Arredamento srl
Group G14 chair, Fiocco (1970), manufactured by Gruppo Industriale Busnelli SpA
Gruppo Architetti Urbanisti Citta Nova lamp, Nesso (1962), manufactured by Artemide SpA
Takenobu Igarashi calendar, Zanders Momentum (1989)
Hisatoshi Iwata tableware (1991), manufactured by Iwata Glass Company Ltd
Ugo La Pietra boxes (1988), manufactured by Artieri Alabastro
Michael Lax various tableware and lights (1960s–80s), manufactured by Mikasa Inc, Lightolier Inc., Amcor Ltd, Centrum
Vico Magistretti lamp, Atollo (1977), manufactured by O'Luce srl
Vico Magistretti lamp, Eclisse (1965), manufactured by Artemide SpA
Vico Magistretti armchair, Gaudi (1970–71)
Vico Magistretti lounge chair, Sindbad (1981)
Angelo Mangiarotti various drinking vessels (1980s), manufactured by Colle srl
Enzo Mari fruit stand, L (1982), manufactured by Bruno Danese srl
Enzo Mari various tableware (1960s), manufactured by Bruno Danese srl
Alberto Meda chair, Frame (1991), manufactured by Alias srl
Alberto Meda/Paolo Rizzatto various lamps (1986–87), manufactured by Luce Plan SpA
Luca Meda chaise, Les Beaux Jours (1987), manufactured by Molteni SpA
Alessandro Mendini bottles, Arsos (1989), manufactured by Venini SpA
Alessandro Mendini sofa, Kandissi (1979), manufactured by Studio Alchimia
Alessandro Mendini centrepiece, Peonia (1993), manufactured by Design Gallery
Alessandro Mendini stool, Trick (1988), manufactured by Vanini
Piero Palange/Werther Toffoioni bowl, manufactured by Alfredo Barbini srl
David Palterer goblet, Fiore dal cuore d'oro for the Riflessioni Collection (1993), manufactured by Edizioni Galleria Colombari
David Palterer vase (1989), manufactured by Alterego
Maurizio Peregalli side chair, Sedia, for the Zeus Collection (1984), manufactured by Noto-Zeus srl
Gaetano Pesce side chair, Dalila (1980), manufactured by Cassina SpA
Gaetano Pesce armchair and ottoman, Up 5, Up 6 (1969), manufactured by B & B Italia, SpA
Gaetano Pesce sofa, Tramonto a New York (1980), manufactured by Cassina SpA
Franco Poli side chair, Flying (1990), manufactured by Montina International srl
Gio Ponti armchair, Novedra (1968), manufactured by B & B Italia SpA
Progetti Studio champagne goblets (1981), manufactured by Progetti srl
Franco Raggi centrepiece, Colpo di Vento (1986), manufactured by Tendentse SpA
Prospero Rasulo side chair, Perlaria (prototype), (1989), manufactured by Masterly srl
Prospero Rasulo urn, Narciso from the Terranea Series, manufactured by the Fine Factory srl
Guglielmo Renzi urn, Noble (1990), manufactured by Manifattura Artistica Le Porcellane
Aldo Rossi espresso pot, La Conica (1984), manufactured by Alessi SpA
Aldo Rossi cooking box, La Cubica (1988–91), manufactured by Alessi SpA
Aldo Rossi/Luca Meda armchair, Teatro (1982), manufactured by Molteni & Co.

Lino Sabattini silver-plated tableware (1960s–70s), manufactured by Sabattini Argenteria SpA
Valerio Sacchetti pitcher, Agilulfo (1984), manufactured by Fratelli Cassetti Corporation
Roberto Sambonet ashtray (1992), manufactured by G.F.R. srl
Roberto Sambonet cooking set, Centre Line (1964), manufactured by Sambonet SpA
Roberto Sambonet cups (1981), manufactured by Cleto Munari Design Associati srl
Denis Santachiara sofa, Lumière (1989), manufactured by Zerodisegno srl
Richard Sapper lamp, Tizio (1973), manufactured by Artemide SpA
Richard Sapper/Marco Zanuso television, Black 201 (1969–70), manufactured by Brionvega SpA
Richard Sapper/Marco Zanuso telephone, Grillo (1965–67), manufactured by Siemens
Richard Sapper/Marco Zanuso radio (1964–65), manufactured by Brionvega SpA
Luca Scacchetti urn, Helsinki (1989), manufactured by Mangani Ars
Afra Scarpa/Tobia Scarpa lamp, Pierrot (1990), manufactured by Flos Incorporated
Carlo Scarpa table, Doge (1969), manufactured by Simon International SpA
Carlo Scarpa flatware (1977), manufactured by Cleto Munari Design Associati srl
Carlo Scarpa carafe, Interno d'Oro (1978), manufactured by Cleto Munari Design Associati srl
Ettore Sottsass lamp, tableware, furniture (1960s–80s) manufactured by Memphis srl, Poltronova, Alessio Sarri Ceramiche, Studio Alchimia and Vetreria Vistosi
Philippe Starck armchair, J. Lang (1984), manufactured by Driade SpA
Studio 65 seating, Capitello (1971), manufactured by Gufram Industria Arredamento srl
Superstudio table, Quaderna (1970–71), manufactured by Zanotta SpA
Yukio Ueno vase (1990), manufactured by Iwata Glass Company Ltd
UFO Paramount Lamp (1969–1976), manufactured by Lapo Binazzi
Massimo Vignelli dinner-ware, Compact (revised model) (1964), manufactured by Heller Incorporated
Massimo Vignelli dinner-ware, Compact (original model) (1964), manufactured by Articoli Plastici Elettric
Massimo Vignelli/Lella Vignelli flatware, Ciga (1979), manufactured by Calegaro
Luciano Vistosi lamps (1972), manufactured by Vetreria Vistosi SpA
Marco Zanini vase, Simeon (1991), manufactured by Venini SpA

Los Angeles County Museum of Art, California

Donald T. Chadwick Equa Chair (1984)
Donald T. Chadwick White Chair (1965)
Donald T. Chadwick Aeron Chair (1994)
Donald T. Chadwick modular seating (prototype)
John Luebtow chair, LF-F4-93/1 (1992)
Richard Neutra Cantilever Chair (1929) redesigned in early 1990s
Richard Neutra Boomerang Chair (1929) re-manufactured (1993)
Peter Shire Adjustable Chaise (1989–90)
Peter Shire table, Breakfast Crunch (1989–90)
Peter Shire swivel table, Double Crunch (1989–90)
Peter Shire six side chairs (1989–90)
Peter Shire round table (1981–82)

Metropolitan Museum of Art, New York

Timo Sarpaneva dinnerplate, Marcel (1991), manufactured by Iittala
Philippe Starck prototype for a knife (1987), manufactured by Sasaki
Lella and Massimo Vignelli flatware, Forma (1979), manufactured by Calegaro for Ciga Hotels

Museum of Modern Art, New York

Athos Bergamachi disposable foldable razor (1975), manufactured by Elberel Italiana
Rodolfo Bretzel lights, Eola (1993), manufactured by Bilumen
Donald Chadwick office chair, Aeron (1994), manufactured by Herman Miller, Inc.
Vincent de Rijk cup (1985)
Thomas Eriksson medicine cabinet (1992), manufactured by Cappellini SpA
Marco Ferreri stool, Is (1993), manufactured by Nemo srl
frogdesign home computer, Macintosh SE (1987), manufactured by Apple Computer, Inc.
Steve Jobs/Jerry Manock home computer, Macintosh 128K, manufactured by Apple Computer, Inc.
Kazuo Kawasaki wheelchair, Carna (1989), manufactured by SIG Workshop Co. Ltd
Makoto Komatsu sake pitcher and cups (1992), manufactured by COM, Japan
Ross Lovegrove chairs, Figure of Eight (1993), manufactured by Cappellini SpA
Alberto Meda side chair, Softlight (1988), manufactured by Alias srl
Jean Nouvel table, Less (1994), manufactured by Unifor SpA
Carl Pott corncob holder (1961), manufactured by C. Hugo Pott
Alejandro Ruiz cheese grater (1994), manufactured by Alessi SpA
Smart Design Good Grips, paring knife, peeler, bottle-opener, manufactured by Oxo International
Superstudio lamp, Gherpe (1967), manufactured by Poltronova
Synthetic Industries American erosion matrix, Pyramat (1992)
Synthetic Industries erosion mat, Landlok (1990)
Synthetic Industries spacer fabric for athletic shoes
Synthetic Industries fuel filter medium
Synthetic Industries wastewater treatment filter media
Marc van de Loo/Tim Parsey digital camera, Quicktake 100 (1994), manufactured by Apple Computer, Inc.
Massimo Vignelli/Lella Vignelli chairs, Handkerchief (1985), manufactured by The Knoll Group
Mary Ann Toots Zynsky vase, Waterspout (1994)

Philadelphia Museum of Art, Pennsylvania

Morison S. Cousins colander (1994), One Touch canisters (1992), One Touch serving bowl set (1992), Thatsa bowl (1992), Wondelier bowls (1992), Zuppa a Noci bowl (1991), manufactured by Tupperware
Hiroshi Egawa cutlery set, Will (1990), manufactured by Aoyoshi Company
Sheila Hicks fabric, Badagara (1968)
Takenobu Igarashi desk set, Fisso (1988), manufactured by Raymay Fujii Corporation
Satoru Hibino Ikebana speaker (1989), manufactured by Yamaha Corporation
International Industrial Design television and radio (1972), manufactured by Japan Victor Company
Kyoichiro Kawakami Arare Plates (1965), manufactured by Hoya Glass Corporation
Motomi Kawakami floor lamps, Ariake (1983), manufactured by Bushy Company
Kazuo Kawasaki scissors and case, X&I (1985); scissors, R&R (1985); knife, Artus (1983); knife and stand, Fluctus (1983), manufactured by Takefu Knife Village
Toshiyuki Kita chair, Wink (1980), manufactured by Cassina
Toshiyuki Kita lamps, Kyo (1983), manufactured by IDK Design Laboratory Ltd
Setsuo Kitaoka cabinet, Yoshiko (1984), manufactured by Build Company
Shiro Kuramata chest of drawers, Furniture in Irregular Forms (1970), manufactured by Cappellini
Masayuki Kurokawa metal Wave desk accessories (1985), manufactured by Daichi Company
Masayuki Kurokawa GOM collection (1973), clocks for GOM collection (1983) manufactured by Fuso Gomu Industry Company
Masahiro Mori trays (1976), manufactured by Hakusan Toki K.K.
Hiroshi Morishima table lamp, Wagami Andon (1986), manufactured by Time-Space-Art
Masanori Umeda cabinet, Ginza Robot (1982), manufactured by Memphis Milano